Since *The social logic of space* was
published in 1984, Bill Hillier and
his colleagues at University College
London have been conducting research
on how space features in the form and
functioning of buildings and cities. A
key outcome is the concept of 'spatial
configuration' – meaning relations
which take account of other relations
in a complex. New techniques have
been developed and applied to a wide
range of architectural and urban
problems. The aim of this book is to
assemble some of this work and show
how it leads the way to a new type of
theory of architecture: an 'analytic'
theory in which understanding and
design advance together. The success
of configurational ideas in bringing
to light the spatial logic of buildings
and cities suggests that it might be
possible to extend these ideas to
other areas of the human sciences
where problems of configuration
and pattern are critical.

Space is the machine

Bill Hillier **Space is the machine**

A configurational theory of architecture

CAMBRIDGE
UNIVERSITY PRESS

Published by the Press Syndicate of the University of Cambridge
The Pitt Building, Trumpington Street, Cambridge CB2 IRP
40 West 20th Street, New York, NY 10011–4211, USA
10 Stamford Road, Oakleigh, Melbourne 3166, Australia

© Cambridge University Press 1996

First published 1996

Printed in Great Britain at the University Press, Cambridge

TAG

'A house is a machine for living in …'   *Le Corbusier (1923)*

'But I thought that all that functional stuff had been
 refuted. Buildings aren't machines.'   *Student*

'You haven't understood. The building
 isn't the machine. Space is the machine.'
 Nick Dalton, Computer Programmer at
 University College London (1994)

Contents

Acknowledgements

Acknowledgements and thanks are due first to the many friends and colleagues who have, over the years, made an enormous contribution to the ideas and research set out in this book, most notably Dr Julienne Hanson, Alan Penn and Dr John Peponis, each of whose contributions has been too large and diverse to acknowledge in detail; to Nick 'Sheep' Dalton for the title of the book, and also for the brilliant software on which much of the research is founded, the outward and visible sign of which is in the plates in the book; to Mark David Major for masterminding the gradual and painful evolution of the text and illustrations; to Myrto-Gabriella (Petunia) Exacoustou for reading, criticising and helping me substantially improve the final draft; to Professor Pat O'Sullivan, Head of the Bartlett, for a six months sabbatical in 1992, when I said I would finish but he knew I would not; to the Engineering and Physical Sciences Research Council for continued research funding; to the many contributors to the research, and especially Tim Stonor, Kayvan Karimi, Beatriz de Campos, Xu Jianming, Gordon Brown, John Miller, Tad Grajewski, Lena Tsoskounoglou, Laura Vaughan, Martine de Maesseneer, Guido Stegen and Chang Hua Yoo (who drew the first version of the map of London); to the MSc and doctoral students of the Bartlett School of Graduate Studies who continue to give so much intellectual buzz to the department; to Professors Philip Steadman, Tom Markus and Mike Batty for sustained intellectual support over the years; to Stuart Lipton and his team at Stanhope Properties Plc for providing us with so many opportunities to apply our research on real development and design projects, and to learn so much from them, and also to Gordon Graham of the London Regeneration Consortium, the South Bank Employers Group, Chesterfield Properties Plc, Ove Arup and Partners, and Peter Palumbo; to the many public bodies who have invited us to contribute to their work through applied research, including National Health Service Estates, British Railways, British Airways, Powergen, the Department of Education and Science, Technical Aid for Nottingham Communities, the London Boroughs of Croydon and Camden, and the Tate Gallery; to the many architectural practices who have invited us to work with them on their projects, but most especially Sir Norman Foster and Partners, the Richard Rogers Partnership, Terry Farrell and Company, Skidmore,

Owings and Merrill, Nicholas Grimshaw and Partners, Bennetts Associates, SW Architects, and Avanti Architects; to Professor Sheila Hillier and Martha Hillier for tolerating an obsessive lap-topper in the house for longer than was reasonable; to Kate, Charlotte and Ben Hillier for continuing to be the good friends and supporters of a preoccupied and inconsiderate father; to the thief who took all the copies of the draft of the first four chapters from my home when stealing my computer, thus saving me from premature publication; to Rose Shawe-Taylor, Karl Howe, Emma Smith, Susan Beer and Josie Dixon of Cambridge University Press; and finally to UCL for continuing to be the most tolerant and supportive of Universities. I also acknowledge that minor errors in figure 8.11 may puzzle the perceptive reader. They were discovered too late to alter.

Introduction

In 1984, in *The social logic of space*, written in collaboration with
Julienne Hanson and published by Cambridge University Press, I set out
a new theory of space as an aspect of social life. Since then the theory has
developed into an extensive research programme into the spatial nature
and functioning of buildings and cities, into computer software linking
'space syntax' analytic tools with graphical representation and output for
researchers and designers, and into an expanding range of applications in
architectural and urban design. During this time, a large number of arti-
cles, reports and features have appeared, theses have been written in many
universities using the theory and methods of 'space syntax', and research
has been initiated in many parts of the world into areas as diverse as the
analysis of archaeological remains and the design of hospitals.

   During this time, many theoretical advances have also been made,
often in symbiosis with the development of new techniques for the computer
representation and analysis of space. One key outcome of these advances
is that the concept of 'configuration' has moved to centre stage. Configuration means, put simply, relations taking into account other relations. The
techniques of 'configurational analysis' - of which the various 'space syntax' techniques are exemplars - that have been built from this idea have
made it possible to bring the elusive 'pattern aspect' of things in architecture and urban design into the light of day, and to give quantitative expression to the age-old idea that it is 'how things are put together' that matters.

   This has in turn led to a clear articulation of a philosophy of design.
Architectural and urban design, both in their formal and spatial aspects,
are seen as fundamentally configurational in that the way the parts are put
together to form the whole is more important than any of the parts taken
in isolation. The configurational techniques developed for research can,
in fact, just as easily be turned round and used to support experimentation
and simulation in design. In linking theoretical research to design in
this way, we are following a historical tradition in architectural theory
which has both attempted to subject the pattern aspect of things in
architecture to rational analysis, and to test these analyses by embodying
them in real designs. The difference now is only that the advent of
computers allows us to bring a much greater degree of rigour and testing
to theoretical ideas.

The aim of this book is to bring together some of these recent developments in applying configurational analysis to issues of architectural and urban theory into a single volume. The surprising success of configurational ideas in capturing the inner logic of at least some aspects of the form and functioning of built environments, suggests that it might in due course be useful to extend these ideas to other areas where similar problems of describing and quantifying configuration seem to be central, including some aspects of cognitive psychology, but also perhaps sociology itself. At present we are encouraged by the present interest in these ideas across a range of disciplines and, just as the last decade has been devoted to the development and testing of techniques of configurational analysis within architecture and urban design, so we hope that the coming decade will see collaborations amongst disciplines where configuration is identified as a significant problem, and where some development of the configurational methodology could conceivably play a useful role.

The immediate context of the book is the changing theoretical debate within and around architecture. Looking back, it is easy to see that in spite of the attention paid to theory in architecture in the twentieth century, and in spite of the great influence that theories have had on our built environment, architectural theories in the last decades have in general suffered from two debilitating weaknesses. First, most have been strongly normative, and weakly analytic, in that they have been too much concerned to tell designers how buildings and environments should be, and too little concerned with how they actually are. As a result, theories of architecture have influenced our built environment enormously, sometimes for good, sometimes for ill, but they have done little to advance our understanding of architecture.

Second, there has been an explosion of the historic tendency to form architectural theories out of ideas and concepts borrowed from other disciplines. As a result, architectural discourse has been dominated by a series of borrowings, first from engineering and biology, then from psychology and the social sciences, then from linguistics and semiology, and most recently of all from literary theory. Each of these has had the merit that it allowed architecture to become part of wider intellectual debate. But there has been a price, in that very little attention has been given to the internal

development of architecture as a discipline. Through this turning away,
architecture has increasingly ignored the lessons waiting to be learned
from the intensive study of experimental twentieth-century architecture,
and acquired what now amounts to a hidden history in which key aspects
of recent architectural reality have been suppressed as though they were
too painful to talk about.

The aim of this book is to begin the process of remedying this bias
towards overly normative theories based on concept borrowing from other
disciplines, by initiating the search for a genuinely analytic and internal
theory of architecture, that is, one based on the direct study of buildings
and built environments, and guided by concepts formed out of the necessities of this study. The guiding belief is that what we need at the end of the
twentieth century is a better and deeper understanding of the phenomenon
of architecture and how it affects people's lives, and how this relates to
innovative possibility in architecture, and the central role of the architectural imagination.

This book is therefore concerned with what buildings and cities are
like, why they are as they are, how they work, how they come about
through design, and how they might be different. The word 'theory' is used
not in the common architectural sense of seeking some set of rules which,
if followed, will guarantee architectural success, but in the philosophical
and scientific sense that theories are the abstractions through which we
understand the world. An architectural theory, as we see it, should deepen
our grasp of architectural phenomena, and only subsequently and with
great modesty, suggest possible principles on which to base speculation
and innovation in design. Such a theory is analytic before it is normative.
Its primary role is to enquire into the puzzle that we see and experience
architecture, but we do not understand what we see and experience.
However strongly we may feel that architecture may be wrong or right, we
rarely understand the architectural grounds on which such judgments are
made. This book therefore seeks an understanding of the theoretical content of architecture.

The book is in four parts. The first, THEORETICAL PRELIMINARIES,
deals with the most basic of all questions which architectural theory tries
to answer: what is architecture, and what are theories, that they can be

needed in architecture? In the first chapter, 'What architecture adds to building', the key concepts of the book are set out on the way to a definition of architecture. The argument is that in addition to functioning as bodily protection, buildings operate socially in two ways: they constitute the social organisation of everyday life as the spatial configurations of space in which we live and move, and represent social organisation as physical configurations of forms and elements that we see. Both social dimensions of building are therefore configurational in nature, and it is the habit of the human mind to handle configuration unconsciously and intuitively, in much the same way as we handle the grammatical and semantic structures of a language intuitively. Our minds are very effective in handling configuration in this way, but because we do work this way, we find it very difficult to analyse and talk rationally about the configurational aspects of things. Configuration is in general 'non-discursive', meaning that we do not know how to talk about it and do not in general talk about it even when we are most actively using it. In vernacular buildings, the configurational, or non-discursive, aspects of space and form are handled exactly like the grammar of language, that is, as an implication of the manipulation of the surface elements, or words and groups of words in the language case, building elements and geometrical coordinations in building. In the vernacular the act of building reproduces cultural given spatial and formal patterns. This is why it seldom seems 'wrong'. Architecture, in contrast, is the taking into conscious, reflective thought of these non-discursive and configurational aspects of space and form, leading to the exercise of choice within a wide field of possibility, rather than the reduplication of the patterns specific to a culture. Architecture is, in essence, the application of speculative and abstract thought to the non-discursive aspects of building, and because it is so, it is also its application to the social and cultural contents of building.

Chapter 2, 'The need for an analytic theory of architecture', then takes this argument into architectural theory. Architectural theories are essentially attempts to subject the non-discursive aspects of space and form to rational analysis, and to establish principles to guide design in the field of choice, principles which are now needed as cultural guidance is no longer automatic as it is in a vernacular tradition. Architectural theories are both analytic in that they always depend on conjectures about what human beings are like, but they are also normative, and say how the world should be rather more strongly than they say how it is. This means that architecture can be innovative and experimental through the agency of theories, but it can also be wrong. Because theories can be wrong, architects need to be able to evaluate how good their theories are in practice, since the repetition of theoretical error – as in much of the modernist housing programme – will inevitably lead to the curtailment of architectural free-dom. The consequence of this is the need for a truly analytic theory of archi-tecture, that is one which permits the investigation of the non-discursive without bias towards one or other specific non-discursive style.

Chapter 3, 'Non-discursive technique', outlines the prime require-ment for permitting architects to begin this theoretical learning: the need for neutral techniques for the description and analysis of the non-discur-sive aspects of space and form , that is techniques that are not simply expressions of partisanship for a particular type of configuration, as most architectural theories have been in the past. The chapter notes a critical difference between regularities and theories. Regularities are repeated phe-nomena, either in the form of apparent typing or apparent consistencies in the time order in which events occur. Regularities are patterns in surface phenomena. Theories are attempts to model the underlying processes that produce regularities. Every science theorises on the basis of its regularities. Social sciences tend to be weak not because they lack theories but because they lack regularities which theories can seek to explain and which there-fore offer the prime test of theories. The first task in the quest for an ana-lytic theory of architecture is therefore to seek regularities. The first purpose of 'non-discursive technique' is to pursue this task.

Part II of the book, NON-DISCURSIVE REGULARITIES, then sets out a number of studies in which regularities in the relation between spatial configuration and the observed functioning of built environments have been established using 'non-discursive techniques' of analysis to control the architectural variables. Chapter 4, 'Cities as movement economies', reports a fundamental research finding: that movement in the urban grid is, other things being equal, generated by the configuration of the grid itself. This finding allows completely new insights into the structure of urban grids, and the way these structures relate to urban functioning. The relation between grid and movement in fact underlies many other aspects of urban form: the distribution of land uses, such as retail and residence, the spatial patterning of crime, the evolution of different densities and even the part-whole structure of cities. The influence of the fundamental grid-movement relation is so pervasive that cities are conceptualised in the chapter as 'movement economies', in which the structuring of movement by the grid leads, through multiplier effects, to dense patterns of mixed use encounter that characterise the spatially successful city.

Chapter 5, 'Can architecture cause social malaise?' then discusses how this can go wrong. Focussing on specific studies of housing estates using configurational analysis coupled to intensive observation as well as social data it is shown how the overly complex and poorly structured internal space of many housing estates, including low-rise estates, leads to impoverishment of the 'virtual community' – that is the system of natural co-presence and co-awareness created by spatial design and realised through movement - and this in turn leads to anti-social uses of space, which are the first stage in decline towards the 'sink estate'. Because the role of space in this process is to create a disorderly and unsafe pattern of space use, and this is then perceived and experienced, it is possible to conceptualise how architecture works alongside social processes to create social decline. In a sense, the creation of disorderly space use through maladroit space design creates the first symptoms of decline, even before any real decline has occurred. In a sense, then, it is argued, we find that the symptoms help to bring about the disease.

Chapter 6, 'Time as an aspect of space', then considers another fundamental difference between urban forms: that between cities which serve the needs of production, distribution and trade, and those which serve the needs of social reproduction, that is of government, major social institutions and bureaucracies. A series of 'strange towns' are examined, and it is shown how in their spatial properties, they are in many senses the opposite to the 'normal' towns considered in chapter 5. The detailed spatial mechanisms of these towns are examined, and a 'genotype' proposed. An explanation is then suggested as to why 'cities of social reproduction' tend to construct these distinctive types of spatial patterns.

Chapter 7, 'Visible colleges', then turns to the interiors of buildings. It begins by setting out a general theory of space in buildings, taking into account the results of settlement analysis, and then highlights a series of studies of buildings. A key distinction is made between 'long and short models', that is, between cases where space is strongly governed by rules, and therefore acts to conserve given social statuses and relationships and cases where space acts to generate relations over and above those given by the social situation. The concept of long and short models permits social relations and spatial configuration to be conceptualised in an analogous way. A ritual is a long model social event, since all that happens is governed by rules, and a ritual typically generates a precise system of spatial relationships and movements through time, that is a spatial 'long model'. A party is a short model event, since its object is to generate new relationships by shuffling them in space, and this means that rules must be minimised by using a spatial 'short model'. In a long model situation space is adapted to support the rules, and behavioural rules must also support it. In a short model situation, space evolves to structure, and often to maximise, encounter density.

Part III of the book, THE LAWS OF THE FIELD, then uses these noted regularities to reconsider the most fundamental question of all in architectural theory: how is the vast field of possible spatial complexes constrained to create those that are actually found as buildings? First, in chapter 8, 'Is architecture an *ars combinatoria*?', a general theory of 'partitioning' is proposed, in which it is shown that local physical changes in a spatial system always have more or less global configurational effects. It is the laws governing this passage from local physical moves to global spatial effects that are the spatial laws that underlie building. These local-to-global spatial laws are linked to the evolution of real buildings through what will be called 'generic function', by which is meant the spatial implications of the most fundamental aspects of human use of space, that is the fact of occupation and the fact of movement. At this generic level, function imposes restraints on what is spatially viable, and this is responsible for what all buildings have in common as spatial designs. Generic function is the 'first filter' between the field of possibility and architectural actuality. The second filter is then the cultural or programmatic requirement of that type of building. The third filter is the idiosyncrasies of structure and expression that then distinguish that building from all others. The passage from the possible to the real passes through these three filters, and without an understanding of each we cannot decipher the form-function relation. Most of all, without a knowledge of generic function and its spatial implications we cannot understand that what all buildings have in common in their spatial structures is already profoundly influenced by human functioning in space.

In Chapter 9, 'The fundamental city', the theory of generic function and the three filters is applied to cities to show how much of the growth of settlements is governed by these basic laws. A new computer modelling technique of 'all line analysis', which begins by conceptualising vacant space as an infinitely dense matrix of lines, containing all possible structures, is used to show how the observable regularities in urban forms from the most local to the most global can be seen to be products of the same underlying processes. A fundamental settlement process is proposed, of which particular cultural types are parameterisations. Finally, it is shown how the fundamental settlement process is essentially realised through a small number of spatial ideas which have an essentially geometrical nature.

Part IV of the book, THEORETICAL SYNTHESES, then begins to draw together some of the questions raised in Part I, the regularities shown in Part II and the laws proposed in Part III, to suggest how the two central problems in architectural theory, namely the form-function problem and the form-meaning problem, can be reconceptualised. Chapter 10, 'Space is the machine', reviews the form-function theory in architecture and attempts to establish a pathology of its formulation: how it came to be set up in such a way that it could not be solved. It then proposes how the configuration paradigm permits a reformulation, through which we can not only make sense of the relation between form and function in buildings, but also we can make sense of how and why buildings, in a powerful sense, are 'social objects' and in fact play a powerful role in the realisation and sustaining of human society.

Finally, in chapter 11, 'The reasoning art', the notion of configuration is applied to the study of what architects do, that is design. Previous models of the design process are reviewed, and it is shown that without knowledge of configuration and the concept of the non-discursive, we cannot understand the internalities of the design process. A new knowledge-based model of design is proposed, with configuration at its centre. It is argued from this that because design is a configurational process, and because it is the characteristic of configuration that local changes make global differences, design is necessarily a top down process. This does not mean that it cannot be analysed, or supported by research. It shows however that only configurationally biased knowledge can really support the design process, and this, essentially, is theoretical knowledge. It follows from this that attempts to support designers by building methods and systems for bottom up construction of designs must eventually fail as explanatory systems. They can serve to create specific architectural identities, but not to advance general architectural understanding.

In pursuing an analytic rather than a normative theory of architecture, the book might be thought by some to have pretensions to make the art of architecture into a science. This is not what is intended. One effect of a better scientific understanding of architecture is to show that although architecture as a phenomenon is capable of considerable scientific understanding, this does not mean that as a practice architecture is not an art. On the contrary, it shows quite clearly why it is an art and what the nature and limits of that art are. Architecture is an art because, although in key respects its forms can be analysed and understood by scientific means, its forms can only be prescribed by scientific means in a very restricted sense. Architecture is law governed but it is not determinate. What is governed by the laws is not the form of individual buildings but the field of possibility within which the choice of form is made. This means that the impact of these laws on the passage from problem statement to solution is not direct but indirect. It lies deep in the spatial and physical forms of buildings, in their genotypes, not their phenotypes.

Architecture is therefore not part art, and part science, in the sense that it has both technical and aesthetic aspect, but is both art and science in the sense that it requires both the processes of abstraction by which we know science and the processes of concretion by which we know art. The architect as scientist and as theorist seeks to establish the laws of the spatial and formal materials with which the architect as artist then composes. The greater scientific content of architecture over art is simply a function of the far greater complexity of the raw materials of space and form, and their far greater reverberations for other aspects of life, than any materials that an artist uses. It is the fact that the architect designs with the spatial stuff of living that builds the science of architecture into the art of architecture.

It may seem curious to argue that the quest for a scientific understanding of architecture does not lead to the conclusion that architecture is a science, but nevertheless it is the case. In the last analysis, architectural theory is a matter of understanding architecture as a system of possibilities, and how these are restricted by laws which link this system of possibilities to the spatial potentialities of human life. At this level, and perhaps only at this level, architecture is analogous to language. Language is often naively conceptualised as a set of words and meanings, set out in a dictionary, and syntactic rules by which they may be combined into meaningful sentences, set out in grammars. This is not what language is, and the laws that govern language are not of this kind. This can be seen from the simple fact that if we take the words of the dictionary and combine them in grammatically correct sentences, virtually all are utterly meaningless and do not count as legitimate sentences. The structures of language are the laws which restrict the combinatorial possibilities of words, and through these restrictions construct the sayable and the meaningful. The laws of language do not therefore tell us what to say, but prescribe the structure and limits of the sayable. It is within these limits that we use language as the prime means to our individuality and creativity.

In this sense architecture does resemble language. The laws of the field of architecture do not tell designers what to do. By restricting and structuring the field of combinatorial possibility, they prescribe the limits within which architecture is possible. As with language, what is left from this restrictive structuring is rich beyond imagination. Even so, without these laws buildings would not be human products, any more than meaningless but syntactically correct concatenations of words are human sentences.

The case for a theoretical understanding of architecture then rests eventually not on aspiration to philosophical or scientific status, but on

the nature of architecture itself. The foundational proposition of the book
is that architecture is an inherently theoretical subject. The very act of
building raises issues about the relations of the form of the material world
and the way in which we live in it which (as any archaeologist knows who
has tried to puzzle out a culture from material remains) are unavoidably
both philosophical and scientific. Architecture is the most everyday, the
most enveloping, the largest and the most culturally determined human
artefact. The act of building implies the transmission of cultural conventions answering these questions through custom and habit. Architecture
is their rendering explicit, and their transmutation into a realm of innovation and, at its best, of art. In a sense, architecture is abstract thought
applied to building, even therefore in a sense theory applied to building.
This is why, in the end, architecture must have analytic theories.

Part one

Theoretical preliminaries

chapter one

What architecture adds to building

*The visual impression, the image
produced by differences of light and
colour, is primary in our perception of
a building. We empirically reinterpret
this image into a conception of corpo-
reality, and this defines the form of
the space within ... Once we have
reinterpreted the optical image into
a conception of space enclosed by
mass, we read its purpose from its
spatial form. We thus grasp ... its
content, its meaning.*

PAUL FRANKL

Defining architecture

What is architecture? One thing is clear: if the word is to serve a useful
purpose we must be able to distinguish architecture from building. Since
building is the more basic term, it follows that we must say in what sense
architecture is more than building. The essence of our definition must
say what architecture adds to building.

The commonest 'additive' theory is that architecture adds art to
building. In this analysis, building is an essentially practical and functional
activity on to which architecture superimposes an artistic preoccupation
which, while respecting the practical and functional, is restricted by neither. The extreme version of this view is that architecture is the addition
to building of the practically useless and functionally unnecessary.[1] The
more common is that builders make buildings while architects add style.

From the point of view of finding what people 'really mean' when
they say 'architecture', there are serious problems with these views. The
most obvious is that it defines architecture in terms of what is normally
thought of as its degeneration, that is, that architecture is no more than
the addition of a surface appearance to building. Even if we take the view
that this is what architecture has become, it is surely unacceptable as
a definition of what it should be. Architects believe, and clients on the
whole buy, the idea that architecture is a way of being concerned with the
whole building, and a means of engaging the deepest aspects of what a
building is. If architecture is defined as an add-on which ignores the main
substance of building, then architecture would be an addition to building,
but would not be more than building. On the contrary, it would be considerably less. If we accuse architecture of being no more than this, we
imply that architecture ought to be much more. We are therefore back
to the beginning in our pursuit of a definition.

An equally difficult problem with this view is that it is very hard
to find examples of building with a purely practical and functional aim.
Wherever we find building, we tend to find a preoccupation with style
and expression, however modest. Some of the most striking instances of
this have come from our growing awareness of building by technological-
ly simple societies, where we do not find that simplicity of technique is
associated with simplicity of cultural intent or the elimination of the

preoccupation with style. On the contrary, we find that through the idiosyncrasies of style, building and settlement form becomes one of the primary – though most puzzling and variable – expressions of culture.[2] The term that expresses this discovery, 'architecture without architects', confirms the existence of architecture as something over and above building, even though at the same time it affirms the absence of architects.[3]

It is the awareness of the cultural richness of everyday building that lead Roger Scruton, in his *The aesthetics of architecture* to try to solve the definition problem for architecture by arguing that since all building shares a preoccupation with the aesthetic and the meaningful, all building should be seen as architecture.[4] Scruton seeks to reintegrate architecture with the whole of building. In his view, all that we ever find in architecture is found, at least in embryonic form, in the everyday vernacular in which most of us participate through our everyday lives. Thus: 'Even when architects have a definite "aesthetic" purpose, it may not be more than the desire that their work should "look right" in just the way that tables and chairs, the lay of places at a table, the folds in a napkin, an arrangement of books, may "look right" to a casual observer.' This leads him to a definition: 'Architecture is primarily a vernacular art: it exists first and foremost as a process of arrangement in which every normal man [sic] may participate.'[5]

The difficulty with this definition is that it leads to exactly the wrong kind of distinction between, for example, the careful formal and spatial rules that governed the English suburban house as built endlessly and repetitiously between the wars by speculative builders, and the works of, say, Palladio or Le Corbusier. The work of both of these architects is characterised by radical innovation in exactly those areas of formal and spatial organisation where according to Scruton's definition, there should be a preoccupation with cultural continuity and reduplication. It would seem to follow that Scruton's definition of architecture would cover the familiar English spec builders' vernacular more easily than it would the works of major architectural innovators.

While it may be reasonable, then, to *prefer* the English inter-war vernacular to the works of Palladio and Le Corbusier, it does not seem likely that a *definition* of the ordinary use of the word architecture lies in this direction. On the contrary, Scruton's definition seems to lead us exactly the wrong way. Architecture seems to be exactly not this preoccupation with cultural continuity, but a preference for innovation. Far from using this as a basis for a definition then Scruton's preoccupation with the vernacular seems to accomplish the opposite. It tells us more how to distinguish everyday building from the more ambitious aspirations of what we call architecture.

Is architecture a thing or an activity?

In what direction should we look then for a definition of architecture as more than building? Reflecting on the common meanings of the word, we find little help and more difficulties. The word 'architecture' seems to mean both a *thing* and an *activity*. On the one hand it seems to imply buildings with certain 'architectural' attributes imposed on them. On the other, it seems to describe what architects do, a certain way of going about the process of making buildings. This double meaning raises serious problems for a definition of architecture. If 'architecture' means both attributes of things and attributes of activities, then which 'really is' architecture? The definition surely cannot encompass both. Properties of things seem to exist regardless of the activity that creates them, and activities are what they are regardless of their product. Is architecture, then, 'essentially' a thing or an activity? It must, it seems, be one or the other.

However, when we try each definition in isolation we quickly run into paradoxes. Let us experiment first with the idea that architecture is essentially a thing, that is certain attributes found in some, but not all, buildings. If that is what architecture 'essentially' is, then it would follow that a copy of a building which possesses the architectural attributes will also be architecture, to exactly the same degree and in the same way as the original building. But we baulk at this idea. Copies of architectural buildings seem not themselves to be architecture, but what we have named them as, that is copies of architecture. Certainly we would not normally expect to win an architectural prize with a deliberate copy. On the contrary, we would expect to be disqualified, or at least ridiculed.

What then is missing in the copy? By definition, it cannot be properties of the building since these are identical in both cases. The disqualifying factor must lie in the act of copying. The act of copying somehow makes a building with architectural attributes no longer, in itself, architecture. This means that what is missing in the copy is not to do with the building but to do with the process that created the building. Copying is therefore in some crucial sense not 'architectural'. Even if we start from the proposition that architecture is attributes of building, and therefore in some sense, 'in the object', the problem of the copy shows that after all architecture implies a certain kind of activity, one which is missing in the act of copying.

What then is missing in the act of copying? It can only be that which copying denies, that is the intention to *create*, rather than simply to reproduce, architecture. Without this intention, it seems, a building cannot be architecture. So let us call this the 'creative intention' and try to make it the focus of a definition of architecture. We may experiment with the idea as before. This time, let there be an ambitious but talentless architect who intends as hard as possible to make architecture. Is the product of this intention automatically architecture? Whether it is or not depends on whether it is possible to approve the intention as architectural but disqualify the result. In fact this is a very common form for architectural judgments to take. The products of aspiring architects are often judged by their peers to have failed in exactly this way. A jury may legitimately say: 'We understand your intention but do not think you have succeeded.' How are such judgments made? Clearly there is only one answer: by reference to the objective attributes of the proposed buildings that our would-be architect has designed.

It seems then the normal use of words and common practice has led us in a circle. Creative intention fails as a definition of architecture by reference to positive attributes of things, just as positive attributes of things previously failed by reference to intentions. Yet architecture seems at the same time to mean both. It seems it can only be that the idea of architecture is at once a thing and an activity, certain attributes of buildings and a certain way of arriving at them. Product and process are not, it seems, independent. In judging architecture we note both the attributes of the thing and the intellectual process by which the thing is arrived at.

This may seem at first sight rather odd. It violates the common conception that attributes of things are independent of the processes that put them there. But it does reflect how people talk about architecture. Architectural talk, whether by lay people or by critics, typically mixes comment on product with comment on process. For example, we hear: 'This is an ingenious solution to the problem of…', or 'This is a clever detail', or 'This spatial organisation is boldly conceived', 'I like the way the architect has…', and so on. Each of these is at one and the same time a comment on the objective attributes of the building and a comment on the creative intellectual process that gave rise to it. In spite of the unlikelihood of product and process somehow being interdependent in the idea of architecture, this does seem to be exactly the case. In describing our experience of architecture we describe not only the attributes of things, but also the intellectual processes of which the thing is a manifestation. Only with the simultaneous presence of both do we acknowledge architecture.

There is, it seems, some inconsistency between our normal way of reasoning about things and the way we talk, reasonably and reasoningly, about architecture. We might even say that the idea of architecture exhibits some confusion between subjects and objects, since the judgment that a building is architecture seems at one and the same time to depend on the attributes of the 'objective' thing and on attributes of the 'subjective' process that give rise to the thing. It might be reasonable to expect, then, that further analysis would show that this strangeness in the idea of architecture was pathological and that, with a more careful definition, product and process, and object and subject, could and should be separated.

In fact, we will find the contrary. As we proceed with our exploration of what architecture is and what it adds to building we will find that the inseparability of products and processes and of subject and objects is the essence of what architecture is. It is our intellectual expectations that it should be otherwise that are at fault. Architecture is at once product and process, at once attribute of things and attribute of activity, so that we actually see, or think we see, both when we see and name architecture.

How does this apparent interdependence of product and process then arise as architecture from the act of making a building? To understand this we must first know what building, the allegedly lesser activity, is, and we must understand it both as product and as process. Only this will allow us to see what is distinctive about architecture, and how this distinctiveness involves both product and process. To allow this to become fully clear, the argument that follows will be taken in two stages. First we will look at building as a product, in order to ask what it is about the building as product that architecture takes hold of and adds something to. Then we will look at building as a process, in order to ask how the process of architecture, as adding something to building, is different.

So what is a building?

The question 'what is a building?' tends to provoke two kinds of simplification. The first is that because buildings are purposeful objects we can say what they are by saying what their purpose is. The second is that there must be some simple primordial purpose which was the original reason for buildings and therefore constitutes a kind of continuing essence of building. The first simplification is a logical error, the second a historical one. Both find their commonest, but not only, expression in such ideas as that buildings are essentially 'shelter'.

   Both simplifications arise because purposes are seen to be anterior to objects and therefore in some sense explanatory of them. But logically, functional definitions are absurd. In defining building in terms of a function rather than an object no distinction is made between buildings as objects and other entities which also can or do provide that function, as for example trees, tents, caves and parasols also provide shelter. Functional definitions are also dishonest. One who defines a building as a shelter has a picture of a building in mind, but one which is implicit rather than explicit, so that the imprecision of the definition is never revealed to the definer. If we say 'a building is a shelter' we mentally see a building and conceive of it functioning as a shelter, so that the function seems to 'explain' the object. Functional definitions only appear to work because they conceal an implicit idea of the object. This prevents the imprecision of the definition from being apparent to the definer. Even if the function were thought to be unique to the object, the definition of an object through its function would never be satisfactory since we could never be sure either that this function is necessarily unique to this object, or that this is the only 'essential' function of this object.

Historically in fact all the evidence is that neither is the case. If we consider the phenomenon of building even in the earliest and simplest societies, one of the most striking things that we find is that buildings are normally multifunctional: they provide shelter from the elements, they provide some kind of spatial scheme for ordering social relations and activities, they provide a framework for the arrangement of objects, they provide a diversity of internal and external opportunities for aesthetic and cultural expression, and so on. On the evidence we have, it is difficult to find historical or anthropological grounds for believing that buildings are not in their very nature multifunctional.

Nor is there any reason why we should expect them to be. In spite of the persistence of the absurd belief that humankind lived in caves until neolithic times (beginning about 10–12,000 years ago), and then used the cave as the model for the building,[6] there is evidence that human beings have created recognisable buildings for a very long time, perhaps as long as at least three hundred thousand years.[7] We do not know how the antiquity of building compares with that of language, but it is clear that the evolutionary history of each is very long, and that conjectural historical ontologies are equally irrelevant to both in trying to understand the complex nature of either as social and cultural phenomenon. The speculation that buildings are somehow 'explained' by being defined as shelters, because we imagine that there must have been a time when this was *all* that building was, is about as useful in understanding the social and cultural complexities of building as the idea that language began with pointing and grunting is to theories of the structure and functioning of language.

But it is not only time that has given buildings their variety of cultural expression. The nature of the building as an object itself has complexities which in themselves naturally tend to multifunctionality and diversity of cultural expression. It is only by understanding the complex nature of the building as object that we can begin to understand its natural tendency to multifunctionality. At the most elementary level, a building is a construction of physical elements or materials into a more or less stable form, as a result of which a space is created which is distinct from the ambient space. At the very least, then, a building is both a physical and a spatial transformation of the situation that existed before the building was built. Each aspect of this transformation, the physical and the spatial, already has, as we shall see, a social value, and provides opportunity for the further elaboration of this value, in that the physical form of the building may be given further cultural significance by the shaping and decoration of elements, and the spatial form may be made more complex, by conceptual or physical distinctions, to provide a spatial patterning of activities and relationships.

However, even in the most primitive, unelaborated state, the effect of this elementary transformation of material and space on human beings – that is its 'functional' effect – is complex. Part, but only part, of this complexity is the functional effect that the 'shelter' theorists have noted, namely the physical effect that bodies are protected from ambient elements that in the absence of the building might be experienced as hostile. These elements include inclement weather conditions, hostile species or unwelcome conspecifics. When we say that a building is a 'shelter', we mean that it is a kind of protection for the body. To be a protective shelter a building must create a protected space through a stable construction. What is protective is the physical form of the building. What is protected is the space. Buildings have a bodily function, broad and non-specific, but classifiable as bodily, as a result of which the building has space able to contain bodies, and certain physical properties through which bodies are protected.

However, even the simplest bodily act of making a shelter is more complex than might appear at first sight. To enclose a space by a construction creates not only a physical distinction on the surface of the earth, but also a logical, or categoric distinction. We acknowledge this through terms like 'inside' and 'outside'. These are relational notions with an essentially logical nature, not simple physical facts. They arise as a kind of 'logical emergence' from the more elementary physical fact of making a boundary. The relationality of these 'logical emergents' can be demonstrated by simply pointing to the interdependence of 'inside' and 'outside'. One implies the other, and we cannot create a space inside

without also making a space outside. Logicality can be demonstrated by
direct analogy. The physical process of drawing a boundary is analogous
to naming a category, since when we do so we also by implication name
all that is not that category, that is we imply the complement of that category, in the same sense that when we name the space inside we also imply
all the space that is outside. In that sense the space outside is the complement of the space inside. Logicians confirm this analogy by drawing Venn
diagrams, that represent concepts as all that falls within the space of a circle, an exactly analogous logical gesture to the creation of a boundary in
real space.

As Russell has pointed out,[8] relations, especially spatial relations,
are very puzzling entities. They seem to exist 'objectively', in the sense
(to use the example given by Russell) that 'Edinburgh is to the north of
London', but we cannot point directly to the relation in the way that we
can to other entities which seem to 'really exist'. We must accept, Russell
argues, that 'the relation, like the terms it relates, is not dependent on
thought, but belongs to the independent world which thought apprehends,
but does not create'. We must then accept, he continues, that a relation
'is neither in space nor in time, neither material nor mental, yet it is
something'.

The 'objectivity' of relations, and of the more complex relational
schemes we call 'configurations', will be a continuing theme in this book.
However, even at the simplest level of the creation of a boundary by the
simplest act of building, matters are yet more complex. The logical distinctions made by drawing boundaries are also sociological distinctions,
in that the distinction between inside and outside is made by a social being,
whose power to make this distinction becomes recognised not only in the
physical making of the boundary and the creation of the protected space
but also in the logical consequences that arise from that distinction. This
is best expressed as a right. The drawing of a boundary establishes not
only a physical separateness, but also the social separateness of a domain
– the protected space – identified with an individual or collectivity which
creates and claims special rights in that domain. The logical distinction
and the sociological distinction in that sense emerge from the act of making a shelter even if they are not intended. The primary act of building, we

might say, is already complex in that minds, and even social relations, are
engaged by bodily transformations.

As is the case with the logical complexity, the sociological complexity implied by the boundary is in its very nature relational. Indeed, it is
the logic of the relational complex that gives rise to the sociological distinctions through which building first begins to reflect and intervene in
social relations. It is this essential relationality of form and of space
which is appropriated in the processes by which buildings are transformed from bodily objects to social and cultural objects. The fundamental relational complex of form and space created by the act of making the
simplest built object is the seed of all future relational properties of
spaces through which buildings become fully social objects.

A building then becomes socially significant over and above its bodily functions in two ways: first by elaborating spaces into socially work-
able patterns to generate and constrain some socially sanctioned – and
therefore normative – pattern of encounter and avoidance; and second by
elaborating physical forms and surfaces into patterns through which culturally or aesthetically sanctioned identities are expressed. The fundamental duality of form and space that we noted in the most elementary
forms of the building thus continues into its complex forms. By the elaboration of space, a social domain is constituted as a lived milieu. By the
elaboration of form a social domain is represented as significant identities
and encounters. In both senses, buildings create more complex patterns
from the basic bodily stuff of form and space. It is through these patterns
that buildings acquire their potential at once to constitute and represent
– and thus in time to appear as the very foundation of – our social and
cultural existence.

We may summarise what we have said about the nature of buildings
as objects in a diagram which we will use from now on as a kind of fundamental diagram of the building as object (see fig. 1.1). The essence of the
diagram is that a building even at the most basic level embodies two dualities, one between physical form and spatial form and the other between
bodily function and socio-cultural function. The link between the two is
that the socio-cultural function arises from the ways in which forms and
spaces are elaborated into patterns, or, as we will in due course describe

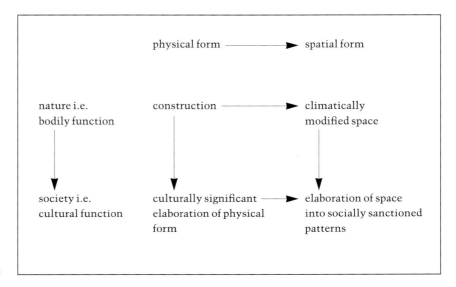

Figure 1.1

them, into configurations. We must now look more carefully at what we mean by the elaboration of form and space into configuration, since this will be the key to our argument not only about the nature of buildings, but also, in due course, to how architecture arises from building.

Let us begin with a simple and familiar case of the elaboration of the physical form of the building: the doric column. When we look at a doric column, we see a plinth, a pedestal, a shaft, a capital, and so on, that is, we see a construction. The elements rest one upon the other, and their relation to each other takes advantage of and depends on the natural law of gravity. But this is not all that we see. The relations of the elements of a column governed by the law of gravity would hold regardless of the 'doric-ness' of the elements. If, for example, we were to replace the doric capital with an ionian capital, the effect on the construction would be negligible, but the effect on the 'doricness' of the ensemble would be devastating.

So what is doricness? Clearly it is not a type of construction, since we may substitute non-doric elements in the ensemble without construc-tional penalty. We must acknowledge that doricness is not then in itself a set of physical relations, although it depends on them. Doricness is a scheme in which elements with certain kinds of elaboration are 'above' and 'below' others in a certain relational sequence which emerges from construction but is not given by construction. On the contrary, the notion of 'above' and 'below' as we find them in doricness seem to be 'logical emergents' from the act of construction in exactly the same sense that 'inside' and 'outside' were logical emergents from the physical construction of a boundary. Doricness is then a logical construction, one built on the back of a physical construction but a logical construction nonetheless. Through the logical doricness of the ensemble, we may say that we move from the simple visuality of the physically interdependent system, to enter the realm of the intelligible. Doricness is a configuration of properties that we understand, over and above what we see as physical interdependencies, a form of relational elaboration to something which exists in physical form, but which through this elaboration stands clear of its physicality. This process of moving from the visible to the intelligible is, we will see in due course, very basic to our experience both of building and of architecture, and, even more so, to the difference between one and the other.

Spatial patterns in buildings also arise as elaborations on primitive logical emergents from the physical act of building. As with doricness, they depend on but cannot be explained by natural law (as many have tried to do by appeal to biological 'imperatives' such as 'territoriality'). The origins of relational schemes of space lie somewhere between the ordering capacities of the mind and the spatial ordering inherent in the ways in which social relationships are realised in space. With space as with form, we therefore find a split in building between a bodily nature, albeit with a rudimentary relational nature, and a more elaborated configurational nature which relates to minds and social experience rather than to bodies and individual experience. The passage from the simple space to a configuration of space is also the passage from the visible to the intelligible.

Space is, however, a more inherently difficult topic than physical form, for two reasons. First, space is vacancy rather than thing, so even its bodily nature is not obvious, and cannot be taken for granted in the way that we think we can take objects for granted. (See chapter 10 for a further discussion of this assumption.) Second, related spaces, almost by definition, cannot be seen all at once, but require movement from one to other to experience the whole. This is to say that relationality in space is rarely accessible to us as a single experience. We must therefore digress for a moment to talk about space as a phenomenon, and how we can overcome the difficulties that exist in talking about it. We will take this in two stages. First, we will talk about the problem of how far space can be seen as an objective, independent 'thing-in-itself'. We must do this because there is great confusion about the status of space and how far it can be regarded as an independent entity rather than simply as a by-product of, say, the arrangement of physical things. Second, we will talk about space as configuration, since it is as configuration that it has its most powerful and independent effects on the way buildings and built environments formed and how they function for their purposes.

About space

It is far from obvious that space is, in some important sense, an objective property of buildings, describable independently of the building as a physical thing. Most of our common notions of space do not deal with space as an entity in itself but tie it in some way to entities that are not space. For example, even amongst those with an interest in the field, the idea of 'space' will usually be transcribed as the 'use of space', the 'perception of space', the 'production of space' or as 'concepts of space'. In all these common expressions, the idea of space is given significance by linking it directly to human behaviour or intentionality. Common spatial concepts from the social sciences such as 'personal space' and 'human territoriality' also tie space to the human agent, and do not acknowledge its existence independently of the human agent. In architecture, where concepts of space are sometimes unlinked from direct human agency, through notions such as 'spatial hierarchy' and 'spatial scale' we still find that space is rarely described in a fully independent way. The concept of 'spatial enclosure' for example, which describes space by reference to the physical forms that define it rather than as a thing in itself, is the commonest architectural way of describing space.

All these concepts confirm the difficulty of conceptualising space as a thing in itself. On occasion, this difficulty finds an extreme expression.

For example, Roger Scruton believes that the idea of space is a category mistake made by pretentious architects, who have failed to understand that space is not a thing in itself, but merely the obverse side of the physical object, the vacancy left over by the building. For Scruton, it is self-evident that space in a field and in a cathedral are the same thing except insofar as the interior built surfaces of the cathedral make it appear that the interior space has distinctive properties of its own. All talk about space is error, he argues, because it can be reduced to talk about buildings as physical things.[9]

In fact, even at a practical level, this is a bizarre view. Space is, quite simply, what we use in buildings. It is also what we sell. No developer offers to rent walls. Walls make the space, and cost the money, but space is the rentable commodity. Why then is Scruton embarrassed by the concept of space? Let me suggest that Scruton is making an educated error, one that he would not have made if he had not been so deeply imbued with the western philosophical tradition in which he has earned his living – and to which, incidentally, he has written an outstanding introduction.[10]

The dominant view of space in western culture has been one we might loosely call the 'Galilean-Cartesian'. This view arises from a scheme of reasoning first set out in full clarity by Descartes.[11] The primary properties of physical objects are, he argued, their 'extension', that is, their measurable properties like length, breadth and width. Because extension can be quantified by measuring devices which do not depend on human agency, extensions can be seen as the indubitably objective properties of things, unlike 'secondary' properties like 'green' or 'nice' which seem to depend in some way on interaction with observers.

Now if extension is the primary property of objects, then it is a short step to see it also as the primary property of the space within which objects sit. As Descartes says: 'After examination we shall find that there is nothing remaining in the idea of body excepting that it is extended in length, breadth and depth; and this is comprised in our idea of space, not only of that which is full of body, but also that which is called a vacuum.'[12] In other words, when we take the object away from its space its extension is still present as an attribute of space. Space is therefore generalised extension, or extension without objects. Descartes again: 'In space...

we attribute to extension a generic unity, so that after having removed from a certain space the body which occupied it, we do not suppose we have also removed the extension of that space.'[13]

Following this reasoning, space comes to be seen as the general abstract framework of extension against which the properties of objects are defined, a metric background to the material objects that occupy space. This view of space seems to most of us quite natural, no more than an extrapolation of commonsense. Unfortunately, once we see space in this way, we are doomed not to understand how it plays a role in human affairs. Culturally and socially, space is never simply the inert background of our material existence. It is a key aspect of how societies and cultures are constituted in the real world, and, through this constitution, structured for us as 'objective' realities. Space is more than a neutral framework for social and cultural forms. It is built into those very forms. Human behaviour does not simply happen in space. It has its own spatial forms. Encountering, congregating, avoiding, interacting, dwelling, teaching, eating, conferring are not just activities that happen in space. In themselves they constitute spatial patterns.

It is because this is so that spatial organisation through buildings and built environments becomes one of the principle ways in which culture is made real for us in the material world, and it is because this is so that buildings can and normally do carry social ideas within their spatial forms. To say this does not imply determinism between space to society, simply that space is always likely to be structured in the spatial image of a social process of some kind. The question is: how exactly does this happen, and what are these structures like?

Space as configuration

One thing is clear. Encountering, congregating, avoiding, interacting, dwelling, conferring are not attributes of individuals, but patterns, or configurations, formed by groups or collections of people. They depend on an engineered pattern of co-presence, and indeed co-absence. Very few of the purposes for which we build buildings and environments are not 'people configurations' in this sense. We should therefore in principle expect that the relation between people and space, if there is one, will

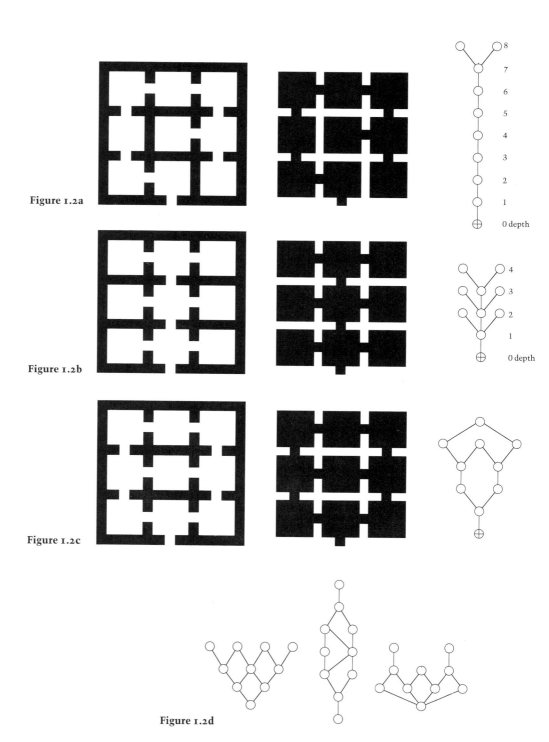

Figure 1.2a

Figure 1.2b

Figure 1.2c

Figure 1.2d

be found at the level of the configuration of space rather than the individual space. This is confirmed by commonsense. Individual spaces place little limit on human activity, except for those of size and perhaps shape. In
most reasonable spaces, most human activities can be carried out. But the
relation between space and social existence does not lie at the level of the
individual space, or individual activity. It lies in the relations between
configurations of people and configurations of space.

   To take the first steps towards understanding how this happens,
we must understand how, in principle, a configuration of space can be
influenced by, or influence, a configuration of people. Let us therefore
consider some simple hypothetical examples. The two notional 'courtyard' buildings of figure 1.2a and b show in the first column in black, in
the normal way, the pattern of physical elements of the buildings. The
corresponding figures in the second column then show in black the corresponding pattern of spatial elements. The basic physical structures and
cell divisions of the two 'buildings' are the same, and each has the same
pattern of adjacencies between cells and the same number of internal and
external openings. All that differs is the locations of cell entrances. But
this is enough to ensure that from the point of view of how a collection of
individuals could use the space, the spatial patterns, or 'configurations',
are about as different as they could be. The pattern of permeability created
by the disposition of entrances is the critical thing. Seen this way, one
layout is a near perfect single sequence, with a minimal branch at the
end. The other is branched everywhere about the strong central spaces.

   Now the pattern of permeability would make relatively little difference to the building structurally or climatically, that is to the bodily aspect
of buildings, especially if we assume similar patterns of external fenestra-
tion, and insert windows wherever the other had entrances onto the courtyard. But it would make a dramatic difference to how the layout would
work as, say, a domestic interior. For example, it is very difficult for more
than one person to use a single sequence of spaces. It offers little in the
way of community or privacy, but much in the way of potential intrusion.
The branched pattern, on the other hand, offers a definite set of potential
relations between community and privacy, and many more resources
against intrusion. These differences are inherent in the space patterns,

and would apply to whole classes of human activity patterns. In themselves the spatial layouts offer a range of limitations and potentialities. They suggest the possibility that architectural space might be subject to limiting laws, not of a deterministic kind, but such as to set morphological bounds within which the relations between form and function in buildings are worked out.

We will see from chapter 3 onwards that it is by expressing these pattern properties in a numerical way that we can find clear relations between space patterns and how collections of people use them. However, before we embark on numbers, there is a visually useful way of capturing some of the key differences between the two spatial patterns. This is a device we call a justified graph, or j-graph. In this we imagine that we are in a space which we call the root or base of the graph, and represent this as a circle with a cross inscribed. Then, representing spaces as circles, and relations of access as lines connecting them, we align immediately above the root all spaces which are directly connected to the root, and draw in the connections. These are the spaces at 'depth one' from the root. Then an equal distance above the 'depth one' row we align the spaces that connect directly to first row spaces, forming the line of 'depth two' spaces, and connect these to the depth one spaces, and so on. Sometimes we will have to draw rather long and circuitous lines to link spaces at different levels, but this does not matter. It is the fact of connection that matters. The laws of graphs guarantee that if the layout is all at one level then we can make all the required connections by drawing lines connecting the spaces without crossing other lines.[14]

The resulting j-graph is a picture of the 'depth' of all spaces in a pattern from a particular point in it. The third column in figure 1.2a and b shows j-graphs for the corresponding spatial structures, drawn using the exterior space as root. We can immediately see that the first is a 'deep tree' form, and the second a 'shallow tree' form. By 'tree' we mean that there is one link less than the number of cells linked, and that there are therefore no rings of circulation in the graph. All trees, even two as different as in the two in the figures, share the characteristic that there is only one route from each space to each other space – a property that is highly relevant to how building layouts function. However, where 'rings' are found, the justified graph makes them as clear as the 'depth' properties, showing them in a very simple and clear way as what they are, that is alternative route choices from one part of the pattern to another. The series of figures in figure 1.2c shows a hypothetical case, based on the same basic 'building' as the previous figures.

We do not have to justify the graph using the outside space as root. This is only one way – though a singularly useful way – of looking at a building. We can of course justify the graph from any space within it, and this will tell us what layout is like from the point of view of that space, taking into account both depth and ring properties. When we do this we discover a fact about the spatial layouts of buildings and settlements that is so fundamental that it is probably in itself the key to most aspects of human spatial organisation. This is the simple fact that a pattern of space not only looks different but actually is different when justified from the point of view of its different constituent elements. The three notional j-graphs shown in figure 1.2d appear very different from each other, but all three are in fact the same graph justified from the point of view of different constituent spaces. The depth and ring properties could hardly appear more different if they were different configurations. It is through the creation and distribution of such differences that space becomes such a powerful raw material for the transmission of culture through buildings and settlement forms, and also a potent means of architectural discovery and creation. Let us see how.

Formally defining configuration

First we need to bring a little more formality into the definition of 'configuration'. Like the word 'pattern' (which we do not use because it implies more regularity than we will find in most spatial arrangements), configuration seems to be a concept addressed to the whole of a complex rather than to its parts. Intuitively, it seems to mean a set of relationships among things all of which interdepend in an overall structure of some kind. There is a way of formalising this idea that is as simple as it is necessary. If we define spatial relations as existing when there is any type of link – say adjacency or permeability – between two spaces, then configuration exists when relations between two spaces are changed according to how we relate one or other or both to at least one other space.

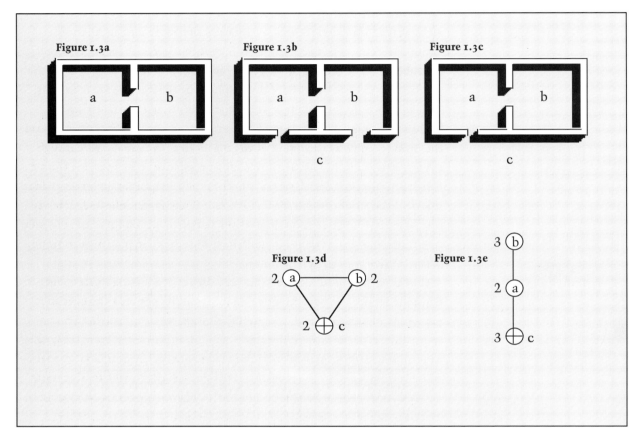

Figure 1.3a

Figure 1.3b

Figure 1.3c

Figure 1.3d

Figure 1.3e

Figure 1.3

This rather odd sounding definition can be explained through a simple graphic example. Figure 1.3a shows a cell divided by a partition into two, sub-cell *a* and sub-cell *b*, with a door creating a relation of permeability between the two. It is clear that the relation is formally 'symmetrical' in the sense that cell *a* is to cell *b* as *b* is to *a*. The same would be true of two cells which were adjacent and therefore in the relation of neighbour to each other. If *a* is *b*'s neighbour, then *b* must also be *a*'s neighbour. This 'symmetry', which follows the algebraic rather than the geometrical definition, is clearly an objective property of the relation of a and b and does not depend on how we choose to see the relation.

Now consider figures 1.3b and c in which we have added relations to a third space, c (which is in fact the outside space), but in a different way so that in 1.3b both a and b are directly permeable to c, whereas in 1.3c, only a is directly permeable to c. This means that in 1.3c we must pass through a to get to b from c, whereas in 1.3b we can go either way. In 1.3c therefore, a and b are different with respect to c. We must pass through a to get to b from c, but we do not need to pass through b to get to a from c. *With respect to c*, the relation has become asymmetrical. In other words, the relation between a and b has been redefined by the relation each has to a third space. This is a configurational difference. Configuration is a set of interdependent relations in which each is determined by its relation to all the others.

We can show such configurational differences rather neatly, and clarify their nature, by using the j-graph, as in figures 1.3d and e, corresponding to 1.3b and 1.3c respectively. Compared to 1.3a, spaces b and c in 1.3e have acquired 'depth' with respect to each other, in that their relation is now indirect and only exists by virtue of a. The numbers adjacent to each space in the j-graph index this by showing the total depth of each space from the other two. In contrast, 1.3d has acquired a 'ring' that links all three spaces, meaning that each has a choice of route to each of the others. The graph of 1.3d is identical when seen from each of its spaces, while in 1.3e, b and c are identical, but a is different.

Society in the form of the object

Now let us use this concept of configuration, and its key spatial dimensions of depth and rings, to try to detect the presence of cultural and social ideas in the spatial forms of buildings. Figures 1.4a, b and c show, on the left, the ground-floor plans of three French houses, and to their immediate right, their j-graphs drawn initially from the outside, treating it as a single space, then to the right again three further j-graphs justified from three different internal spaces.[15] Looking at the j-graphs drawn from the outside, we can see that in spite of the geometrical differences in the houses there are strong similarities in the configurations. This can be seen most easily by concentrating on the space marked sc, or salle commune, which is the main everyday living space, in which cooking also occurs and everyday visitors are received. In each case, we can see that the salle commune lies on all non-trivial rings (a trivial ring is one which links the same pair of spaces twice), links directly to an exterior space – that is, it is at depth one in the complex – and acts as a link between the living spaces and various spaces associated with domestic work carried out by women.

The salle commune also has a more fundamental property, one which arises from its relation to the spatial configuration of the house as a whole. If we count the number of spaces we must pass through to go from the salle commune to all other spaces, we find that it comes to a total which is less than for any other space – that is, it has less depth than any other space in the complex. The general form of this measure [16] is called *integration*, and can be applied to any space in any configuration: the less depth from the complex as a whole, the more integrating the space, and vice versa. This means that every space in the three complexes can be assigned an 'integration value'.[17]

Now once we have done this we can ask questions about how the different functions in the house are 'spatialised', that is how they are embedded in the overall spatial configuration. When we do this, we find that it is very common that different functions are spatialised in different ways, and that this can often be expressed clearly through 'integration' analysis. In the three French houses, for example, we find that there is a certain order of integration among the spaces where different functions are carried out, always with the salle commune as the most integrated, as can be seen in the j-graphs beside each plan. If all the functions of the three houses are set out in order of the integration values of the spaces in which they occur, beginning with the most integrated space, we can read this, from left to right, as: the salle commune is more integrated (i.e. has less depth to all other spaces) than the corridor, which is more integrated than the exterior, and so on. To the extent that there are commonalities in the sequence of inequalities, then we can say that there is a common pattern to the way in which different functions are spatialised in the house. We call such common patterns 'inequality genotypes',

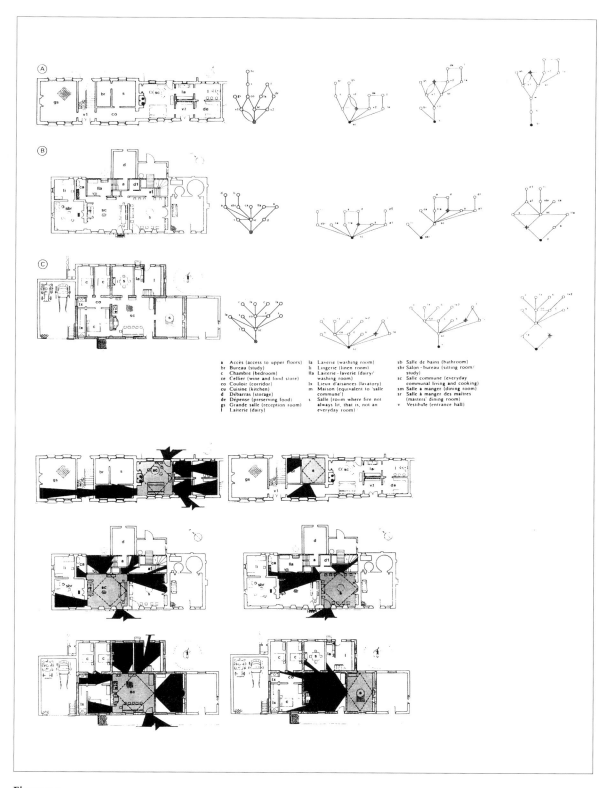

a   Accès (access to upper floors)
br Bureau (study)
c   Chambre (bedroom)
ce Cellier (wine and food store)
co Couloir (corridor)
cu Cuisine (kitchen)
d   Débarras (storage)
de Dépense (preserving food)
gs Grande salle (reception room)
l   Laiterie (dairy)

la Laverie (washing room)
li Lingerie (linen room)
lla Laiterie - laverie (dairy/
    washing room)
lx Lieux d'aisances (lavatory)
m   Maison (equivalent to 'salle
    commune')
s   Salle (room where fire not
    always lit, that is, not an
    everyday room)

sb Salle de bains (bathroom)
sbr Salon - bureau (sitting room/
    study)
sc Salle commune (everyday
    communal living and cooking)
sm Salle à manger (dining room)
sr Salle à manger des maîtres
    (masters' dining room)
v   Vestibule (entrance hall)

Figure 1.4

because they refer not to the surface appearances of forms but to deep structures underlying spatial configurations and their relation to living patterns.[18]

These results flow from an analysis of space-to-space permeability. But what about the relation of visibility, which passes through spaces? The three rows of figures on the right in figure 1.4 show all the space that can be seen with the doors open from a diamond-shaped space within each salle commune and one other space, drawn by joining the centre points of each wall of a room, and thus covering half of the space in the room. The idea of the diamond shape is that space use (in most western cultures) is normally concentrated within this diamond shape, the corners commonly being reserved for objects. The diagrams show that in each case the salle commune has a far more powerful visual field than the salle. In other words, the spatial and functional differences between spaces that we find through the analysis of permeability in the houses also appear in the analysis of visibility. These visibility differences can also form the basis for quantitative and statistical analysis.

This type of method allows us to retrieve from house plans configurational properties that relate directly to the social and cultural functioning of the house. In other words, through spatial configuration culturally determined patterns are embedded in the material and spatial 'objectivity' of buildings. By the analysis of spaces and functions in terms of their configurational relations within the house, and the search for common patterns across samples, we can see how buildings can transmit common cultural tendencies through spatial form. We must now ask how and why this is the case, and what follows from it?

The non-discursivity of configuration: ideas we think of and ideas we think with

The answer will take us to the centre of our argument: the non-discursivity of configuration. Non-discursivity means that we do not know how to talk about it. The difficulty of talking about spatial or formal configurations in architecture has always seemed a rather peripheral problem to architectural theory. I suggest it is the central problem, and part of a much more general problem in human affairs.

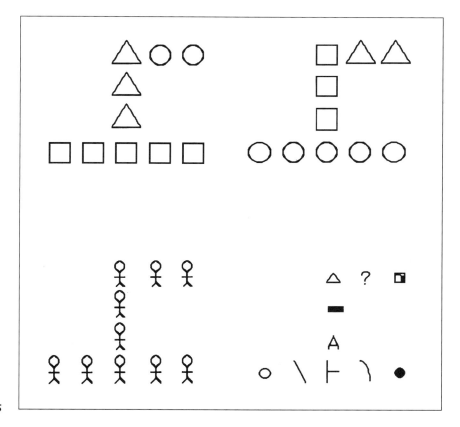

Figure 1.5

Let us begin to explore the intuitive aspects of the idea of configuration a little further. Consider the four groups of elements in figure 1.5. Each group is a different set of 'things', but placed in more or less the same overall 'configuration'. The human mind has no difficulty in seeing that the configurations are the same, in spite of the differences in the constituent 'things', and this shows that we easily recognise a configuration, even where we have no way of giving it a name and thus assigning it to a category – although we might try to do so by making analogies with configurations for which names are already at hand, such as 'L-shaped', or 'star-shaped'. However, the fact that our minds recognised configurations as being the same even when there is no name at hand to link them shows that our ability to recognise and understand configuration is prior to the assignment of names.

Configuration seems in fact to be what the human mind is good at intuitively, but bad at analytically. We easily recognise configuration without conscious thought, and just as easily use configurations in everyday life without thinking of them, but we do not know what it is we recognise and we are not conscious of what it is we use and how we use it. We have no language for describing configurations, that is, we have no means of saying what it is we know. This problem is particularly salient in buildings and architecture, because both have the effect of imposing spatial and formal configuration on the world in which we live. But the problem is not confined to architecture. On the contrary it appears to be present to some degree in most cultural and social behaviours. In using language, for example, we are aware of words and believe that in speaking and hearing we are handling words. However, language only works because we are able to use the configurational aspects of language, that is the syntactic and semantic rules which govern how words are to be assembled into meaningful complexes, in a way which makes their operation automatic and unconscious. In language we can therefore distinguish ideas we think *of*, that is the words and what they represent, and ideas we think *with*, that is syntactic and semantic rules which govern how we deploy words to create meaning. The words we think *of* seem to us like things, and are at the level of conscious thought. The hidden structures we think *with* have the nature of configurational rules, in that they tell us how things are to be assembled, and work below the level of consciousness. This 'unconscious configurationality' seems to prevail in all areas where we use rule systems to behave in ways which are recognisable as social. Behaviour at table, or the playing of games, appear to us as spatio-temporal events, but they are given order and purpose by the underlying configurational 'ideas-to-think-with' through which these events are generated. We acknowledge the importance of this unseen configurationality labelling it as a form of knowledge. We talk about 'knowing how to behave', or 'knowing a language'.

We can call this kind of knowledge 'social knowledge', and note that its purpose is to create, order and make intelligible the spatio-temporal events through which we recognise the presence of culture in everyday life. We must of course take care to distinguish social knowledge from forms of knowledge which we learn in schools and universities whose purpose is to understand the world rather than to behave in it, and which we might therefore call analytic, or scientific knowledge. In itself (though not necessarily in its consequences) analytic knowledge leaves the world as it is, since its purpose is to understand. Analytic knowledge is knowledge where we learn the abstract principles through which spatio-temporal phenomena are related – we might say the 'configurationality' – consciously. We are aware of the principles both when we acquire and when we use the knowledge. As a result, through the intermediary of the abstract, we grasp the concrete. In social knowledge, in contrast, knowledge of abstract configurationality is acquired through the process of creating and experiencing spatio-temporal events. Social knowledge works precisely because the abstract principles through which spatio-temporal phenomena are brought together into meaningful patterns are buried beneath habits of doing, and never need be brought to conscious attention.[19]

In spite of these functional differences, social knowledge and analytic knowledge are made up of the same elements: on the one hand, there is knowledge of spatio-temporal phenomena, on the other, there are abstract 'configurational' structures that link them together. But whereas in social knowledge the abstract ideas are held steady as ideas to think with in order to create spatio-temporal events in the real world, so that the abstract ideas become the normative bases of behaviour, in scientific knowledge, an attempt is made to hold spatio-temporal phenomena steady in order to bring the abstract structures through which we interpret them to the surface in order to examine them critically and, if necessary, to reconstitute them.

This can be usefully clarified by a diagram, see figure 1.6. The difference between the two forms of knowledge lies essentially in the degree to which abstract ideas are at the level of conscious thought and therefore at risk. The whole purpose of science is to put the abstract 'ideas we think with' in making sense of spatio-temporal events at risk. In social knowledge, the whole purpose of the 'knowledge' would be put at risk by bringing them to conscious thought since their function is to be used normatively to create society. However, it is clearly a possibility that the abstract structures of social knowledge could, as with science, themselves become the object of conscious thought. This, in a nutshell, is the programme of

	abstract principles	spacial-temporal events
social knowledge	codes, rules ideas to think	speech, social behaviour, spaces, ideas to think
analytic knowledge	theories, hypotheses paradigms	'facts', phenomena

Figure 1.6

'structuralism'. The essence of the structuralist method is to ask: can we build a model of the abstract principles of a system (e.g. language) that 'generates' all and only the spatio-temporal events that can legitimately happen? Such a model would be a theory of the system. It would, for example, 'explain' our intuitive sense that some strings of words are meaningful sentences and others – most – are not. Structuralism is rather like taking the output of a computer as the phenomena to be explained, and trying to find out what programme could generate all and only these phenomena. Structuralism is an enquiry into the unconscious configurational bases of social knowledge, that is, it is an enquiry into the non-discursive dimensions of social and cultural behaviour.

Building as the transmission of culture through artefacts

The spatial and formal patterns that are created through buildings and settlements are classic instances of the problem of non-discursivity, both in the sense of the configurational nature of ideas we think with in creating and using space, and in the sense of the role these play in social knowledge. As has already been indicated, one of the most pervasive examples of this is the dwelling . Domestic space varies in the degree to which it is subject to social knowledge, but it is not uncommon for it to be patterned according to codes of considerable intricacy which govern what spaces there are, how they are labelled, how bounded they are, how they are connected and sequenced, what activities go together in them and which are separated, what individuals or categories of persons have what kinds of rights in them, how they are decorated, what kinds of objects should be displayed in them and how, and so on. These patterns vary from one cultural group to another, but invariably we handle domestic space patterns without thinking of them and even without being aware of them until they are challenged. In general, we only become aware of the degree of patterning in our own culture when we encounter another form of patterning in another culture.

But domestic space is only the most intensive and complex instance of a more generalised phenomenon. Buildings and settlements of all kinds, and at all levels, are significantly underpinned by configurational non-discursivity. It is through this that buildings – and indeed built environments of all kinds – become part of what Margaret Mead called 'the transmission of culture through artefacts'.[20] This transmission occurs largely through the configurational aspects of space and form in those environments. For example, we think consciously of buildings as physical or spatial objects and we think of their parts as physical or spatial parts, like columns or rooms. But we think of 'buildings' as whole entities through the unconscious intermediary of configuration, in that when we think of a particular kind of building, we are conscious not only of an image of an object, but at the same time of the complex of spatial relations that such a building entails. As space – and also as meaningful forms – buildings are configurational, and because they are configurational their most important social and cultural properties are nondiscursive. It is through non-discursivity that the social nature of buildings is transmitted, because it is through configuration that the raw materials of space and form are given social meaning. The social stuff of buildings, we may say, is the configurational stuff, both in the sense that buildings are configurations of space designed to order in space at least some aspects of social relationships, and in the sense that it is through the creation of some kind of configuration in the form of the building that something like a cultural 'meaning' is transmitted.

Building as process
How then can this help us make the distinction between architecture and building? We note of course that we now begin not from the notion that

buildings prior to architecture are only practical and functional objects, but from the proposition that prior to architecture buildings are already complex instances of the transmission of culture through artefacts. This does not mean of course that buildings of the same type and culture will be identical with each other. On the contrary, it is common for vernacular architectures to exhibit prodigious variety at the level of individual cases, so much so that the grounds for believing that the cases constitute instances of a common vernacular style, either in form or space, can be quite hard to pin down.

The crucial step in arriving at our definition of architecture is to understand first how the vernacular builder succeeds in making a building as a complex relational structure through which culture is transmitted, while at the same time creating what will often be a unique individual building. We do not have to look far for the answer. This combination of common structure and surface variety is exactly what we find where social knowledge is in operation in the form in which we have just described it: complex configurational ideas at the non-discursive level guide the ways in which we handle spatio-temporal things at the surface level, and as a result configurational ideas are realised in the real world. In building terms, the manipulation of the spatial and formal elements which make up the building will, if carried out within the scope of non-discursive configurational 'ideas-to-think-with', which govern key aspects of their formal and spatial arrangement, lead to exactly the combination of underlying common structure and surface variety that characterises vernacular architectures in general.

To understand how this happens in particular cases, we can draw on the remarkable work of Henry Glassie.[21] Glassie proposes that we adapt from Noam Chomsky's studies of language a concept which he calls 'architectural competence'. 'Architectural competence' is a set of technological, geometrical and manipulative skills relating form to use, which constitute 'an account not of how a house is made, but of how a house is thought...set out like a programme...a scheme analogous to a grammar, that will consist of an outline of rule sets interrupted by prosy exegesis'. The analogy with language is apposite. It suggests that the rule sets the vernacular designer uses are tacit and taken for granted in the same way as the rule sets that govern the use of language. They are ideas the designer thinks with rather than of. They therefore have a certain degree of abstraction from the material reality they help to create. They specify not the specific but the generic, so that the vernacular designer may use the rules as the basis of a certain restrained creativity in interpreting the rules in novel ways.

Now the implication of Glassie's idea is that 'architectural competence' provides a set of normative rules about how building should be done, so that a vernacular building reproduces a known and socially accepted pattern. The house built by a builder sharing the culture of a community comes out right because it draws on the normative rules that define the architectural competence of the community. In this way buildings become a natural part of 'the transmission of culture by artefacts'. Through distinctive ways of building, aspects of the social knowledge distinctive of a community are reproduced. Thus the physical act of building, through a system of well defined instrumentalities, becomes the means by which the non-discursive patterns we call culture are transmitted into and through the material and spatial forms of buildings. The non-discursive aspects of building are transmitted exactly as we would expect them to be: as unconscious pattern implications of the manipulation of things.

So what is architecture?

To understand building, then, we must understand it both as a product and as a process. Having done this, we can return to our original question: what is it that architecture adds to building? By unpacking the cultural and cognitive complexity of building, it will turn out that we are at last in sight of an answer. Whatever architecture is, it must in some sense go beyond the process by which the culturally sanctioned non-discursivities are embedded in the spatial and physical forms of buildings. In what sense, then, is it possible to 'go beyond' such a process?

The answer is now virtually implied in the form of the question. Architecture begins when the configurational aspects of form and space, through which buildings become cultural and social objects, are treated not as unconscious rules to be followed, but are raised to the level of conscious, comparative thought, and in this way made part of the object of creative attention. Architecture comes into existence, we may say, as a result of a kind of intellectual *prise de conscience*: we build, but not as cultural automata, reproducing the spatial and physical forms of our culture, but as conscious human beings critically aware of the cultural relativity of built forms and spatial forms. We build, that is, aware of intellectual choice, and we therefore build with reason, giving reasons for these choices. Whereas in the vernacular the non-discursive aspects of architecture are normative and handled autonomically, in architecture these contents become the object of reflective and creative thought. The designer is in effect a configurational thinker. The object of architectural attention is precisely the configurational 'ideas-to-think-with' that in the vernacular govern configurational outcomes. This does not mean that the designer does not think of objects. It means that at the same time the designer thinks of configuration.

The essence of architecture lies therefore in building not by reference to culturally bound competences, and the way in which they guide the non-discursive contents of buildings through programmes of social knowledge specific to one culture, but by reference to a would-be universalistic competence arrived at through the general comparative study of forms aimed at principle rather than cultural idiosyncrasy, and, through this, at innovation rather than cultural reduplication. It is when we see in the non-discursive contents of buildings evidence of this concern for the abstract comparability of forms and functions that building is transcended and architecture is named. This is why the notion of architecture seems to contain within itself aspects of both the product which is created and of the intellectual process through which this creation occurs.

Architecture exists, we might say, where we note as a property of things evidence not only of a certain kind of systematic intent – to borrow an excellent phrase proposed by a colleague in reviewing the archaeological record for the beginning of architecture[22] – in the domain of non-discursivity, but of something like theoretical intent in that domain. In a key sense architecture transcends building in the same way that science transcends the practical crafts of making and doing. It introduces into the creation of buildings an abstract concern for architectural possibility through the principled understanding of form and function. The innovative imperative in architecture is therefore in the nature of the subject. We should no more criticise architects for their penchant towards innovation than we should scientists. In both cases it follows from the social legitimations which give each its name and identity. Both architecture and science use the ground of theoretical understanding to move from past solutions to future possibility, the latter in the direction of new theoretical constructs, the former in the direction of new realities.

The judgment we make that a building is architecture arises when the evidence of systematic intent is evidence of intellectual choice and decision exercised in a field of knowledge of possibility that goes beyond culture into principle. In this sense, architecture is a form of practice recognisable in its product. The judgment we make that a building is architecture comes when we see evidence in the building both of systematic intent which requires the abstract and comparative manipulation of form within the general realm of architectural possibility, and that this exploration and this exercise of intellectual choice has been successfully accomplished.

Architecture is thus both a thing and an activity. In the form of the thing we detect evidence of a systematic intent of the architectural kind. From the built evidence we can judge both that a building is intended to be architecture and, if we are so inclined, that it is architecture. We see now why the definition of architecture is so difficult. Because it is the taking hold of the non-discursive contents of building by abstract, universalistic thought, it is at once an intentional mental act and a property we see in things. It is because we see in things the objectivised record of such thought that we name the result architecture.

It is clear from this analysis that architecture does not depend on architects, but can exist within the context of what we would normally call the vernacular. To the extent that the vernacular shows evidence of reflective thought and innovation at the level of the genotype, then that is evidence of the kind of thought we call architectural within the vernacular. This does not mean that the innovative production of buildings which are phenotypically individual within a vernacular should be thought of as architecture. Such phenotypical variety is normal as the product of

culturally constrained non-discursive codes. It is only when the innovation, and therefore the reflective thought, changes the code that underlies the production of phenotypes that we detect the presence of abstract
and comparative – and therefore architectural – thought within the
confines of vernacular tradition. It is therefore perhaps at times of the
greatest change that we become aware of this type of thought in vernacular traditions, that is when a new vernacular is coming into existence.
This is why the demarcation between the vernacular and architecture
constantly shifts. The reproduction of existing forms, vernacular or otherwise, is not architecture because that requires no exercise of abstract
comparative thought, but the exploitation of vernacular forms in the
creation of new forms can be architecture.

Architecture exists then to the degree that there is genotypical
invention in the non-discursive that is, invention with the rules that
govern the variability that is possible within a style. The precondition
for such invention is an awareness of possibilities which are not contained in contemporary cultural knowing but which are at the same
time within the laws of what is architecturally possible. Architecture is
characterised therefore by a preoccupation with non-discursive means
rather than non-discursive ends. This is not the outcome of a perverse
refusal to understand the cultural nature of building, but a taking hold of
this very fact as a potentiality to explore the interface between human
life and its spatial and physical milieu. In the act of architectural creation, the configurational potentialities of space and form are the raw
materials with which the creator works.

Like any creative artist, therefore, the architect must seek to learn,
through intellectual enquiry, the limits and potentialities of these raw
materials. In the absence of such enquiry, there are manifest and immediate dangers. In the vernacular the pattern of form and the pattern of
space which give the building its social character are recreated through
the manipulation and assembling of objects. We can say then that the
form, the spatial pattern and the functional pattern – the form-function
relation, in short – are known in advance and need only be recreated.
Because architecture of its nature unlinks the pattern aspects of the
building from their dependence on social knowledge these aspects of

the building – and above all their relation to social outcomes – become uncertain.

In architecture then because these crucial relations between non-discursive forms and outcomes are not known in advance, architecture has to recreate in a new, more generalised form, the knowledge conditions that prevail in the vernacular. Because architecture is a creative act, there must be something in the place of the social knowledge structure as ideas to think with. Since architecture is based on the general comparability of possible forms, this knowledge cannot simply encompass particular cases. It must encompass the range of possible cases and if possible cases in general. There is only one term for such knowledge. It is theoretical knowledge. We will see in the next chapter that all architectural theories are attempts to supply principled knowledge of the non-discursive, that is to render the non-discursive discursive in a way that makes it accessible to reason. In the absence of such knowledge, architecture can be, as the twentieth century has seen, a dangerous art.

The passage from building to architecture is summarised in figure 1.7. The implication of this is that, although we know the difference between architecture and building, there is no hard and fast line to be drawn. Either can become the other at any moment. Taking a broader view which encompasses both, we can say that in the evolution of building we note two ways in which things are done: in obedience to a tradition, or in pursuit of innovation. Building contains architecture to the degree that there is non-discursive invention, and architecture becomes building to the degree that there is not. Vernacular innovation is therefore included within architecture, but the reduplication of vernacular forms is not. Architecture is therefore not simply what is done but how it is done.

The bringing of the non-discursive, configuration dimension of built form from cultural reproduction to reflective awareness and abstract exploration of possibility is at once a passage from the normative to the analytic and from the culture bound to the universal, the latter meaning that all possibilities are open rather than simply the permutations and phenotypical innovations that are sanctioned by the vernacular. The passage is also one which transforms the idea of knowledge from cultural principle to theoretical abstraction.

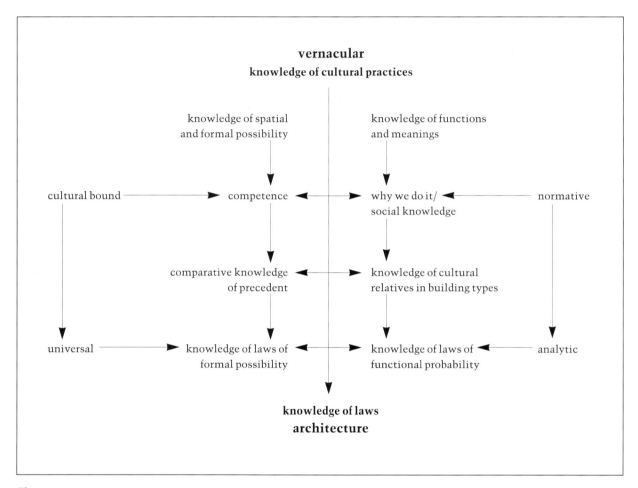

Figure 1.7

In a strong sense, then, architecture requires theory. If it does not have theoretical knowledge, then it will continue to depend on social knowledge. Worse, there is every possibility that architecture can come to be based on social knowledge masquerading as theoretical knowledge, which will be all the more dangerous because architecture operates in the realms of the non-discursive through which society is transmitted through building.[23] Architecture is therefore permanently enjoined to theoretical debate. It is in its nature that it should be so. In that it is the application of reflective abstract thought to the non-discursive dimensions of building, and in that it is through these dimensions that our social and cultural natures are inevitably engaged, architecture is theory applied to building. In the next chapter we will therefore consider what we mean by theory in architecture.

Notes

1   J. Ruskin, *Seven Lamps of Architecture*, London 1849, chap. 1.

2   The literature on vernacular architecture as culture is now extensive, and growing rapidly. Among the seminal texts offering wide coverage are Rudovsky's *Architecture Without Architects*, 1964; Paul Oliver's *Shelter and Society*, Barrie & Rockliff, The Cresset Press, 1969 and its follow-up *Shelter in Africa*, Barrie & Jenkins, London, 1971; Amos Rapoport's *House Form and Culture*, Prentice Hall, 1969; Labelle Prussin's classic review of the contrasting vernaculars within a region, *Architecture in Northern Ghana*, University of California Press, 1969; Susan Denyer's *African Traditional Architecture*, Heineman, 1978; and Kaj Andersen's *African Traditional Architecture*, Oxford University Press, 1977; in addition to earlier anthropological classics such as C. Daryll Forde's *Habitat, Economy and Society*, Methuen, 1934. Studies of specific cultures are now too numerous to mention, as are the much larger number of texts which have now dealt with the architecture of particular cultures and regions, but which are not yet available in English. Among recent studies of the vernacular, the most important to my mind – and by far the most influential in this text – has been the work of Henry Glassie, and in particular his *Folk Housing in Middle Virginia*, University of Tennessee Press, 1975, references to which, explicit and implicit, recur throughout this text.

3   The same has often been said of 'industrial' architecture. J. M. Richards, for example, in his *An Introduction to Modern Architecture*, Penguin, 1940, describes Thomas Telford's St Katharine's Dock as 'Typical of the simple but noble engineer's architecture of his time'.

4   Roger Scruton, *The Aesthetics of Architecture*, Methuen, 1977.

5   Ibid., p. 16.

6   For a recent restatement of this belief see S. Gardiner, *The Evolution of the House*, Paladin, 1976.

7   See for example prehistorical sections of the most recent (nineteenth) edition of Sir Banister Fletcher's *A History of Architecture* (edited by Professor John Musgrove) written by my colleague Dr Julienne Hanson. It is a comment on architectural history that it is only very recently that the true antiquity of building has been reflected in the histories of world architecture. Some of Dr Hanson's sources are in themselves remarkable

texts which if better known would entirely change popular conception of the history not only of building but also of human society. The key texts are given in Dr Hanson's bibliography, but I would suggest the remarkable R. G. Klein, *Ice Age Hunters of the Ukraine*, Chicago and London, 1973 as a good starting point.

8   B. Russell, *The Problems of Philosophy*, Home University Library, 1912, Oxford University Press paperback, 1959; chapter 9 'The world of universals'.

9   R. A. Scruton, *The Aesthetics of Architecture*, p. 43 et seq.

10 R. A. Scruton, *A Short History of Modern Philosophy: from Descartes to Wittgenstein*, ARK Paperbacks,1984.

11 R. Descartes, *The Principles of Philosophy*, Part 2, Principle X in *The Philosophical Works of Descartes*, Cambridge University Press, vol. 1, p. 259.

12 Descartes, Principle XI, p. 259.

13 Descartes, Principle X , p. 259.

14 Graphs which have this property are called 'planar' graphs. Any spatial layout on one level, considered as a graph of the permeability relations, is bound to be planar.

15 These examples are taken from a study of seventeen houses in Normandy carried out for the Centre Nationale de Recherche Scientifique, and published as 'Ideas are in things' in *Environment and Planning B, Planning and Design* 1987, vol. 14, pp. 363–85. This article then formed one of the basic sources for a much more extended treatment in J. Cuisenier, *La Maison Rustique: logique social et composition architecturale*, Presses Universitaires de France, 1991.

16 The 'normalisation' formula for taking the effect of the number elements in the graph out of the total depth calculation from an element is $2(md-1)/k-2$, where md is the mean depth of other elements from the root element, and k is the number of elements. There is a discussion of this measure in P. Steadman, *Architectural Morphology*, Pion, 1983, p. 217. The measure was first published in Hillier et al., 'Space Syntax: a new urban perspective' in the *Architect's Journal*, no 48, vol. 178, 30.11.83. There is an extensive discussion of its theoretical foundations and why it is so important in space in Hillier and Hanson, *The Social Logic of Space*, Cambridge University Press, 1984. The measure theoretically eliminates the effect of the numbers of elements in the system. However, in architectural and urban reality there is an additional problem: both buildings and settlements, for practical and empirical reasons (as will be fully discussed in chapter 9) tend to become relatively less deep as they grow. A second, 'empirical' normalisation formula is therefore required to take account of this. Such a formula is set out in *The Social Logic of Space,* which has proved robust in use, but has been extensively discussed, for example in J. Teklenberg, H. Timmermans & A. van Wagenberg, 'Space syntax: standardised integration measures and some simulations', *Environment & Planning B: Planning & Design*, vol. 20, 1993, pp. 347–57. See also M. Kruger, 'On node and axial grid maps: distance measures and related topics', paper for the European Conference on the Representation and Management of Urban Change,

Cambridge, September 1989, Unit for Architectural Studies, University College London.

17   There is a further measure called 'difference factor', which expresses how strong these differences are, set out in 'Ideas are in things', cited in note 15 above.

18   It should be noted that the argument in the paper from which these examples are taken, 'Ideas are in things' is a great deal more complex than that presented here to illustrate the technique. In fact, it was proposed that two fundamental typological tendencies would be identified within the sample, which were more to do with differences in the relations of the sexes than anything else. A new version of this paper will be published in J. Hanson, *The Social Logic of Houses*, forthcoming from Cambridge University Press.

19   These issues are dealt with at greater length and for a slightly different purpose in chapter 7.

20   Margaret Mead, *Continuities in Cultural Evolution*, Yale University Press, 1964, chapter 5.

21   For example, Henry Glassie, *Folk Housing in Middle Virginia*.

22   J. Hanson, written for the intended *Encyclopaedia of Architecture*, McGraw-Hill, New York, but not yet published.

23   We will see in later chapters, and particularly in chapters 6 and 11, exactly how this can occur and what its consequences are.

chapter two

The need for an analytic theory of architecture

Do architects need theories?

In the previous chapter, architecture was defined as the taking into
reflective thought of the non-discursive, or configurational, aspects of
space and form in buildings. In vernacular traditions, these aspects are
governed by the taken for granted *ideas to think with* of a culture. In
architecture, *ideas to think with* become *ideas to think of*. Spatial and
formal configuration in buildings ceases to be a matter of cultural reproduction and becomes a matter of speculative and imaginative enquiry.

It follows from this definition that architecture is an aspiration, not
a given. To bring to conscious thought the principles that underlie the
spatial and formal patterns that transmit culture through buildings, and
to formulate possible alternatives that work *as though they were culture*
– since architecture must be an addition to culture not simply a removal
of it – is an intellectual as well as a creative task. It requires not only the
conceptualisation of pattern and configuration *in vacuo* , but also comparative knowledge and reflective thought. This is why architecture is a
reflective as well as an imaginative project, one which seeks to replace –
or at least to add to – the social knowledge content of building with an
enquiry into principle and possibility.

Architectural theory is the ultimate aim of this reflection. An architectural theory is an attempt to render one or other of the non-discursive
dimensions of architecture discursive, by describing in concepts, words
or numbers what the configurational aspects of form or space in buildings
are like, and how they contribute to the purposes of building. In a sense,
theory begins at the moment architecture begins, that is, when spatial and
formal configuration in buildings, and their experiential and functional
implications, are no longer given through a tradition of social knowledge
transmitted through the act of building itself. As soon as building moves
free from the safe confines of cultural programming, something like a
theory of architecture is needed to support the creative act by proposing
a more general understanding of the spatial and formal organisation of
buildings than is available within the limits of a single culture.

This is not to say that creative architecture depends on theory. It does
not. But in that architecture is the application of speculative abstract
thought to the material world in which we live, the reflective aspects of

architectural enquiry lead to the formulation if not of theory then at least of theory-like ideas. The need for theory becomes greater as architecture advances. Theory is most required when architecture becomes truly itself, that is when it becomes the free exploration of formal and spatial possibility in the satisfaction of the human need for buildings.

However, the fact that theory is an inevitable aspect of architecture does not mean that all theories will have a positive effect on architecture. On the contrary, the dependence of architecture on theoretical ideas creates a new type of risk: that theories may be wrong, maybe disastrously wrong. The much discussed 'failure' of modernism in architecture is seen as at least the failure of a theory – the most ambitious and comprehensive ever proposed – and even by some as the failure of the very idea of a theory of architecture.

As a result, in the late twentieth century a number of new questions are posed about theories of architecture which are also questions about architecture itself. Does architecture really need theories, or are they just a pretentious adjunct to an essentially practical activity? If architecture does need theories, then what are they like? Are they like scientific theories? Or are they a special kind of theory adapted for architectural purposes? If architectural theories can be wrong, and have apparently adverse consequences, then can they also be right? How can we set about making architectural theories better? And most difficult of all: how can architecture as a creative art be reconciled to the disciplines of theory? Are the two not opposed to each other, in that better theories must lead inevitably to the elimination of architectural freedom?

The answer proposed in this chapter is that once we accept that the object of architectural theory is the non-discursive – that is, the configurational – content of space and form in buildings and built environments, then theories can only be developed by learning to study buildings and built environments *as non-discursive objects* . To have a theory of non-discursivity in architecture in general we must first build a corpus of knowledge about the non-discursive contents of architecture as a phenomenon. This of course runs counter to most current efforts in architectural theory, which seek to build theory either through the borrowing of concepts from other fields, or through introspection and speculation.

However, the product of the first-hand study of non-discursivity in buildings and built environments will lead to a new kind of theory: an analytic theory of architecture, that is one which seeks to understand architecture as a phenomenon, before it seeks to guide the designer. An analytic theory of architecture is, it will be argued, the necessary corollary of architectural autonomy. Without the protection of an analytic theory, architecture is inevitably subject to more and more externally imposed restrictions that substitute social ideology for architectural creativity. Analytic theory is necessary in order to retain the autonomy of creative innovation on which the advance of architecture depends.

Are architectural theories just precepts for builders?
Before we can embark on the task of building an analytic theory of architecture, however, we must first explore the idea of theory in architecture a little to prevent our enquiry being obscured by some of the more common misconceptions. Architectural theories do take a very distinctive form, but all is not as it seems at first sight, and it is important that we do not allow appearances to disguise their true nature and purposes.

    We may usefully begin by examining the views of a well-known critic of architectural theories. In his 1977 polemic against architectural modernism and its intellectual fashions, *The Aesthetics of Architecture*,[1] Roger Scruton is dismissive of the very idea of a theory of architecture: 'Architectural theory', he says in a footnote, is 'usually the gesture of a practical man, unused to words'. Elsewhere he goes further. There is not and cannot be a theory of architecture. What has been called architectural theory are merely '...precepts...which...guide the builder'. While such precepts can be useful canons, they can never amount to a real theory, because they cannot be universal, and it is only with the claim to universality that theory arises.[2]

    At first sight, Scruton seems to be right. For the most part – modernism is one of the few exceptions – we associate theories of architecture with individual architects. When we think of Palladio's or Le Corbusier's theory of architecture we take it to mean something like the intellectual ground of a style, the generic principles underlying an approach to design. It seems self evident that no such principles could ever be universal. The idea even leads to paradox. A universal formula for architecture would, if followed, render architecture the same and unchanging, and therefore ultimately dull.

But does theory in architecture really only mean a formula for architectural success? A scientist would find this a strange use of the word 'theory'. For a scientist a theory is a rational construct intended to capture the lawfulness of how the world *is*, not a set of guidelines as to how it *should be*. Scientific theories help us act on the world, but only because they have first described the world independently of any view of how it should be. The essence of science is that its theories are *analytic,* not *normative* in intent. They describe how the world is, not prescribe how it ought to be.

Might we then suggest that this is exactly the difference between architectural and scientific theories, namely that scientific theories are analytic, and about understanding how things are, whereas architectural theories are normative, and about telling us what to do? There seems to be some truth in this. It is reasonable to say that architecture is about how the world should be rather than how it is, and that its theories should therefore tend to express aspirations rather than realities. In fact, on closer examination, it turns out that this is not and can never be the case. Admittedly, architectural theories are normally presented in normative form, but at a deeper level they are no less analytic than scientific theories.

Take for example, two theories which are about as far apart as they could be in focus and content, Alberti's theory of proportion,[3] and Oscar Newman's theory of 'defensible space'.[4] Both are presented as precepts for successful design, in that both authors' books are aimed primarily at guiding the architectural practitioner in design, rather than explaining the nature of architectural experience as experienced, as Scruton's book is. But if we read the texts carefully, we find that this is not all they are. In each case, the normative content of the work rests on clear, if broad, analytic foundations. Alberti's theory of proportion rests on the Pythagorean notion of mathematical form in nature,[5] and the coincidence it asserts between the principles of natural form and the powers of the mind, as evidenced by the relationship between our sense of harmony in music and the simple numerical ratios on which those harmonies are based.

If architecture follows the mathematical principles found in nature, Alberti argues, then it cannot help reproducing the intelligibility and harmony that we find in natural forms. Similarly, Newman's 'defensible space' theory rests on the theory of 'human territoriality', by which genetic tendencies in certain species to defend territory against others of the species, are generalised to human beings, both as individuals and – mistakenly in my view – as groups. If, Newman argues, architects design space in conformity with 'territorial' principles, then it will be following biological drives built into us by nature.[6]

It is notable that in both of these theories, the principles for design are said to be based on principles to be found in nature. In a very strong sense, then, in both cases the normative content of the theory depends on the analytic. On reflection, it must be so to some degree in all cases. Any theory about how we should act to produce a certain outcome in the world must logically depend on some prior conception of how the world is and how it will respond to our manipulations. Careful examination will show that this is always the case with architectural theories. We invariably find that the precepts about what designers should do are set in a prior framework which describes how the world is. Sometimes this framework is explicitly set out, and rests on a specific scientific or quasi-scientific foundation, as in the two cases we have instanced. Sometimes it is much more implicit, reflecting no more than a currently fashionable way of looking at the world, as for example many recent theories have rested on the fashionable assumption that 'everything is a language' so that designers can and should design following the principles of linguistic theories in making their buildings 'meaningful'.

Although presented normatively, then, architectural theories must have a great deal of analytic content, whether this is explicit or implicit. In point of fact, faced with an architectural theory, our first reaction would usually be to treat it exactly as we would a scientific theory. Offered a general proposition on which to base architectural precepts for design – say a proposition about the psychological impact of certain proportional systems or the behavioural effects of a certain kind of spatial organisation – our first reaction would be to question the general proposition, or at least to subject it to test by a review of cases. We usually find quite quickly

that would-be general propositions run foul of cases known to us, which
we then instance as counter-examples to the theory. In other words, we
treat an architectural theory very much in the same way as we would
treat a scientific theory: that is, we treat it as an analytic theory by trying
to find counter-examples which would refute its generality. Even when it
survives, we would be inclined to treat it with continuing scepticism as
at best a provisional generalisation, which we can make use of until a
better one comes along.

It is a mistake, then, to treat architectural theories simply as normative precepts, as Scruton does. Architectural theories are not and cannot
be simply normative, but are at least analytic-normative complexes, in
which the normative is constructed on the basis of the analytic. It follows
that properly theoretical content of architectural theories is specified by
the analytic. If the analytic theory is wrong, then the likelihood is that
the building will not realise its intention. Architectural theories, we
might say, are about how the world should be, but only in the light of
how it is believed to be.

Theories in design

Why should architectural theories take this distinctive form of combining propositions about how the world should be with propositions about
how it is believed to be? The answer is to be found in the nature of what
architects do, that is design. Through its nature as an activity, design raises issues to which architectural theorists propose solutions in the form of
analytic-normative complexes of theoretical ideas. To understand why
this is so, we must understand a little about design.

Design is of course only a part of the protracted processes by which
buildings come into existence. The 'building process' involves formulat-
ing a need for a possible building, conceptualising what it might be like,
initiating a process of resourcing, negotiating and organising, creating
some kind of representation, or series of representations of increasing
refinement, of what the building will be like, then constructing, fitting,
operationalising, and finally occupying the completed building. Vernacular building is of course a less complex process. But if the circumstances
exist in which 'design' is a function, then the corollary is that this more

complex building process, or something approximating to it, also exists. Design does not exist as a function independent of this larger process. On the contrary, it implies it.

How then do we define design within this process? First, we note that it is only at the end of the process that the object of the process – an occupied building – exists. For most of its duration, the process is organised around a surrogate for the building in the form of an abstract idea or representation which continually changes its form. It begins as an idea *for* the building, then becomes an idea *of* the building, then a more formalised concept, then a series of more and more refined representations, then a set of instructions and finally a building. For the most part, the complex process of building takes place around this shifting, clarifying, gradually materialising idea.

The process of seeking, fixing, and representing a realisable concept of a building from an idea *for* a building is design. Design is what architects do, though it is not all they do, and not only architects do it. But it is design that keeps what architects do – whether or not it is architects that do it – fixed in the process of creating buildings. There has to be a control of the process of searching out, conceptualising, and representing the surrogate building through the process. Let us call this the 'design function', so that we can see that it is independent of who actually carries it out.

The design function exists within the building process for one fundamental reason: because at all stages of the process – though with differing degrees of accuracy – the properties and performance of the building as it will be when built must be foreseen in advance, that is, they must be knowable from the surrogate. Without this foresight, the commitments of resources necessary at each stage of the process cannot be made with confidence. The design function is essentially a matter of stage-managing a constantly changing representation of what will eventually be a building, so that at all stages of the process there is in view a proposal for an object that does not yet exist, and which is probably unique – since if it were a copy there would be no need for design – but whose technical, spatial, functional and aesthetic properties if and when built are, as far as possible, predictable in advance.

The design function in the building process therefore involves on the one hand searching out and creating a representation of a possible

solution for the design problem in hand, and on the other the prediction
of the performance of the building when built from the representation.
The activities that make up the design process reflect this duality. Design
essentially is a cyclic process of generating possible design proposals,
then selecting and refining them by testing them against the objectives
the building must satisfy – to be beautiful, to be cheap, to be ostentatious,
to represent an idea, to repay investment, to function for an organisation
by providing adequate and well-ordered accommodation, and so on.[7]
These two basic aspects to the design process can be called the creative
phases and the predictive phases. In the creative phases the object is to
create possible design proposals. In the predictive phases, the object is
to foresee how proposals will work to satisfy the objectives.

Once we understand the creative-predictive nature of the design
process, then it is easy to see how the normative and analytic aspects of
theories can usefully contribute to the process. Theories can be used, and
often are used, tacitly or explicitly, in two quite distinct modes in the
design process: as aids to the creative process of arriving at a design; and
as aids to the analytic process of predicting how a particular design will
work and be experienced. Often of course these two aspects will be
conflated in an undifferentiated thought process. The normative aspects
of a theory tell the designer where to search for candidate solutions in
the creative phases, the analytic aspects how the solution will work. For
example, if you are a Palladian, then in the creative phases of design you
search for a formal and spatial solution with Palladian properties – a certain range of envelope geometries, certain symmetries of plan and facade,
certain kinds of detailing, and so on – confident that if you proceed in a
Palladian manner then you can predict a Palladian outcome. If you are a
Newmanite, then you search for formal and spatial solutions with a certain layering of spatial hierarchies, certain possibilities of surveillance,
the avoidance of certain formal themes and so on, again confident that by
proceeding this way a safe environment will result. Theory thus structures
the search for a possible design in a solution space that might otherwise
be both vast and unstructured, and it does so in a way that gives the designer
confidence – which may of course be quite misplaced – that the nature
and properties of the eventual building can be known from the theory.

The use of theory is of course only one way of structuring the design process. In fact few designers claim to create designs from theory, and many would go out of their way to deny it. But this does not mean that they do not design under the influence of theory. Much use of theoretical ideas in architecture is tacit rather than explicit. This is not due to malign intent on the part of designers, but much more to do with the need for theory in design, however little this is recognised. Consider, for example, the problem of prediction. Having created a candidate design, the designer now has the task of foreseeing how the 'unknown non-discursivities' of form and space that will be created by the design will work and be experienced when built. Logically there are only two possible bases for such prediction: known precedent and theoretical principle. Prediction by precedent means prediction by reference to known cases that already exist. Prediction by principle means prediction by reference to the generality of known cases. Both are essentially claims based on experience, but the former is specific, and the latter general.

Prediction from precedent raises two problems. The idea of architecture includes the idea that the building to be created will not simply be a copy of one which exists. This means that precedent cannot be used lock, stock and barrel for the whole building. Precedent can therefore only be used piecemeal for aspects or parts of the building. Since formally and spatially buildings are complex configurations, and not simply assemblages of parts, it can never be clear that the new embedding of a precedent attribute or part will not work differently in the context of the new whole. The use of precedent in design is necessary, since it brings in concrete evidence in support of prediction, but it is never sufficient, because each new synthesis recontextualises each aspect of precedent. The use of precedent therefore necessarily involves interpretation.

The pressure on designers to work at least in part from knowledge of theoretical principle is therefore intense. The apparent advantage to the architect of working within a particular theory becomes clear. The solution to the prediction problem appears already to be contained within the theory. The normative theoretical concepts that guide the generation of a candidate design also take the form of analytic concepts which indicate that if the designer follows the precepts of the theory, then it is to be expected that the design will work in the way the architect intends. The analytic foundations of the normative theory return at the predictive stages to appear to guarantee architectural success. This is why architectural theories take the form of normative-analytic complexes. They fulfil the two primary needs of the design process with a single set of propositions.

However, it is clear that these advantages will only exist to the extent that the theory's analytic foundations are not illusory. If they do not offer a realistic picture of how the world works, then it is likely that the designer's predictions will refer only to an illusory reality. A poorly founded analytic theory will not inhibit the designer in the creative phases of design, but it would lead him or her to look in the wrong place. It would also mean that the designer's predictions would be unlikely to be supported by events when the building is built. This is why bad theories are so dangerous in architecture.[8] They make design appear to be much easier, while at the same time making it much less likely to be successful. This, in the last analysis, is why architects need analytically well founded theories.

However, this is not the same as to say that architects simply need scientific theories to guide them in design. The dual use of theory in architecture both to generate designs and to predict their performance permits us to introduce a very important comparison: between theories in art and theories in science, and to argue that architecture needs theories both in the sense that the word is used in art and in the sense that the word is used in science.

Theories in art are not analytic-normative complexes of the kind we typically find in architecture. They are primarily about supporting the creative process, that is, they are in essence about *possibility* . Theories in art expand the realm of the possible, by defining a new way to art or even by defining a new form of art. There need in principle be no constraints on what type of theories are used. The role of a theory in art is not to claim a universal art, or to set up one form of art as superior to another, but to open up one more possible kind of art. Theory in art is then essentially generative. It does not have to take much account of functional or experiential consequences. It uses abstract thought only to generate new possibilities in art that had not been seen before.

If architecture were simply an art, it would need theories only in the sense that painters or sculptors have theories: that is as speculative extensions of the realm of the artistically possible. It is clear that architecture as art has and needs this kind of theory. But this is not all it has and needs. The difference between architecture and art is that when an artist works, he or she works directly with the material that will eventually form the art object – the stone, the paint and so on. What the artist makes is the work of art. Architecture is different. An architect does not work on a building, but a representation of a building we call a design. A design is not simply a picture of a building, but a picture of a potential object and of a potential *social* object – that is an object that is to be experienced, understood and used by people. A design is therefore not only a prediction of an object, rather than an object itself, but, however functionally nonspecific it claims to be, a prediction of people in relation to building. This is where analytic theories are needed, and analytic theories are analogous to scientific theories. Theories in science are sets of general, abstract ideas through which we understand and interpret the material phenomena the world offers to our experience. They deal with how the world is, not how it might be. Because architecture is creative it requires theories of possibility in the sense that they exist in art. But because architecture is also predictive, it needs analytic theories of actuality as well as theories of possibility.

It is this double nature that makes architectural theories unique. They require at once to have the generative power of theories in art and at the same time the analytic power of theories in science. The first deals with the world as it might be, the second with the world as it is. The question then is: how may there be theories of architecture which are at once creative and analytic? One aspect of the answer turns out to be simple: good analytic theories are already likely to be also good theories of possibility. The entire usefulness of scientific theories in their applications in science and technology is in fact founded on the simple but unobvious fact: that analytic theories do not simply describe the world as it is, but also describe the limits of how it can be. Scientific theories are arrived at through the examination of the world as it is. But it is exactly the theoretical understanding of the world as it is that opens up whole realms of new possibility that do not yet exist.

It is this fundamental link between actuality and possibility that opens the way to an analytic theory of architecture. But before we explore it, we must first look a little more carefully at architectural theories to see how they are structured, and why, and how they might eventually move in the direction of becoming more analytic.

The problem of architectural theory

The most common problem with architectural theories is that they have too often been strongly normative and weakly analytic, that is, it has been too easy to use them to generate designs, but they are too weak in predicting what these designs will be like when built. The theories of modernism were, for example, quite easy to follow in generating designs to satisfy normatively stated objectives. The problem was that the architectural means proposed were not the means required to achieve those objectives. The theories were weakly analytic. They did not deal with the world as it actually is. The normative dominated the analytic.

Exactly how normatively strong but analytically weak architectural theories are held in place can be seen by taking one more step in disaggregating what architectural theories are like and how they work. For example, looking a little more closely at our two exemplars of architectural theories – the Albertian and the Newmanite – we find both have two quite distinct components: one in the realm of broad intention, telling architects what they should aim to achieve through architecture, and one in the realm of what we might call architectural technique, telling architects how to realise that intention. Alberti's theory, for example, tells architects that in order to design buildings that people will experience as harmonious, they should aim to reflect in their buildings the mathematical order found in nature. He then goes on to offer a method for calculating proportions to serve as a technique for realising this aim in architectural terms.[9] Newman tells architects they should aim to design spaces beyond the dwelling so that inhabitants may identify with them and control them, then specifies hierarchical techniques of space organisation in order to realise this. We might call these the broad and narrow propositions about architecture contained in a typical architectural theory. The broad proposition, or intention, sets a goal while the narrow proposition, or

architectural technique, proposes a way of designing through which the
intended effect will be realised.

One difference between the broad and narrow propositions lies in
what they engage. The broad proposition engages a world of ideas which
may be very large in its scope and may contain much that is poorly
defined and little understood. The narrow proposition, on the other hand,
engages the realities of architectural design and experience. If in general
theories are abstract propositions which engage the real world of experience, then the broad and narrow propositions of architectural theories
occupy opposite ends of the spectrum covered by theories. The broad
propositions are in the realm of philosophical abstraction, where the
theory engages the vast world of ideas and presuppositions, implicit and
explicit, which eventually rests nowhere but in the evolution of human
minds. The narrow propositions are in the realm of direct experience of
the world where theories engage the minutiae of everyday experience.

Broad proposition and narrow proposition also differ in their intended
universality. Broad propositions are intended to be universalistic in that
they attempt to say things about architecture which are held to be generally true, and to say it in such a broad way as to allow it to be true in quite
different architectural circumstances. But it is clear that we should not
regard the narrow propositions as universalistic.[10] For the most part the
narrow propositions are offered as possible techniques for realising an
abstractly stated aim, not the only such techniques. On reflection, again
this must be so. The narrow propositions of an architectural theory are
techniques for bridging between the abstract and the concrete. Only an
abstraction can be general. We should not mistake a technique for realising
an analytic abstraction for the abstraction itself.

Now consider these broad and narrow propositions in relation to
what is required of theory in the two phases of design, that is, in the first
phase, ideas about possible forms and, in the second phase, ideas about
the relations between forms and performance outcomes. Both of the theories we have been considering appear to supply both needs. Ideas of possible forms are contained in the narrow propositions, that is the constructive techniques through which the theorist advises the designer how to
go about design to ensure success. In the case of Alberti's theory, this

means the systems of worked out proportions which guided the designer
in setting up the building as a physical form. In Newman's case, this
means the diagrams of spatial hierarchy which the designer can follow in
setting up the spatial design. Ideas of the relation between form and functional outcome are then expressed at the more philosophical level of the
broad propositions. In Alberti's case, this means the broad propositions,
based on the analogy with music, about the human experience of visual
harmony.[11] In Newman's case, it means the broad propositions about
'human territoriality' and its spatial implications.[12] In other words, in
both cases, it is the highly specific narrow propositions which guide the
creative process of design, and the very generalised broad propositions
which guide the designer in predicting functional effect from formal
configuration.

Now the problem with most architectural theories is that this is
exactly the opposite of what is required for architecture which is creatively
innovative and functionally successful. In the generative phase of design,
what is needed if architectural creativity is to be maximised is ideas about
formal and spatial configuration which are as unspecific as possible about
specific solutions, in order to leave the solution space as open as possible
to creative invention. In the predictive phases, what is needed is precision
about specific forms since what is at issue is the prediction of the functional outcome of this or that real design. In the generative phases, where
what is required are abstract or genotypical ideas which open up realms of
possibility just as theories do in art, architectural theories of this type
offer a rather narrow range of solution types which are essentially no
more than a set of abstract exemplars to follow – particular systems of
numerical proportions in one case, particular diagrams of hierarchical
spatial relations in the other. Then when in the predictive phases of design
the designer needs a much greater degree of analytic precision in order to
foresee how this or that innovative form will work functionally or experi-
entially, all that the theories offer is the vague analytic generalisations of
the broad propositions.

In other words, architectural theories of this type are over specific
where they should be permissive and vague where they should be precise.
The designer is given concrete models to follow when he or she needs

constructive creative ideas to search the solution space, and vacuous abstractions when he or she ought to be given techniques to predict the performance of particular designs. This is, in a nutshell, the problem with most architectural theories, and this is how, in real design, the normative aspects of theory come to dominate the analytic. What is needed are theories with the reverse properties, that is theories that are as nonspecific as possible to particular solutions in the generative phases of design in order to leave the solution field as large and dense as possible, and as specific and rigorous as possible in the predictive phases in order to be able to deal predictively with unknown forms where the need for effective prediction is greatest. The implication of this is that we need a fully fledged analytic theory which would offer abstract understanding rather than specific models in the creative phases of design, and phenotypical precision rather than vague generalisations at the testing stages.

What exactly, are theories?

How should we go about setting up such a theory? The first step must be to make sure we understand exactly what an analytic theory is. This turns out to be not as easy as looking the word up in a dictionary. Few words are in fact more ambiguous in their origins than 'theory'. In its ancient Greek origins, the verb *theoreein* means to be a spectator, and the products of this speculative activity, *theoremata* , were, not surprisingly, speculations. For Bacon theories were simply errors, the 'received systems of philosophy and doctrine', to be replaced in due course by something altogether better.[13] This meaning is still reflected in everyday use. In common usage, theories are speculations, of lesser status than facts, at best a temporary fix until the facts are known. A fictional detective with a premature 'theory' about a case will almost certainly be shown to be wrong. The expression 'only a theory' clearly expects theory not to be eventually supported by 'facts', but to be replaced by facts. In these senses, theories embody irremediable uncertainties, and appear to constitute a form of thought whose object is to replace itself with a-theoretical, and therefore secure, knowledge. In complete contrast, in modern science the word 'theory' today stands for the deepest level of understanding of phenomena. Successful theories in areas where none had previously prevailed, like evolution theory, are the most epoch making of intellectual events. Conflicts between rival theories of, say, the origins of the universe or the nature of matter, conducted on the obscure battlefields of macro and micro phenomena, are among the epics of the late twentieth-century thought.

So what then is 'theory', that it can be subject to such a range of interpretations and ambiguities? The source of this ambiguity lies of course not in the vagaries of etymological history but in the nature of theories themselves. Theories are found in the realm of speculative thought, because they are at root, speculations. They are not in themselves, for example, statements about observable phenomena, nor even statements about the regularities that are to be found in observable phenomena. They are propositions about hypothetical processes which might be responsible for the regularities we see in phenomena. As such they have a necessarily abstract nature, and are purely conceptual entities. You cannot see a theory, only its consequences, so you cannot verify a theory, only phenomena that are consistent with it. When we test a theory we do not simply look at the theory to see if all the parts are in working order and properly related, though we do also do this. We check the theory by seeing how far the phenomena available in the real world are consistent with the theory, and preferably with no other. To check a theory, in effect, we look away from the theory. Theories are in themselves unobservable and unexperiencable, and this is why in the end even the best and the most durable remain in some sense speculative.

But even when we accept the abstract and speculative nature of theories, we have not yet exhausted the apparent indeterminacy of the idea. No set of concepts which become part of a theory can exist in isolation. On the contrary, concepts can only exist as part of conceptual schemes through which we interpret our experience of the world and turn information into knowledge. No concept or set of concepts can exist in a vacuum. Each must be embedded in a broader range of propositions or assumptions about what the world is like and how it works. These broader frameworks have been known as paradigms since Thomas Kuhn first drew attention to their existence.[14]

With all this indeterminacy in what we mean by theory, how is it that they can be so important and so useful? To answer this we must

understand the circumstances in which theories arise and what purposes
they serve. Theorisation begins when we note a certain type of phenomenon and make a certain type of presupposition. The phenomenon we note
is that of *surface regularity* in the world as we experience it. The presupposition we make is that surface regularity implies *underlying invariance*
in the processes that give rise to the phenomena we see.

The first of these – the noting of regularities – theorisation shares
with language. The fact that language has words for classes of things
rather than simply for individual things assumes that we know the difference between order and chaos, that is that we can discern in the objective
world 'structural stabilities' [15] which are sufficiently well defined and
repetitious to support the assignment of names. These names are, as
philosophers have endlessly noted, abstract terms for classes in the guise
of names for things, with the consequence that even such a simple apparently concrete act as pointing at a thing and naming it depends on the
prior existence not only of the abstract universal constituted by that class
name, but also of the scheme of such abstractions of which that particular abstraction forms a part. These schemes, as we have known since de
Saussure,[16] differ from one language to another so that we are compelled
to acknowledge that names are not neutral, simple handles on things, but
conceptual instruments by which we create an organised picture of the
world. Names *create* understanding, and it is against the background of
the organised picture of the world already given to us by language and
culture that theorisation begins.

Theory begins in the same place as language where we note, in the
flux of experience, regularities, but adds a further presupposition: that
since regularity is unlikely to be the product of chance, there must be
some kind of order not only in the regular phenomena that we observe
but also in the processes that give rise to the phenomena. Why we should
make this presupposition is not clear. But it seems plausible that just as
language seems intimately bound up with how we cognise the world so
theorisation is bound up with how we act in the world. When, for example, we strike stones to make sparks and then fire, the sequence of events
from one to the other is not inscribed on the surface of things but implies
some interior process which is set in motion by our actions. Just as the

world responds to our actions on it by producing regularities, so we presuppose that the existence of regularities which do not result from our actions must be the result of invariant processes analogous to our actions. If then language arises from our being in the world and needing to know its objective persistences, so theorisation seems to arise from our acting in the world and on the world and needing to know the interior processes by which outcome reliably follows from action.

We thus see that regularities are the starting point of theory, but they are not the theory itself. Regularities initiate the process of theorisation since we infer from the existence of regularities that there must be some invariant structure in whatever process it is that produces these surface regularities. Theories are concerned with the nature of that process, more precisely they are attempts to model the invariant structure of processes which are thought to exist for there to be surface regularities. A theory, then, is not a list of regularities. Regularities are what theory seeks to explain, but are not in themselves theory. They initiate the search for theory but are not and cannot be its end point. A theory which seeks to 'explain' regularities is an entity of an altogether different kind from a list of regularities.

Moreover, although theorisation moves on from language by seeking to identify the hidden processes that give rise to surface regularities, it does not begin in a conceptual or linguistic void. It begins in the only place it can, in the evolution of thought and language, and their relation to the space-time phenomena that we experience 'without trying'. Because thought and language already give us a picture of the world which, at some level at least, seems to reflect its order and therefore to explain it, we are compelled to acknowledge that when we begin the process of theorisation we are already in possession of a view of the world which in many ways is very like a theory, in that it makes the world seem a more or less coherent and organised place. The difference is that the theory-like understanding we acquire from culture and language reflects not an interior order which gives rise to the surface regularities but an order in those surface regularities themselves. When for example language tells us that 'the sun rises', it reflects the regularities that we note on the surface of things, not a hidden process which gives rise to this surface regularity. We might

usefully then think of such everyday constructions as 'theory in the weak
sense'. Analytic, or scientific theories, are 'theories in the strong sense'.
They aim at a greater truth because they seek not to bring order to surface
regularities but to show how those surface regularities arise from invariant
necessities buried deep in the nature of things.

Formally defining simple regularities

Because surface regularities are the object of theory, the first step in theorisation is to formalise the idea. In fact, there is a beautifully simple way
to extract the idea of regularity from phenomena and represent it as pure
regularity, independent of the overall qualitative nature of things. The
idea is that of translating the properties of objects in the world as we see
them in real space into an abstract space which allows us to be quite clear
about what these properties are. This is done by the familiar technique
of replacing the space within which the object exists with an abstract co-
ordinate system in which the axes represent those properties of the object
that seem to be of interest as regularities. Thus one co-ordinate might
represent the height of the object, another the length and another the
breadth. We may then represent any object which has these properties
as a single point in the 'property space'.

Once we can represent the properties of an object as a point in a
property space rather than as that set of actual properties in real space, we
can easily represent exactly what we mean by a regularity as far as these
properties are concerned. For example, to the extent that things are comparable to each other in more than one property in the property space, the
points representing them in the property space will cluster in a particular
region of the space. Clusters in the property space give a formal meaning
to the idea of a type or class of things, in so far as those properties are concerned. If things when represented as points in the property space are randomly distributed throughout the space, that is, if there are no clusters,
then we would say either that there were no types, but only individuals,
or that we had selected the wrong properties for analysis. If on the other
hand we see clusters, we infer that things tend to fall into types, by which
we mean that variation on one property tends to be associated with variation
on at least one other, or perhaps many others. This is shown graphically

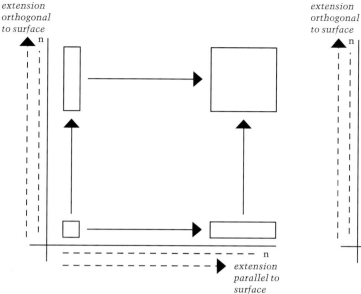

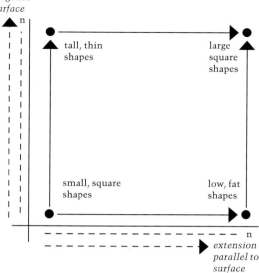

We first create a co-ordinate system in which the vertical axis represents increasing size orthogonal to the surface and the horizontal axis increasing size parallel to the surface. We then draw in the space shapes conforming to the co-ordinates. In the bottom left corner we start with an initial square shape. This becomes extended vertically as we move upwards, laterally as we move horizontally and in both dimensions if we move in both directions.

Because the properties of lateral and vertical expansion are represented in the axes, then the points in the property space represent the changes in shape in the left figure no less than the actual shapes themselves. Other properties not in the co-ordinate system would of course be omitted. The points represent only the properties selected for representation in the property space. The idea of types or classes of shapes can thus be shown by point clusters.

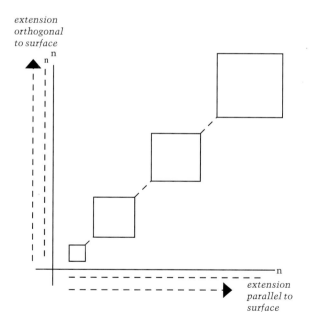

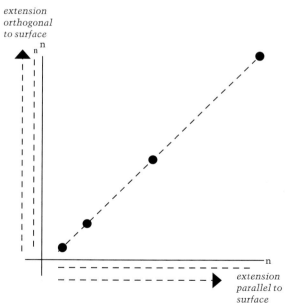

In the above case, the shapes drawn in the co-ordinate space show that an increase on one dimension is always related to an increase in the other. This type of regular association between changes is the surface phenomenon we associate with 'cause and effect' – one change seems to bring about another. But what is shown in the figure is not 'cause and effect', merely the regular association of changes. To 'explain' these regularities we would need to show why they are necessary.

Associated changes can also be represented as points in the property space. The position of points indicates that a change in one dimension is always associated with a change in the other. This representation is also known as a 'scattergram'. The degree to which points form a line from bottom left to top right can be indexed by a 'correlation coefficient', a value between 0 and 1 which indicates how strongly one change implies the other.

Figure 2.1

in the top two diagrams of figure 2.1. We may equally use the property space to formalise the idea that the regularity we see lies not in apparent classes or types of things but sequences of states of things. In this case we ask: when an entity changes on one dimension, does it change in any other? If it does, then the regularity will show itself as a regular pattern in the distribution of entities in the property space. This is shown in the bottom two diagrams in figure 2.1. When we see such a pattern, we would infer that some process if not of cause and effect then at least of regular co-variation was in operation, since each time one variable was changed a change in another variable regularly appeared.

We might then reasonably say that questions about types, that is about similarities and differences, are questions of the form: do entities cluster in particular regions of the property space?; while questions about cause and effect are of the form: when entities move in one dimension of the property space do they move in another? [17] Both of these describe the apparent regularities of surface phenomena, that is the appearance of types and the appearance of cause and effect, in an abstract way. The property space is a means of controlling the attributes that are to be accounted for in the pattern of similarities and differences. Where the real object is present, all its properties are manifest. In the property space, only selected properties are present. Of course, everything depends on our selecting the right properties for the property space in the first place. For this reason we can never be sure from the absence of a regularity that no regularities are present in these phenomena.

But even if we go through a long process of experimenting with different properties until we eventually find the clusters or co-variations that indicate the presence of regularities, it will always still be the surface phenomena that are represented regardless of the degree of abstraction. We are still seeing the surface of things, that is apparent regularities of things as presented to our experience. We are not seeing the theory that purports to account for those regularities, that is we are not seeing the model of the structures of the process which might account for these regularities. What we are doing is recording phenomena in such a way as to be able to see clearly what we mean by regularities, by translating properties into the dimensions of a co-ordinate space and locating objects as points within this space so that only the regular properties are represented in what we see. This both seems to be and is a fundamental way – maybe the fundamental way – of rigorously recording similarities and differences, and constant associations between things, within an objective and independent framework.

The meaning of the word theory can then be made precise. As we have said, just as the a priori given for the noting of regularities is that we know the difference between order and randomness, the a priori given for taking this into theorisation is that regularity on the surface implies some systemic process below the surface, such that the structure of that system is in some sense invariant. A theory is an attempt to model these invariants in a system of interdependent concepts. A theory is a model because it deals with the way in which things must be interrelated in order to produce the surface phenomena, abstract because it represents the system by some means other than that of the system itself. A theory is a model, but not in the sense that a physical model is a model, that is a small copy of the thing itself, but in the contrary sense of a model taking as abstract a form as possible, uncommitted to any particular kind of representation or embodiment. In its purest form, a theory is a kind of abstract machine, since it is an attempt to create an abstract representation of the working of processes which give rise to what we see.

Now the enormous power of theories arises from one very specific property of such 'abstract machines', a property we have already touched upon. Because theories are abstract working models of processes which give rise to the actual, they also give a basis for conjecturing about the possible. Theories in effect allow us to go beyond the accumulated experience of reality and conjecture possible states of reality that are compatible with the model. It is this link between the actual and the possible that makes theories so useful for prediction. To 'apply' a theory is essentially to pose the question: is what is proposed a possible case?

It is too limiting then to call theories 'explanations' of how the world is. A theory defines the invariants that underlie many different states of reality. It is in principle unlikely that all possible states of a particular set of phenomena already exist or are already known. It is likely then that the theory will also predict possible states that do not exist but could according to the model. It is this property above all others that imparts to theory its immense power as a tool of thought and as an agent of human creativity, and also its practical usefulness. However, it is clear that these virtues will arise only to the degree that the theory captures invariants that really are 'out there'. But how can this be? How can an abstraction capture what is really 'out there'? To take this next step, we must know a little more about how theories are put together, how they work, and what they are made of.

What are theories made of?

The first thing we must note is that theories are made of concepts, usually in the form of a system of interdependent concepts with two forms of expression: words, and formal expression, usually mathematical. Since everyday life and language is also run on concepts we must know the difference between a scientific concept and an unscientific one. What then is the difference? We can do no better than to discuss the concepts on which both language and science seem to be founded, that is, the difference between order and randomness.

Order and randomness are both concepts which have a powerful intuitive meaning. Both are very broad indeed in their application, so much so that it is very hard to pin down what the two terms mean with any real clarity. Both terms, and even more the way they are related, express complex intuitions about the way the world is. Each term can be used in a wide range of situations, and the meaning only becomes clear enough to feel understood in the spoken or written context. This is common enough. The intuitive concepts that pervade and give sense to our languages have this richness and imprecision, so they can be used in a great variety of situations, and indeed it is only in the context in which a concept is used that its meaning becomes unambiguous.

In science, it is exactly this richness and imprecision that is restricted. Scientific concepts, although expressed in language, are much narrower in their potential application than normal linguistic concepts. But they are also more systemic, in that they compress and express more interrelationships between concepts. They express more connection between things, but at the cost of a narrowing of the range of application. The

concept of 'entropy' is a good example of this because it relates both order
and chaos in a systemic way, and in doing so restricts the range of application of the new synthetic concept to those situations where precisely
these systemic relations hold. The degree of entropy in a system describes
that system's position in a continuum from order to chaos. Like many
scientific concepts of great profundity and generality it can be explained
simply, though not through words but through a simple model.[18] Imagine
two jars, A and B, with A containing 100 balls numbered 1–100, and B
empty, and some system for selecting a random number between 1 and
100 – say, a pointer on a spindle which can be spun so that it lands with
equal likelihood on the numbers set out in a circle. Spin the pointer and
when the point rests on a number, find the ball with that number and
transfer it from whichever jar it is in to the other one. Then repeat this
operation as many times as necessary. What happens? Intuitively – and
correctly – we say that the process will settle down to about half the balls
in each jar. Why? The answer tells us what entropy is and how it can be
measured. The first time the pointer selects a number, the probability
that the ball selected will go from A to B is 1, that is it is certain, because
all the balls are in A. The second time, there is one chance in 100 that the
single ball in B will return to A, but 99 chances out of 100, that is a probability of .99, that another ball will go from A to B. The next time there is
one chance in 50 that one of the balls in B will return to A, but 98 chances
out of 100 that another ball will go from A to B. Clearly, as the process
goes on, the chances of balls going back from B to A gradually increase
and the chances of balls going from A to B diminish correspondingly.

When about half the balls are in each jar, the probabilities are about
equal, so the system tends to settle down to small variations about this
state. To see why this happens let us define a microstate of the system as
a particular distribution of individual balls in jars and a macrostate as a
particular number of balls in each jar. There are, clearly, only 200 possible
microstates of the system for the macrostate in which one ball is in one jar
and the rest are in the other, that is one for each of the hundred balls in each
jar. For the macrostate with two balls in one jar and 98 in the other there
are all possible combinations of two balls for each jar, that is 200×200.
For the macrostate with three in one and 97 in the other there are all

combinations of three balls. In other words, the number of microstates for the macrostate is maximised when the largest possible number are in the least full jar – that is when half the balls are in each – because beyond that point there will be fewer balls in the other jar and everything happens in reverse.

This is why the system tends to the half and half state. There are far more microstates corresponding to the half and half (or near half and half) macrostates than for those in which a few balls are in one jar and many in the other. In other words all the system does is to tend to its most probable state. This is also the definition of the state of maximum entropy. Entropy is maximal in a system when the system is in one of the macrostates for which there are the largest number of microstates. An example of this is where two gases are each randomly distributed in a container, without regions where one or other gas predominates. There are far more microstates with random distribution than microstates with concentrations of one or other gas in a certain region. Our model of jars and balls is then a statistical representation of the mixing of two gases in a closed compartment – or for the gradual heat death of the universe as the universe tends from its current improbable state to its most probable state, that is one in which heat is more or less evenly dispersed throughout the universe.[19]

In other words, entropy relates the notions of order and chaos into a single concept, but at the same time gives it a much more precise and limited reference to the world. However, it also does something else of no less importance. It permits the concept to be captured in a formal mathematical expression as well as through words. It is through this formal expression that the link between the concept and the observable world is made. This two-way emancipation of concepts, on the one hand reorganising concepts into more precise systems of interdependence and on the other relating them to the real world by associating them with formal expressions, is the essence of what theories are.

Theories are therefore made of two things: words and formal expressions. But both represent concepts. A theory is a system of concepts with one type of expression, the verbal, which links the concepts back into our understanding, necessarily with some imprecision; and another, mathematical form which links the concepts forward into phenomena,

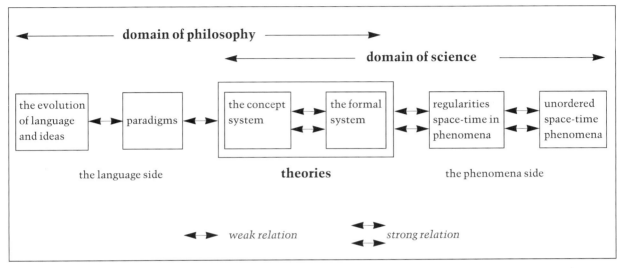

Figure 2.2

necessarily with great exactness. Theories thus link our understanding
to the world, connected to our understanding by linguistic concepts and
connected to phenomena by formal expressions corresponding to the
concepts.

   This two-way relation using language and formalism to link concepts to our understanding on the one hand and to the real world on the
other is the heart of what theories are. We may clarify all these complex
relations in a diagram, see figure 2.2. This figure shows not only how
theories intervene between language and the world, but also how science
relates to philosophy, which overlaps with science in part of this overall
scheme. The overall form of the diagram sets the evolution of language
and ideas on the left and the phenomena of space-time on the right.
Theories are in the centre, defined as a relation between a system of concepts and a system of formal expressions which looks two ways: through
the concepts it looks back first into the broader conceptual schemes we
call paradigms, then into the evolving structure of language and ideas
which are both an inevitable context and an inevitable constraint on
theorisation; and through the formalism it looks forward towards the
regularities in space-time phenomena which theories seek to account

for, and then onwards into the general foreground of space-time phenomena which do not form part of the regularities but which may at any stage
arbitrarily engage the theory by offering phenomena which are inconsistent
with the 'abstract machine' for generating phenomena proposed by the
theory.

The earliest ancestors of what we would recognise as 'scientific'
theories, such as those of the Pythagoreans who are said to have first
noted the relation between numerical ratios and forms occurring in
nature, are probably best seen as paradigms rather than as fully fledged
theories, although in their preoccupation with the relation between
space-time regularities and formal expression they certainly prefigure
theories in the modern sense.[20] Pythagoreanism (as we earlier noted as
influencing Alberti) is a generalisation of a single concept which generated
a way of looking at the world on the basis of a few results. This is legitimately
a precursor to theory but not in itself what we ought to be calling a theory.
However the attraction of such over-generalisation remains, as is seen in
the prevalence of variants on Pythagoreanism in the mystical substitutes
for theory which have continued to occupy the fringes of architectural
thought throughout the twentieth century.[21]

Theories in the scientific sense are one step in from both paradigms
on the one side and regularities on the other in that they are composed of
concepts which are focused and related to each other to form a system,
with precise relations between each concept and formal techniques or
expressions which are used to check how far the regularities implied by
the system of concepts are detectable in space-time phenomena.
Scientific theories thus require three relations to be particularly strong:
the relations among concepts which form the conceptual system; the
relations between concepts and formal techniques of measurement; and
the relations between these formal techniques and space-time phenomena.
In terms of the diagram, we may say then that science needs to be strong
from the 'concept system' in the direction of phenomena.

Science is, and must expect to be, weaker in the other direction, that
is in the passage back through paradigms into the more general evolution
of ideas. This tends to be ground occupied by philosophy. Philosophy overlaps with science in being interested in theories, and relating them back

to broader families of concepts [22] right through to those that prevail in everyday life and social practices,[23] but does not normally preoccupy itself with the rigorous testing of theories against real space-time phenomena. Science and philosophy are rivals in the realm of theory, but only because their preoccupations reach out from theory in contrary directions with the effect that between them science and philosophy cover the ground that needs to be occupied by theoretical thought. However, it is because science moves from concepts to phenomena that its theories eventually come to have a puzzling status, because the intuitive sense that they 'explain' things comes from the relation between the concepts that make up the theory and the sense we have from everyday language that our ideas 'explain' the world. Scientific theories are in this sense psychologically strongest where they are in fact weakest, that is where the concepts that form the theory relate back into the broader conceptual systems which inform everyday life.[24]

Towards an analytic theory of architecture
Given these definitions, how then can there be an analytic theory of architecture? First, let us be completely clear about one thing. If there are no objective regularities in the real world of architectural form and space, linking the configurational aspects of form and space with behavioural and experiential outcomes, then there are no grounds whatsoever for seeking to build an analytic theory. The need for and the possibility of an analytic theory both stand or fall with the existence of such 'non-discursive regularities'.

This means that to build an analytic theory, non-discursive regularities must first be investigated and, if they exist, brought to light. How can this be done? We may first recall that an architectural theory is an attempt to render one or other of the non-discursive aspects of architecture discursive, by describing non-discursivity in concepts, words and numbers. We may say that an architectural theory seeks to create a 'non-discursive technique', that is, a technique for handling those matters of pattern and configuration of form and space that we find it hard to talk about. In research terms we could say that an architectural theory, at least in the 'narrow' aspects through which it describes and prescribes design decisions, is an attempt to control the architectural variable.

Now, as we have seen, architectural theories in the past have tended to be strongly normative and weakly analytic, because the non-discursive techniques proposed are only able to describe certain kinds of configuration. This is why in application they are partisan for that kind of configuration. For example, if a non-discursive technique describes systems of proportion in terms of numerical or geometric ratios, it is unlikely to be able to deal with configurations which lack such proportionality. It will only describe those cases where these proportions hold. In any attempt to apply such partisan techniques generally, they are more likely therefore to act as distorting mirrors than a discovery of new regularities. Likewise, if our non-discursive technique is a system of diagrams expressing spatial hierarchy, it is unlikely that those techniques can be usefully applied to the vast range of cases where such clear hierarchisation is not found. It follows again that such a technique will be useless for investigating spatial patterns in general.

We can say then that a non-discursive technique which is partisan for – usually because it is a product of a preference for – one particular kind of non-discursivity, will not be usable as an analytic tool, and cannot therefore be used for the discovery of non-discursive regularities. This deficiency, however, does point us in the direction of what is needed. To bring to light non-discursive regularities, we need non-discursive techniques for the description of either spatial patterns or formal pattern (or conceivably both) which are uncommitted to any particular type of spatial or formal configuration or pattern, and which are capable of general application to describe all possible types of pattern. For example, it ought to be able to handle spatial patterns or built form patterns which lack geometric regularity as well as those which have it. Unless this can be done with rigour there is little hope that theoretical propositions in architecture can ever be analytic in the sense that we require them to be.

The next chapter of this book will introduce such a set of non-discursive techniques for the analysis of configuration, first developed in spatial form as 'space syntax', but now being broadened to cover other aspects of configuration. These techniques have been used over several years for two principle purposes, first to discover how far it was possible to bring to light and subject to rigorous comparative analyses the configurational aspects of space and form in building through which culture is transmitted, and second, through these comparative studies to develop a corpus of material which would permit the gradual development of a general theory of architectural possibility. The remainder of this book is essentially an account of the progress that has so far been made in this project.

As we will see, what we discover through applying these techniques to the analysis of spatial and formal patterns in architecture, wherever they are found and whatever their embodiment in either buildings or urban systems, are invariants in patterns which lie not on the surface of things but which are buried in the nature of configurations themselves. These invariants we can think of as deep structures or genotypes. Each cultural manifestation through building, whether as a building 'type' for a particular purpose, or a particular architectural ethnos or imprinting of culture on building, does so through such genotypes. For example, seen as systems of organised space, it turns out that towns and cities have deep structures which vary with culture. Likewise, seen as organised space, buildings for different function purposes also have deep structures or genotypes. These genotypes are – or embody – cultural or typological invariants. These are not of course general laws. They are at best the 'covering laws' of cultures. There are the genotypical invariants by which each society and each function in society seeks to express itself through architecture.

However, as we build our corpus of genotypes we gradually begin to see that there is another level of invariance: there are genotypes of the genotypes. Below the level of cultural variation in architecture there exist invariants across cultures and types. These 'genotypes of genotypes' are not the covering laws of cultures but the invariant laws that bind humankind in general to its artificial material world. They are the abstract raw material out of which all configurational possibility in space and form in the built world are constructed. It is at this level of invariance – and only at this level – that we can build a genuine analytic theory. These possibilities will be dealt with in chapters 8 and 9.

Architecture as art and as science
If this theoretical project is eventually to succeed – and it is beyond the scope of any single book to do more than take a few faltering steps towards

such a theory – then it is clear that such a theory would liberate rather than constrain design. At root, the need for architectural theory arises from the need to formulate principles from the experience of having built to inform and guide us on how we might build. This dynamic between the actual and possible is the essence of architectural theorising. Architectural theory arises from the fact that architects can neither forget the architectural tradition, nor repeat it. In architecture, theory is not simply a means to fix a picture of the world in a certain form. It is also the means by which form is destabilised and a new future is conceived. Architecture progresses by incorporating its reflection on the past into an abstract frame of possibility. This frame is theory. Without it, historical thought is sterile, and can only lead to imitation of the past. Through the intermediary of theory, reflection on the past becomes possible future. History constrains, but theory liberates, and the more general the theory, the greater the liberation.

Does this mean then that the line between architecture as science and architecture as art needs to be redrawn closer to science? I do not believe so. We can call on the beautiful ideas of Ernst Cassirer on the relation between art and science.[25] 'Language and science', he writes, 'are the two main processes by which we ascertain and determine our concepts of the external world. We must classify our sense perceptions and bring them under general notions and general rules in order to give them an objective meaning. Such classification is the result of a persistent effort towards simplification. The work of art in like manner implies such an act of condensation and concentration…But in the two cases there is a difference of stress. Language and science are abbreviations of reality; art is an intensification of reality. Language and science depend on one and the same process of abstraction; art may be described as a continuous process of concretion… art does not admit of…conceptual simplification and deductive generalisation. It does not inquire into the qualities or causes of things; it gives the intuition of the form of things…The artist is just as much the discoverer of the forms of nature as the scientist is the discoverer of facts or natural laws.'

Those of us who believe that science is on the whole a good thing, accept that science is in one sense an impoverishment – though in others an enhancement – of our experience of the world in that it cannot cope with the density of situational experience. It has to be so. It is not in the nature of science to seek to explain the richness of particular realities, since these are, as wholes, invariably so diverse as to be beyond the useful grasp of theoretical simplifications. What science is about is the dimensions of structure and order that underlie complexity. Here the abstract simplifications of science can be the most powerful source of greater insight. Every moment of our experience is dense and, as such, unanalysable as a complete experience. But this does not mean to say that some of its constituent dimensions are not analysable, and that deeper insight may not be gained from such analysis.

This distinction is crucial to our understanding of architecture. That architectural realities are dense and, as wholes, unanalysable does not mean to say that the role of spatial configuration (for example) in architectural realities cannot be analysed and even generalised. The idea that science is to be rejected because it does not give an account of the richness of experience is a persistent but elementary error. Science gives us quite a different kind of experience of reality, one that is partial and analytic rather than whole and intuitive. As such it is in itself that it is valuable. It needs to be accepted or rejected on its own terms, not in terms of its failure to be like life or like art.

It is in any case clear that the dependence of architecture on theories, covert or explicit, does not diminish its participation in Cassirer's definition of art. This is true both in the sense that architecture is, like art, a continuous process of concretion, and also in the sense that, like art, 'its aspects are innumerable'. But there are also differences. The thing 'whose aspects are innumerable' is not a representation but a reality, and a very special kind of reality, one through which our forms of social being are transformed and put at risk. The pervasive involvement of theory in architecture, and the fact that architecture's 'continuous concretion' involves our social existence, defines the peculiar status and nature of 'systematic intent of the architectural kind': architecture is theoretical concretion. Architects are enjoined both to create the new, since that is the nature of their task, but also to render the theories that tie their creation to our social existence better and clearer. It is this that makes architecture distinct and unique. It is as impossible to reduce architecture to theory as it is to eliminate theory from it.

Architecture is thus both art and science not in that it has both technical and aesthetic aspects but in that it requires both the processes of abstraction by which we know science and the processes of concretion by which we know art. The difficulty and the glory of architecture lie in the realisation of both: in the creation of a theoretical realm through building, and in the creation of an experienced reality 'whose aspects are innumerable'. This is the difficulty of architecture and this is why we acclaim it.

Notes

1   Roger Scruton, *The Aesthetics of Architecture*, Methuen, 1977.

2   Ibid., p. 4.

3   L. B. Alberti, *De Re Aedificatoria*, 1486; translation referred to: Rykwert et al. (1988), MIT Press, 1991.

4   O. Newman, *Defensible Space*; Architectural Press, 1972.

5   Alberti, chapter 9.

6   Newman, pp. 3–9.

7   How this happens as a cognitive process is the subject of chapter 11: 'The reasoning art'.

8   Chapter 11 includes a case study in the dangers of bad theory.

9   Alberti, for example, Book 9.

10   Scruton's fundamental error is to confuse these two aspects, and in effect to believe that the narrow propositions of architectural theory are intended to be universalistic. See Scruton, *The Aesthetics of Architecture*, p. 4.

11   Alberti, Book 9.

12   Newman, pp. 3–9.

13   F. Bacon, *The New Organon* (1620), Bobbs Merrill 1960, Aphorisms Book 1, Aphorism cxv, p. 105.

14   T. Kuhn, *The Structure of Scientific Revolutions*, University of Chicago Press, 1962.

15   To use Rene Thom's admirable expression for what we observe – see *Structural Stability and Morphogenesis*, Benjamin, New York, 1975 – originally in French 1972 as *Stabilité Structurelle et Morphogenese*. See for example p. 320.

16   F. De Saussure, (originally in French 1915) version used *Course in General Linguistics*, McGraw Hill, 1966, translated by C. Bally and A. Sechahaye with A. Riedlinger – see for example pp. 103–12.

17   These examples of course deal with linear variation, but the basic arguments also apply to non-linear variation.

18   This model, the 'Ehrenfest game', is taken from M. Kac and S. Ulam, *Mathematics and Logic*, Pelican Books, 1971, p. 168. Originally Praeger, 1968.

19   For a further discussion see H. Reichenbach, *The Direction of Time*, University
      of California Press, 1971, particularly chapter 4.

20   See K. Popper, *Conjectures and Refutations*, Routledge and Kegan Paul, 1963,
      chapter 5: 'Back to the presocratics'.

21   See for example M. Ghyka, *Geometrical Composition and Design*, Tiranti,
      London, 1956.

22   For example in the work of Alexander Koyre, e.g. *Metaphysics and Measurement*,
      Chapman and Hall, 1968 (originally in French) and *Newtonian Studies*, Chapman
      and Hall, 1965, or Georges Canguilhem, e.g. *La Connaissance de la Vie*, Librairie
      Philosophique J.Vrin, Paris, 1971.

23   As pioneered in the work of Michel Foucault.

24   In the past, this has led to a quite rapid permeation by new scientific concepts of the
      conceptual schemes of everyday life, bringing changes in consciousness which may
      seem entirely progressive, as for example with the theories of Newton or Darwin. It
      may indeed be the loss of this illusory strength that has brought about much of the
      alienation from science in the late twentieth century. As science has progressed
      farther into micro and macro phenomena and discovered patterns which are utterly
      remote from everyday intuition the concepts that make up scientific theories become
      so strange that they cannot even be formulated so as to interface effectively with the
      established conceptual system of linguistic normality. This has happened with
      quantum theory. But what has happened with quantum theory confirms our model as
      set out in the diagram: science intervenes through formalisms between concepts and
      phenomena. It is no part of its function or its morality that these concepts should 'fall
      within the lighted circle of intuition' (to use Herman Weyl's admirable phrase – see
      his *Philosophy of Mathematics and Natural Science*, Atheneum, New York, 1963, p. 66)
      and so be translatable into the available concepts of everyday life and language. There
      is no greater arrogance than that we should expect them to be, except perhaps the
      belief that the world itself in its deepest operations should conform itself to the
      apparatus of our intuitions.

25   Ernst Cassirer, *An Essay on Man*, Yale University Press, 1944. Edition used: Bantam
      Matrix, 1970. Chapter 9, 'On art', pp. 152–88.

chapter three

Non-discursive technique

'Environments are invisible. Their…
ground rules…evade easy perception.'
MARSHALL MCLUHAN

Object artefacts and abstract artefacts

One of the durable intellectual achievements of the twentieth century
has been to initiate the scientific study of human artefacts. At first sight,
such a study might seem paradoxical. Most artefacts are physical objects
that adapt natural laws to human purposes. To make an object for a purpose surely presupposes that we understand it. But twenty-five years ago,
Herbert Simon, in his *The Sciences of the Artificial*, showed that this was
far from the whole story.[1] Even if the objects we make are not puzzling in
themselves, they are so when seen in the context of the ramifying effects
of their dispersion throughout our socio-technical ecosystem. He was
thinking, amongst other things, of computers. It would be as enlighten-
ing, he argued, to have a natural history of computers in our increasingly
artificial world, as of any natural phenomenon. Empirical sciences of
artefacts were therefore not only a possibility, but a necessity.

But object artefacts are only the lesser aspect of the puzzle of the
artificial. There also exists a class of artefacts which are no less dramatic
in their impact on human life, but which are also puzzling in themselves
precisely because they are not objects, but, on the contrary, seem to take
a primarily abstract form. Language is the paradigm case. Language seems
to exist in an objective sense, since it lies outside individuals and belongs
to a community. But we cannot find language in any region of space-time.
Language seems real, but it lacks location. It thus seems both real and
abstract at the same time. Other artefacts which share some of the
attributes of language, such as cultures, social institutions, and even,
some would argue, society itself, all seem to raise this central puzzle
of being, it seems, 'abstract artefacts'.

It cannot of course be said that 'abstract artefacts' are not manifested in space-time. They appear in the form of linguistic acts, social behaviours, cultural practices, and so on. But these space-time appearances are
not the artefact itself, only its momentary and fragmentary realisations.
We apprehend speech, as de Saussure would say, but not language.[2] In the
same way, we see social behaviours, but we never see social institutions,
and we see cultural events but we never see cultures. Yet in all these
cases, the space-time events that we witness seem to be governed in their
form by the abstract, unrealisable artefacts that we give a name to. The

material world provides the milieu within which the abstract artefact is
realised, but these realisations are dispersed and incomplete. The existence
of languages, social institutions and cultures can be inferred from space-
time events but not seen in them.

In spite of this strange mode of existence, abstract artefacts seem to
be the stuff of which society is made. We cannot conceive what a society
would be like if deprived of its languages, its characteristic social behaviours, its cultural forms and its institutions. It is not clear that anything
would be left which we could reasonably call 'society'. We may conjecture,
perhaps, that abstract artefacts are the way they are precisely *because* their
purpose is to generate and govern dispersed events, and through this to convert a dispersed collectivity of speakers, behaviours or social actors into
some semblance of a system. The multipositionality of the space-time
realisation of abstract artefacts seems to be an essential part of how
they work.

However, to say this is to restate the problem, not to solve it. In fact,
in spite of their apparent oddity, abstract artefacts pose many of the puzzles
which science seeks to explain for natural systems. For example, they seem
able both to reproduce themselves over time, and also to undergo morphogenesis, though whether this is by a constant or sudden process is
entirely obscure. If abstract artefacts have such properties, then it would
seem to follow that they must therefore have some kind of internal principles or laws which give rise to stability and change, as do natural systems.[3]
Yet whatever these laws are like, they must also pass through the human
mind, since it is only through human mental activity that the self reproduction and morphogenesis of these systems occurs. It seems inconceiv-
able, therefore, that the laws which govern the forms of abstract artefacts
are similar to, or even commensurable with, the laws that govern natural
systems. At the same time, such laws must be part of nature, since they
cannot be otherwise. They must reflect some potentialities within nature.

In view of all these apparent paradoxes, it was the great merit of Levi-
Strauss and other pioneers of the study of abstract artefacts to have both
identified the key insight necessary for their study, and to have pointed
to a possible methodology for research.[4] The insight was to have seen the
dependence of the concrete on the abstract in systems like language and

culture, as clearly as Plato once noted it for the natural world.[5] Now, as then, this fundamental insight provides the starting point and initial stance for the setting up of sciences. The methodology was that, as with natural systems, we would expect to find clues to the nature of these organising laws by studying the regularities that abstract artefacts generate in space-time, that is, in speech, behaviour, cultural practices and institutional forms. Accordingly, the movement called structuralism aimed to assign abstract formal models with the structure and variety manifested in the space-time output of such systems - observed speech, social behaviour, organisational dynamics and so on - and through this to account not only for the internal systemness of such phenomena, but also to show how the human mind was capable of holding and creatively transforming such powerfully structured information. In this sense, structuralism was no more or less than orthodox science rewritten for the study of abstract artefacts.[6]

This research strategy reflects the fundamental fact that abstract artefacts manifest themselves to us in two ways: through the space-time events they generate; and through the configurational patterns which seem to support them and which enable us both to generate and interpret them. These two ways in which we experience abstract artefacts are bound together by the fact that in using configurational structures to generate space-time events we also project these configurational structures into space-time and in doing so help to transmit them into the future. This double take between the conscious manipulation of space-time events and the transmission of configurational structure is the defining characteristic of the abstract artefact and the reason it is able to be the stuff of society. By deploying objects and creating space-time events we necessarily transmit structures, and through them the abstract artefacts which hold society together as a communicative system. The object of structuralism is to capture the dynamics of these processes.

Formal methods were therefore critical to structuralism. However, as Heisenberg once remarked: 'Our scientific work in physics consists in asking questions about nature in the language that we possess and trying to get an answer from experiment by the means that are at our disposal.'[7] This is surely true of all scientific enquiry. Unfortunately, it seems to point directly to the failure of structuralism to deliver on its promises.

Examining the space-time regularities of the phenomena generated by abstract artefacts, we cannot fail to note one overwhelming consistency; that they seem to be governed by *pattern* laws of some kind. The words that make up speech and the behaviours that seem social are all manifested in space-time as sequences or dispositions of apparent elements whose interdependencies seem to be multiplex, and irreducible to simple rules of combination. For example, to say, as Chomsky did,[8] that sentences, which appear to be sequences of words, cannot be generated by a left-right grammar, is a configurational proposition. Some degree of syncretic co-presence of many relations is involved whose nature cannot be reduced to an additive list of pairwise relations. This is to say that the laws governing abstract artefacts seem to be *configurational* in something like the sense we have defined it in the previous chapters.

It is in this respect that structuralism seems to have lacked methodology. Its formal techniques did not try to drive straight to the problem of configuration, but confined themselves to the more elementary aspects of logic and set theory, those branches of mathematics that is that sought to axiomatise the thinking processes of minds, rather than to model real world complexity.[9] Consequently, just as the 'languages' available for Plato in his time were inadequate for his vision of nature,[10] so the tools picked up in the mid-twentieth century by structuralism were too frail for the vision of artificial phenomena that had initiated their search. The phenomena that structuralist analysis sought to explain were in the main configurational, but the formal techniques through which investigators sought to demonstrate this rarely were.

Built environments as artefacts
The purposes of this digression into abstract artefacts are two: first, to draw attention to certain properties of built environments that might otherwise be missed; second, to point to certain advantages of the built environment in providing a platform for taking on the problem of configuration in a new way. First, however, we must understand the very peculiar status of built environments as artefacts.

Built environments appear to us as collections of object artefacts, that is, of buildings, and as such subject to ordinary physical laws, and deserving of Simonian enquiry. But that is not all that they are. As we noted in chapter 1, in terms of spatial and formal organisation, built environments are also configurational entities, whose forms are not given by natural laws. If we wish to consider built environments as organised systems, then their primary nature is configurational, principally because it is through spatial configuration that the social purposes for which the built environment is created are expressed. The collections of object artefacts in space-time that we see, are then a means through which socially meaningful configurational entities are realised. In other words, in spite of appearances, built environments possess a key property of abstract artefacts. Its objects are more durable than, say, the spoken words of a language, or the rule-influenced individual behaviours that make up a social event, but they are of the same kind. They are space-time manifestations of configurational ideas which also have an abstract form. The built environment is only the most durable of the space-time manifestations of the human predilection for configuration. This has an epistemological consequence. We should not expect the built environment merely to be the material backdrop to individual and social behaviour, as it is often taken to be. It *is* a social behaviour, just as the use of language is a social behaviour and not just a means to social behaviour. We cannot therefore regard the built environment as merely an inert thing, and seek to understand it without understanding the 'social logic' of its generation.

But just as we cannot treat a built environment as a thing, we can no more treat it as though it were no more than a language. The built environment is, apart from society itself, the largest and most complex artefact that human beings make. Its complexity and its scale emerge together, because, like society, a built environment is not so much a thing as a process of spatio-temporal aggregation subject to continual change and carried out by innumerable agencies over a long period of time. Although these processes of aggregation may be locally characterised by the same kind of autonomic rule following as we find for individual acts of building, there are other no less fundamental attributes that make the built environment a special case.

The most obvious, and the most important, is that the spatio-temporal outputs of built environment processes are not ephemeral like those of language or social behaviour. They are long-lasting, and they aggregate by occupying a particular region of space for a long time. This means that over and above thinking of built environments as the products of abstract rule systems, we must also recognise that they have an aggregative dynamics which is to some extent independent of these rule systems, although, as we will see, it is rarely quite out of their control. These aggregative processes have quite distinctive properties. Spatio-temporal additions to a system usually occur locally, but the dynamics of the system tend to work at the more global aggregative levels.[11] Complexity arises in part from the recursive application, in increasingly complex aggregations, of rules which may initially be simple, but themselves may be transformed by the evolving context in which they are applied. A locally driven aggregative process often produces a global state which is not understood [12] but which needs to be understood in order for the locally driven process to be effective. This is the essential nature of the large aggregates of buildings which form most built environments.

This complex, processual aetiology is the main reason why built environments have proved so resistant to orthodox attempts to model their structure mathematically. Buildings and cities are not crystalline objects, unfolding under the influence only of laws of growth. The elementary spatial gestuaries of humankind and its cultures may construct local elemental configurations, but these then operate as local orderings within growth processes and act as constraints on the 'natural' evolution of global patterns. Architectural and even more so urban forms occur at the interface between natural processes and human interventions. Human actions restrict and structure the natural growth processes, so that they cannot be understood without insight into both, and into the relations between the two. The intervention of the mind in the evolving complexity must be understood, but so must its limitations.

The built environment may then be the most obvious of objects, and the one that forms our familiar milieu, but at the same time its inner logic and structure is as inaccessible to us as anything in nature. However, it has one great advantage as an object of study. Its very scale, manifestness and slow rate of change offer it up as the paradigm case for configurational investigation. The essence of the problem is to capture the local-to-global dynamics of architectural and urban system, that is to show how the elementary generators which express the human ability to cognise and structure an immediate spatial reality, unfold into the ramified complexities of large-scale systems.

In this, methodological difficulties are central. The aim of a method must be to capture the local or elemental ordering, the emergence of global complexity, and how both relate to the human mind. For any of these, the manifest problem of configuration must be tackled head on, and must be approached first and foremost as an empirical problem. If the space-time products of abstract artefacts are held together by configuration, then configuration can be found by examining them. The corpus of configurations that can be built through the study of real cases must be some indicator of where we might seek for the configurational invariants of built environment processes. For this task, the very scale, relative stability and availability of built environments make them the ideal vehicle for an enquiry. All we need are techniques that permit the extraction of configuration from its space-time embodiments - that is, non-discursive technique.

Simplicity as a means to complexity

The configurational formalisms proposed here as the basis for non-discursive technique are in some ways much simpler than others proposed for the similar classes of phenomena over the last twenty years.[13] Yet they have proved the most powerful in detecting formal and functional regularities in real systems. There are probably three reasons for this. First, the quantitative methods proposed are directed straight at the problem of *configuration*, that is the problem of understanding the simultaneous effects of a whole complex of entities on each other through their pattern of relationships. Lack of attention to this central problem is the prime reason why past formalism often seemed to offer mathematical sophistication out of proportion to the empirical results achieved. With configurational analysis it is the other way round. Exceedingly simple quantitative techniques have led to a disproportionate success in finding significant formal and form-functional regularities. Configuration, as defined below, seems to be at least one of the things that architectural and urban patterns are about.

Second, in configurational analysis, as much theoretical attention has been given to the *representation* of the spatial or formal system that is to be analysed as to the method of quantification. As we will see, this quite normally gives rise to a whole family of representations of the same spatial system, each one relevant to some aspect of its functioning. It is also normal to combine representations, literally by laying one representation on top of the other and treating the resulting connections as real connections in the system. Through this, we find that pairs or even triples of representations taken together yield formally or functionally informative results. In terms of research strategy, this means trying to represent space in terms of the type of function in which we are interested. For example, simple line structures drawn through spaces, temporarily discounting other properties, have proved sufficient (as we will see in the next chapter) to account for many aspects of movement within buildings and urban areas.

Third, and synthesising the previous two, much attention has been given to the graphic representation of the results of mathematical analysis, so that the formal structures identified in spatial or formal complexes can be intuitively seen and understood without the intermediary of the mathematical formalism. This means that much can be understood by those whose temperaments lead them to prefer a graphical rather than a mathematical understanding. By representing mathematical results graphically, a level of communication is possible that permits large numbers of people to be interested and knowledgeable who would otherwise fall at the first fence of mathematical analysis. In parallel to this graphical representation of results, usually drawn by computer, there is a parallel emphasis in the initial stages of investigation to the drawing of spatial or formal ideas by investigators and by students as a constant adjunct to and check on formal analysis.

No apology is then offered for the simplicity of some of the notions presented here. Others have discussed some of these properties but have not been minded to explore their full empirical or theoretical relevance, or how they might be fitted into the overall form-function picture. Perhaps one reason for researchers to miss key relations while 'going close', has been what we would see as an overarching and in some ways premature concern with design at the expense of the empirical investigation of buildings. The 'space syntax' research at UCL has been driven by a remark of Lionel March's: 'The only thing you can apply is a good theory.'[14] Another possible reason why formal exploration has missed theoretical insight has been the frequent lack of a close enough relation between mathematical and empirical aspects of the problems posed by real buildings and cities. In contrast, the techniques of spatial representation and quantification proposed here are essentially survivors of an intensive programme of empirical investigation spread over the best part of two decades in which formal questions have been explored in parallel to the empirical puzzles posed by architectural and urban realities.

We have already discussed the idea of configuration at some length in chapter 1. Now we need to define it formally, and to show some of its power to say simple things about space and form. It should be noted that what follows is not a methodological cook book, but a theoretical exploration of the *idea* of configuration. At this stage, the examples given are illustrations of ideas, not worked examples of analysis. Case studies will come in ensuing chapters. The relation of this chapter to those that follow is that of a quarry, which future chapters return to to pick up one of the possibilities set out here, and refine it for the purposes of that chapter. This chapter shows the bases and connection of the whole family of methods.

Defining configuration

Let us begin by defining exactly what we mean by configuration, using an example directly analogous to figure 1.3 in chapter 1, but taking a slightly different form. We may recall that in chapter 1, a *simple* relation was defined as a relation - say, adjacency or permeability - between any pair of elements in a complex. A *configurational* relation was then defined as a relation insofar as it is affected by the simultaneous co-presence of at least a third element, and possibly all other elements, in a complex. In figure 3.1 i, for example, *a* and *b* are two cubes standing on a surface. In 3.1 ii, the cubes are brought together full facewise to make a conjoint object. The relation of *a* and *b* is symmetrical in that *a* being the (contiguous) neighbour of *b* implies that *b* is the (contiguous) neighbour of *a*. One

Figure 3.1

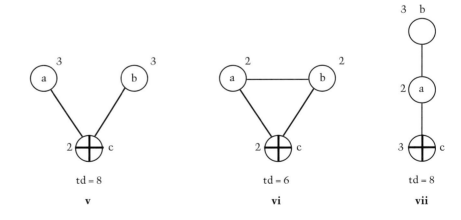

could equally say, though with less obviousness, that in 3.1 i *a* and *b* were noncontiguous neighbours, and were therefore symmetrical in this sense. Either way, the relation of the two remains symmetrical, and in fact this is implicit in the 'neighbour' relation. In 3.1 iii, the conjoint object formed by a and b in 3.1 ii is taken and rested on one of its ends, without changing the relation of *a* to *b* . But *b* now appears to be 'above' *a* , and the relation of 'being above', unlike that of 'being the neighbour of', is not symmetrical but asymmetrical: *b* being above *a* implies that *a* is not above *b* .

How has this happened? The temptation is to say that relations like 'above' and 'below' depend on an exogenous frame of reference, like 'east' and 'west', or 'up' and 'down'. In fact, what has happened can be said more simply, as shown in 3.1 iiii. The surface on which the cubes stand - say, the surface of the earth - was not referred to in describing the relation between *a* and *b* in 3.1 i and ii. It should have been, had we wanted to foresee the effects of standing the conjoint object on its end. Let us call it *c* . In 3.1 ii, the relation of both *a* and *b* , taken separately, to the third object, *c* , is also symmetrical, as is their relation to each other. So, incidentally, is the relation of the conjoint object formed by a and b to the third object. These are all simple relations. But we can also say something more complex: that in 3.1 ii, *a* and *b* are symmetrical with *respect to c* , as well as with respect to each other. This is a configurational statement, since it describes a simple spatial relation in terms of at least a third. What happens in 3.1 iii is now clear. Although *a* and *b* remain symmetrical with respect to each other, they are no longer symmetrical with respect to *c* . On the contrary, they are asymmetrical with respect to c. The difference between 3.1 ii and iii is then a configurational difference. The relation of *a* and *b* to each other is changed if we add the 'with respect to' clause which embeds the two cubes in a larger complex which includes *c* .

The situation is clarified by the justified graphs (or j-graphs: graphs in which nodes are aligned above a root according to their 'depth' from the root (see chapter 1) of the configurations shown in 3.1 v, vi and vii. In each, the bottom node is the earth, and is inscribed with a cross to indicate that it is the root. In 3.1 v, *a* and *b* are each independently connected as neighbours to the earth. In 3.1 vi, the relation of neighbour between *a* and *b* is added. In 3.1 vii, the relation between *b* and *c* , the earth, is

Figure 3.2

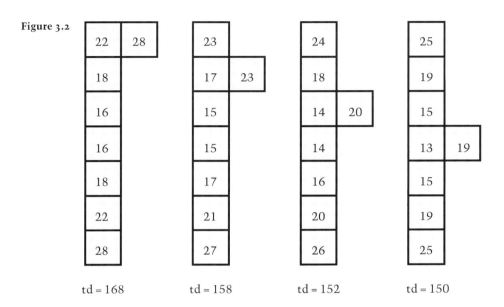

td = 168   td = 158   td = 152   td = 150

broken creating a 'two deep' relation between *b* and *c* . One may note that this set-up already exists in 3.1 v between the two noncontiguous cubes with respect to the earth. In this sense, 3.1 vii recreates a graph which already exists in v. This is also shown in the numbers attached to each of the nodes of the graph, which indicate the sum of 'depth' from that node to the other nodes in the system. The total depth of 3.1 v and vii is therefore 8, while that of vi is 6. We might say, then, that the distributions of total depths and their overall sum describe at least some configurational characteristics of these composite objects.

Now let us explore this simple technique a little further by examining figure 3.2, a series of simple figures composed of square cells joined together through their faces (but not their corners) with 'total depths' for each cell to all others inscribed in each cell, and the sums of these total depths for each figure below the figure. The figures are all composed of seven identically related cells, plus an eighth which is joined to the original block of seven initially at the top end in the leftmost figure, then progressively more centrally from left to right. There are two principal effects from changing the position of this single element. First, the total depth values and their distributions all change. Second, the sums of total depth for each figure change, reducing from left to right as the eighth element moves to a more central location. The effects, however, are quite complex. This is not of course surprising, but it illustrates two key principles of configurational analysis. First, changing one element in a configuration can change the configurational properties of many others, and perhaps all others in a complex. Second, the overall characteristics of a complex can be changed by changing a single element, that is, changes do not somehow cancel out their relations to different elements and leave the overall properties invariant. On the contrary, virtually any change to elements that is not simply a symmetrical change, will alter the overall properties of the configuration. We will see in due course that configurational changes of this kind, even small ones, play a vital role in the form and functioning of buildings and built environments.

Shapes as configurations
Another way of saying this, is that different arrangements of the same numbers of elements will have different configurational properties. For example, figure 3.3 is a set of rearrangements of the same eight square cells that we considered in figure 3.2, again with 'total depths' inscribed in each cell, but also with a number of other simple properties, including the total depth, set out close to the figure: td is total depth, d bar is the average for each cell, sd is the standard deviation, df is the 'difference factor' indicating the degree of difference between the minimum, maximum and mean depth in each complex (Hillier et al. 1987a), and t/t is the number of different depth values over the number of cells.

In treating shapes as configurations in this sense, that is as composites made up of standardised elements, we are in effect treating a shape as a graph, that is as a purely relational complex of some kind in which we temporarily ignore other attributes of the elements and their relations. It is clear that such descriptions are very much less than a full description of the shape. For many shape properties, and for many of the purposes for which we might seek to understand shape, a configurational description of this kind would be quite inadequate or inappropriate. But there is one sense in which the configurational structure of the shape is a uniquely

Figure 3.3

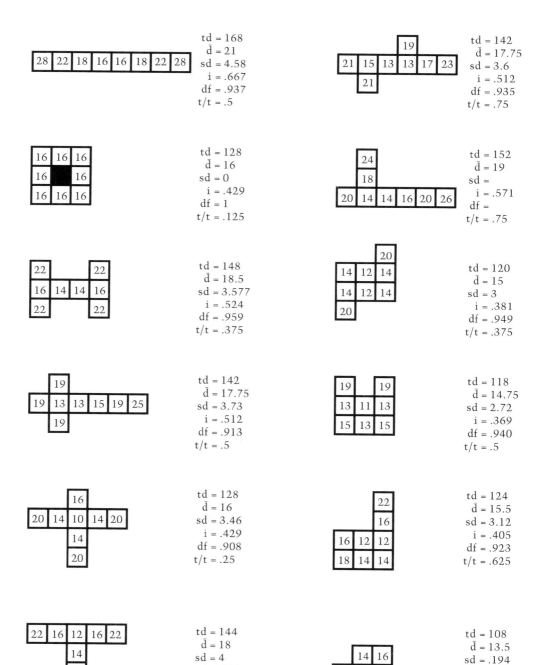

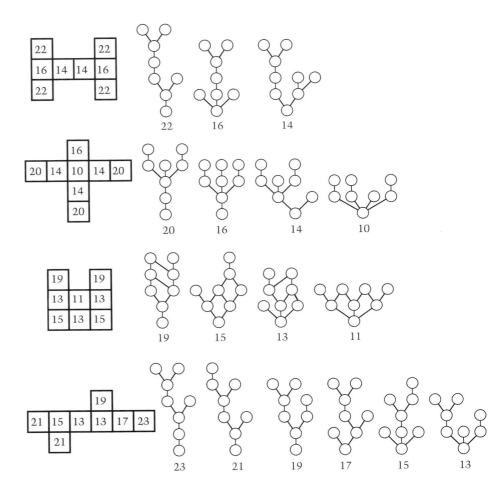

Figure 3.4

powerful property, and gives insights into properties of spatial and formal shapes which are increasingly manifesting themselves as the most fundamental, especially in studies of architectural and urban objects. This property is that graphs of shapes and spatial layouts are significantly different when seen from different points of view within the graph. This can be demonstrated visually by using the j-graph. By drawing j-graphs from all nodes in a shape, then, we can picture some quite deep properties of shapes.

For example, a highly interesting property of shapes is the number of different j-graphs they have, and how strong the differences are. For example, figure 3.4 shows all different j-graphs for a selection of the shapes in figure 3.3. The number varies from 3 to 6. The reason for this is that if we find that the j-graphs from two nodes are identical, then this means that from these two points of view, the shape has a structural identity, which we intuitively call symmetry. This is why in the shapes in figure 3.4, the smaller the number of different j-graphs as a proportion of the total number of j-graphs (that is the number of elements in the graph) then the more the shapes appear regular because there are more symmetries in the shape. This is the ratio given as t/t (types over total) in figure 3.3. This aspect of the structure of the graph thus seems to reflect our sense that shapes can be regular or irregular to different degrees.

This analogy can be made more precise. In fact, the symmetry properties of shapes can be exactly translated as configurational properties. Mathematically, symmetry is defined in terms of invariance under transformation. In their book *Fearful Symmetry*, Ian Stewart and Martin Golubitsky illustrate this with singular clarity. 'To a mathematician' they argue, 'an object possesses symmetry if it retains its form after some transformation.'[15] They illustrate this with a diagram showing the symmetries of the square, as in figure 3.5, in which 'a typical point in the plane is mapped into eight different images by the…eight rigid motions that leave the square invariant'. Thinking of symmetries in terms of points in a shape is useful configurationally, since we may immediately ask what will be the characteristics of j-graphs drawn from each of the points. It is immediately clear that the j-graphs drawn from each of Stewart's points will be identical, and that this would also be the case for any other comparable set of points which Stewart had selected. It is also clear that once a point has been selected there will only be seven other points in the shape from which j-graphs will be identical. The principle is in fact very simple: in a shape, every symmetry will create exactly one point from which the j-graph is isomorphic. In effect, j-graph isomorphism is a test for symmetry. The j-graph

Figure 3.5

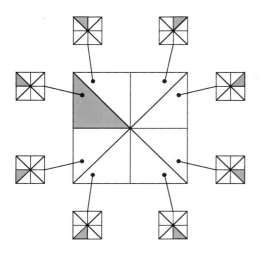

allows us to look at symmetry as an internal property, in contrast to
the more external view presupposed by the 'invariance under motion'
definition. In a sense, the invariance under motion exists because there
are different points within the shape from which the shape is identical.
We might say that in a shape with symmetry there are points within the
shape with identity of positional information in relation to the object
as a whole and this is demonstrated by j-graph isomorphism.

Universal distances

The distributions of depths that are shown through the j-graphs, and which
underlie both architectural and geometrical effects - are in fact the most
fundamental idea in quantifying the configuration properties of spatial or
formal complexes. The idea first made its appearance in the literature of
applied graph theory in 1959 when Harary applied it to sociometry under
the name of 'status'. 'Status' is defined by Buckley and Harary[16] thus: 'The
status s(v) of a node v in G (a graph) is the sum of distances from v to each
other node in G', distance meaning the fewest number of nodes intervening
between one node and another. The problem with status defined in this
way as 'total depth' is that the value will be very substantially affected by
the number of nodes in the graph. Accordingly, as discussed in chapter 1
(see note 17) a normalisation formula was proposed in *The Social Logic of
Space*[17] which eliminates the bias due to the number of nodes in the graph.
With this normalisation, numerical values can be assigned expressing 'total
depth' independently of the size of the system. This normalisation formula
was discussed and clarified by Steadman in *Architectural Morphology*.[18] We
will call these normalised values i-values, to express the idea of the degree of
'integration' of an element in a complex, which we believe these values express.

The need for the normalisation formula and the intuition of the
form it might take in fact came from using the justified representation
of the graph, or j-graph. Simply as a consistently used representation, the
j-graph makes the structure of graphs, and more importantly the differences
in their structures extraordinarily clear. However, by representing them
in a standard format, it also makes clear the need for comparative numerical analysis and how it might be done. For example, it is immediately
clear what graph will be maximally and what minimally deep. It is a

simple matter from there to find the normalisation. The fact that no one
found this useful expression before, when it opens up whole new vistas
for the empirical analysis and comparison of forms, is presumably
because no one saw either its necessity or possibility.

However, although the i-value formula allows the theoretical elimination of the effects of the size of the system, it does not deal with the fact
that, empirically, architectural and urban spatial complexes use only a
small proportion of those theoretically possible, and this proportion shrinks
as the size of the system grows. These effects are discussed in full in chapter 9, and in fact become the basis of a full theory of urban spatial form. A
second, empirical normalisation formula was therefore introduced to cope
with this empirical fact.[19] The second formula is an empirical approxima-
tion with some theoretical justification (that it approximates a normal
distribution of depth values from any node in a graph) and as such it lacks
elegance. However its robustness has been demonstrated in large numbers
of empirical studies over the years, during which time no need has arisen
to call it into question.[20] No doubt, as studies advance, it will be possible to
eliminate this second normalisation formula and replace it with an expression with more theoretical elegance. In the meantime, 'integration' will
refer to the outcomes of both normalisations, unless 'total depth' (status,
with no normalisation) or 'i-value' (status with the first, theoretical normalisation for size) are specified. All these terms are different ways of
referring to the same quantity.

Why has this quantity proved so fundamental in the empirical
study of spatial and formal configurations? It is possible that its simplicity
conceals a very fundamental theoretical property: that it is essentially a
generalisation of the idea of distance. Our common concept of distance is
that of a specific number of metric units between one point and another
within some system of spatial reference. We can call this a specific distance.
Total depth sums all specific distances from a node to all others. We may
therefore think of it as a 'universal distance' from that node. If specific
distance is about the metric properties of shapes and complexes, universal distances seem to be the key to configurational properties. Universal
distance seems to be a generalisation of the idea of depth that permits
configuration to become the central focus of analysis.

Theoretical preliminaries

Figure 3.6

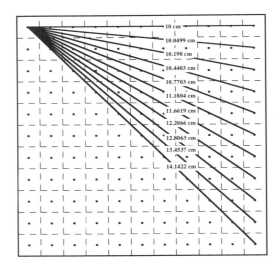

Figure 3.7

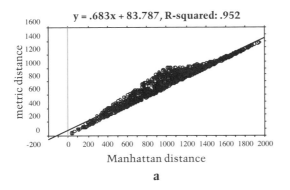

y = .683x + 83.787, R-squared: .952

a

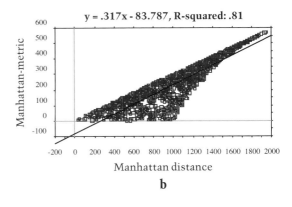

y = .317x - 83.787, R-squared: .81

b

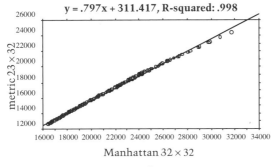

y = .797x + 311.417, R-squared: .998

c

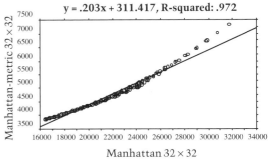

y = .203x + 311.417, R-squared: .972

d

It may be objected that that concept of universal distance has only
been made possible through an unacceptable simplification of the idea
of a shape to that of a graph, rather than an infinite set of points. This is
a difficulty, but it seems that it might not be as great as might at first
appear. If we consider a square shape made up of square cells, and therefore representable as a graph, as in figure 3.6, and measure distances from
and to the centroid of each cell, it is clear that graph distances will
approximate metric distances only when they are orthogonally related.
On the diagonal, metric distances will be either shorter or longer than
graph distances, depending on whether or not we connect the graph diagonally across cell corners, or only allow joins through the faces. If corner
links are not allowed, then graph distances will be n + m (or 'Manhattan'
distances, by analogy with the Manhattan grid) where m is the horizontal
distance and n the vertical distance, while the metric (or 'as the crow
flies') distance will be the square root of m squared + n squared. This will
be maximal between opposite top and bottom corners. If diagonal links to
adjacent nodes are allowed, then the distance between opposite top and
bottom corners will be m or n, whichever is the greater, which equally
misrepresents the metric distance. If we plot graph distance against metric specific distances in such a system we will find that not only are the
differences substantial, but also that they vary in different parts of the
system. In other words, graph and metric specific distances are not linearly related, so we cannot use one as a proxy for the other. Figure 3.7a is a
plot of metric specific distance against graph (Manhattan) specific distance for 1000 randomly selected pairs of points in a 100×100 square cell
arrangement of the type shown in the previous figure, and figure 3.7b
plots the difference between metric and graph specific distance on the
vertical axis for increasing graph distance on the horizontal axis.

However, if we substitute universal for specific distances, and carry
out the same analysis, this problem is significantly diminished. Figure
3.7c shows graph (Manhattan) against metric universal distances for all
nodes in a 32×32 (i.e. 1024 cells) square cell complex, and figure 3.7d plots
graph distance against the difference between metric and graph distances.
Although the values are still exactly as different overall, they are now
more or less linearly related, so that it is much more reasonable to use

one as a proxy for the other. This fortunate fact permits a far more flexible use of graph based measure of configuration than would otherwise be the case. As we will see, such matters as shape and scale, area and distance can all be brought, as approximations at least, within the scope of the configurational method. All will be in some sense the outcome of seeing a complex of related elements as a set of j-graphs. The j-graph in effect redefines the element of a complex in terms of its relation to all other elements in the complex. Summing the properties of j-graphs to express properties of the whole complex means summing the different points of view from which the complex can be seen internally. The eventual justification of this formalism is that architectural and urban systems are exactly this kind of complex. They are global systems whose structure, functioning and growth dynamics are manufactured out of the innumerable different points of view from which they can be seen.

Regular shapes as configurations
Now let us take the idea a little further, and closer to everyday experience. It is clear that any shape can be represented as a regularly constructed mesh of cellular elements, or tessellation, provided we can scale the mesh as finely as we need. This can then be treated as a graph,and thus expressed as a pattern of universal graph distances. By describing simple everyday shapes in this way, it turns out that we can capture important aspects of how they fit into everyday living patterns.

Suppose, for example, we create an (approximately) circular tessellation of arbitrarily small square cells, as in figure 3.8a. We may calculate the mean depth of each cell from all others, and express the results in a distribution of dot densities for the square elements in which the higher densities, or darker colours, stand for greater integration - that is, less depth – graded through to lightest colours for the least integration, or greatest depth. It is clear that the centre has the highest integration, and that integration reduces evenly in concentric rings around the centre. In a perfect circle, all edge locations will have an identical degree of integration.

If we then consider the square tessellation in figure 3.8c we find that the pattern of integration not only runs from centre to edge, but also from the centre of the edge to the corners. The square form is thus more complex

Figure 3.8

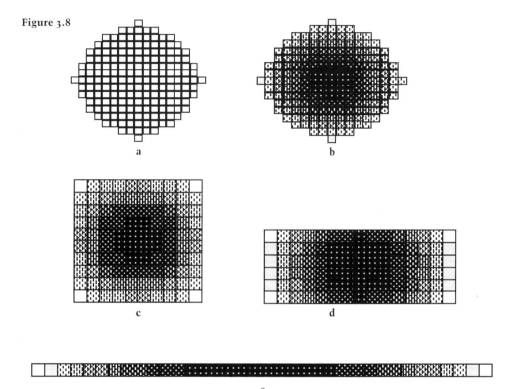

than the circular form in a simple, but critical way. We may say that in the square form, the 'central integration' effect occurs twice: once in the global structure from centre to edge, and once more locally on each side of the form. We can also easily calculate that the square form is less integrated - that is, has greater average universal distances per tessellation element - than the circular form.

As we elongate the square into a rectangle, as in figure 3.8d, the overall form is even less integrated, and the properties first found in the square become more exaggerated. The global structure of the form is now a group of integrated central squares which includes some on or near the periphery of the object, with the two 'ends' substantially less integrated than other parts. Each side has a central distribution of integration, but one in which the long sides have much greater differentiation than the short sides, and correspond increasingly to the global structure of the tessellation as we elongate it. In the limiting rectangular tessellation, the single sequence of squares, then the local and global structures are identical, as in figure 3.8e.

We may summarise this by saying that while all these forms are globally structured from centre to edge, in the circular form the local or lateral structure is uniform, in the square form the lateral structure is maximally different from the global structure, while in the rectangular form the local lateral structure tends to become the global structure as we elongate it, until the limiting form of the single sequence is reached when the two structures become identical. The correspondence between these 'structures' of shapes and the ways in which shape is exploited for social purposes in everyday life is intriguing. For example, on square dining tables the centre side is more advantageous than corner locations, because it is a more integrated location. Similarly, the English prime minister sits in the centre of the long side of a broad rectangular table, maximising this advantage in integration. In contrast, where status rather than interaction is the issue, caricature dukes and duchesses sit at opposite ends of a long table, maximising proxemic segregation but also surveillance, while students and monks classically sit on the sides of a long thin 'refectory' table with no one at the ends, thus making all but localised conversations difficult. The politics of landholding knights with a peripatetic king sitting at a round table are equally manifest, as are the endless political debates over the shapes of conference tables and parliament chambers. The ways in which shapes are exploited and used all follow the pattern of integration in some way, though with opposite tendencies depending on whether interactive status or symbolic status is more critical.

Plans as shaped space
Now let us consider the more complex case of the house plan. In the sequence of plans in figure 3.9i, is a slightly simplified version of the plan of one of the farm houses in rural France that were considered in chapter 1. The salle commune is the everyday space where cooking, eating and the reception of everyday visitors take place. The grande salle is a space

the front of the house is a more critical element than appeared in the earlier analysis, and in effect imparts to the house a front-back organisation that had not emerged from the earlier analysis. Also, we can see that the relation between what we might call the 'energy economy' of the house plan, that is the amount of effort needed to go from one location to another as shown in the metric tessellation, and the higher-level organisation is quite subtle. In effect, convex space integration for the major spaces is displaced from the metric centre of gravity, and the degree of displacement is to some extent compensated by size. Thus the grande salle is more displaced than the salle commune, but compensates for this greater displacement by its greater size.

Multi-layered analysis suggests then that we should not see a system of space as one thing. A spatial layout is a shape which contains many configurational potentials, each of which seems to relate to a different aspect of function. These potentials may be treated as independent systems of space by choosing to analyse the layout on the basis of one particular representation rather than another, or they may be treated in selective combinations, or even altogether. It all depends on what we are trying to find out.

Facades as configurations

If the distribution of the various layers of integration in a shape relates to the ways in which we use shapes, then an intriguing possibility might be that it could also be implicated in how we understand shapes. For example, building facades seen as shapes seem capable of being 'understood' as communicators of information in some sense. Could configuration be involved in this type of apparent communication?

Consider in a very elementary way how we recognise objects. The top row of figure 3.10 shows three figures which are constructed by arranging thirty square elements in different ways. Recognising these figures seems to happen in two stages. In the first stage, we identify a distinct shape, different from others, in the second we assign that shape to a category by giving it a name. In figure 3.10a and b, we see two shapes. We easily recognise the difference between the two shapes, that is, we readily make a pure configurational distinction between the two objects. But we have

Figure 3.10

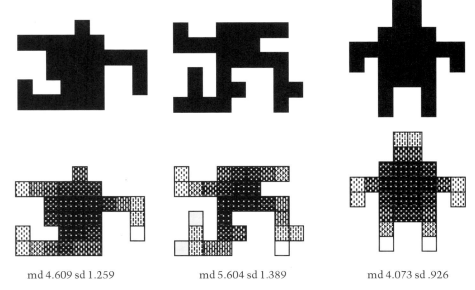

md 4.609 sd 1.259　　　　md 5.604 sd 1.389　　　　md 4.073 sd .926

6×5 rectangle: md 3.554 sd .543

a　　　　　　　　b　　　　　　　　c

Line chart for columns: $X_1 ... X_4$

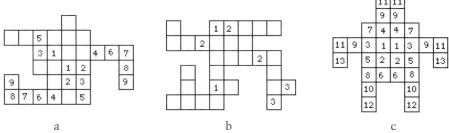

○ 6×5rectangle

◇ Fig 1 a

△ Fig 1 b

□ Fig 1 c

Observations

a:si=21/30=.7; b:si=26/30=.867; c:si=11/30=.367

6×5 rectangle si=9/30=.3

no category to which we can assign either object. The process of object recognition is therefore ended at the first stage. In figure 3.10c we also see a shape, but this time we conjecture a category: the shape looks like an over-regularised humanoid, so we conjecture it is meant to be either a robot, a caricature human, or perhaps a toy.

Of course, the figure does not really bear much resemblance to a human being or humanoid. The evidence on which our category conjecture is based is, to say the least, flimsy. However the nature of the evidence is interesting. It seems to be configurational. Figures 3.10a, b and c are no more than outlines produced by rearranging 30 square cells into different configurations. We have, it seems, a clear ability to distinguish pure shapes or configurations from each other, prior to any intuition of the category of thing to which the configuration might belong.

We can call the first the syntactic stage of object recognition, and the second the semantic stage. The second stage has been extensively dealt with by philosophers and others, but what about the first, 'syntactic' stage, only now being investigated by cognitive psychologists? [21] What does it mean to recognise a configuration? One approach to this is to reverse the question and ask what properties configurations have that might allow them to be recognised. Suppose, for example, we analyse the configurations as distributions of total depth values as in the second row of figure 3.10.

This gives us several kinds of useful information about the configuration. First, there is the distribution of integration in each form, as shown by the dark-to-light pattern. This can be thought of as a structure within the shape. Second, there are the integration characteristics of the form as a whole, as indexed by the mean depth values and their standard deviation as shown beneath each form. For comparison, the mean depth and standard deviation for a six by five rectangle (that is, a regular form with the same number of elements and approximating a square as closely as possible) is also noted. We see that 3.10c is more integrated than 3.10a, which is more integrated than 3.10b, and that all are less integrated than the six by five rectangle. Standard deviations follow a similar pattern. These depth values seem to correspond to certain intuitions we have about the forms, as do the standard deviations, which shows that 3.10b has greater

variation in the mean depths of individual elements than 3.10a, which
has more than 3.10c, and all have more than the six by five rectangle.

However, there is another intuition which is not expressed in these
measures. It is obvious that 3.10c is more 'symmetric' than either 3.10a
or 3.10b, since it has the property of bilateral symmetry, one of the commonest and most easily recognisable types of symmetry found in artefacts
or in nature. However, while figures 3.10a and 3.10b both lack formal
symmetries, they do not seem to be entirely equivalent from this point
of view. In some sense, figure 3.10a seems to be closer to symmetric
organisation than 3.10b. There is a possible quantification for this property. To explain it, we must consider the whole idea of symmetry from a
configurational point of view.

We have already seen that pure symmetries in shapes could be interpreted as configurational properties, namely j-graph isomorphisms. From
an architectural point of view, it is very useful to formulate properties of
symmetry in this way, since, unlike the normal 'invariance under motion'
definitions of symmetry, it opens the way to weaker definitions of symmetry,
and permits an account of intuitively important architectural properties
which approach symmetry but cannot be so formally defined. For example,
we can specify identity of positional information with respect not to the
whole object but to a region within the object, that is, local rather than
global j-graph isomorphism, and discuss the relation between local and
global j-graph isomorphism. Buildings are full of local symmetries – the form
of a window, or of a particular mass within a complex – which sometimes
are and sometimes are not reflected in a global symmetry. The relation
between local and global symmetry seems a natural way to express this.

Most significantly, we can specify similarity, rather than identity,
of positional information, and do so in a precise way. For example, j-graph
isomorphism means that j-graphs share not only the same number of elements and the same total depth, but also the same number of elements
at each level of the j-graph and the same connections between elements.
One way of weakening this property would be to maintain all properties
except the requirement that the connections be identical. Another would
be to vary the number at each level (from which it follows that connections
would be different) but to maintain the total depth the same.[22]

Figure 3.11

The second of these seems particularly interesting, since it offers
a possible formalisation of the property of 'balanced' asymmetry often
discussed in the literature on the formal properties of architecture.[23] For
example, in figure 3.11 we load a simple linear shape with two sets of four
by two cells, one horizontal, the other vertical, but each joined to exactly
two cells in the basic form. Although the two end shapes created are
different, and in themselves have different distributions of total depth
values (or i-values), all the values in the bottom two rows are paired in
that each cell has exactly one other cell which is 'symmetrically' located
and has the same i-value. This i-value equality seems to give a rather
precise meaning to the idea of 'balanced asymmetry'.

    We may apply this analysis to the three shapes shown in figure 3.10.
The third row shows each shape with cells with equal i-values marked
with the same number, from the most to the least integrating. We see that
3.10a has far more equal i-values than 3.10b. Also, in 3.10a the equal values
reach well into the integration core of the shape, whereas in 3.10b they
are distinctly peripheral. Both of these properties, as well as the degree
of integration, can be represented through a simple statistical device: the
line chart shown in the final row of 3.10. Here each shape is represented
by a series of i-values, plotted from most to least integrated (shown as
least to most depth), together with a series representing the six by five
rectangle (shown as circles) to provide a baseline for comparison: 3.10a
is represented as diamonds, 3.10b as triangles, and 3.10c as squares.

Evidently, the overall degree of integration is indexed by the location of
the series on the vertical axis. Thus the rectangle is the most integrated,
3.10c next, then 3.10a and finally 3.10b. Also, the shapes diverge as they
move from integrated to segregated elements, so that the most integrated
elements in each shape are much closer together than the least. The line
charts also show the degree of 'balanced asymmetry' in the shape by align-
ing elements with the same i-value next to each other to form a horizontal
line. The ratio of the total number of elements to the number of elements
that form part of such lines will index the degree of balanced asymmetry
in the shape. The simplest index is the number of i-values over the number of elements. Identical i-values will include both those resulting from
perfect symmetry as shown by isomorphic j-graphs, and those that only
share the same total depth. This summary figure may then be thought of
as a broad 'symmetry index'. Si's for 3.10a,b and c are below the line chart.

   Integration analysis of shapes, then, permits us to retrieve some useful descriptions of shape properties in a consistent way, though without
any pretence that this is a full account of those properties. One area
where this approach is useful, however, is in considering buildings as
shapes. The key point here is that buildings are not pure shapes, in the
geometric sense of freestanding forms in a uniform context, but oriented
shapes, in the sense that they are oriented to and away from the ground on
which they stand. If we take this simple fact into account in analysing
building facades as shapes then we easily find some very suggestive
results. This can be demonstrated by simply standing shapes on a line,
which we will call the 'earth-line'. The three figures of figure 3.12 are the
square and rectangular forms shown earlier with earthlines added. In the
case of the rectangular form, the earthline is added twice, once to create a
shape horizontally aligned to the earth and once to create a shape vertically aligned.

   The first effect that must be noted is that in the case of the square,
adding the earthline has the effect of reducing the original eight symmetries of the square to a simple bilateral symmetry. This can be seen visually if we compare the shading patterns of the square with an earthline to
the original square form. The concentric pattern is still quite marked, but
now an additional bilaterally symmetric pattern is detectable. This effect

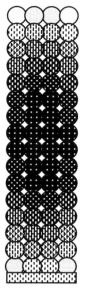
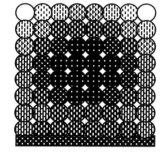
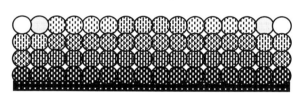

i=.178 si=.477   i=.124 si=.446   i=.095 si=.308

Figure 3.12

results, of course, from the earthline, as it were, drawing integration down towards itself. This confirms intuition. It is clear that we do not regard a square facade as having the symmetries of a free-standing geometrical square. We see it as a form anchored to the earth and having left-right symmetry, but not top-bottom symmetry. Indeed the language in which we describe the form - top and bottom, left and right, shows which relations we see as symmetrical and which asymmetrical.

The 'bilateral effect' of the earthline is far more marked in a square form than in an elongated form, whether we elongate the form horizontally or vertically. In the vertical form, the effect of the earthline is to make integration run from the bottom of the form to segregation at the top. This obliterates any sense of a bilateral symmetric effect in the shading pattern, and substitutes a differentiation from bottom to top. Adding an earthline to a horizontally elongated form, we again find the bilateral effect is barely noticeable in the shading pattern, and instead there is a tendency to form broad layers in the form, but with much weaker differentiation from bottom to top.

In terms of integration and symmetry index the differences between the vertical and horizontal forms are also striking. The vertical form, because of the greater distance of most elements from the earthline and the fact that far fewer connect directly to it, is almost as segregated as the elongated form without the earthline. In the horizontal form, however, most elements are now closer to the earthline, with many actually touching it, and the effect is that the shape has now become much more integrated than the square form, the opposite of the case without the earthline.

When we consider the symmetry index the effects are no less striking. Whereas in the original shapes, the square form had more 'symmetry' than the elongated form, the addition of the earthline has opposite effects on the vertical and horizontal forms. The vertical form has less symmetry than the square form, because fewer elements are on the same level, while the horizontal form has substantially more, for the contrary reason. Again, there is a common-sense reason for these effects. The addition of an earthline to a vertical form converts a pattern of integration that in the original form went from centre to edge to one that also now goes from the earthline - which, as it were, now anchors the form - upwards through the form, from more integration at the bottom, closest to the earthline, to least at the top, farthest from the earthline. The vertical form in effect now runs vertically from integration to segregation. In the horizontal form, on the other hand, insofar as elements are horizontally related, they will tend to become more similar to each other, by virtue of their closeness to the earthline. This corresponds to the intuition that the more shapes are aligned along a surface, the more equal they become. In contrast, the vertical dimension stresses difference, in that the relations of above and below are asymmetrical. Horizontality, we may say, equalises and integrates, while verticality segregates and differentiates.

The analysis of facades as layers is also suggestive. For example, if we take a simplified representation of a classical facade, we can represent it first as a shape, that is, as a metric tessellation, then by drawing the dominant elements in the facade, as a pattern of convex elements. By analysing each separately, as in figure 3.13 a and b, we see that the shape, as represented by the tessellation shows a centralised pattern of integration focussed above, and running down into, the central column, giving

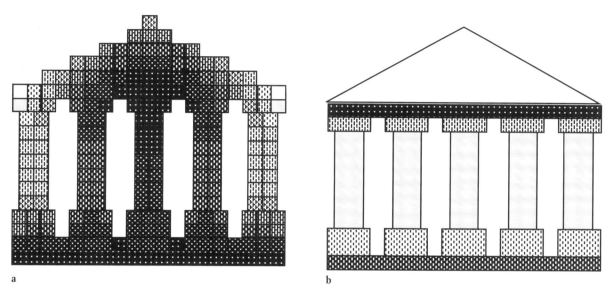

a   b

Figure 3.13

the distribution a strongly vertical emphasis. In contrast, the convex
analysis focusses integration on the frieze, creating a horizontal emphasis. One might conjecture that in looking at a facade we see a shape, and
our view of that shape is then modified by the larger-scale organisation of
elements imposed on that shape.

    These centralised vertical and linear horizontal structures which
are revealed by the analysis are, taken separately, among the commonest -
perhaps the commonest - formal themes which builders and designers
have created in whole classes of building facades across many cultures.
The fact that analysis 'discovers' these structures seems, at least, a
remarkable confirmation of intuition. The analysis perhaps suggests that
one reason why the classical facade has often, from Laugier onwards[24]
been argued to constitute a fundamental mode of facade organisation,
is exactly because through its shape and convex organisation it both
expresses and creates a tension between the two most fundamental
modes of facade organisation. If this were the case, then it would suggest
that what the human mind 'reads' when it looks at the form of a building
is, or at least includes, the pattern of integration at more than one level,
and the interrelations between the levels.

Urban space as layers: the problem of intelligibility

Whatever the case with facades, one area where substantial empirical research has established the need to consider layers of configurational potential, and their inter-relations, is urban space. Consider, for example, the two hypothetical urban layouts in figure 3.14a and b. The two layouts are composed of the same 'blocks' or 'islands' of buildings. In the first case, they are arranged in a way which has a certain degree of irregularity, but looks more or less 'urban', in that the pattern of space created by the arrangement of the blocks - and this is all that urban space essentially is – seems to have the right kinds of spaces in the right kinds of relations, and as a result appears 'intelligible' as an 'urban' system. In the second layout, all the 'blocks' are the same but each has been moved slightly with the effect that the system of space seems much less 'urban', and much less easily 'intelligible'. It is clear that any useful analysis of urban space must either capture these intuitions or show why they are illusory. It will turn out that they are not illusory at all, and that they arise from well-defined relations amongst the different spatial potentials that make up the layout.[25]

In one sense, both layouts represent the commonest type of urban space structure. We can call it the 'deformed grid', because while made up of outward facing islands of buildings each surrounded on all sides by continuous space in the manner of a regular grid, the structure of that space is deformed in two ways: it is linearly, or axially deformed, in that lines of sight and access do not continue right through the grid from one side to the other, as they would in a perfectly regular grid, but continually strike the surfaces of the building blocks and change direction as a result; secondly it is convexly deformed in that two-dimensional spaces continuously vary in their dimensions and shape, making a pattern of wider and narrower spaces. The visibility field at any point in the space for someone moving in the grid will be made up of both kinds of element. Wherever the observer is, there will always be a local convex element of some kind, in which every point is visible from every other point, plus the shape made by all lines of sight and access passing through the point. The easiest way to describe the differences between the two layouts intuitively is to say that a moving observer in either layout would experience continuous changes in the visibility field, but that the kinds of visibility field experienced in the first are quite different to those in the second. The apparent differences in intelligibility in the two layouts will turn out to be related to these formal differences in the succession of visibility fields.

We can build up an analysis of the two layouts by investigating these different potentials. First, we will consider the 'overlapping' convex elements that are defined by the surface of this block.[26] Here convex elements are defined by reference to the surface of each block, each of which defines its maximal convex field. These fields will inevitably overlap, and where they do, the area of overlap will itself form a smaller convex element from which both overlapping convex spaces will be fully visible, that is, will be convex, although these spaces are not convex to each other. The same will be true when further overlapping spaces are added. Certain small spaces will indeed be convex to a substantial number of convex spaces because all those spaces overlap in that area. Such areas will as a result have large visibility fields, whereas areas where there is no overlap will tend to have much smaller visibility fields. Overlapping convex elements are virtually impossible to intuit, because the overlapping is so difficult to represent. Computer analysis is therefore required.

Let us look first at the pattern of overlapping convex spaces generated in our two layouts. Figures 3.14c and d, are the result of the analysis of the open-space structure of the two layouts. The computer has first drawn all the overlapping convex elements defined by the faces of each 'block' and then carried out an 'integration' analysis of the pattern, with integration to segregation shown from dark-to-light, as before. In the first 'urban' layout, the darkest spaces of the resulting 'integration core' (the shape made by the darkest areas) cross each other in the informal 'market square', and dark spaces link the market square towards the edge of the 'town'. In the second, there is no longer a strong focus of integration linking a 'square' to the edges of the system, and in effect, the integration core has become diffused. In fact, the most integrating spaces are now found at the edge, and no longer get to the heart of the system. On average, the layout as a whole is much less 'integrated' than the first, that is it has much greater total depth from all spaces to all others.

In other words, the marginal rearrangement of the urban blocks from the first to the second layout resulting in a spatial structure which is

Figure 3.14

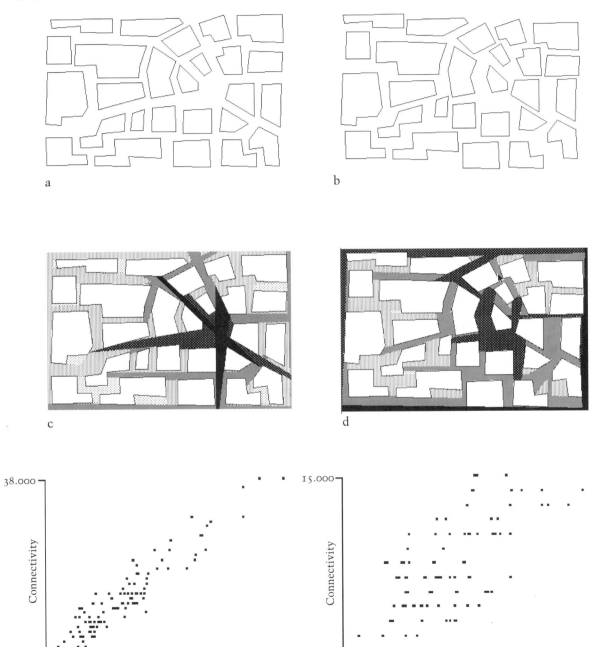

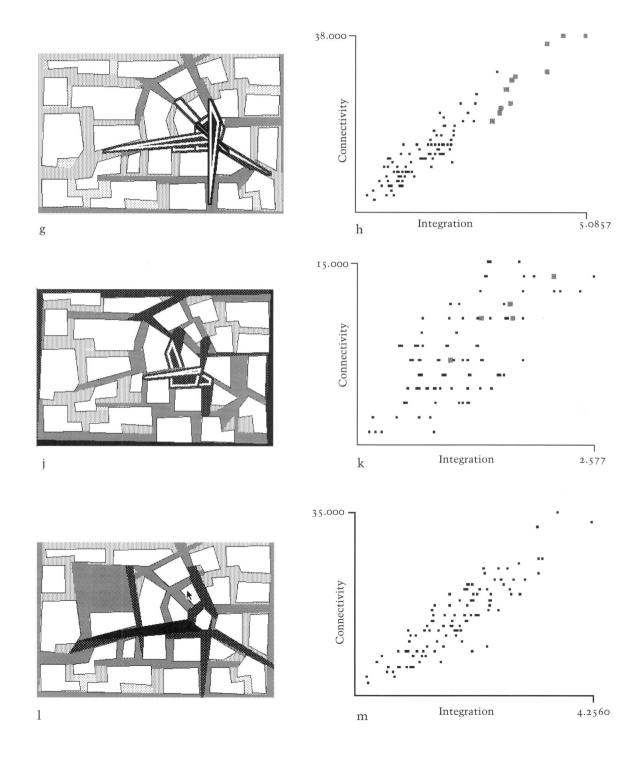

g

h   Integration   5.0857

j

k   Integration   2.577

l

m   Integration   4.2560

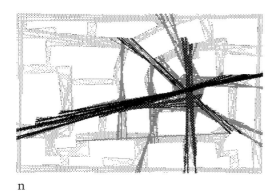

n

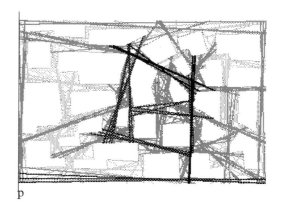

p

176.000   101.0000

Connectivity   Connectivity

q   Integration   10.5161   r   Integration   6.4007

quite different both in the distribution and in the degree of integration. Intuitively, we might suspect that the edge-to-centre integration core structure of the first layout has much to do with the overall sense of urban intelligibility, and its loss in the second layout. Intelligibility is a challenging property in an urban system. Since by definition urban space at ground level cannot be seen and experienced all at once, but requires the observer to move around the system building up a picture of it piece by piece, we might suspect that intelligibility has something to do with the way in which a picture of the whole urban system can be built up from its parts, and more specifically, from moving around from one part to another.

There is in fact a simple and powerful way in which we can represent exactly this property. It is illustrated in the two 'scattergrams' in figures 3.14a and b, corresponding to the two layouts. Each point in the scatter represents one of the overlapping convex spaces in the figure above. The location of the point on the vertical axis is given by the number of other convex spaces that space overlaps with, that is, the 'connectivity' of the space with other spaces, and on the horizontal axis by the 'integration' value of the space, that is its 'depth' from all others. Now 'connectivity' is clearly a property that can be seen from each space, in that wherever one is in the space one can see how many neighbouring spaces it connects to. Integration, on the other hand, cannot be seen from a space, since it sums up the depth of that space from all others, most of which cannot be seen from that space. The property of 'intelligibility' in a deformed grid means the degree to which what we can see from the spaces that make up the system - that is how many other spaces are connected to - is a good guide to what we cannot see, that is the integration of each space into the system as a whole. An intelligible system is one in which well-connected spaces also tend to be well-integrated spaces. An unintelligible system is one where well-connected spaces are not well integrated, so that what we can see of their connections misleads us about the status of that space in the system as a whole.

We can read the degree of intelligibility by looking at the shape of the scatter. If the points (representing the spaces) form a straight line rising at 45 per cent from bottom left to top right, then it would mean that every time a space was a little more connected, then it would also become a little more integrated - that is to say, there would be a perfect 'correlation' between what you can see and what you can't see. The system would then be perfectly intelligible. In figure 3.14e, the points do not form a perfect line, but they do form a tight scatter around the 'regression line', which is evidence of a strong degree of correlation, and therefore good intelligibility. In figure 3.14h we find that the points have become diffused well away from any line, and no longer form a tight fit about the 'regression line'. This means that connectivity is no longer a good guide to integration and therefore as we move around the system we will get very poor information about the layout as a whole from what we see locally. This agrees remarkably well with our intuition of what it would be like to move around this 'labyrinthian' layout.[27]

Now let us explore the two layouts in more detail. In figure 3.14g and h, we have selected a point in the 'square' in the analysis of the first layout, and drawn all the overlapping convex elements that include this point. The scatter then selects these spaces in the scattergram by making them darker and larger. We can see that the spaces that overlap at this point are among the best connected and most integrated in the layout and that the points also form a reasonable linear scatter in themselves, meaning that for these spaces more visible connectivity means more integration. Both the shape made by the set of spaces, reaching out from the square in several directions towards the edge of the system, and the scattergram properties confirm that this point in the 'square' space has a high 'strategic' value in the layout as a whole. If we try to do the same for points in the second layout, as in figure 3.14j and k, we find that the points are buried in the scatter and have no special strategic value. By experimentally clicking on a series of points, and checking both the visual fields and the scattergrams, one can establish that there are no comparable strategic points from which a series of key spatial elements in the layout can be seen.

We may also experiment with the effects of changes to the layout. Suppose, for example, we decide that the current 'market square', although strategically placed, is too small and that it should therefore be moved elsewhere in order to enlarge it. In figure 3.14l and m, the old market square has been built over and a new, larger square has been created towards the top left of the layout. The layout has been analysed and the convex elements overlapping in the new square picked out. In spite of its size, the new square has poor integration, and its overlapping spaces occupy a poor position in the scatter. The most integrated spaces remain those pointing into the old market square. In other words, the spatial configuration as a whole continues to 'point to' the old square. An important conclusion from this, amply confirmed by the examination of real town plans, is that a square is more than a local element. How it is embedded in the configuration as a whole is equally, if not more, important. If we were to seek to exploit this by expanding the old market square by removing adjacent blocks, we would find the square becomes much more dominant, and that the largest space within the square (i.e. as opposed to those entering and leaving which are normally more dominant) is now itself the second most integrated space. In other words, we would begin to shift the emphasis of integration from linear elements to the open space itself. Again, this would distort the essential nature of layout. The size, location, and embedding of major open spaces are all formally confirmed as aspects of what we intuitively read as the urban nature of the layout.

Convex elements are not, of course, the most 'global' spatial elements in a layout, and do not exhaust all relationships of visibility and permeability. These limits are found by looking not at two-dimensional convex elements, but at one-dimensional line elements. In a deformed grid, the elements most spatially extended linearly will be the set of straight lines that are tangent to the vertices of blocks of buildings. Relations between pairs of these vertices in effect define the limits of visibility from points within the system. This can be explored through 'axial' or 'all line' analysis, and in figure 3.14n–r where the computer has found and carried out an integration analysis of all the line elements tangent to block vertices. We find that the intelligibility of the system seen axially is better than seen convexly, because lines are more 'global' spatial elements than convex elements, in that they explore the full limits of visibility and permeability within the layout. Lines therefore make the relation between the local spatial element and the global pattern of space look as good as possible. The differences between the two layouts that we found through the overlapping convex analysis are however more or less reproduced in the all-line analysis. This agreement between the two kinds of analysis is itself a significant property of the layouts.

From the point of view of how layouts work, both types of analysis are important. Movement, for example, can be predicted from a stripped down version of the axial analysis in which only the longest and fewest lines needed to cover the whole system form the line matrix. Similarly, many aspects of 'static' urban behaviours, especially the informal use of open spaces, exploit the two-dimensional 'visibility field' properties of space, with the highest levels of use normally adjacent to the most strategic spaces.

Designing with configurational models

Because these techniques allow us to deal graphically with the numerical properties of spatial layouts, we can also use the technique creatively in design, bringing in much new knowledge about space and function as we do so. For example, extensive research has shown [28] that patterns of movement in urban areas are strongly predicted by the distribution of integration in a simple line representation of the street grid. By using configurational analysis technique in simulation mode, we can exploit both this knowledge, and the potential for configurational analysis to give insight into possible urban patterns that will not be at all clear to intuition. This potential has now been exploited in a large number of urban design projects, often involving the modelling of whole cities in order to simulate the effects of new designs.[29]

To demonstrate the essentials of the technique, a simplified hypothetical model will suffice. The top left figure of figure 3.15 is an analysed axial map (the longest and fewest lines that cover the street grid) of a small area around a hypothetical redevelopment site, with integration from dark to light as before, with, to its right, the scattergram of its intelligibility, showing a weakly intelligible system. We can experiment by asking, what would happen if, for example, we imposed a regular grid on the site without taking too much account of the surrounding structure, as the second-row figure and scatter. We see that in spite of the geometric regularity, our lack of concern for the global pattern has left us with a rather uniformly segregated space pattern within the site, with too poor

Figure 3.15

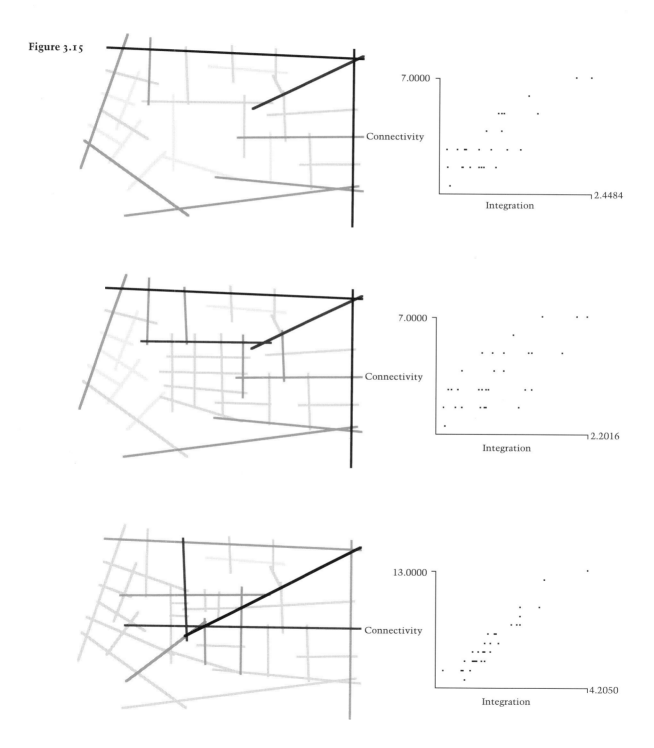

a relation to the surrounding areas. As a consequence, we see from the scatter that the area as a whole has become even more unintelligible.

Suppose we then go the other way, and try to design the site by extending strong lines, and linking them to others, as in the third row figure and scatter. The result is an integrating site, and good intelligibility. The spatial structure in the site also has a good range of integrated and segregated space, in close proximity to each other. As we will in later chapters see this is an important urban property. (See chapters 4 and 5.) This is a simple example, but it shows the ability of configurational analysis not only to aid the designers' intuition in thinking about patterns, and in particular in trying to understand the pattern consequences of individual design moves, but also its ability to permit the designer to think more effectively about the relation of new and existing patterns, and in general about the relation of parts and wholes in cities.

We may again illustrate this by a simplified simulation. Plate 1 is the axial map of a hypothetical urban system with well-defined sub-areas. Research has shown that the critical thing about urban sub-areas is how their internal structures relate to the larger-scale system in which they are embedded. The best way to bring this out is to analyse the system for its integration at two levels. First we do ordinary integration, which counts how deep or shallow each line is from every other line. Second we count how deep or shallow each line is from all lines up to three steps away. The latter we call radius-3 integration, since it looks at each line up to a radius of 3. The former we can call radius-n integration. Radius 3 integration presents a localised picture of integration, and we can therefore think of it also as local integration, while radius-n integration presents a picture of integration at the largest scale, and we can therefore call it global integration.

We will see in due course that local integration in urban systems is the best predictor of smaller-scale movement - that usually means pedestrian movement because pedestrian trips tend to be shorter and read the grid in a relatively localised way - while global integration is the best predictor of larger-scale movement, including some vehicular movement, because people on longer trips will tend to read the grid in a more globalised way. In historical cities, as will be shown, the relationship

between these two levels of integration has been a critical determinant of
the part-whole structure of cities, because it governs the degree of natural
interface there would naturally be between more local, and therefore
more internal movement, and more global and therefore more in-out
movement and through movement.

Some of the different effects on this relationship that different types
of local area design will have can be shown by highlighting the areas in
scattergrams of the whole system and examining the scatter of local
against global integration. The area shown in the bottom row, for example, is a classically structured area for a European city, with strong lines
in all directions from edge to centre, with a less integrated structure of
lines related both to this internal core and to the outside. This ensures
that those moving in the area will be conscious of both the local and global
scales of space as they move around, and there will be a good interface
between local and global movement. The scatter formed by the sub-areas
is shown to the right. The points of the area form a good linear scatter,
showing that local integration is a good predictor of global integration,
and cross the regression line for urban area as a whole at a steeper angle,
showing that there is a stronger degree of local integration for the degree
of global integration. A line on the core of the whole settlement will, in
contrast, lie at the top end of the main regression line. This shows how
subtly urban areas create a sense of local structure without losing touch
with the larger-scale structure of the system. (See chapter 4 for an examination of real cases.)

The area shown immediately above, in the second from bottom
row, is typical of the layouts we tend to find in housing estates, with few
connections to the edge and little relation between the edge to centre
structure and the internal structure of the layout. This type of layout is
invariably shown as a series of layers in the red point scatter with virtually
no correlation between local and global integration. Such layouts invariably freeze all our natural movement and become structurally segregated
lumps in the urban fabric. [30] The areas in the top two rows show other
variations on local area structure, one producing effects rather similar to
those in the experimental grid in the design experiment of figure 3.16,
while the other is a random scatter of lines, showing that in spite of the

apparent informality of much good urban design, random lines simply do
not work except by chance.

Future urban models: intelligent analogues of cities
In addition to their role in design, configurational models are now being
developed as a basis for researching into the multidimensional dynamics
of cities. Consider, for example, one of the broadest and least tractable of
issues facing the built environment industry: that of the economic, social
and environmental 'sustainability' of cities. Even to monitor effectively
and compare cities on sustainability criteria, whatever they might turn
out to be, we must bring data on the physical and environmental performance of cities together with data on their economic and social performance, and relate both to some kind of description of the city. For
example, energy consumption and pollution production depend, among
other factors, on settlement patterns. Should settlements be dense or
sparse, nucleated or dispersed, monocentric or polycentric, or a mix of all
types? For research to give an answer, measurement data on environmental performance, and data on the implications of different behavioural
assumptions (for example about the distribution of work and home) and
'knock-on' effects such as the economic, social and cultural consequences of spatial aggregation and disaggregation policies, must be related to descriptions of the physical and spatial form of cities which reflect
the range of variation found in the real world.

To work towards a theoretical model of how this might be done, we
may begin with the purely 'configurational' models we have presented,
and show how other key spatial attributes such as metric distance, area,
density, plot ratios, shape, political boundaries, and so on can be expressed
within the configurational model by using the idea of integrating 'layered'
representations of space into a single system. For the purposes of illustration we will again use notional, simplified examples. First, we represent
a street network as a series of lines or strips, and analyse their pattern of
integration, as in the top-left figure in figure 3.16a and b. In this analysis,
no account has yet been taken of metric distance. However, in some circumstances at least, this seems likely to be an important variable. We can
supply this by selecting an arbitrary module - say a ten-metre square –

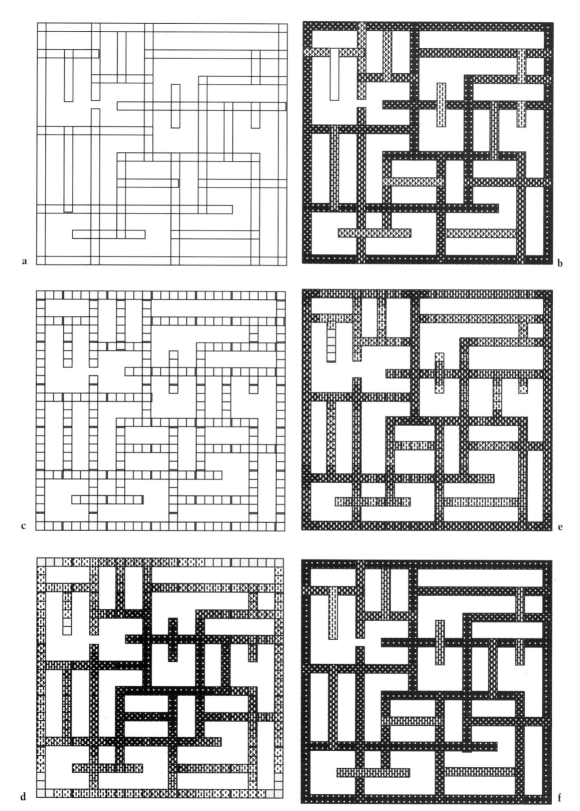

Figure 3.16

and linking modules into the pattern of the grid and analysing this as a tessellation shape, as in figure 3.16c. On its own, this is not of great interest, since it inevitably reflects the pattern of metric centrality in the grid, as in 3.16d, but if we superimpose the line network onto the metric modular system and analyse the two layers as a single system, then the effect is to weight each line with a number of modules directly related to its length. The outcome of this 'length weighted' integration analysis is shown at both levels of the combined analysis: in terms of the modular units in the left figure of the second row of figure 3.16e, and in terms of the 'line superstructure' of strips in 3.16f. The strip level is much the same as previously, but the modular elements show an interesting - and very lifelike - localised structure in which greater integration is concentrated at the 'street intersections', with less integrated modules in the centres of links away from the intersections. This immediately enables us to capture a new and functionally significant aspect of space organisation in a representation.

The relationship between metric area and configuration can be dealt with in an analogous way by underlaying convex elements with a two-dimensional modular layer, as in figure 3.17a-f. In a–c we see a simple system in which four convex spaces of equal size and shape and the connections between them are represented as a layer of modular elements with four convex elements and four strips for the connection superimposed. The two-layer system is then analysed. Whether we look at the result with the convex layer uppermost or the modular layer, the results will be a symmetrical distribution of integration dominated by the strips. In figure 3.30 d–f we give the convex elements different areas and underlay modular elements accordingly, so that each is now weighted by the number of modular elements it overlays. Analysis separately then together shows that integration is drawn into the convex elements according to their area. Note however that the integration of the two smaller convex areas (on the top) in the 'wrong' order. This is because the one on the left is closer to the largest-scale convex area (bottom left) and this affects its own integration with respect to the rest of the system. Thus the results show a combination of configurational effects and metric area effects. From this we can see that if we make a

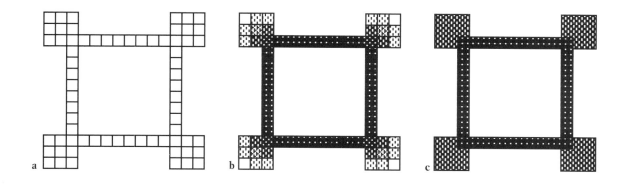

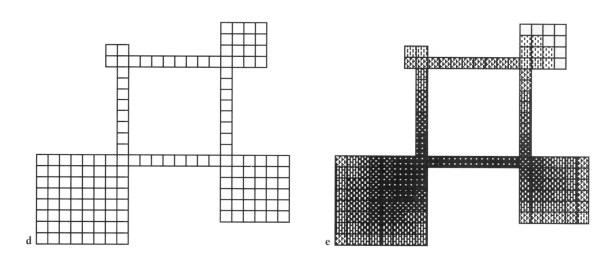

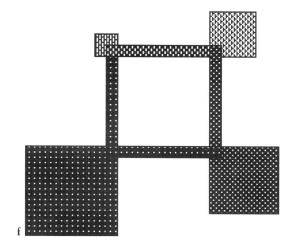

Figure 3.17

large and small square configurationally equivalent in an urban system then the large square will integrate more. Metric area, it turns out is like distance, a property capable of expression as an aspect of configuration.

We may simulate the effect of plot ratios and densities by equally simple means. For example, if we wish to attach a building with a given number of floors to a street network, all we need to do is attach a convex space the size of the ground area of the building to the appropriate position in the street system, then overlay on that a convex element for each floor, making sure that each element above the ground is detached from the street and only connected through the ground layer as it would be in real life. This will not appear visually as a three-dimensional structure, but it will exactly represent the addition of above ground floor space to the urban system.

We may now build a model of an urban system in the following way. First, we divide the city up into an arbitrary number of areas and represent them as non-contiguous polygons. These may be as small or as large as we need, according to the level of resolution required by the research question. The polygons may be based on political boundaries, like wards, administrative boundaries like enumeration districts, segments defined by an arbitrarily fine grid, or they may be defined by objective morphological properties of the built environment. These polygons representing areas are the fundamental units of analysis for the technique.

Figure 3.18a shows our imaginary simplified case in which the street network of the city (or part-city) is superimposed on the patchwork of polygons so that each polygon is linked into the urban system by all the streets or part-streets that pass through it or alongside it. This two-level spatial system is analysed 'configurationally' to find the pattern of integration in the whole system. Evidently, the street pattern will tend to dominate the area polygons simply because the streets are connectors. However, the street system can then be 'peeled off' the polygons, as in figure 3.18b, leaving a pattern of polygons with their spatial characteristics in relation to the city area around them, and to the city system as a whole, recorded as a set of numbers.

This basic process of linking areas together by the street network in a single configurational model is the basis of what we call an 'intelligent

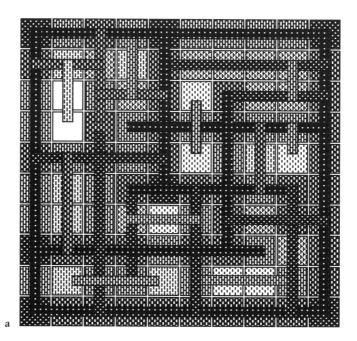

a

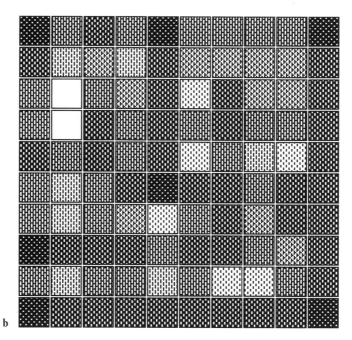

b

Figure 3.18

urban analogue' model. Once this is established, we can then complicate the model in all the ways we have described previously. For example, we can underlay the street network with metric modules so that the analysis of the street system takes distances into account. We can underlay the polygons with metric modules so that the metric area of a polygon is taken into account. We can also, if we wish, superimpose layers on the polygons representing off the ground floor space.

There is also an easy way of further disaggregating any model from the level of resolution originally selected. Each of the original area polygons can be itself subdivided into much smaller polygons and analysed as before. This more localised analysis will give a much richer and denser picture of the detailed characteristics of the area. These may then be fed into a larger-scale model as more detailed environmental descriptors. There is no reason in fact why both levels of the model should not be analysed as a single system. The principal barrier would be computing time. In our experience adding a new level of fine structure to an existing model leaves the larger-scale picture more or less intact provided that the disaggregation is done uniformly and is not confined to particular regions.

At the other end of the scale, we may also derive new measures of the most macro-properties of the city system, such as shape, and shape loaded with different densities in different regions. This can be done by simply linking the area polygons together and analysing the distribution of integration in the system without the superimposed street system. Shape will be indexed by the degree and distribution of integration, and can be shown both by direct graphical representation of the city system, or by statistical representations such as frequency distributions, or simply by numbers. The effects of weighting shapes by loading different regions with higher densities can be explored by simply overlaying the spaces representing the additional densities onto the relevant polygons of the contiguous polygon system, then proceeding as before. By varying the pattern and density of centres we can explore their effects on total distance travelled, other things being equal, in different kinds of three-dimensional urban system. The effects of other nearby settlements can also be investigated by simply adding them as extensions to the model.

The numerical data resulting from the analysis of the urban system can then be used in a number of ways. First, most obviously, the parametric descriptors for the polygons resulting from analysis, reflecting as they do the position and configuration of each 'finite element' in the city system as a whole, then become the frame for other kinds of data which can be assigned as descriptors to the polygons. This can be done with any functional variable that can be numerically indexed for that area such as population densities, pollution levels, traffic movement, pedestrian movement, unemployment rates, crime rates, council tax banding, and so on. Because spatial and other descriptors are now all in numerical form, simple statistical analysis can begin to reveal patterns. Second, the distribution of any property may be represented graphically in the urban system as a visual distribution of that property in the city system. This means, in practice, that all the visualising and cartographical potentials that have been developed in the past few years through 'geographic information systems' can be interfaced with and potentially brought within the scope of an analytic model with proven ability to link morphological and functional properties of built environment systems, hopefully in a more predictive way.

Layered models are the future of configurational modelling of space. These new techniques arise from the results of research over several years in which various types of configurational modelling have been used: first to identify non-discursive regularities in the ways in which architectural and urban systems are put together spatially and identify the 'genotypes' of spatial form; second to correlate these non-discursive regularities with aspects of how human beings can be observed to function in space; and third, to begin to build from these regularities a picture of higher generality of how spatial systems in general are put together and function in response to the demands that human beings and their collectivities make of them. In the next chapter we introduce the most fundamental of all correlates with spatial configuration: human movement.

Notes

1   H. Simon, *The Sciences of the Artificial*, MIT, 1969.

2   F. De Saussure, *Course in General Linguistics*, McGraw Hill, 1966 translated by
     C. Bally and A. Sechahaye with A. Riedlinger. See pp. 9–15 (originally in French
     1915).

3   It has of course become fashionable to follow the later Wittgenstein's
     Philosophical Investigations (Basil Blackwell 1953; Edition used 1968) and deny
     any systemic properties to such things as languages, and see in them only shift-
     ing contingencies. For example: 'Instead of producing something common to all
     that we call language, I am saying that these phenomena have no one thing in
     common which makes us use the same word for all, but they are all related to
     each other in many different ways. And it is because of this relationship, or
     these relationships, that we call them all "language".' – Wittgenstein, para 65.
     Or: 'Language is a labyrinth of paths. You approach from one side and know your
     way about; you approach the same place from another side and no longer know
     your way about' – Wittgenstein, para 203. The use of the urban analogy is inter-
     esting. As we will see in later chapters, this is the one type of artefact where it
     can be shown quite clearly that Wittgenstein was wrong.

4   The clearest statement is still probably the 'Overture' to Claude Levi-Strauss's
     The Raw and the Cooked, Jonathon Cape, London 1970, originally in French as
     Le Cru et le Cuit, Plon, 1964.

5   Plato, *The Republic*, for example VI, 509–11, pp. 744–7 in Plato, *The Collected
     Dialogues*, eds. E. Hamilton and H. Cairns, Princeton University Press,
     Bollingen Series, 1961. See also ed. F. M. Cornford, *The Republic of Plato*,
     Oxford University Press, 1941, pp. 216–21.

6   For the clearest formulation, see R. Thom, 'Structuralism and Biology', in ed.
     C. H. Waddington, *Theoretical Biology 4*, Edinburgh University Press, 1972,
     pp. 68–82.

7   W. Heisenberg, *Physics and Philosophy*, George Allen & Unwin, 1959 p. 57.

8   N. Chomsky, *Syntactic Structures*, Mouton, The Hague, 1957.

9   There are important exceptions to this, for example Levi-Strauss's attempt, in
     collaboration with Andre Weil, to model certain marriage systems as Abelian
     groups. See Levi-Strauss, *The Elementary Structures of Kinship*, Eyre &
     Spottiswoode, 1969, pp. 221–9. Originally in French as *Les Structures
     Elementaire de la Parente*, Mouton, 1949.

10   For example, his ingenious attempt to model the elementary properties of mat-
     ter through the five regular solids in the *Timaeus*. See Plato, *Timaeus*, 33 et seq.
     p. 1165 in *The Collected Dialogues* (see note 5 above)

11   This process is the subject of chapter 9.

12   As described, for example, in chapter 2 of *The Social Logic of Space*.

13   For a lucid summary, see P. Steadman, *Architectural Morphology*, Pion, 1983.

14   L. March, in conversation.

15   I. Stewart and M. Golubitsky, *Fearful Symmetry*, Penguin, 1993, p 229.

16   F. Buckley and F. Harary, *Distance in Graphs*, Addison Wesley, 1990, p. 42.

17   B. Hillier and J. Hanson , *The Social Logic of Space*, Cambridge University Press, 1984, p 108. See also note 16 in chapter 1.

18   Steadman, p. 217.

19   Hillier & Hanson, pp. 109–13.

20   However, see the references in note 16 of chapter 1.

21   For example, I. Biederman, 'Higher level vision', in eds. D. Osherson et al., *Visual Cognition and Action*, MIT Press, 1990.

22   For a discussion of some of these variations from the point of view of graph theory see Buckley and Harary, *Distance in Graphs*, pp. 179–85.

23   For example, P. Tabor, 'Fearful symmetry', *Architectural Review*, May 1982.

24   Abbé Marc-Antoine Laugier, *Essai sur l'architecture*, Paris 1755.

25   See Hillier & Hanson, *The Logic of Space*, p 90.

26   It should be noted at the outset that these overlapping convex elements are unlike the convex elements described in *The Social Logic of Space*, which were not allowed to overlap. See Hillier & Hanson, pp. 97–8.

27   It is exactly this property that labyrinths exploit. At every point the space you see gives no information – or misleading information – about the structure of the labyrinth as a whole. In general – though not invariably – a good urban form does exactly the opposite.

28   See chapter 4. Also B. Hillier et al., 'Natural movement: or configuration and attraction in urban pedestrian movement', *Environment & Planning B, Planning & Design*, vol. 20, 1993.

29   As, for example, in the case of the new Shanghai Central Business District on which we collaborated with Sir Richard Rogers and Partners, or the original plan for the King's Cross Railways Lands, London with Sir Norman Foster and Partners. See for example B. Hillier, 'Specifically Architectural Theory', *Harvard Architectural Review*, vol. 9, 1993. Also published as B. Hillier, 'Specifically architectural knowledge', *Nordic Journal of Architectural Research*, 2, 1993.

30   The problems generated by this type of layout are examined in detail in chapter 5.

Part two

Non-discursive regularities

chapter four

Cities as movement economies

The human understanding is of its own nature prone to suppose the existence of more order and regularity in the world than it finds.

FRANCIS BACON,
APHORISM XLV, P. 50

An axis is perhaps the first human manifestation; it is the means of every human act. The toddling child moves along an axis, the man striving in the tempest of life traces for himself an axis. The axis is the regulator of architecture.

LE CORBUSIER,
'VERS UNE ARCHITECTURE'

The physical city and the functional city

It is a truism to say that how we design cities depends on how we understand them. In the late twentieth century, this truism has a disquieting force. Cities are the largest and most complex artefacts that humankind makes. We have learned long and hard lessons about how we can damage them by insensitive interventions. But the growth of knowledge limps painfully along through a process of trial and error in which the slow timescale of our efforts and the even slower timescale of our understanding, make it almost impossible to maintain the continuity of experience and study which we might hope, in time, would give rise to a deeper, more theoretical understanding of cities.

Even so, a deeper theoretical understanding is what we need. We are at a juncture where fundamental questions about the future of our cities – should settlements be dense or sparse, nucleated or dispersed, monocentric or polycentric, or a mix of all types? – have been raised by the issue of sustainability.[1] It is widely acknowledged that to make cities sustainable we must base decisions about them on a more secure understanding of them than we have now. What is unclear is what we mean by a better understanding. Physically, cities are stocks of buildings linked by space and infrastructure. Functionally, they support economic, social, cultural and environmental processes. In effect, they are means-ends systems in which the means are physical and the ends functional. Our most critical area of ignorance is about the relation of means to ends, that is of the physical city to the functional city. The fact that sustainability is about ends and the controls largely about means has exposed our ignorance in this critical area.

One reason for this ignorance is the compartmentalisation that has developed over the past quarter century among the disciplines concerned with the city. There is now a deep split between those who are preoccupied with analysis and control of the social and economic processes which animate the city, and who for the most part call themselves planners, and those concerned with physical and spatial synthesis in the city, who call themselves urban designers. This split is now, in effect, a split between understanding and design, between thought and action.

From the point of view of our ability to act on the city, there are two consequences. The first is a form-function gap: those who analyse urban function cannot conceptualise design, while those who can conceptualise design guess about function. The second is a scale gap. Planning begins with the region, deals reasonably with the 'functional city', that is the city and its 'dependences' (as the French say of outlying buildings) but barely gets to the urban area in which we live. Urban design begins with a group of buildings, gets to the urban area, but hesitates at the whole city for fear of repeating the errors of the past when whole city design meant over-orderly towns which never quite became places. Neither applies itself to our need to understand the city as a spatial and functional whole.

One effect of this disciplinary apartheid has been a complete failure to come to terms conceptually with what seems at first to be the simplest thing about the city: the fact that it is a large, apparently complex physical and spatial object, one which is at once a record of the functional processes which historically created it, and at the same time the strongest constraint on future development. Most attempts to use computers to model the ways in which cities work, for example, have dealt with the physical aspects of the city only at the grossest level, far above the level at which most interventions are made. Since the aim of an urban model is to try to bring the structural and dynamic complexities of cities as means-ends systems within the scope of reasoned decision-making about physical and spatial interventions, this has been a critical weakness.[2]

The fact that the physical city has proved most difficult to model effectively is probably due to two things. First, the physical and spatial structure of cities appears, for the most part, to be the rather disorderly outcome of a long history of small-scale, incremental changes, which accumulate over time to produce patterns with neither geometrical nor functional simplicity. Until recently, the types of pattern that result from these quasi-organic processes have not seemed tractable to any obvious method of analysis. Consequently they were neglected. Second, the incremental processes by which economic and social processes create the city's physical and spatial patterns seem in themselves to be quite complex, involving feedback and multiplier effects, and interaction between different scales. Processes of urban growth and change seem to exhibit both 'emergence', by which unforeseen macro changes result from a series of micro-changes, and the contrary effect, by which macro changes produce unforeseen effects at the micro scale. Again, until recently, there have not been obvious ways of modelling such processes.

The apparent intractability of the city as a physical and spatial object afflicts the synthesists as much as the analysts. If we look to urban designers for an analysis of the object of their design attention, we find much moral earnestness about such matters as the creation of 'places' as rich and complex as those found in traditional cities, but little analytic endeavour to understand how the physical and functional cities of the past gave rise to such 'places'. The current preoccupation with 'place' seems no more than the most recent version of the urban designer's preference for the local and apparently tractable at the expense of the global and intractable in cities. However, both practical experience and research suggest that the preoccupation with local place gets priorities in the wrong order. Places are not local things. They are moments in large-scale things, the large-scale things we call cities. Places do not make cities. It is cities that make places. The distinction is vital. We cannot make places without understanding cities. Once again we find ourselves needing, above all, an understanding of the city as a functioning physical and spatial object.

Multifunctionality and the part-whole problem
Where should we then find a starting point for an enquiry into the form and functioning of cities, in the hope of founding a theory of cities as means-ends systems? In situations where new theories are needed, there is a useful rule. At every stage in the development of our understanding of phenomena, we already have in our minds some conceptual scheme through which we interpret and interrelate the phenomena that we see.[3] Usually there are irritating anomalies and problems at the edges of these conceptual schemes. The rule is that instead of keeping these problems at the edge of our field of vision, and accepting them as anomalies, we should bring them centre stage and make them our starting point. We should, in effect, start from what we cannot explain rather than what we think we can.

There are two such great anomalies in our current ways of seeing cities. The first is the problem of multifunctionality. Every aspect of the spatial and physical configuration of the city form seems to have to work in many different ways – climatically, economically, socially, aesthetically, and so on – with the additional difficulty that form changes only slowly while function changes rapidly. The second is the part-whole problem, or as some might prefer, the place-city problem, that is, the fact that in most cities made up of parts with a strong sense of local place it is almost impossible to make a clear morphological distinction between one part and another, at least not at the level at which it could inform design.

If the theory set out in this chapter is anywhere near right, then it will become clear that these two issues are rather more than closely related: they really are the same problem, because all functions relate to the form of the city through two generic functional factors: how we as individuals find the city intelligible, and how we move around in it. These generic factors are so powerful that all other aspects of function pass through them and influence the urban form through them. They are so because in cities, as in buildings, the relationship between form and function passes through space. How we organise space into configuration is the key both to the forms of the city, and how human beings function in cities.

The theory to be set out in this chapter is based on one central proposition: that the fundamental correlate of the spatial configuration is movement. This is the case both in terms of the determination of spatial form, in that movement largely dictates the configuring of space in the city, and in terms of the effects of spatial form, in that movement is largely determined by spatial configuration. The principal generator of the theory set out here is the discovery, through recent research, that the structure of the urban grid considered purely as a spatial configuration, is itself the most powerful single determinant of urban movement, both pedestrian and vehicular. Because this relation is fundamental and lawful, it has already been a powerful force in shaping our historically evolved cities, by its effect on land-use patterns, building densities, the mixing of uses in urban areas and the part-whole structure of the city.[4]

The result now available suggests that socio-economic forces shape the city primarily through the relations between movement and the structure of the urban grid. Well-functioning cities can therefore, it will be suggested, be thought of as 'movement economies'. By this is meant that it is the reciprocal effects of space and movement on each other (and not, for example, aesthetic or symbolic intentions), and the multiplier effects on both that arise from patterns of land use and building densities, which are themselves influenced by the space-movement relation, that give cities their characteristic structures, and give rise to the sense that everything is working together to create the special kinds of well-being and excitement that we associate with cities at their best.

It will be suggested as a consequence of these arguments that our view of the city in the recent past has been afflicted by conceptions of space which are at once too static and too localised. We need to replace these by concepts which are dynamic and global. Both can be achieved through the configurational modelling of space, using the power it gives us both to capture the complexities of urban form, and bring these analyses to bear on design.

Form and function in space are not independent

We must begin by making a few basic observations about space and its relation to function. We tend to think of the form and function of space as two quite independent things. Space is a shape, and function is what we do in it. Set up this way, it is hard to see why there should be any relation between the two, and even harder to see how any relation could be a necessary one.

But if we think a little more carefully about how human beings operate in space, we find everywhere a kind of natural geometry to what people do in space. Consider, for example, figure 4.1. At the most elementary level, people move in lines, and tend to approximate lines in more complex routes, as in the first figure. Then if an individual stops to talk to a group of people, the group will collectively define a space in which all the people the first person can see can see each other, and this is a mathematical definition of convexity in space, except that a mathematician would say points rather than people. The more complex shape of the third figure defines all the points in space, and therefore the potential people, that can be seen by any of the people in the convex space who can also see each other. We call this type of irregular, but well defined, shape a 'convex isovist'. Such shapes vary as we move about in cities, and therefore define a key aspect of our spatial experience of them.

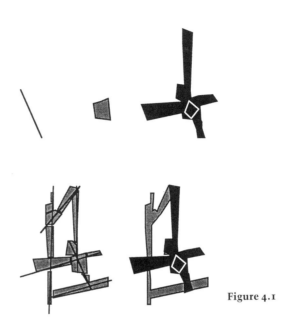

Figure 4.1

There are relationships, then, between the formal describability of
space and how people use it. These elementary relationships between the
form of space and its use suggest that the proper way to formulate the
relation is to say that space is given to us as a set of potentials, and that
we exploit these potentials as individuals and collectivities in using
space. It is this that makes the relation between space and function
analysable, and to some extent predictable. By dividing up urban space,
which is necessarily continuous, in different formal ways we are likely to
be dividing it up according to some aspect of how human beings function.

Consider, for example, figure 4.2a which is the plan of Rome, in
which the customary representation with the buildings in black and the
space white has been reversed to draw attention to the fact that it is the
black structure of space that is our focus of concern.[5] Figure 4.2b is then
one possible structure within figure 4.2, the fewest and longest lines that
cover the open space of Rome, and therefore form its potential route
matrix. Figure 4.2c is another such structure: all the convex elements we
call public open spaces together with their isovists. By definition, this

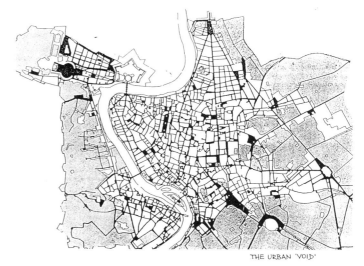

THE URBAN 'VOID'

Figure 4.2a Plan of Rome, Italy

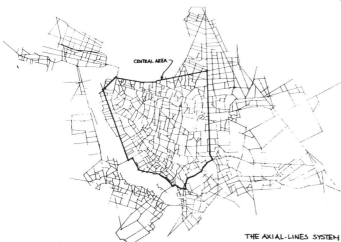

CENTRAL AREA

THE AXIAL-LINES SYSTEM

Figure 4.2b Axial map of Rome, Italy

Figure 4.2c Isovist map of Rome, Italy

includes all the lines that pass through the spaces and relate them in the urban structure as a whole. Note how they link up to form global clusters. We immediately see how mistaken we would be to see Roman squares as local elements. The isovists show they also form a global pattern.

All these ways of looking at space can be seen as layers of spatial structuring, co-existing within the same plan, each with its own contribution to intelligibility and function. A spatial layout can thus be seen as offering different functional potentials. What is it like to move around in it? Does it have potential to generate interaction? Can strangers understand it? and so on. All these questions are about the relationship of space as formal potentials to different aspects of function. A layout can thus be represented as a different kind of spatial system according to what aspects of function we are interested in.

The shape of space in the City of London

Let us now look in more detail at a case that is much closer to home: the City of London, for no better reason than that it has been as often criticised as 'haphazard' as praised as 'organic' – but never explained properly. The plan of the 'square mile' (in fact it is neither square nor a mile) is shown in figure 4.3a using the black on white convention to emphasise that it is space we are looking at. Figure 4.3b homes in on one of the allegedly 'labyrinthian' back areas of the City between Cornhill and Lombard Street, taken from the Rocque map of 1746. We say allegedly because although it looks so in plan, it does not seem in the least labyrinthian to the person moving at ground level. On the contrary, it seems highly intelligible. How does this happen? The technique is simple. The space structure is admittedly highly broken up into 'convex' spaces – but there are always lines which link the convex spaces together, usually several at a time. Sometimes the line 'just about' gets through the spaces formed by the buildings, sometimes more easily. But because people move in lines, and need to understand lines in order to know where they can go, this means that the space structure is easily intelligible from the point of view of movement.

In fact, the pattern is slightly subtler. There is for the most part a 'two-line logic' in that if you pass down a line that you can see from the

Figure 4.3

a Black and white illustration of the public open space of the City of London as it is today

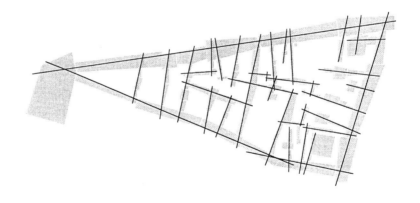

b Close-up of the one- and two-dimensional space structure of the area between Cornhill and Lombard Street in 1677.

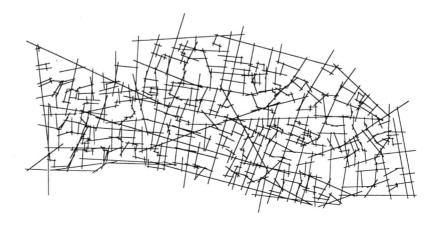

c Axial map of the City of London as it is today

main grid, the next line will take you either out of the back area again or to some significant spatial event – say a larger piece of space or a significant building – within the back area. This means that wherever you go, there is usually a point from which you can see where you have come from and where your next point of aim might be. This is the opposite of labyrinthi-an. As observation will confirm, the effect of this spatial technique is that the back areas become normally and naturally used for movement as part of the urban space pattern. There is no inhibition or sense of territorial intrusion in these areas.

This two-line logic is not the only constant property of these small-scale complexes. We also find that nearly every convex element, including the narrow ones that enter the back areas, as well as the fatter ones we find within the areas, has building entrances opening onto it. In the city, a fascinating cultural practice has augmented this: even in inclement weather, doors to buildings tend to be left open, often showing to the outside world one-way up stairs or down and another into the ground-level premises.

The effect of these apparent rules about how buildings relate to open space is to create two 'interfaces'. First, there is a close relation between those within the building, and those outside. Second, there is a natural mingling between those who are using the space outside the buildings, and those who are passing through. There is no sense of lack of privacy or intrusion. Nor is there any pressure to interact, though this is available if required. All we have is a relation of co-presence between groups doing different things. Such co-presence seems unforced, even relaxed. It is the product of a two-way relation from the convex spatial element: one into the building, the other to the larger scale through the line structure. The larger and smaller scales of a space are held together by this spatial technique.

Now let us zoom out to the larger scale. Figure 4.3c is an 'axial map' of the City as a whole, that is, the least set of straight lines that pass through all the open space in figure 4.3a. The first thing we see when looking at the larger scale – that is at the longer lines – is that the tendency of lines to 'just about' pass through convex space is still there. It is just possible, in spite of the sinuous curves of the buildings, to see down

Lombard Street from one end to the other, and it is just about possible to see from the Bank interchange through the whole of Cornhill into Leadenhall Street as far as Billiter Street. In both cases the line ends by striking the facade of a building at a very open angle, and from this it seems natural to infer continuation of potential movement in that general direction.

These improbably extended 'just about' lines create another effect which one must search a little to find, and perhaps go back to the old map to verify. It is that if one enters any of the old City gates and proceeds following only a rule that requires you to take the longest line available at any time (without going back on yourself) then in each case from somewhere on the second line a line opens up from which the Bank interchange, the old centre of the City can be seen. Again, we find a simple two-line logic underlying apparent complexity, and again we need have no doubt about its functional implication. It accesses the stranger to the heart of the city. An automaton could find the centre – so a stranger could.

However, when we compare the two levels at which we find this two-line logic, there is a geometric difference which we can summarise in a simple principle: the longer the line the more likely it is to strike a building facade at an open angle, the shorter the line, the more likely it is to strike a building at a right angle. This is exactly the opposite of the current rather pompous urban fashion to end major axes at right angles on major building facades. Historically this usually occurs where urban space is taken over for the symbolic expression of power, whereas the City's urban space structure is about the movement required to create a dense encounter field. The right-angle relation of facade to line is used in the City to, as it were, illuminate the smaller-scale and spatially more complex areas, and to make them visible from the larger-scale grid. Thus we begin to see not only that there is an interior logic to the City's apparently disorderly grid, but that this inner logic is fundamentally about movement, and the potential that movement gives for creating co-presence. We see that many of the properties of urban space that we value aesthetically are a product of this functional shaping of space.

These consistencies in spatial patterning show how the City is put together locally, and how it therefore works as a series of experiences. But the City also acquires a global form. To understand this, and why it is important, we must begin to formalise our understanding a little. It will turn out that the line pattern of the City is the most important to its global structure, and we must therefore begin by examining this if we wish to move the focus of our analysis from the local to the global. We may begin by a simple observation: that to go from any line to any other one must pass through a certain number of intervening lines (unless of course the origin line directly intersects the destination line). Each line thus has a certain minimum line 'depth' from another, which is not necessarily a function of distance. It follows that each line has a minimum average line 'depth' from *all* other lines in the system. Because lines will always be shallow from some lines and deep from others, one might expect that this would average itself out. The surprising thing is that it does not. There are substantial differences in the mean depth of lines from all others, and it is these differences that govern the influence of the grid on movement in the system: roughly, the less depth to all other lines, the more movement; the more depth the less.

These configurational pictures of the City from the point of view of its constituent lines can be measured exactly through the measure of 'integration'. (See chapters 1 and 3.) The 'integration value' of each line reflects its mean linear 'depth' from all other lines in the system. We can then map these integration values from red through purple, and produce a global integration map of the whole of a city, as in plate 2a. We can also produce another highly informative map, one in which we calculate integration only up to three lines away from each line in every direction, and which we therefore call 'local integration', or radius-3 integration, in contrast to 'global' or radius-n integration. (plate 2b)

Integration values in line maps are of great importance in understanding how urban systems function because it turns out that how much movement passes down each line is very strongly influenced by its 'integration value' calculated in this way, that is by how the line is positioned with respect to the system as a whole.[6] In fact it is slightly more subtle and depends on the typical length of journeys. Pedestrian densities on lines in local areas can usually be best predicted by calculating integration for the system of lines up to three lines away from each line (radius-3 integration), while cars on larger-scale routes (though not in local areas, where radius-3 is the best predictor) depend on higher radius integration because car journeys are on the whole longer and motorists therefore read the matrix of possible routes according to a larger-scale logic than pedestrians.[7]

The principle of natural movement

This relationship between the structure of the urban grid and movement densities along lines can be called the principle of 'natural movement'. Natural movement is the proportion of movement on each line that is determined by the structure of the urban grid itself rather than by the presence of specific attractors or magnets. This is not initially obvious, but on reflection does seem natural. In a large and well developed urban grid people move in lines, but start and finish everywhere. We cannot easily conceive of an urban structure as complex as the city in terms of specific generators and attractors, or even origins and destinations but we do not need to because the city is a structure in which origins and destinations tend to be diffused everywhere, though with obvious biases toward higher density areas and major traffic interchanges. So movement tends to be broadly from everywhere to everywhere else. To the extent that this is the case in most cities, the structure of the grid itself accounts for much of the variation in movement densities.

We should then expect that the distribution of colours in axial maps will foreshadow densities of moving people. Because the colours are really rough indexes of precise numerical values, this proposition can of course be tested by selecting areas and correlating movement rates against integration values. However, because movement along a particular line is influenced in the main by its position in the larger-scale urban grid, we must take care to include enough of the whole urban grid in our analysis to ensure that each line in the area we are studying is embedded in all the urban structure that may influence its movement. We cannot then do better than to begin with the whole of an urban system, or at least a very much larger part of it in order to ensure that our study area is sufficiently well embedded.

In order to analyse an area in inner London, then, we begin with an axial representation of the very large part of London shown in figure 4.4,

Figure 4.4 Axial map of Greater London within the North and South Circular roads

which covers the area approximately within the North and South
Circular Roads. Plate 2c–e is then a series of analyses of integration at
different radii. Plate 2c is the radius-n analysis, and as such shows the
most global structure of London, with a strong edge-to-centre pattern
centred on Oxford Street, which is the most integrated line. Plate 2d is
the radius-3 analysis, which highlights a much more localised structure,
including most local shopping streets, but also picks out Oxford Street as

the dominant integrator. This implies that Oxford Street is not only the strongest global integrator in London as a whole, but also the strongest local integrator of its surrounding area. Plate 2e is then a radius-10 (or radius-radius) analysis, meaning that the integration analysis is set at the mean depth of the whole system from the main integrator, which in this case is 10. The effect of setting the radius of analysis at that of the main integrator is that each line is analysed at the same radius which is at the same time the maximum radius possible without differences in radius between lines. The effect of a radius-radius analysis is to maximise the globality of the analysis without inducing 'edge effect', that is the tendency for the edges of spatial systems to be different from interior area because they are close to the edge. Taken together, the figures show a remarkably true-to-life functional picture of London as a whole, highlighting all the main in and out routes and shopping high streets.

The reason that a spatial analysis can give such a true-to-life functional picture is due to the powerful influence that natural movement – the tendency of the structure of the grid itself to be the main influence on the pattern of movement – has on the evolution of the urban pattern and its distribution of land uses. To test this properly we must translate back from graphics to numbers. Figure 4.5a selects a small area within the system, more or less coterminous with the named area of Barnsbury, and assigns precise 'integration values' to each line. Figure 4.5b then indexes observed movement rates of adult pedestrians on each line segment throughout the working day.[8] Figure 4.5c is a scattergram plotting pedestrian movement rates against radius-3 integration. The R-squared value shows that about three-quarters of the differences between line segments in their movement rates are due to their configurational position in the larger-scale grid. Note, by the way, that we are still calculating integration with respect to a much larger system than shown in figure 4.5a. Movement is not only largely determined by configuration, but also by configuration on a fairly large scale.

Readers can consult published texts for detailed results, but similar results have been achieved across a great range of studies, and even better – though slightly different – results have been found from studies relating vehicular movement to spatial configuration.[9] These studies show that

Figure 4.5

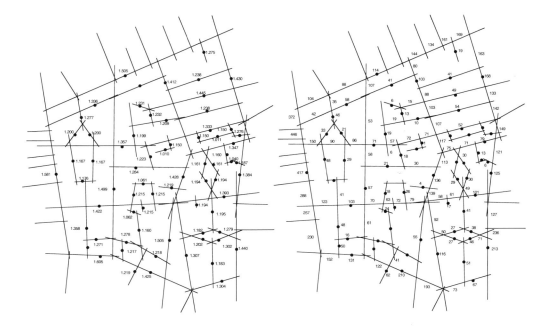

a The integration value of each axial line in Barnsbury   **b** Average number of pedestrians per hour for all periods

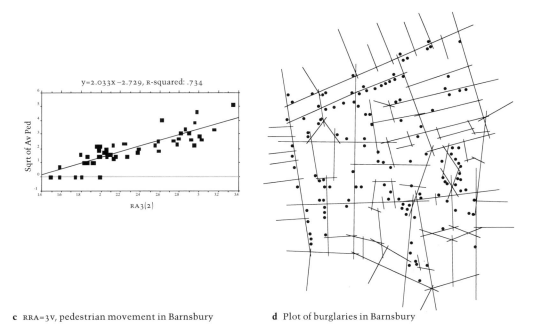

c RRA=3V, pedestrian movement in Barnsbury   **d** Plot of burglaries in Barnsbury

the distribution of pedestrian movement in the urban grid is to a considerable extent determined by spatial configuration, with the actual levels
also strongly influenced by area building densities (though the effects of
building density are not in general found at the level of the individual
line), while vehicular movement is strongly influenced by spatial integration in association with net road width, that is the width of the road less
the permitted car parking. In the case of vehicular movement the second
variable, net road width, does influence movement on a line-by-line basis
and plays a more significant part in the larger scale road network.[10]

We may investigate another key component of successful urbanism,
the informal use of open spaces for stopping and taking pleasure, by using
a similar technique. Figure 4.6 is a 'convex isovist' representation of the
City of London's few, rather informal open spaces, which vary remarkably in their degree of informal use. Attempts to account for the pattern
of well and poorly used spaces in the City in terms of commonly canvassed
explanations have been singularly unsuccessful. For example, some
spaces hemmed in by traffic are several times better used than adjacent
spaces without traffic, exposed spaces often perform better than spaces
with good enclosure, some of the most successful spaces are in the shadow of tall buildings, and so on. The only variable that correlates consistently with the degree of observed informal spaces is, in fact, a measure of
the 'Roman property', noted in figure 4.2c, which we call the 'strategic
value' of the isovist. This is calculated by summing the integration
values of all the lines which pass through the body of the space (as
opposed to skirting its edges). This makes intuitive sense. The primary
activity of those who stop to sit in urban spaces seems to be to watch others pass by. For this, strategic spaces with areas close to, but not actually
lying on, the main lines of movement are optimal. The main fault in most
of the modern open spaces we have observed (with the most notable
exception of Broadgate, which has the most successful spaces in the City
of London) is that the designers have given too much attention to local
enclosure of the space, and too little to strategic visual fields – yet another instance of an overly localised view of space. The general rule seems to
be that a space must not be too enclosed for its size. The visibility field
must be scaled up in proportion to the scale of the space.

Once we have the trick of correlating numbers indexing observed
function with numbers indexing spatial patterns we can extend it to anything that can be represented as a number and located in space. When we
do so, it turns out that everything seems to relate to space, and therefore
to movement in some way: retail, building densities, indeed most types
of land use seem to have some spatial logic which can be expressed as a
statistical relation between spatial and function measures. Even crime
can be spatially correlated. Figure 4.5d plots burglaries within a twelve-
month period in the Barnsbury area. Visually, it looks as though there
may be some effect from configuration, in that the densest concentrations seem to be in less integrated locations, while some of the more integrating lines are relatively free. Is this true? By assigning each dwelling
the integration value of the line on which it opens we can ask if burgled
dwellings are significantly more segregated or integrated than unburgled
dwellings. It turns out that burgled dwellings are significantly more
segregated on average than unburgled dwellings.

Now let us look at other aspects of how things are distributed in the
urban grid. Take, for example, the well-known Booth map of London,
part of which is shown in plate 3 in which socio-economic classes are
plotted from gold for the best off (there are none in the part of London
shown), through red for merchant grade houses, then through pink to grey
and black for the poorest. The most integrated streets are lined with red,
and as you move into the less important, and less integrating streets, the
grade of housing falls off, leaving the poorest in the most segregated areas.
There is also a subtler organisation concealed in the Booth map, one
which provides an important clue to one of the hidden secrets of urban
space: how different uses and economic classes are mixed in the same
area by using a principle that can be summarised as 'marginal separation
by linear integration'. If we look carefully we can see that different grades
of housing – and in other situations we will find different land uses – may
often be in close proximity but separated effectively by being on different
alignments, often as part of the same urban block. The fundamental land
use element is not the zone or even the urban block but the line: land use
changes slowly as you progress along particular lines of movement, but
can change quite sharply with ninety-degree turns onto different align-

Figure 4.6 Convex isovists from eight city of London squares

ments. Since we know that the pattern of alignments is the fundamental
determinant of movement, we can begin to see that the structure of the
urban grid, the distribution of land uses, and built form densities are in
the historically evolving city bound up with each other in a dynamic
process centred on the relation of the grid structure to movement.

Which then is primary? Let us argue this through the spatial distribution of retail, the commonest non-residential land use. We may already
have been suspected of having confused the effects of spatial configuration on movement with the effect of shops. Are not the shops the main
attractors of movement? And do they not lie on the main integrators?
This is of course true. But it does not undermine what is being said about
the structure of the grid as the prime determinant of movement. On the
contrary it makes the argument far more powerful. Both the shops and

the people are found on main integrators, but the question is: why are the shops there? The presence of shops can attract people but they cannot change the integration value of a line, since this is purely a spatial measure of the position of the line in the grid. It can only be that the shops were selectively located on integrating lines, and this must be because they are the lines which naturally carry the most movement. So, far from explaining away the relation between grid structure and movement by pointing to the shops, we have explained the location of the shops by pointing to the relation between grid and movement.[11]

Now of course in a sense to say this is to say the obvious. Every retailer knows that you should put the shop where people are going to be anyway, and it is no surprise if we find that the structure of the urban grid influences at least some land uses as it evolves. It would be surprising if it were not the case. However, a little more than this is being claimed. It is being suggested that there is an underlying principle which, other things being equal, relates grid structure to movement pattern not only on the main lines in and out of a city, but also in the fine structure, and through this gives rise to a whole multiplicity of inter-relationships between grid structure, land uses, densities, and even the sense of urban well-being and fear.

Multiplier effects and the movement economy

We can pursue this by thinking carefully about what it would take to produce this degree of agreement between grid structure, movement, land uses and densities. We find ourselves unavoidably led towards a theory of the general formation of the city through the functional shaping of its space by movement. Let us begin by thinking about that. An urban system, by definition, is one which has at least some origins and destinations more or less everywhere. Every trip in an urban system has three elements: an origin, a destination, and the series of spaces that are passed through on the way from one to the other. We can think of passage through these spaces as the by-product of going from a to b. We already know that this by-product, when taken at the aggregate level, is determined by the structure of the grid, even if the location of all the a's and b's is not.

Location in the grid therefore has a crucial effect. It either increases or diminishes the degree to which movement by-product is available as potential contact. As we saw in the coloured-up maps, this applies not only to individual lines, but to the groups of lines that make up local areas. Thus there will be more integrating and less integrating areas, depending on how the internal structure of the area is married into the larger-scale structure of the grid, and this will mean also areas with more by-product and areas with less.

Now if cities are, as they were always said to be, 'mechanisms for generating contact', then this means that some locations have more potential than others because they have more by-product and this will depend on the structure of the grid and how they relate to it. Such locations will therefore tend to have higher densities of development to take advantage of this, and higher densities will in turn have a multiplier effect. This will in turn attract new buildings and uses, to take advantage of the multiplier effect. It is this positive feedback loop built on a foundation of the relation between the grid structure and movement which gives rise to the urban buzz, which we prefer to be romantic or mystical about, but which arises from the co-incidence in certain locations of large numbers of different activities involving people going about their business in different ways. Such situations invariably arise through multiplier effects generated from the basic relation between space structure and movement, and ultimately this depends on the structure of the urban grid itself. In other words, how the urban system is put together spatially is the source of everything else.

We may illustrate this negatively through a notorious case where the urban buzz does not occur, in spite of the co-existence in a small area of many major functions. The example is the area of the South Bank cultural centre in London, where, within a few hundred metres can be found Europe's largest and most diverse cultural complex, a major international railway terminus, extensive office development, significant residential development and a famous riverside walk. Why do all these facilities not add up into an urban area with the qualities called for by these high-level facilities? It can only be the way it is put together. This is indeed the case. Our studies have shown that each of the various constituencies of space users – travellers, residents, office workers, tourists, concert-goers and gallery visitors all use space in a different way and, as it were, move through the area largely on separate routes passing each other like ships in the night. It is the failure of the configuration of space to bring these different constituencies into patterns of movement and space use where all are prioritising the same space, that deprive the area of the multiplier effects that occur when different constituencies of space use all spark off each other.

If these arguments are right, it means that all the primary elements of urban form, that is the structure of the urban grid, the distribution of land uses and the assignment of development densities are bound together in the historical city by the principle that relates the structure of the urban grid to the by-product of movement. It means that under certain conditions of density and integration of the grid structure things can happen that will not happen elsewhere. Movement is so central to this process that we should forthwith cease to see cities as being made up of fixed elements and movement elements and instead see the physical and spatial structure as being bound up to create what we have called the 'movement economy', in which the usefulness of the by-product of movement is everywhere maximised by integration in order to maximise the multiplier effects which are the root source of the life of cities.

Urbanity, we suggest, is not so mysterious. Good space is used space. Most urban space use is movement. Most movement is through movement, that is, the by-product of how the grid offers routes from everywhere to everywhere else. Most informal space use is also movement related, as is the sense and fact of urban safety. Land uses and building density follow movement in the grid, both adapting to and multiplying its effects. The urban buzz, or the lack of it when it suits us, is the combination of these, and the fundamental determinant is the structure of the grid itself. The urban grid through its influence on the movement economy is the fundamental source of the multifunctionality that gives life to cities.

Parts and wholes
We can also show how the movement economy creates the part-whole structure of cities. We have already noted that movement occurs at different scales: some localised and some more globalised. Long journeys will tend to naturally prioritise spaces which are globally more integrated, more local journeys those which are more locally integrated. The space

system is literally read – and readable – at a different scale. Since different radii of integration reflect different scales of the urban system, it will turn out that the key to understanding parts and whole is understanding the relations between the different radii of integration.

Consider, for example, the relation between the City of London and London as a whole. Figure 4.7a is a close up of the axial map of the City of London in context. Figure 4.7b is a scattergram plotting each line in the London axial map as a whole as a point located according to its degree of global (radius-n) integration on the horizontal axis and its degree of local (radius-3) integration on the vertical axis. The dark points are the lines which make up the City of London. The dark points form a good linear scatter about their own (invisible) regression line, and cross the main regression line at a steeper angle. The linearity implies a good relation between local and global integration, the steeper slope across the regression line implies that the most integrated lines within the city, which are the lines from the outside towards the centre, are more locally than globally integrated. Their local integration is, as it were, intensified for their degree of global integration. Repeating this experiment with all of the well-known named London areas, such as Soho, Covent Garden, Bloomsbury, and even Barnsbury – yields this kind of scatter. In other words, the relation of part and whole in the axial map is made up at least in part of the relation between local and global integration. The reason this is so is that each local area has its heart linked to the supergrid lines that surround it by strong integrators. These form an edge-to-centre structure in all directions, and the less-integrated areas are within the interstices formed by the structure. The strong local integrators which define the slope of the dark points for the local area are invariably these edge-to-centre lines.[12]

Remarkably, we find exactly the same phenomenon on a much smaller scale, for example within the City of London. Figure 4.7c homes in on the Leadenhall Market area, and figure 4.7d shows the City scatter with the Leadenhall Market area as the dark points. Once again we find the local area effect. The effect of this is that as you move down the supergrid lines – Gracechurch Street or Leadenhall Street – then Leadenhall Market is available as a well-structured local intensification of the grid, itself laid

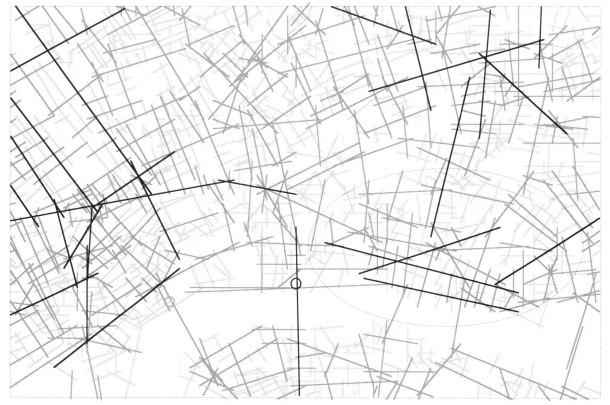

Figure 4.7a City of London within the context of Greater London

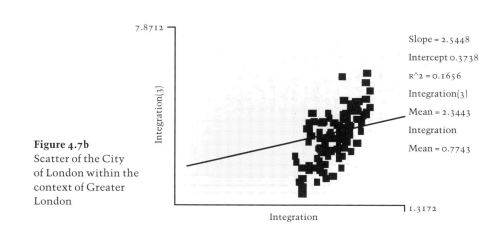

Figure 4.7b
Scatter of the City
of London within the
context of Greater
London

Figure 4.7c
Leadenhall Market,
City of London

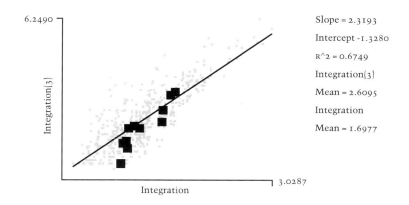

Slope = 2.3193

Intercept -1.3280

R^2 = 0.6749

Integration(3)

Mean = 2.6095

Integration

Mean = 1.6977

Figure 4.7d
Scatter (in black dots) of
Leadenhall Market with-
in the context of the City
of London

out in much the same way as the town is laid out. Once you are near it in the adjacent streets, it becomes a powerful attractor.

We can draw a simple conclusion from these results, one which I believe agrees with intuition: that the more the set of dark points forms a line crossing the regression lines for the whole city but tending to greater steepness, there is more that is local integration than global, then the more the sub-area is distinctive; while the more the dark points lie on the City regression lines, the more they are simply sets of smaller spaces related to the main grid, but not forming a distinctive sub-area away from it. This depends, however, on the dark points themselves forming a good line, since without that we do not have a good integration interface – that is a good relation between the different scales of movement – in the first place, regardless of where it is in relation to the main City. It depends also on the dark points including points well up the scale of integration. A clutch of points bottom left will be very segregated, and not function as a sub-area. (Chapter 5 deals with this problem in detail.)

We have found an objective spatial meaning, it seems, to the areas we name as areas, and in such a way as to have a good idea of the functional generators of their distinctive urban patterns. We have a key to how at least some cities can be put together as cities of parts without losing the sense of the whole. Historically, it seems, cities exploited movement constructively to create dense, but variable, encounter zones to become what made them useful: to be 'mechanisms for generating contact'. How they did this was by using space to generate multiplier effects on the relation between movement and encounter. This was achieved by quite precise spatial techniques, applied now this way now that (for example, in Arabic cities we find a quite different development of the same underlying laws), but always having the effect of creating well-defined relationships between different levels of movement: between the movement within buildings and the movement on the street, between localised movement in less important streets and the more globalised pattern of movement, and between the movement of inhabitants and the movement of strangers entering and leaving the city. In a sense, cities were constructed to be, in the words of Dr John Peponis,[13] interfaces between scales of movement.

The interface between different radii of integration was the spatial

means to the functional end. It created a close relation between more localised
and more globalised movement. It is therefore the key to the local by-product
effect, and the means to create local advantage from global movement. The
spatial technique by which this was done was to maintain a number of spatial
interfaces: between building entrances and all spaces, at whatever scale; between
smaller spaces and the larger urban scale through the relation between the
convex and linear structures; and between different scales of the linear
structure, especially between parts and the whole.

Disurbanism
The urban movement economy, arising from the multiplier effect of space,
depends on certain conditions: a certain size, a certain density, a certain distribution of land uses, a specific type of grid that maintains the interface between
local and global, and so on. Once this is spelled out, it is easy to see how thoroughly some of our recent efforts have disrupted it, so much so that we must
think of many developments of recent years as exercise in the spatial techniques
of disurbanism. 'Disurbanism' is intended to convey the reverse of the urban
spatial techniques we have identified: the breaking of the relation between
buildings and public space; the breaking of the relation between scales of
movement; and the breaking of the interface between inhabitant and stranger.

Consider, for example, the integration map of an area around Barnsbury,
which includes three housing estates around the King's Cross railway lands
site (the empty area), as in figure 4.8a The estates are easy to pick out: they
are more complex and at a smaller spatial scale than the surrounding street-
based areas, and each is marked by its density of light shaded, that is segregated,
lines. If we try to plot these estates as dark point scatters of local against global
integration, as in 4.8b, c and d then we find that in each case the estate scatter
forms a series of layers, each distributed in a more or less vertical pattern. This
phenomenon will be dealt with in detail in the next chapter. Here we note
three consequences of this type of spatial design. First, the estate is substantially
more segregated than the rest of the urban surface and, what is more problematic,
segregated as a lump. Good urban space has segregated lines, but they are close
to integrated lines, so that there is a good mix of integrated and segregated lines
locally. Second, there is a poor relation between local and global integration,
that means a very unclear relation between the local and global structure.

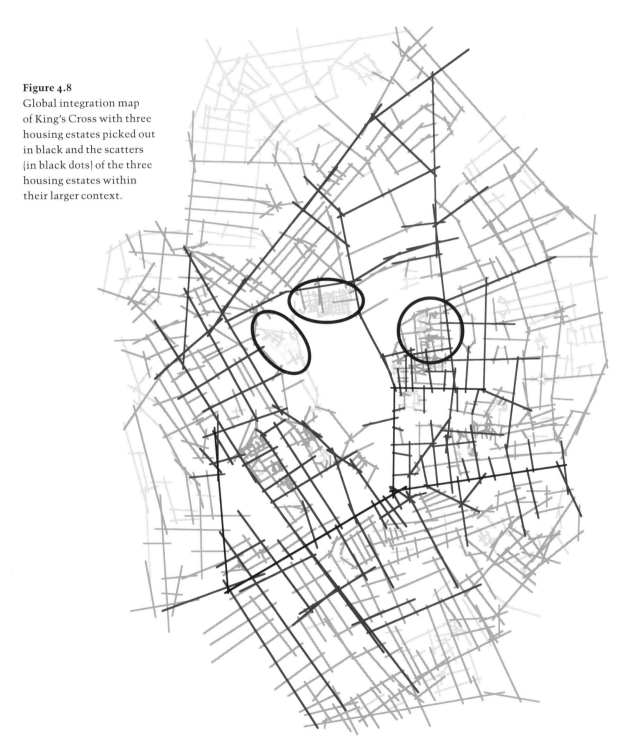

a

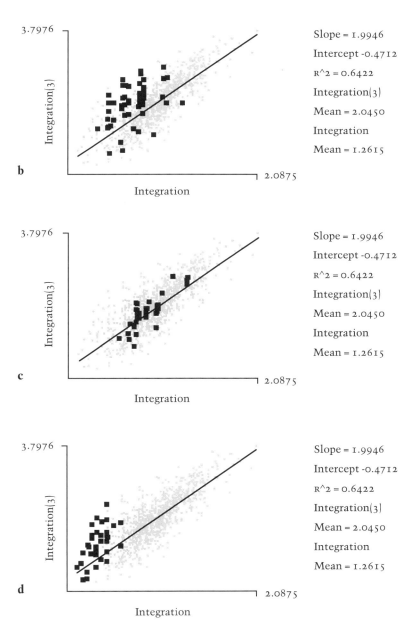

Slope = 1.9946

Intercept -0.4712

R^2 = 0.6422

Integration(3)

Mean = 2.0450

Integration

Mean = 1.2615

Slope = 1.9946

Intercept -0.4712

R^2 = 0.6422

Integration(3)

Mean = 2.0450

Integration

Mean = 1.2615

Slope = 1.9946

Intercept -0.4712

R^2 = 0.6422

Integration(3)

Mean = 2.0450

Integration

Mean = 1.2615

Third, the scatter does not cross the line to create a well-structured local intensification of the grid.

What this means in functional terms is that all interfaces are broken: between building and public space; between localised and less localised movement; and between inhabitant and stranger. Of course life is possible in such a place. But there is now evidence to suggest that we ought to be more pessimistic. Efforts to trace the path that such designs can have over a long period on the type of life that goes on in them suggest that there is a pattern of long-term development in which spatial designs create serious lacunas in natural movement, which then attract anti-social uses and behaviours. As we will see in chapter 5, in extreme cases, where the lacunas of natural movement are the integration core of the estate itself, then the situation may become pathological.

These 'disurban' places arise from a poorly structured local configuration of space as a consequence of which the main elements of the movement economy are lost. A similar pattern of loss can also arise through dispersion. If we move from an urban system that is dense and nucleated to one that is dispersed and fragmentary, it is obvious that the mean length of journeys will, other things being equal, increase. It is less obvious, but equally true, that the by-product effect will also be diminished. As dispersion increases, it becomes less and less likely that connected locations will benefit from the byproduct of movement. In effect, as dispersion increases, the movement system becomes more like a pure origin-destination system. Instead of one journey accomplishing a number of purposes, more journeys, each one accomplishing fewer purposes, must be made to attain the same goals. These are the basic reasons why people travel farther in the country, and why most of this extra travel is in private cars.[14]

A similar effect can arise even in a comparatively dense urban system through an urban design policy of replacing continuous urban structure with specialised enclaves. This will also tend to eliminate by-product. Enclaves are, almost by definition, destinations which are not available for natural movement. They form discontinuities in the urban grid. Because this is so they are in many ways comparable in their effects to the physical dispersion, and similarly disruptive of the movement economy. Any tendency in an urban structure towards 'precinctisation' must also be a tendency to a lessening of the useful by-product, and therefore of the multiplier effect on which urban vibrancy depends.

These arguments suggest that the culturally sanctioned values that are embedded in attitudes towards urban design that until quite recently were taken for granted – lowering densities wherever possible, breaking up urban continuity into well-defined and specialised enclaves, reducing spatial scale, separating and restricting different forms of movement, even restricting the ability to stop travellers from moving and taking advantage of the by-product effect – are fundamentally inimical to the natural functioning of the city and its movement economy. It is not density that undermines the sense of well-being and safety in urban spaces, but sparseness, not large spatial scale, but its insensitive reduction, not lack of order but its superficial imposition, not the 'unplanned chaos' of the deformed grid, but its planned fragmentation. Without an understanding of the spatial and functional nature of the city as a whole, we are in danger of eliminating all the properties of density, good spatial scale, controlled juxtaposition of uses, continuity, and integration of the urban grid on which the well-ordering and well-functioning of the city depends.

Reflections on the origins of urbanism and the transformation of the city

These conclusions can only reinforce the thought with which we began: our interventions in the city can only be based on our understanding of the city. Where this understanding is deficient, the effects can be destructive, and this will be more the case to the degree that this false understanding is held in place by a value system. The value system according to which we have been transforming our cities over much of the past century has always appeared as a kind of urban rationality, but it was never based on the study of the city. Where then did it come from?

Let us first reflect a little on the nature and origins of cities, why we have them and what made them possible. Towns, as physical objects, are clearly specialised forms of spatial engineering which permit large numbers of people to live in dense concentrations without getting on each other's nerves, and minimise the effort and energy needed for face-to- face contact with each other and with the providers of needs. Towns, we suggest, were in fact made functionally possible in the first instance by a transmutation in the way energy flowed through society. It is most easily explained through the geographer Richard Wagner's distinction between two kinds of energy-related artifact: *implements* which transmit or accelerate kinetic energy, and *facilities* which store up potential energy and slow down its transfer.[15] For example, a flint knife is an implement, whereas a dam is a facility. Whatever else made towns possible, there is no doubt that they were usually marked by a radical increase in facilities, most especially irrigation systems and food storage facilities.

What made towns possible socially was an invention we are so familiar with that we tend to take it for granted and forget it is there: the urban grid. The urban grid is the organisation of groups of contiguous buildings in outward-facing, fairly regular clumps, amongst which is defined a continuous system of space in the form of intersecting rings, with a greater or lesser degree of overall regularity. Urban grids were never inevitable. In fact, the archaeological record reveals many proto-towns with quite different morphologies.

The urban grid was, however, the first powerful theorem of urban spatial engineering. Its crucial characteristic is that it is itself a facility – one that takes the potential movement of the system and makes it as efficient and useful as possible. The grid is the means by which the town becomes a 'mechanism for generating contact', and it does this by ensuring that origin-destination trips take one past outward-facing building blocks *en route*. That is, they allow the by-product effect to maximise contact over and above that for which trips are originally intended.

In the nineteenth century, however, under the impact of industrialisation and rapid urban expansion, two things happened. First, to cope with sheer scale, the urban spatial grid was thought of as more of an implement than a facility. That is, it was seen as a means to accelerate movement in order to overcome size. Alongside this it was envisaged as a set of point-to-point origins and destinations, rather than as an 'all points to all points' grid, which is the product of an urban movement economy.

Second, the city began to be seen not as a grid-based civilisation, but as the overheated epicentre of focal movement into and out of the city, and as such the most undesirable of locations. A social problem was seen in the disorderly accumulation, in and around city centres, of people brought in to serve the new forms of production. Big became synonymous with bad, and density became synonymous with moral depravity and political disorder. It was this that gave rise to much of the value system of nineteenth-century urban planning, as well as the more extreme proposals for the dispersion and ruralisation of the city and its population.

Unfortunately, much of this nineteenth-century value system survived into the twentieth century, not so much in the form of consciously expressed beliefs and policy objectives as in assumptions as to what constituted the good city. For much of the twentieth century, nineteenth-century anti-urbanism provided the paradigm for urban design and planning. It would be good to believe that this may have now changed, and that cities are again being taken seriously. But this is not the nature of human beliefs when they become embedded in institutional forms and structures. Many aspects of the nineteenth-century urban paradigm have not yet been dismantled, and are still to be found enshrined in such everyday policies towards density, in novel ways of breaking up urban continuity into well-defined and specialised enclaves, in continuing to reduce spatial scale, and in separating and restricting different forms of movement. These relics of an outdated paradigm do not derive from an understanding of cities. On the contrary, they threaten the natural functioning and sustainability of the city.

Notes

1   The best recent review of these issues is S. Owens, 'Land-use planning for energy efficiency', in *Applied Energy*, 43, 1–3, Special issue on the rational use of energy in urban regeneration eds. R. Hackett & J. Bindon, Elsevier Applied Science, 1992; an important source on settlement forms on which she draws is P. Rickaby, 'Six settlement patterns compared', *Environment & Planning B, Planning & Design*, 14, 1987, pp. 193–223; significant recent contributions include D. Banister, 'Energy use, transport and settlement patterns', in ed. M. Breheny, *Sustainable Development and Urban Form*, Pion, 1992, and P. Hall, 'Squaring the circle; can we resolve the Clarkian paradox?' *Environment & Planning B: Planning & Design*, 21, 1994, pp. 79–94.

2   For a discussion see M. Batty, 'Urban modelling and planning: reflections, retrodictions and prescriptions', in B. Macmillan, ed., *Remodelling Geography*, Basil

Blackwell, Oxford, 1989, pp. 147–169. See also M. Batty and P. Longley, *Fractal Cities*, Academic Press, London, 1994.

3   B. Hillier et al., 'Natural movement: or configuration and attraction in urban pedestrian movement', *Environment & Planning B, Planning & Design*, vol. 20, 1993; and A. Penn & N. Dalton, 'The architecture of society: stochastic simulation of urban movement', in eds. N. Gilbert & J. Doran, *Simulating Societies: The Computer Simulation of Social Phenomena*, UCL Press, 1994, pp. 85–125.

4   In this sense, it is an instance of what Ian Hacking calls 'the creation of phenomena', which then leads to the evolution of theory – I. Hacking, *Representing and Intervening*, Cambridge University Press, 1983, chapter 13, 'The creation of phenomena', pp. 220–32.

5   The figures are taken from a case study carried out by Marios Pelekanos while a student on the MSc in Advanced Architectural Studies in the Bartlett School of Graduate Studies, UCL, in 1989.

6   B. Hillier, et al., 'Natural movement'.

7   A. Penn. et al., 'Configurational modelling of urban movement networks', 1995. Submitted for publication, but currently available from the Bartlett School of Graduate Studies.

8   In this study, each line segment was observed in total for about 50 minutes, spread during five different time periods: 8–10 am, 10–12 noon, 12–2 pm, 2–4 pm and 4–6 pm. The data is therefore of very high quality. Experiments have shown however, that comparatively short periods of observation can be sufficient where there are reasonable numbers of people to be observed. In sparse environments, more protracted observations are required.

9   See for example A. Penn & B. Hillier, 'Configurational modelling' (see n. 7).

10   Penn & Hillier (see n. 7).

11   This issue is discussed in greater detail in Hillier et al. 1993, 'Natural movement' (see n. 3).

12   This structure has also been found in small towns and called a 'deformed wheel', since there is always a semigrid, or hub, of lines near the centre, strong integrators which link this semi-grid to the edges, like spokes, and some edge lines are also integrated, forming a partial rim. This structure is usually the main public space structure, while less integrated residential areas form in the interstices form by the wheel. See B. Hillier, 'The architecture of the urban object', *Ekistics* – Special issue on space syntax research, vol. 56, no. 334/5, 1989.

13   Dr John Peponis of the Georgia Institute of Technology and the Polytechnic University of Athens, in conversation.

14   See for example Department of Transport, National Transport Survey: 1978/79 Report, HMSO, Norwich, 1983, Table 10.4, p. 71. (See also NTS: 1975/76 Report, Table 3.17, p. 37.)

15   R. Wagner, *The Human Use of the Earth*, New York, Chapter 6, for a further discussion see K. Flannery, 'The origins of the village as a settlement type in Mesoamerica and the Near East: a comparative study', in eds. P. Ucko et al., *Man, settlement and urbanism*, Duckworth, 1972, pp. 23–53.

chapter five

Can architecture cause social malaise?

Architectural determinism as a mind-body problem

There is a widespread belief that architecture can cause social malaise,
either by directly bringing about anti-social behaviour, or by inducing
stress and depression in individuals, or by creating vulnerability to crime.[1]
In fact, little is known about these effects. We cannot even be sure if any of
them genuinely exist. The long-term and large-scale studies that would be
necessary to settle the questions have not been done. As a result, although
these effects are widely believed in, they are equally widely discounted as
incredible, either on common sense grounds – how could building possibly
have such far-reaching effect on people's minds – or methodological
grounds – how can the vast variety of factors that can affect social malaise
be sorted out one from the other when they are all so inextricably bound
up together in the lives of the alleged victims of bad design.

From a research point of view, there are good grounds for scepticism,
at least on the basis of current evidence. There is a problem of method in
establishing any kind of link between architecture and social outcomes,
which studies have not usually convincingly broached. Housing is invariably a social process as well as a physical product. Both markets and
bureaucracies assign poor people to poor housing, making bad housing a
dependent variable in a process of social disadvantagement. How then can
we ever hope to extract any effects there may be from architecture as an
independent variable, when the social process in which architecture is
embedded is already likely to be operating with architecture as a dependent variable? In short, if we do find bad design associated with social disadvantagement, how can we ever be sure that the former is determining –
or even contributing to – the latter, when the broader social process is likely already to have brought about the association of both? Since all we can
study are real cases, and every estate or housing area selected for study will
already be a continuing social process, it is not clear how this difficulty
can ever be circumvented.

If this were not enough, there is a second difficulty, no less fundamental, but theoretical – even philosophical – rather than methodological.
Building is the creation of a physical and spatial milieu. If we are to believe
that this physical milieu can somehow invade people's minds and have
effects that are strong and systematic enough to influence behaviour, then

we must have some conception of a plausible chain of sensorial or mental events through which this could come about. There are no credible models for such mechanisms. Even for individuals, it is hard to conceive of a process by which such effects could occur. The idea that they can be extended to the level of whole communities is frankly incredible.

In fact, the very idea of 'architectural determinism' – that buildings can have systematic effects on human behaviour, individually or collectively – seems to lead directly into the quagmire of mind–body problems which have plagued philosophy for centuries. Whether we conceptualise minds as immaterial entities or as physical brain states, it is equally difficult to see how physical objects like buildings could affect minds in such a way as to produce durable and systematic behavioural effects. Without some conception of how such chains of events might come about, it is difficult to see how research can proceed.

The two difficulties taken together – the methodological and the theoretical – combine to make architectural determinism a surprisingly deep and complex issue. However, it is hard to see how it can be avoided. To argue in principle against any kind of architectural determinism, that is any kind of positive or negative effects of architecture, leads to the odd proposition that it does not matter at all how environments are designed, since they are behaviourally neutral. This proposition seems even less credible than architectural determinism. We are, it seems, caught between two contrary and mutually exclusive possibilities, each of which seems as unlikely as the other. As a result, architectural determinism seems more paradoxical than problematic, in the sense that these rather abstruse difficulties stand in the way of a clear problem identification that would allow research to proceed.

Fortunately, when human thought finds itself in such situations, there is always a simple third possibility: that the problem has been set up in the wrong way. It is through this third possibility that both of these apparent difficulties will be addressed in this chapter. There are, it will be argued, perfectly credible mechanisms by which architecture can get into heads and come out as individual behaviour and equally credible mechanisms for generalising these to effects on communities. Moreover, in setting these mechanisms out with care, we can also show how the effects of architecture can be extricated from those of the social disadvantagement process. In other words, the methodological and theoretical problems can be solved together because they stand or fall together. The two can be reformulated, and converted from a form in which neither can be solved into one in which both are, if not obviously solvable, then at least tractable to systematic enquiry.

A careful look at methodology

The argument begins with methodology. We must first be a little clearer about the methodological difficulties that studies of the effects of architecture on people have always encountered. Strangely, perhaps, the key difficulty has not so much been one of investigating what goes on in human minds. Architectural and social psychologists have generally been quite adept at this. The difficulty has been one of controlling the architectural variable, that is of arriving at descriptions of the differences between one built environment and another that are sufficiently precise and consistent to permit correlation with attitudinal or behavioural variables. Most studies have sought to solve this problem by physical descriptors at the gross level of the estate or block – size of estate, numbers of stories per block, number of entrances, existence of walkways, and so on. Unfortunately, it is exactly at this gross level that the social process of disadvantagement is likely to be most active. The only level at which it might be expected to be less active would be at the much smaller scale of the different types of location within the estate – this section of walkway, this cul-de-sac, this courtyard, and so on. However, the type of descriptors that have been used do not easily permit such disaggregation in a systematic way. It is partly as a result of the failure to control the architectural variable with sufficient precision that many suggestive results apparently linking architecture to social disadvantagement are challenged. The gross level at which the architectural variables are handled makes it easy – and proper – to argue that studies have failed to distinguish architectural effects from social process effects convincingly, because it is exactly at this gross level that the social processes are most manifest and easiest to point to.[2]

  This problem can be solved, if at all, only by treating both the architectural and social variables at a much finer level of resolution, so that the units of analysis are, at most, small groups of households – we can call them location groups – which are sufficiently large so that individual variation is not dominant, but not so large that social process differences between one location group and another are likely to be dominant. If it is the case that bureaucratic allocation processes and market forces alike tend to work most virulently at the grosser levels of the bad area, the notorious estate, or the unpopular block, then we may reasonably expect them to be much less obtrusive at the level of the numerous small groups of households which will be found on every estate or in every area.

It is exactly this finer level of resolution of both architectural and social data that can be achieved and made systematic by using configurational modelling of space, as the basic means for controlling the architectural variable. This allows parametric descriptors of spaces to be assigned at whatever level of resolution we choose. We have already seen that configurational properties of spaces are crucial to the ways in which space 'works' at the level of patterns of movement, and the knock-on effects these have over time on other aspects of urban form which are sensitive to movement, such as the distribution of certain types of land use, such as retail, and some types of crime, as well as the fear of crime. In the studies shown in chapter 4, the ability to control the architectural variable parametrically through spatial modelling allowed us to distinguish the effects of spatial configurations on behavioural variables such as movement rates from other possible explanations of the same phenomena. It was simply a matter of doing the analysis carefully.

Architecture and the virtual community

From the point of view of our present interest in social malaise, however, the regularities between space and movement that we have noted are at a rather 'low level', in the sense that although they are clearly 'system effects' from architectural design to patterns of behaviour amongst collections of people, it is not clear that they have implications for the forming of communities, which are 'high level' in the sense that they involve more or less complex structures of interactions and relationships amongst collections of people. However, in the previous chapter we were able to look outwards from these low-level system effects and find that they were

related to many other key features of urban structure, such as the evolution of the urban grid, land use distributions and building densities. In
other words, at the level of the city as a complex physical and spatial structure we were able to find a way from low-level regularities linking space
and movement to some quite high-level effects on the structure and
functioning of the city as a whole.

In what follows, the argument will be taken in the contrary direction,
and we will look for the possible implications of these low-level system
effects on the microstructure of the urban spatial environment, that is the
immediate spatial milieu in which many people live out much of their
everyday lives. The basis of the argument is simple. Spatial configuration
influences patterns of movement in space, and movement is by far the
dominant form of space use. Through its effects on movement, spatial
configuration tends naturally to define certain patterns of co-presence
and therefore co-awareness amongst the individuals living in and passing
through an area. Co-present individuals may not know each other, or even
acknowledge each other, but it will be argued that this does not mean to
say that co-presence is not a social fact and a social resource. Co-present
people are not a community, but they are part of the raw material for community, which may in due course become activated, and can be activated if
it becomes necessary. However, even without conversion into interaction,
patterns of co-presence are a psychological resource, precisely because
co-presence is the primitive form of our awareness of others. Patterns of
co-presence and co-awareness are the distinctive product of spatial design,
and constitute, it will be argued, the prime constituents of what will be
called the 'virtual community'. The 'virtual community' in a given area is
no more nor less than the pattern of natural co-presence brought about
through the influence of spatial design on movement and other related
aspects of space use.

Because virtual communities are no more than physical distributions
of people in space, careful observation can tell us a great deal about them.
First, virtual communities have certain obvious properties such as density,
but also less obvious properties such as a certain structure, that is a certain
pattern of co-presence between people of different categories and using
space for different purposes; for example inhabitants and strangers, men

and women, adults and children, and so on. Second, it is easy to establish that the density and structure of virtual communities is observably quite different in most housing estates compared with street-based urban areas, and seems to become more so in quite systematic ways as housing estates become 'worse'. Third, there seem to be clear associations between the nature of virtual communities in different types of environment and key outcome variables: how much vandalism and where it occurs, where crimes occur, where anti-social uses of space develop, and so on.

Through its low-level effects on patterns of movement, it will be argued that there are also high-level implications for space at the micro-level which come about through the creation – or elimination – by spatial design of the patterns of natural co-presence and co-awareness of individuals that make up virtual communities. Whatever the long-term effects of architecture are, it will be proposed that they pass through this central fact, that architecture, through the design of space, creates a virtual community with a certain structure and a certain density. This is what architecture does and can be seen to do, and it may be all that architecture does. If space is designed wrongly, then natural patterns of social co-presence in space are not achieved. In such circumstances, space is at best empty, at worst abused and a source of fear. If too much space in the local milieu is like this, everyday experience of others is an experience of a disordered 'virtual community'. It is this that links architecture to social malaise. The intervening variables between architecture and behaviour are, in effect, the design of space and the consequent use of space.

In this chapter it will be argued that through configurational analysis of space, coupled to careful observation of the use of space, we can isolate certain suggestive regularities in the structure of virtual communities, and show that these differences are the outcome of differences in the architectural design of space. Co-presence and co-awareness are therefore the key operation concepts, and the virtual community the key theoretical concept. These differences, it will be argued, are both systematic effects of the design of spatial configuration, and also far more important to the long-term development of the spatial community than has hitherto been realised, not the least because social scientists have normally seen social interaction as the elementary social unit, and co-presence as merely prior

to social interaction. However, the pattern of co-presence does result
largely from design and its analysis therefore offers the most promising
path from architecture to its social effects.

The formula for urban safety

We may begin by considering the results in the last chapter a little more
carefully from the point of view of the micro-structures of local space. From
hourly rates of pedestrian movement in the area shown in the study of
Barnsbury in chapter 4, we can work out the rates of movement per minute,
which is about the time it takes to walk 100 metres at normal speed. We can
then take the average line length, and work out the probabilities of co-presence
in space for individuals moving around the area. The comparatively long
average length of lines, coupled with the fact that the average movement
rate is around 2.6 adults per minute in this area, means that on average an
individual will be in visual contact with at least one other person more or
less constantly. In fact, for most of the time, a walking individual is likely
to be in visual contact with more than one other person. The merits of this
combination of numbers and length of lines of sight are obvious. It provides
the moving individual not only with the security of more or less constant
visual contact with more than one other person, but also with sufficient
warning of encounter to take evasive action if necessary. The interface with
others is both dense and to some extent controllable by the individual.

Now consider the parallel situation in one of the nearby housing
estates shown in chapter 4. Here the mean encounter rate in the estate
interior is .272, an order of magnitude less than in the street area, even
though the streets surrounding the estate approximate the rates in the
street area. It is also the case that the mean length of sightlines within the
estate is a great deal shorter than in the street area. From these two pieces
of information we may easily calculate that an individual walking in the
interior of the estate will be on their own for most of the time. The sparsity
of encounters, coupled with the shortness of sightline, also means that
most encounters, when they occur, will be relatively sudden, with little
time to evaluate the coming encounter and take appropriate action.

In these conditions, individual behaviour changes. We may illustrate
this with a thought experiment. Imagine an individual, x, living in an ordi-

nary street. It is midday. x comes out of his or her front door. A stranger is about to pass by the door. Another is slightly farther away, but will also pass the door shortly. A third is passing in the opposite direction on the other side of the road. In these circumstances, the presence of strangers seems natural. x even finds it reassuring. Certainly x does not approach the person passing the door and ask what he or she is doing here. If x did this, others would think x's behaviour odd, even threatening. Unless there were special circumstances, someone might even send for the police if x persisted.

Now consider y, who lives on a short upper-level walkway remote from the public street within a housing estate. Like x, y comes out of his or her front door, and looks down the walkway. Suddenly a stranger appears round the corner in exactly the same position relative to y's doorway as in the previous case the stranger was to x's. Due to the local structure of the space, of course, it is very likely that no one else is present. Unlike x, y is nervous, and probably does one of two things: either he or she goes back inside the house, if that is easiest, or if not asks the stranger if he or she is lost. The encounter is tense. Both parties are nervous. y is being 'territorial', defending local space, and the stranger is being asked for his or her credentials.

Now the curious thing is that in the prevailing spatial circumstances, y's behaviour, which, if it had occurred on the street, would have seemed bizarre, seems normal, even virtuous. In different environmental conditions, it seems, not only do we find different behaviours, but different legitimations of behaviour. What is expected in one circumstance is read as bizarre in another. So what exactly has changed? There seem to be two possibilities. First, the overall characteristics of the spatial configuration – not the immediate space which is more or less the same – of which the space y was in is a part has changed, compared with x's. Second, y's expectation of the presence of people has changed.

These two changes are strictly related to each other. Changes in configuration produce, quite systematically, different natural patterns of presence and co-presence of people. People know this and make inferences about people from the configuration of the environment. An environment's configuration therefore creates a pattern of normal expectation about people. These expectations guide our behaviour. Where they are violated, we are uncomfortable, and behave accordingly. What is environmentally normal in one circumstance is unexpected in another. This is both an objective fact of environmental functioning, and a subjective fact of 'description retrieval',[3] that is, of the mental processes by which we read objective circumstances and make inferences from them.

The behavioural difference we have noted is therefore environmentally induced, not directly, but via the relation between configurational facts and configurational expectations. One effect of this is that it can induce environmental fear, often to a greater degree than is justified by the facts of crime, because it takes the form of an inference from environment rather than from an actual presence of people. It is these inferences from the structure of space to the pattern of probable co-presence that influence behaviour and are also responsible for the high levels of fear that prevail in many housing estates. This is the fundamental reason that the urban normality of street-based systems usually seem relatively safer than most housing estates.

Let us then reflect on how the reduction of the mean encounter rate by an order of magnitude in the housing estate when compared with the street-based system actually occurs. Figure 5.1a shows a black on white of the space of the housing estate in question within its urban context, and figure 5.1b shows its global integration into its urban context. There are two aspects to the answer. The first is that the complexity and down-scaling of the spatial design of the estate ensures that natural movement is virtually eliminated. The simplest way to show this is simply to correlate movement with axial depth from the outside into the estate. Figure 5.1c is the scattergram.[4] This fall off of movement from the edge of the estate towards the interior is common to the majority of housing estates, most of which down-scale and destructure estate space in a similar way. It is noteworthy that in this case, as in other cases, the movement pattern directly reflects the layered local spatial system shown in figure 4.8 in chapter 4.

The second reason has to do with the number and distribution of dwelling entrances. In this estate, as in most others, entrances only occur on certain lines, and most of these are relatively deep from the outside. Each line will have perhaps ten or twelve dwellings opening onto it, and it will be connected to the outside not by other lines with dwellings opening onto them, but in general by lines without dwellings. In other words, even

Figure 5.1a Figure ground of
space of the housing estate.

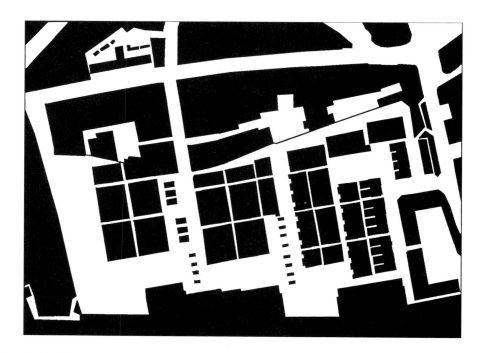

Figure 5.1b Global integration
of housing estate within its
urban context.

Figure 5.1c

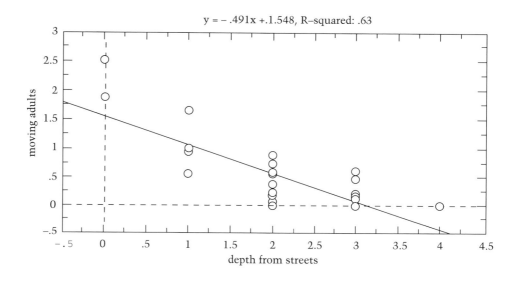

Figure 5.1d

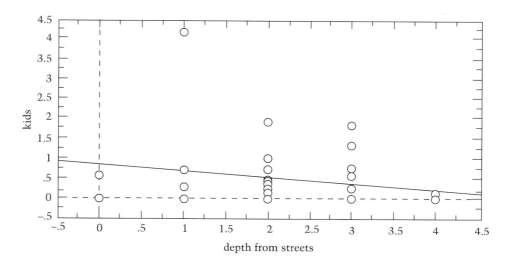

lines with dwellings will only have the movement on them generated by the dwellings themselves. Suppose there are two adults per dwelling and each makes, say, to be generous, four movements a day. This means less than ten per hour, or about one every five minutes – that is, the observed encounter rate. Since the residential lines are relatively short, the probability of encounter on any trip on that line will be no more than ten per cent.

In other words, the encounter rates on the estate, with all their implication for the generation of fear and nervous behaviours, are implicit in the design.

We can now see that the formula for urban safety must depend, for simple numerical reasons, on the presence of strangers as well as inhabitants, and is therefore a little more complex than 'defensible space'. We need to replace a static conception of space by a movement-based one. The main idea behind defensible space was that inhabitants who were static and in their dwellings had to be put into a position, by design, to have natural surveillance of the spaces leading to their doors in order to see and deter potential wrongdoers, who were strangers and moving. Our results suggest that what really happens is that the natural movement of moving strangers maintains natural surveillance on space, while the static inhabitants, through their dwelling entrances and windows, maintain natural surveillance of moving strangers. This formula clearly depends on the spatial configuration creating a strong probabilistic interface between inhabitants and strangers. In short, it is the mix of inhabitants and strangers in space that is the source of safety. Environments will tend to lack of safety and environmental fear to the extent that they separate the two. Put more succinctly, the formula for urban safety is a certain aspect of the structure of the virtual community – that is the pattern of probabilistic interfaces – created by spatial design.

Social structures of space and the L-shaped problem
Now the heart of my argument is that through more complex effects on virtual communities, these still rather low-level effects of space reach much further into our social lives than we realise. They can create or fail to create certain subtle and complex system effects, which are so suggestive that we might even think of them as the 'social structures' of space – though at some risk of criticism from social scientists who would not think of these effects as social at all. These social structures of space are simply generalisation of the ideas we have so far developed on how space interfaces inhabitants and strangers to different categories of people in general: men and women, adults and children, the young and the old, and so on.

These 'multiple interfaces' in space can be objectivised by using, as before, the simple statistical technique of the scattergram, though now we will be more interested in the visual pattern of the scatter than in correlation coefficients. Figures 5.2a and 5.2b are scattergrams in which instead of setting functional against spatial parameters, we set two functional parameters against each other, in this case the movement of men against the movement of women. By checking the axes for the average degree to which each space is used by each category, we can work out the probability of co-presence in each space. The correlation co-efficient thus indexes something like a probabilistic interface between two different categories of people.

Now the point of the pair of scattergrams is that the first represents the situation in the street pattern area shown in chapter 4, which is near the housing estate under consideration, while the second shows the situation within the housing estate. It is easy to see that the 'probabilistic interface' between men and women is much stronger in the street area than within the estate. In the street area, the linearity of the scatter shows that men and women are using space more or less in the same way, and are more or less equally likely to be co-present in all space. There are no spaces in which men are more likely to be present than women, and vice versa. Within the estate, the situation is quite changed. The irregularity of the scatter shows that many spaces prioritised by men are poorly used by women, and vice versa.

By using this simple technique to explore interfaces between different categories of people using space, we can show that ordinary urban space, even in predominantly residential areas, is characterised by multiple interfaces: between inhabitant and stranger, between men and women, between old and young and between adults and children. We can be confident that these multiple interfaces are produced by spatial design, because they are essentially a product of the natural movement patterns which we have already shown are predominantly produced by the structure of the urban grid. This is such a consistent phenomenon, that it is difficult to see it as purposeless or accidental. In fact, the more we find out about how space works socially and economically, the more these multiple interface patterns seem implicated in all the good things and the loss of multiple interfaces in all the bad.

One of the most critical of these interfaces – because it may be implicated in socialisation – is that between adults and children. Figure 5.2c is

Figure 5.2a Street pattern

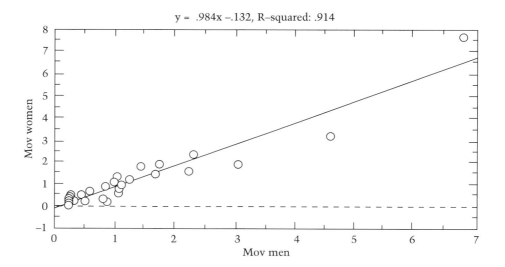

y = .984x −.132, R−squared: .914

Figure 5.2b Housing estate

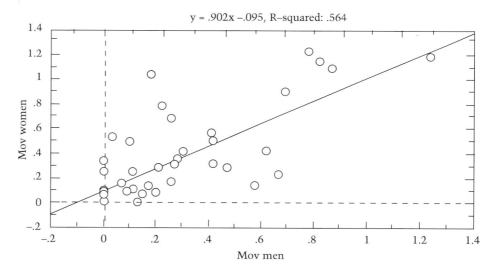

y = .902x −.095, R−squared: .564

the interface between moving adults and 'static' children (i.e. those who are more or less staying in the same space) in the urban areas and figure 5.2d the same for the housing estate. The scatter for the urban area is far from perfect, but it shows unambiguously that moving adults and children are present in spaces in a fairly constant ratio, with adults outnumbering children by at least five to one, and more commonly ten to one. Wherever

Figure 5.2c Street pattern

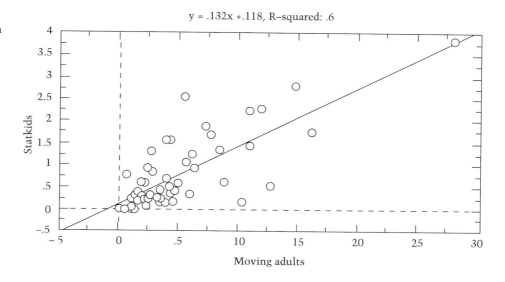

Figure 5.2d Housing estate

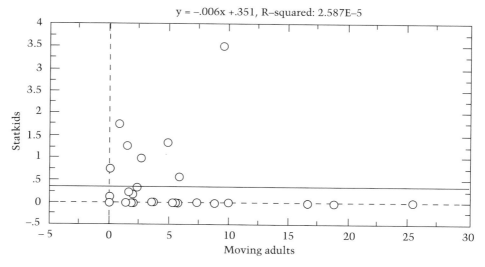

there is a child or a group of children, there are also likely to be significantly more adults in the space. This is not deterministic, but it is a powerful
enough probabilistic regularity in the system to be a fairly reliable experiential property.

Within the estate, the scatters show a dramatically different picture.
The L-shaped scatter shows that adults and children are completely out of

Figure 5.3a. A 'ten minute'
map plotting numbers of
adults on a route with each
dot representing one adult
per ten minute period.

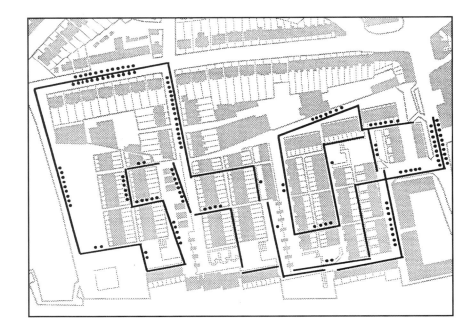

Figure 5.3b. A 'ten minute'
map plotting numbers of
children on a route with each
dot representing one child per
ten minute period.

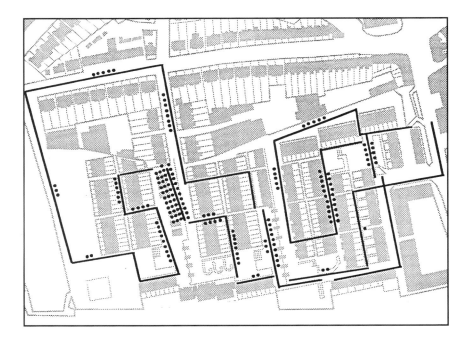

synchronisation with each other. This is not a random relation, but a highly structured non-relation. Spaces prioritised by adults are in general not well used by children and spaces prioritised by children are usually poorly used by adults for movement. This means that the probabilistic interface between the two categories is very poor indeed. This is why we call this the L-shaped problem. L-shaped distributions mean ruptured interfaces between different kinds of people. The more the scatter moves from a linear scatter to an L-shape, the less there is a natural probabilistic interface between those categories of people through the effects of the space pattern on everyday movement.

This effect may also be shown graphically in the plan. Figures 5.3a and 5.3b plot the presence of adults and children respectively in the plan of the housing estate by recording one dot per individual present during an average ten-minute time period during the working day – hence the name 'ten minute' maps. For adults the pattern is clear. Movement densities fall off rapidly with linear depth into the estate, so that in the deepest lines towards the centre of the estate, there is very little movement indeed. In particular, the north-south lines where most dwelling entrances are located have very low rates of movement. The children's ten minute map is quite different. The main concentrations of children are in exactly the north to south lines that are so poorly used for adult movement. In fact, the younger children use the constituted (with dwelling entrances) north-south spaces off the main east-west axis, while teenagers, especially boys, use the more integrated, largely unconstituted spaces on the upper levels just off the integration core. In general, we see that children tend to occupy spaces with low adult movement one step away from the natural movement spaces (such as they are).

The pattern becomes clear if we plot the presence of children against linear depth from the outside of the estate, as in figure 5.1d. The peak is not near the edge as with adults but a good deal deeper. This can be checked numerically by first calculating the mean axial depth of adults from outside the estate, which is .563, and then children which is .953. We can then recalculate subtracting one axial step per observed child. This yields .459, which is more or less the same as for adults. In other words children are on average one step deeper than adults. Because the effect of spatial

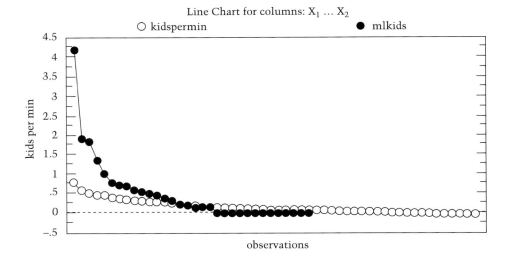

Figure 5.4

complexity on such estates is such that every axial step into the estate
means greater segregation from the surrounding area as a whole this means
that children are, on average, a little less integrated than adults, but about
as integrated as they could be without occupying the natural movement
spaces most used by adults. They are in effect as integrated as they can be
without being where adults are. This is what we sense moving about the
estate. We are very aware of children, but we are not among them. Again,
by checking the same distributions across housing estates, we find that
this is a fairly general pattern. Children do not seek out segregated spaces.
They seek out the most integrated spaces that are not used by adults for
natural movement. The loss of interface between adults and children in
effect depends on the availability of such spaces. In urban street systems ,
such spaces do not exist because all spaces are used to a greater or lesser
extent for adult movement.

   This is not the end of the matter. If we look at the actual counts of
children in the various spaces of the urban street area and the estate then
we find a very high degree of diffusion among the children in the urban area.
This can be seen in figure 5.4 which plots the numbers of children found in
each space from the most to the least with circles representing the pattern
in the urban area, and dots for the housing estate. In the urban area, there
are no significant concentrations, and very few spaces are without children

altogether. Numerically, there are no spaces without adults and only 11 per cent of spaces without children. In the housing estate, in contrast, children are much more concentrated. 41 per cent of the spaces have no children and the much higher overall average number of children are concentrated in a very much smaller proportion of the spaces, with some very large peaks, so much so that some spaces are dominated by children or teenagers. As we have seen, these spaces are lacunas in the movement system for smaller children and lacunas on the movement and related-to-entrances system for older kids. In other words, we can see clearly that children on the estate spend more time away from adults and in larger groups in spaces which they control by occupying them unchallenged. We might describe such a process as emergent, or probabilistic, territorialisation, and note that it is a system effect, the outcome of a pattern of space use, rather than the product of a hypothetical inner drive in individuals. At present, we can only speculate on the effects of these spatial regularities on the long-term socialisation of children into the adult world. At this stage, we can only note that children spend longer times in larger groups, well away from natural surveillance by adults. Not surprisingly perhaps these patterns have also been correlated with patterns of petty crime and vandalism.[5]

More worryingly, observations of other 'interfaces', admittedly less rigorous than the one reported above, have suggested that other, more obviously anti-social uses of space also follow similar patterns, in that these uses tend to concentrate not on the most integrated lines of natural movement, nor on the most segregated lines, but on the most integrated lines available that are not dominated by natural movement. Anti-social uses of space seem to seek out the most integrated spaces available after those taken up by natural movement.

Other estates

What is clear is the generality of the loss of interfaces and the relation of this to the degree of integration of an estate. These findings are due to the work of a doctoral student in the Bartlett, Xu Jianming. He studied ten housing estates, including the one above, selected to cover a range of morphological types and historical periods since the second world war. He

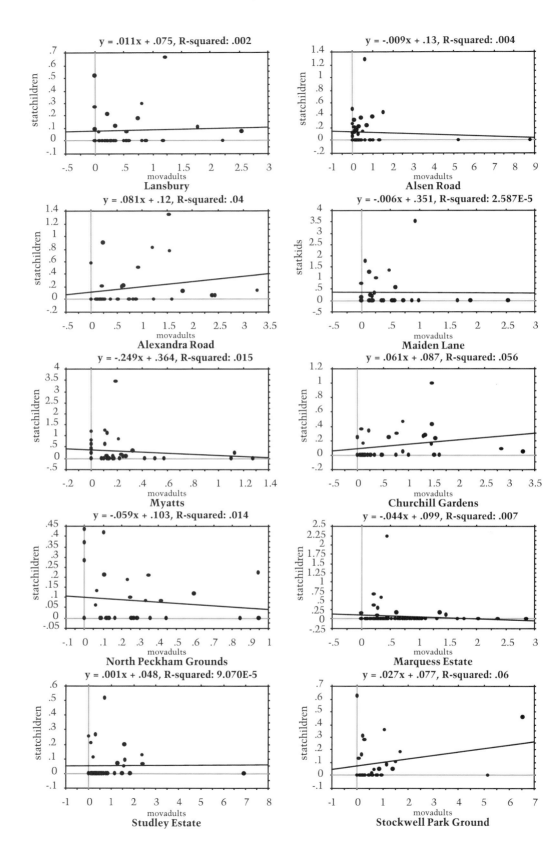

Figure 5.5

divides his types in to three main historical phases. His early period covers the typical mixed high- and low-rise estates of the early modern post-war period, his second the 'streets in the air' phase, when designers, following the criticism of early modern solutions by Team 10 and others, sought to recreate above the ground the space and space use types characteristic of traditional streets, and his third the neo-vernacular phase, when designers retreated from above-ground solutions and tried to recreate traditional space at ground level, though usually with over-complex, labyrinthian designs imitating imaginary small town and village space types.

The full range of this still incomplete study will not be reviewed here. However, as part of his research Xu observed space use and move-ment patterns, and plotted scattergrams of interfaces between all major constituencies of space users. The results are quite remarkable, from two points of view. First, the L-shaped scatter for the moving adults to static children relation is highly general, though occurring to a different degree, as shown in the series of scatters for the ground level of estates in figure 5.5. Second, the degree to which the L-shaped scatter is present, as indi-cated by a poorer correlation coefficient (the effect can also be checked visually), is strongly correlated with the degree of internal integration of the estate, that is, not with its degree of integration into the surrounding area, but with the degree of integration of the internal structure, as shown in figure 5.6a. The L-shaped factor was also correlated against the average 'feelgood' rank of the estates, an admittedly dubious measure obtained by asking researchers familiar with all the estates to rank them in 'feelgood' order. The correlation is strong, as in figure 5.6b, and does correlate well with common reaction to the estates noted by observers.

Even more remarkably, in another study of the King's Cross area [6] in which seven housing areas and three housing estates were studied, again (including the present estate), adult movement against static children was plotted separately for all street areas and estates. The results are shown in the scattergrams in figures 5.6c and 5.6d. Nothing could more graphically express how dramatically the interface between adults and children changes from ordinary streets to housing estates. Without exception, the spaces in the estates have concentrations of children where there are few adults, while in streets this is never the case.

Figure 5.6

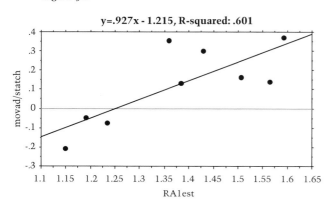

a Integration of ground level estate against
adult-child interface.

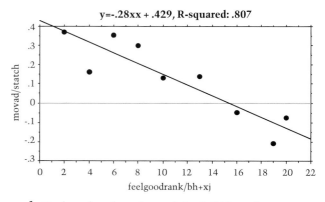

b Feelgood rank against adult-child interface

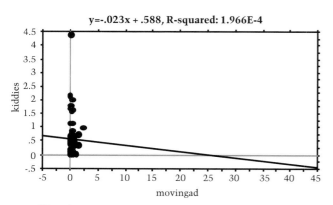

c Housing estates

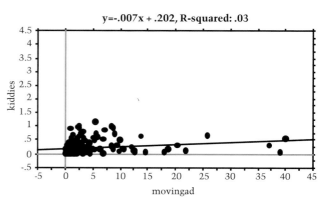

d Street-based housing areas

Citizens and space explorers

How can we generalise these results? The evidence suggests that the users of space naturally tend to divide themselves into two kinds: ordinary citizens, who use space as an everyday instrument to go about their business; and space explorers, like children, who are not so intent on everyday goals, and whose spatial purposes are essentially about discovering the potential of space – just as children's games like hide and seek explore potentials of space.[7] Now in ordinary urban space children are constrained by the spatial pattern to use space in ways which are not too dissimilar to those of adults. There simply is no other space available, except space specially provided like parks and playgrounds, and so children in the streets tend to remain within the scope of the multiple interfaces. When presented with exploration opportunities, however, children quickly find the lacunas in the natural movement system, creating probabilistic group territories which then attract others, and this usually occurs in the most integrating lacunas in the natural movement system.

Children are not the only space explorers. Junkies and methsheads are also space explorers, as in their way are muggers and burglars. Junkies and methsheads, however, like children, are social space explorers, and use space to create and form localised social solidarities. I suggest that all social space explorers tend to follow the same principle of occupying the most integrating lacunas available in the natural movement system. On an admittedly all too cursory examination of evidence it may even be conjectured that it is where the design of space is such that the lacunas in the natural movement system occur in the local integration core itself that an explosive potential is created. In spite of their huge differences in spatial geometry and density, from a syntactic point of view both the Broadwater Farm estate in north London and the Blackbird Leys estate in ex-urban Oxford, both loci of notorious, and notoriously sudden, riots share this structural feature in common.

It seems a characteristic of such space structures that when natural movement retreats from the integration core, as it does in both after the closing of shops, then the integration core becomes dominated not by multiple interfaces, but by its opposite: the domination of space use by a single category of user, in these cases teenage boys and youths. It is in such cases that confrontations seem to develop which easily turn into worse disorder. This is not to say of course that spatial design causes the eventual explosion into riot. It does not. But it does seem likely that badly designed space can create a pathology in the ways in which space is used, which a random spark may then ignite. Space does not direct events, but it does shape possibility. We should perhaps be no more surprised at the form anti-social events take in Blackbird Leys or Broadwater Farm than we should be surprised if people windsurf on open water or skateboard under the South Bank walkways.

The more common outcome by such unwelcome effects of spatial design is however chronic rather than acute. The pattern of space use in itself creates unease, untidiness and in due course fear, but not riot. We do not then need to invoke the deficiencies of state education, or the welfare state, or the decline in family life to understand these phenomena. They can be produced among ordinary families provided they live in extraordinary spatial conditions. They are systematic products of the pattern of space use arising in specific spatial conditions.

Distinguishing social from architectural effects

Before drawing too many premature conclusions, let us look again at the original housing estate from the point of view of distinguishing the effects of architecture from those of social processes. We may do this because it is one of the few cases where we have not only spatial and space use data, as we have seen, but also extensive social data gained from a study [8] carried out by others and aimed at diagnosing the cause of the estate's apparent precipitate decline from wonder estate to 'problem estate' in a little over four years.

The estate is a visually striking, all white and low rise, the last throw, it has been said, of the Camden school of modernism. It opened in 1983 to praise not only from critics but also from the new residents, 80 per cent of whom approved the hyper-modern white architecture, using words from 'palace, paradise, fantastic' to 'modern, clean, bright' . Less than five years later, the social survey commissioned under urgent pressure from local police reports, reported that '71 per cent (of residents) give descriptions of the estate in negative terms, often with a menacing element: prison, concentration camp, forbidden city, criminal dreamland, battery farm, mental institution in southern Spain…' How had such a change in reported attitudes come about?[9]

In fact, a closer examination of the evidence [10] showed that one thing that had happened was that those who had interpreted the evidence provided by the social survey had indulged in a certain amount of 'architectural licence'. Most of the negative comments about the estate turned out to be about 'rubbish and dirt' and other management failures, and only about 30 per cent had made negative comments on the architectural appearance of the estate, and of these only a small minority were as readily headlinable as the ones quoted. 69 per cent in fact approved the appearance of their dwelling, and opinion was about evenly divided on the appearance of the estate as a whole. It seems in fact a matter of some research interest that those who were commissioned to survey social breakdown on an estate reported exactly that, with all the trimmings, even where the data did not support it. It will be suggested shortly that this tendency to overstatement may itself be no small aspect of the processes by which estate stigmatisation and degeneration typically occurs.

A careful reanalysis of the survey data, coupled with the results of the spatial analytic and space-use study, in fact showed a much more instructive story. Figure 5.7a is a matrix showing the correlation of various attitudes on the estate distributed according to small 'location groups' defined by the lines that make up the syntactic analysis. There are in fact two quite separate clusters of attitudes. Negative attitudes to the estate such as 'not liking the estate' formed a dominant cluster, which we might call the 'affect' cluster. But these do not correlate with other attitudes where we might expect a correlation, such as feeling unsafe, or fear of crime. These form a quite separate cluster. Factors like finding the estate friendly were not correlated with either major cluster, but only with having children, nor was 'being on the transfer list', which correlates only with not having wanted to come to the estate in the first place.

The 'affect' variables were not on the whole well correlated with spatial variables such as integration or depth in the estate, but the 'fear and crime' cluster were so correlated, most strongly with depth from the outside which, because co-presence falls with depth, is the prime determinant

	6 adequate bedrm	pep/bedrm	10 est like sum	14 home satis	16a dwell app sat	feel unsafe	lot anx burglary	lot anx attack
6 adequate bedrm	1.0							
pep/bedrm	-0.999	1.0						
10 est like sum	0.837	-836	1.0					
14 home satis	0.981	-0.981	0.925	1.0				
16a dwell app sat	0.983	-0.977	0.892	0.983	1.0			
feel unsafe	-0.083	0.073	0.453	0.113	0.001	1.0		
lot anx burglary	0.102	-0.065	0.199	0.098	0.256	-0.086	1.0	
lot anx attack	-0.054	0.091	0.12	-0.036	0.111	0.025	0.983	1.0

Figure 5.7a Correlation matrix for variables: x1 … x8

	depth surround	loxanxburg	feel unsafe	21s dirty	children prob …	appearance di …
Depth surround	1.0					
lotanxburg	0.755	1.0				
feel unsafe	0.572	0.716	1.0			
21s dirty	0.741	0.823	0.604	1.0		
childrenprob…	0.879	0.708	0.649	0.742	1.0	
appearancedi…	0.804	0.755	0.669	0.68	0.932	1.0

Figure 5.7b Correlation matrix for variables: x_1 … x_8

of the structure of the virtual community. The 'fear and crime' cluster were also correlated strongly with 'finding children a problem', which was itself correlated with depth in the estate, as shown in figure 5.7b. In contrast to the 'fear and crime' cluster, the 'affect' cluster was spatially distributed, but not according to integration or depth in the estate. In fact it

Figure 5.8

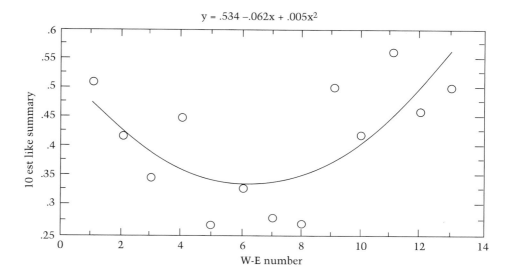

$$y = .534 - .062x + .005x^2$$

showed a most curious distribution. If this group of attitudes among location groups was plotted from west to east in the plan, that is, according to
the order of building the blocks on the estate, then the result is always the
inverted U-shape distribution shown in figure 5.8. Examination of the
data shows that this closely follows the changing policies pursued by the
local authority as building progressed on the estate.

This can be shown most clearly by considering the 'affect' cluster
of attitudes alongside two other variables with which they also cluster,
namely the subjective perception of overcrowding and the objective calculation of the number of people per bedroom in the dwellings making up
each location group. In fact, these two latter variables correlate so exactly
that we may treat them as one. As figure 5.7a shows, both subjective and
objective overcrowding increase as each block is built successively, and
both are correlated exactly with attitudes. The agreement between subjective and objective factors shows in fact that as building progressed, the same-
sized dwellings were being allocated to larger families, clearly reflecting
the pressures on the local authority to respond to housing need first and
foremost. After the first phase was complete, the 'affect' cluster of attitudes
begins to pick up, following the U-shaped curve shown in figure 5.8, and
in fact following the elimination of further overcrowding on the estate by

building flats and single person accommodation, rather than houses for families.

In short, the concentration of negative attitudes to the estate in the central areas of the estate is clearly related to increasing overcrowding (both real and perceived) as larger families who didn't ask to come to the estate were allocated to the same-sized houses. In fact, in this case we are able to distinguish the effects of the social process from the effects of spatial design. The social process – that is the changing allocation policies which sent larger and more single-parent families to the same-sized houses as the estate progressed – governs the dominant negative attitude cluster, but not fear and crime, which are largely determined by the patterning of space, and its consequent effects on the pattern of co-presence and co-awareness.

The contrast between the two dominant attitude clusters is then most striking. One group, which is less spatial in that there would be no obvious grounds for expecting these attitudes to correlate with space, but which do express the most general stated attitudes, are clearly the outcome of the social process. The other group, which we would expect to be correlated with space because fear and crime are spatially located events, are correlated with space, and in the way we would expect. Attitudes to children are also critical. That spatial factors are implicated in finding children a problem lends further support to the possibility that the spatial design of the estate and the objective facts of co-presence, that is the dramatic reduction in natural co-presence and the elimination of social interfaces with depth in the estate, are related to this attitude cluster. Other studies suggest that in general this is the case. Environmental fear is in the main an effect of the de-structuring of the virtual community. Such fear is an inference about people drawn from the structure of space. Fear, it seems, can be designed into estates, but only through the effects of spatial configuration on the virtual community.

Are the symptoms then the causes?

We may then in this case be fairly clear about the respective roles of space and social process in estate degeneration. How can the two be fitted together? It may be quite simple. First, the effects of spatial design are both systematic and quick to operate. Because they are systematic products of design, we must accord them some independence and probably some logical priority in the process. We do not require a pathological community to create a pathological use of space. It arises from consistent and predictable patterns of behaviour in particular spatial circumstances. However, we must also remember that the pathology of space produced by design is complex and social in nature, rendering many patterns of spatial relationship abnormal. Put simply, we can say that spatial design, operating independently, can create *symptoms* – that is the external manifestation of what appears to be a disorder.

What could be more natural than that people should infer the disease from the symptoms – infer, that is, a pathological community from the appearances of pathology in the use, and subsequent abuse, of space. Now the heart of my argument is that such inferences, though as natural as inferring internal disease from surface symptoms, are usually illegitimate. The symptoms we see are a pathological product of an innovative and poorly understood spatial design. Unfortunately, they can all too easily appear to be signs of an underlying disorder in the community itself. In most cases, these inferences are probably an insult to communities who are struggling against the odds. Even so, sometimes the inference will also be made by the community itself, as well as by outsiders. A process of social demonisation can begin, instigated by the spatial process.

The people most likely to infer a pathological community from pathological appearances are those with responsibility for controlling the estate: local authority estate managers, social workers, the police, and so on. If an estate begins to acquire a bad name with any or all of these, then it is very likely that this in itself will initiate, engage, accelerate or even precipitate the policies and signs of the unpopular, then sink, estate: allocation of problem families, increased, though probably sporadic, police attention, public expressions of concern, and so on. One must ask: when the managers in the local authority began to assign unwilling 'problem families' to the Maiden Lane estate in significant numbers, did they believe that they were assigning them to the pristine paradise of the first occupants of the estate, or to an estate that was already acquiring a dubious reputation? If the latter was the case to any significant extent, then it seems likely that the appearance

of spatially determined symptoms might actually help to activate the
very social processes of labelling and social stigmatisation which will in
due course ensure that the pathology of the community on the estate does
eventually come to pass. To assign the socially weak and disadvantaged
to places where the visual signs of disorder are already present, is a further
event confirming the inferences that people are already making from the
visible signs of disorder.

The apparent decay of the estate, we might suggest, initiates a
process of stigmatisation which is then multiplied by the actual assignment
of problem families. Theoretically, this implies that in a non-trivial sense
the symptoms cause the disease. The outward and visible signs of pathology are the preconditions and perhaps sometimes the initiators of the social
process of degeneration. If this is right then we must conclude that architecture should be seen more as a set of preconditions in which social
processes can trigger social pathology, than a fully fledged cause of social
pathology in itself. But nevertheless the independent effects of architecture are powerful, predictable, logically prior – and remediable. Probably
they don't work without the social process. But without architectural effects,
perhaps, the social process will tend less to pathology. Spatial design, we
may suggest, lowers the thresholds of social pathology.

We may reasonably infer from this that the ordering and use of space
is the linking mechanism between buildings and social effects. The use of
space is determined by the ordering of space to a far greater extent than has
been realised, and space use is more complex than has been realised,
embodying subtle social patterns which become a pervasive feature of the
experience of others in everyday life. Through architectural design, the use
of space can either develop in a well-ordered way, or in a pathological way.
Where it is pathological then it tends to become implicated in and even to
spark off the social process by which estates degenerate. As such, space is
neither necessary nor sufficient for social decline, but it is nevertheless
frequently a strong contributing or initiating mechanism.

Architectural determinism and the virtual community
If the sole effect of spatial design is to create some kind of – virtuous or
pathological – virtual community, then it seems that this would be enough

Plate 1

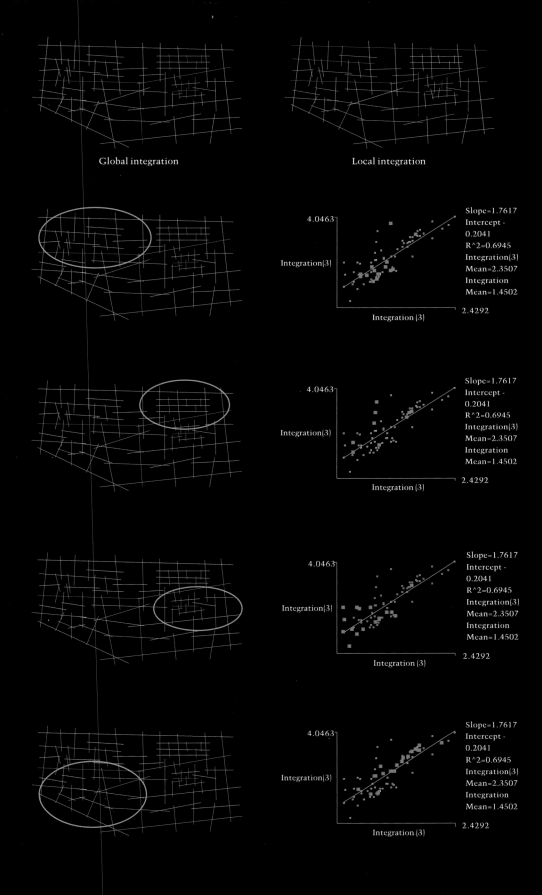

Global integration

Local integration

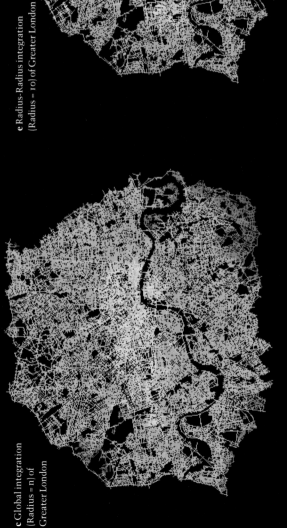

a Distribution of global integration (Radius = n) in the City of London

b Distribution of local integration (Radius = 3) in the City of London

c Global integration (Radius = n) of Greater London

d Local integration (Radius = 3) of Greater London

e Radius-Radius integration (Radius = 10) of Greater London

Plate 2

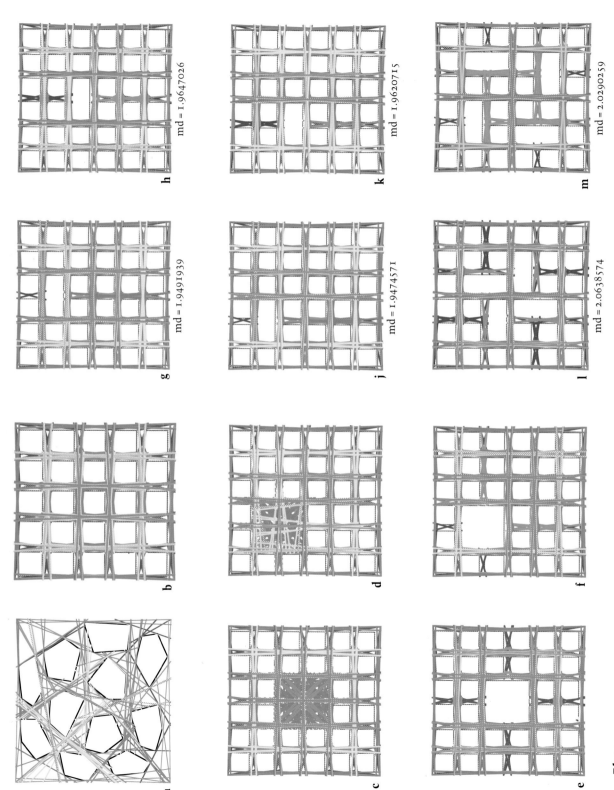

md = 1.9647026

md = 1.9491939

md = 1.9620715

md = 1.9474571

md = 2.0290259

md = 2.0638574

Plate 3

Plate 3 (continued)

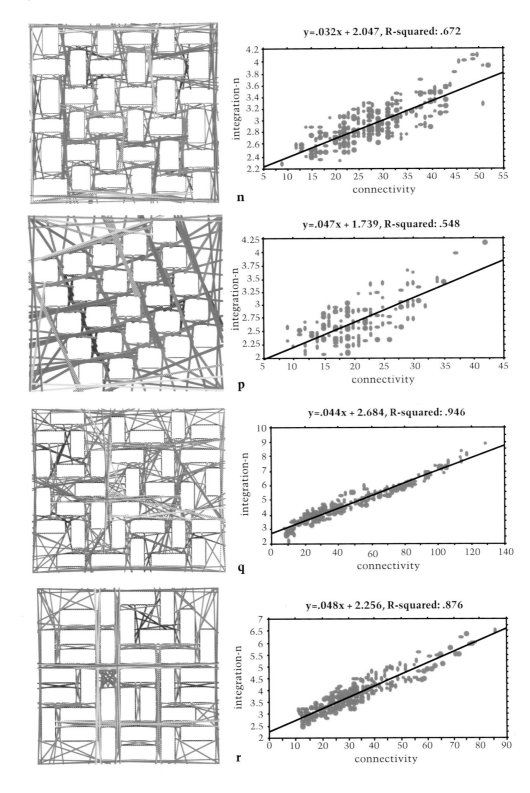

y=.032x + 2.047, R-squared: .672

n

y=.047x + 1.739, R-squared: .548

p

y=.044x + 2.684, R-squared: .946

q

y=.048x + 2.256, R-squared: .876

r

Plate 4

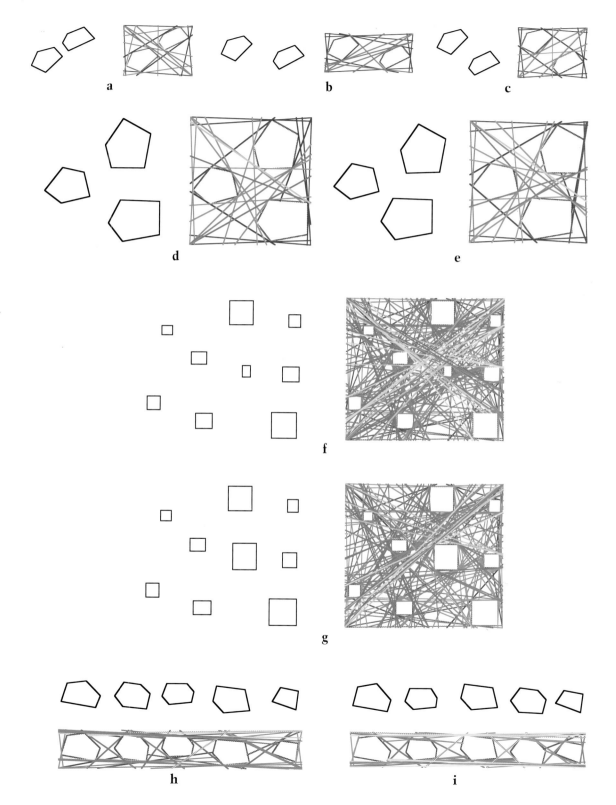

Plate 5

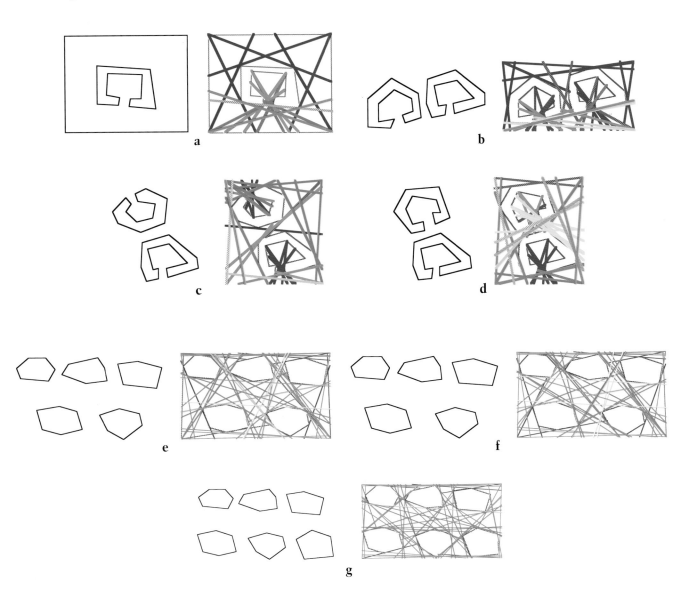

a

b

c

d

e

f

g

Plate 6

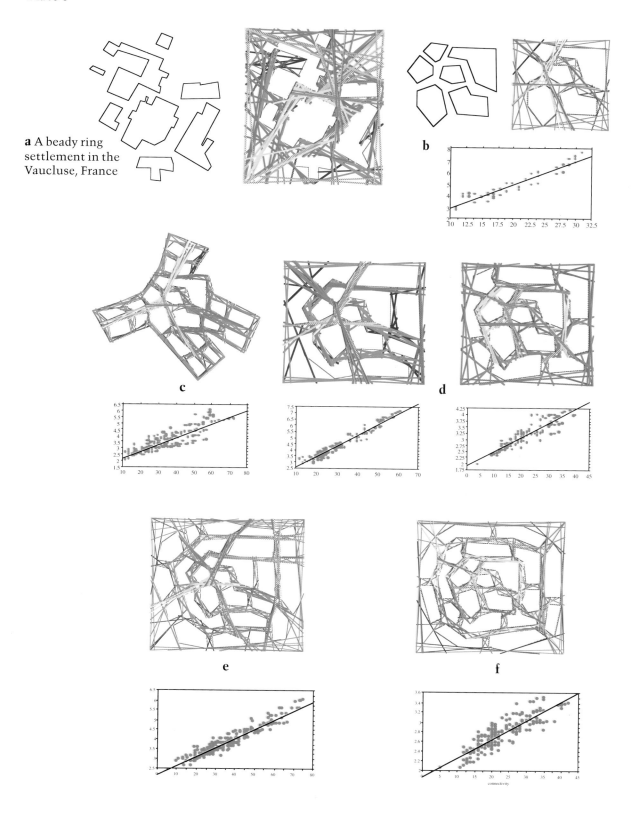

a A beady ring settlement in the Vaucluse, France

b

c

d

e

f

Plate 7

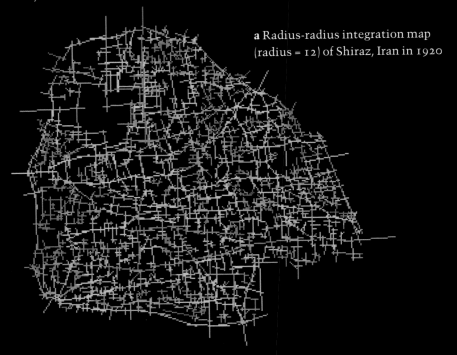

a Radius-radius integration map
(radius = 12) of Shiraz, Iran in 1920

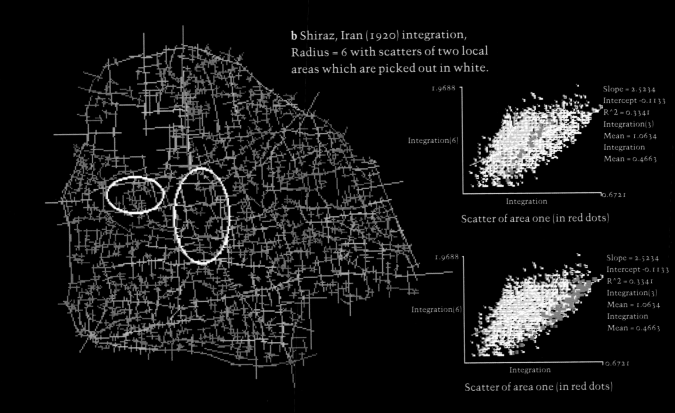

b Shiraz, Iran (1920) integration,
Radius = 6 with scatters of two local
areas which are picked out in white.

1.9688

Integration(6)

Slope = 2.5234
Intercept -0.1133
R^2 = 0.3341
Integration(3)
Mean = 1.0634
Integration
Mean = 0.4663

0.6721

Integration

Scatter of area one (in red dots)

1.9688

Integration(6)

Slope = 2.5234
Intercept -0.1133
R^2 = 0.3341
Integration(3)
Mean = 1.0634
Integration
Mean = 0.4663

0.6721

Integration

Scatter of area one (in red dots)

to account for all the apparent effects of architectural determinism. At the very least, we no longer have a problem with a credible mechanism by which architecture and society might in general be related. All the relations between space and society that we have noted as regularities seem to pass through this basic fact. This does not mean that space is a determinant of society, though it could come to that. A virtual community is the product of space and is an as yet unrealised community, that is, it has not yet become the field of encounter and interaction which most social scientists would take as the most elementary of social phenomena. Because it is prior to interaction, the virtual community falls outside what social scientists have conceptualised as society.

However, there are now strong grounds for believing that the virtual community, and how it is structured, may be a far more significant social resource than has been realised until now. The first set of reasons stem from the effects of spatial design on the structure and density of the virtual community which seem to be involved in the pathology of spatial communities. These effects are powerful not because space is a strong determinant of society but because space and its effects on the virtual community are pervasive and insistent. In their very nature they are never absent. They come to be built into the very detailed patterns of everyday life so that although they are rarely obtrusive, they are never absent.

In the last analysis, then, all of the apparent effects of architecture on social outcomes seem to pass through the relation of spatial configuration and natural co-presence. This is perhaps because movement is not simply the unintended by-product of spatial organisation but its very reason for existence. By its power to generate movement, spatial design creates a fundamental pattern of co-presence and co-awareness, and therefore potential encounter amongst people that is the most rudimentary form of our awareness of others. As we have shown, virtual communities have a certain density and structure, and are made up of probabilistic interfaces between many different types of person: inhabitants and strangers, relative inhabitants and relative strangers, men and women, old and young, adults and children, and so on.

Spatial design can change the structure of these patterns of co-awareness, and lead to such pathological phenomena as the radical reduction in the density of the virtual community so that people live in space which makes them aware of almost no one (earlier we called this the 'perpetual night' syndrome, since in some housing estates awareness of others during the day was little better than normal residential areas during the night), and which changes the structure of patterns of co-presence and co-awareness, leading to fear, the domination of some spaces by single categories of user and the emptying out of other spaces. The long-term effects of these 'social structures of space' are perhaps the key to the spatial pathology of communities. We see now also that they were all changes in the structure of the virtual community.

Notes

1   For a recent review see H. Freeman, *Mental Health and the Environment*, Churchill Livingstone, 1984.
2   The two best known studies, Oscar Newman's *Defensible Space*, Architectural Press, 1972 and Alice Coleman's *Utopia on Trial*, Shipman, 1984 have both been criticised on these grounds.
3   B. Hillier & J. Hanson, *The Social Logic of Space*, CUP, 1984.
4   The movement pattern correlates strongly with integration, but only when the estate is embedded in the larger scale surrounding area and integration values within the estate are read from the whole system. With spatial designs of the type found on this estate, this has the effect that integration values fall off with depth into the estate, as shown by the layers in the dark point scatter. If analysed on its own as an isolated system, the correlation between integration and movement is poor. All these effects are common for housing estates.
5   Hillier et al., *The Pattern of Crime on a South London Estate*, Unit for Architectural Studies, UCL, 1990.
6   Reported in Hillier et al., 1993, referred to in Chapter 4.
7   See *The Social Logic of Space*, chapter 1.
8   See Hunt Thompson Associates, *Maiden Lane: Feasibility Study for the London Borough of Camden*, 1988.
9   Ibid.
10 B. Hillier et al., *Maiden Lane: A Second Opinion*, Unit for Architectural Studies 1990.

chapter six

Time as an aspect of space

How can space be ideological?

Frederic Jameson

Strange towns

Let us first establish the phenomenon which we will address in this chapter: the phenomenon of 'strange towns' – towns that seem to contradict all the orthodoxies for the construction of urban forms set out in chapter 4. Here, towns and cities were defined as variations on certain common themes. Buildings are arranged in outward facing blocks so that building entrances continuously open to the space of public access. The space of public access is arranged in a series of intersecting rings which are regularised by a greater or lesser degree of linearisation of space to form the – more or less deformed – grid of the town. Through this linearisation the larger-scale structure of the town is made intelligible both to the peripatetic individual moving about within the town and to the stranger arriving at its edges. The linear structure links the building entrances directly to a pattern of space which also links closely to the edges of the town. The effect of this control of the linear organisation of space is to create a structure in the 'axial map' of the town, that is a distribution of local and global 'integration', which becomes the most powerful functional mechanism driving first the pattern of movement and, through this, the distribution of land uses, building densities and larger-scale spatial and physical elements such as open spaces and landmarks. The essence of urban form is that it is spatially structured and functionally driven. Between structure and function is the notion of intelligibility, defined as the degree to which what can be seen and experienced locally in the system allows the large-scale system to be learnt without conscious effort. Structure, intelligibility and function permit us to see the town as social process, and the fundamental element in all three is the linear spatial element, or axis.

Strange towns are towns – and proto-towns in the archaeological and anthropological record – which appear to flout all these principles. Historical examples from pre-Columbian America include Teotihuacan, figure 6.1a, and Tikal, figure 6.1b, and modern examples would include Brasilia, figure 6.1c. How should we seek to understand these towns, morphologically, functionally and as expressions of social processes? First, we must address the question of how we should describe them at the same level as we have described more orthodox towns. Only when we understand exactly how they are different can we hope to find an answer to the

Figure 6.1a Teotihuacan. General map of the central zone of the city showing cruciform plan and location of the principal constructions

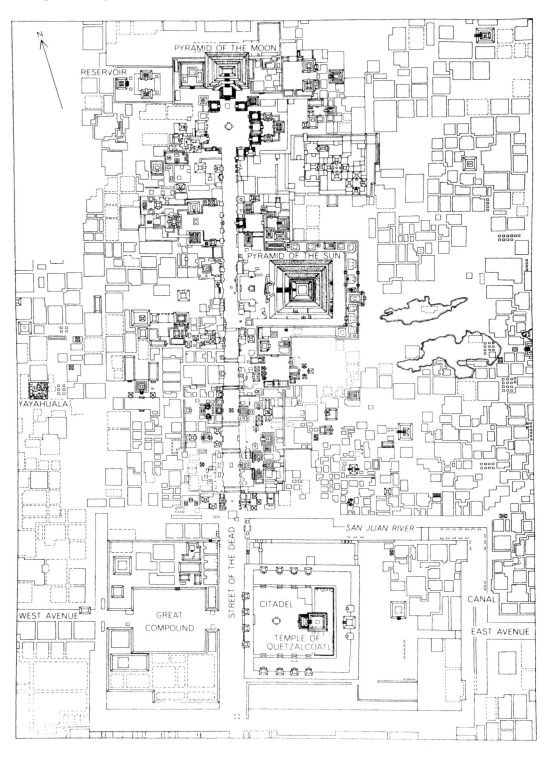

Figure 6.1b Tikal

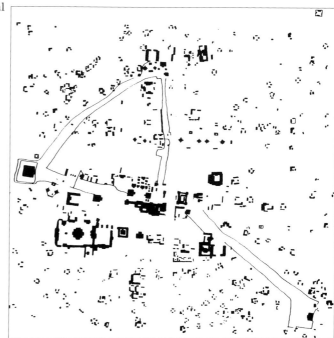

Figure 6.1c Brasília

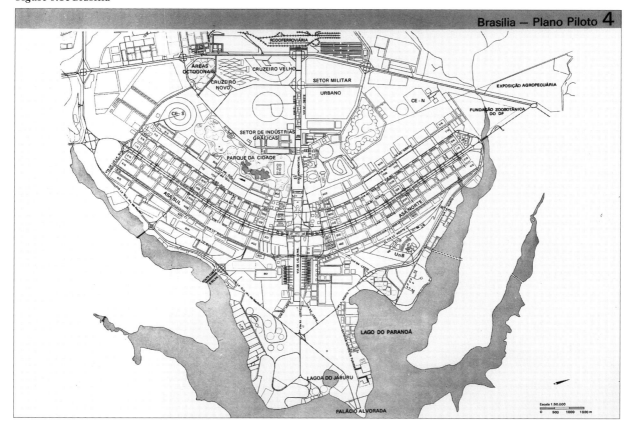

question as to why are they different – in some ways almost the inverse, one suspects – of the towns we are familiar with.

The answer will, I suggest, tell us something quite fundamental about the potential of space to express human intentions and to relate to social forms. This in turn will suggest a more familiar distinction: between towns which act as centres for the processes by which society produces its existence by making, distributing and exchanging goods, and those which act as centres for governing institutions, regulating bureaucracies and dominant ceremonial forms, and through which society reproduces its essential structures. Just as the axial structure is the key to understanding the first, more common type of town, so in quite another sense, it is also the key to understanding the second type – the strange town. Let us then begin with some thoughts about the axis.

The axis as symbol and as instrument

In common urban space, the most familiar property of the axis is that it usually passes through a series of convex spaces. This is the means by which towns create a more global awareness of the urban form in the peripatetic observer than is available from the convex organisation. We associate this property therefore with the practicalities of understanding towns well enough to move around them effectively.

Paradoxically, an almost identical description can be given to the use of the axis in quite different circumstances: to express the relation between the sacred and the profane in religious buildings. For example, figure 6.2 shows three ancient Egyptian temples, from a collection illustrated in Banister Fletcher.[1] In each case, as in the others in the Banister Fletcher set, the religious epicentre of the buildings is in the deepest space, that is, at the limit of a sequence of boundaries. In each case also there is a single direct line of sight passing through each boundary and linking the innermost sacred space to the most public space of the entrance. In *The Social Logic of Space* it was noted that the same phenomenon common in European churches and cathedrals can also be detected in such an arcane type as the Ashanti 'abosomfie'.[2]

When such common themes are detected we might of course be attracted by a diffusionist explanation. In this case, it is barely conceivable

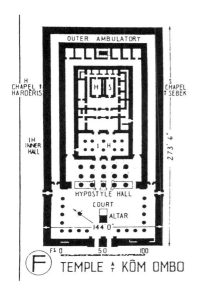

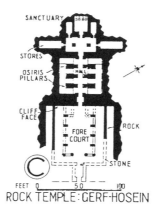

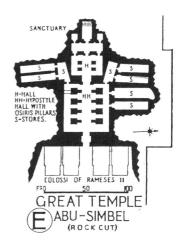

Figure 6.2

that diffusion could make links across such vast tracts of space and time. The 'genotype' in question arises, surely, from the discovery of the same potentials in space to solve a certain kind of commonly occurring architectural problem: how to combine the need for the sacred to be separated from the everyday by spatial depth, as it always seems to be, with the need to make this depth visible and therefore intelligible to the people to whom the sacredness is addressed, that is, the 'congregation' of that particular sacredness. The fact that it is common practice for this distant visibility to be replaced by concealment at certain times of the ritual calendar supports this analysis.

What then do profane urban spaces, in which lines pass through a series of spaces to guide movement and to make them intelligible, have in common with sacred spaces where the same axial device is used to express the sacred? Are the spatial phenomena really the same and dependent entirely on the context for their interpretation? Or are they in some more subtle sense distinct spatial phenomena? In one sense, they are of course the same phenomenon. What we see in both cases is a certain potential in space, the potential to use lines of sight to overcome the physical separation of metric or topological distance. It is the same phenomenon in that one of the two most fundamental of all spatial devices is being used to overcome what we might call the metric limits of our presence in space. If our visual presence was limited to our metric presence, then there is no doubt towns and buildings would not be as they are. They are as they are because we can use the convex and axial superstructures to provide visual extensions to our metric presence, and through them make available locations to which we might wish to go. Convex and axial structures, built on the basis of the metric geometry of space, are the fundamental means through which we make the structure of space intelligible, and pretty well the only means. We can hardly be surprised when similar elementary strategies are deployed in different cultures.

However, although the two types of case – the urban and the sacred – are using the same potential in this respect, in most other respects they are quite different. One is enclosed, the other open. In one the line of sight strikes the building at an open angle, suggesting continuity, in the other at a right angle suggesting that the line stops at that point. In one the line makes us aware of a whole series of potentials, space as well as buildings; in the other it seems to point to one thing only. In one there is no relation between any order present in the facades of the building and the shape of the space defined by the facade; in the other there is often a clear relation between the bilateral symmetry of the line and the bilateral symmetry of the sacred object. These distinctions show that the same spatial device is only being used in a very limited sense. If we view the whole 'configuration' of the situation, then, it is clear that certain common elements are being embedded in quite different configurations. The same syntactic elements, we might say, are being used in different contexts. We must then expect them to express different meanings.

Symbolic axiality in urbanism

Now consider the first of our strange towns, Teotihuacan. If one thinks about its plan in relation to the types of axial organisation found in ordinary towns, then it seems in most respects to be exactly the opposite. In spite of the fact that there is an underlying geometrical organisation in the plan – according to archaeologists, there is a 57-metre grid underlying the block structure – there is an almost complete absence of the types of

improbably extended axiality that is the norm in most towns. In the
evolution of the town plan, it is clear that, in most parts of the town, no
attention at all is given to extending axiality much beyond the individual
block-compound. The same is true of the convex organisation, and of the
relation between the convex and axial organisation.

However, there *is* axiality in the plan of Teotihuacan: the single axis
passing almost from one side of the town centre to the other, and directly
linking the Great Compound-Citadel complex with the Pyramid of the
Moon. Axiality, which is a generic and diffused property in most towns, is
here concentrated into a single axis. At the same time, the space through
which the axis passes is expanded laterally and more or less uniformly
to create an elongated convex strip more or less as long as the axis.

But in spite of its dominance, the main axis has very little relation
to the rest of the axial organisation of the plan. The line is more or less
isolated. It gathers no significant laterals. It connects to no significant
continuities. It is on its own, the only case of significant axis in the plan.
Similarly, it has no relation to building entrances. The edifices with which
it is lined are not buildings, but for the most part interiorless monuments.
Not a single one of the large number of compounds opens onto the main
axis. All entrances are, as it were, axially concealed in the labyrinthian
complexity of the bulk of the plan.

If we were to compare this to the plan of Brasilia in figure 6.1c, we
would find certain striking similarities. Brasilia has no formal or geometrical resemblance to Teotihuacan, yet in many respects the genotypical
resemblance is considerable. It too has a single dominant axis, one which
does not organise the plan by connecting to significant laterals (apart from
the 'road axes') or continuities, one which has no everyday buildings
opening onto it, and one which does not link edge to syntactic centre but
is end-stopped near the edge of the town, having passed through almost
its entire length. The rest of the plan is not as axially complex as Teotihuacan but it is complex in a way quite unlike most traditional towns.

Now consider the third case, the proto-town of Tikal, figure 6.1b,
a major centre of the ancient Maya. In this town we discern no global
spatial organisation at all apart from the 'causeways' linking the various
parts of the ceremonial complex together. There is of course a local logic

governing the aggregation of built forms at the very localised level. But this serves to point out the complete lack of global concern in how these elements are arranged on the larger scale.

Some comparisons and consistencies

How can we give a theoretical explanation of these strange phenomena? First, we must note one obvious commonality. All three of our strange towns are centres which are in some way concerned with social reproduction. Teotihuacan is dominated by symbolic monuments and ceremonial buildings, while its domestic arrangements appear to be geared to a quite substantial priestly caste. Brasilia is a purpose-built centre of government, intended to express the structure and continuity of Brazil. Tikal is described by archaeologists as a 'ceremonial centre' – though one whose role in the functioning of its parent society remains largely mysterious.

Spatially, however, the three towns appear remarkably heterogeneous. They seem to have in common only that they *lack* the spatial properties common to most normal towns. However if we look a little more carefully we will find that there is a certain consistency and even a certain structure in these differences, one which when explicated will be seen to have as natural a relation to the spatial requirement of social reproduction as the spatial themes of normal towns do to the needs of production. Social reproduction, we might say, requires symbolic forms of space, social production instrumental forms of space. Both express themselves fundamentally through how the axis is handled. The axis can be symbol, or it can be instrument. The key to strange towns is the conversion of the axis from instrument to symbol.

How is this done? And are there invariants in the way in which symbolic axiality is used to express the various aspects of social reproduction? Let us explore this first by looking carefully at some more familiar, closer to home examples. Figure 6.3a is the ground plan of the City of London as it was around the year 1800.[3] The most obvious thing one would notice about it in comparison with some of the previous examples is its lack of any underlying geometry. If it is irregular, then it is so in quite a different way to Teotihuacan. From the point of view of symbolic axiality, there seems to be little to speak of. The facade of St Paul's Cathedral, close to the western edge of the City, does have a tentative visual link in the direction of Fleet Street, away from the main body of the City, but it is half-hearted compared with what we have seen.

On reflection, we might take the view that it is the very *lack* of axial lines striking the facades of major buildings at anything like a right angle which is rather puzzling. St Paul's is a case in point. Apart from its vague axial gesture towards the west, the cathedral is axially disconnected from the surrounding city in all other directions – a property which many planners and urban designers have identified as a deficiency and sought to rectify by 'opening up views to St Paul's', as though the axial disconnection of the cathedral were an error of history. In fact, in the City shown by the 1800 map not only the facades but also the dome of St Paul's are more or less invisible at ground level from anywhere in the City. Such consistencies are unlikely to happen by chance. The axial and visual isolation of St Paul's seems, prima facie, to be a structural property of the City plan.

The group of major buildings in the centre of the City, the Royal Exchange, the Mansion House and the Bank of England, which are the only free-standing buildings in the City, are equally distinctive in their lack of right-angle relations to major axes. The most prominent of these, the Royal Exchange, in spite of its location at the geometric heart of the City where several strong lines intersect, does not stop any of these lines. On the contrary, the lines slip by leaving the building almost unnoticed. The Bank of England is even more axially obscured. Even the more prominent Mansion House is neatly avoided by the mesh of lines intersecting directly in front of its portico. More remarkably, in the modern plan after the Victorian modifications to the street structure of the city increased the number of lines meeting at this point from four to seven,[4] all seven major axes avoid end-stopping themselves on any of the major building facades (see figures 4.3 a and c). Again, this can hardly be accidental. On the contrary, to assemble so many axes and so many facades without anything remotely resembling a right-angle relation between facade and line is a significant feat of spatial engineering.

Equally puzzling is the consistency with which we find that minor public buildings, such as the many guild buildings, are unobtrusive in the axial structure of the plan. Take for example the Apothecaries' Hall, marked in black in the south-east corner of figure 6.3a. Not only is it located in a spatially segregated part of the City, but, also its axial relation to the street is so unobtrusive as to lead the exploring visitor to be taken by surprise when he discovers the beautiful court that intervenes between the building and the outside world. Why is so much symbolic expense in architecture invested in spaces which are almost invisible from the public domain, especially as it is in these highly localised spaces that one does after all find the right-angle relation between facade and axis which seems to be a hallmark of symbolic axiality? It seems that symbolic axiality is only applied on the most localised level, remote from the main axes where public life takes place, and confined to out-of-the-way corners in the urban complex.

After prolonged inspection, an exception to this rule can be found, though it is far from obvious. The facade of the Guildhall (to be found just south-east of the right-angle of the indent on the north boundary) has, in spite of being buried deep in the backlands of an urban block well to the north of the City, a more or less right angle axial line linking its facade directly to the riverside area, perhaps even to the river itself, though it is hard to be sure if this was actually the case at the time. The reason why this is hard to decide lies in the extraordinary nature of the line. Several times on its route from the Guildhall building to the 'Vintner's Quay', which lies at the point where the line appears to strike the river, the line just manages to squeeze through, past buildings which would break the line if they protruded even a short distance further. Such a series of narrow escapes, again, can hardly be an accident. But why should such length in a line be achieved so unobtrusively, as though the line had to exist but not really be noticeable?

Once seen, the Guildhall line looks as though it might actually be the longest axial line in the City, until we notice that it intersects with Upper Thames Street just short of the river, which turns out to be substantially longer. Again our ideas about urban normality are thwarted, because this line combines considerable length with surprising narrowness. It is of course the line that in earlier times linked all the quays together. We might then expect that it would follow the line of the river. But it does not. The river curves, but the line does not. Here as elsewhere it does not appear possible to explain axial structure through either of the common explanations of symbolisation or topography.

What then are the axial properties of the City of London? Is, for example, the property of 'just–about' axiality that we noted for the Guildhall line (and which was discussed in chapter 4) exceptional, or is it the general rule? We have only to look carefully at the main and secondary street structures to see that this property is present to a quite remarkable degree. Take, for example, the line that goes from Poultry (at the eastern end of Cheapside) to half way down Leadenhall Street in the east part of the plan, skimming the surfaces of buildings both to the south and to the north of the line as it goes. Or the line that links the lower end of Bishopsgate to its wider market area in the south. Or the line that links Smithfield to Ludgate Hill. Or the narrow alley line that links Birchin Lane to the interior of the block bounded by Cornhill and Gracechurch Street. 'Just about' axiality is, it seems, a consistent property of the spatial structure of the City at several scale levels. Nor does it quite end there. Where we do not find 'just-about' lines linking key places, then we often find that there are two 'just-about' lines making the link. This is particularly true in the smaller-scale back areas and the system of allegedly 'labyrinthian' back alleys, which for this reason are not in fact labyrinthian at all. This 'two-step' logic of 'just-about' axial lines imparts a natural intelligibility to these seemingly complex sub-areas.

The social reasoning behind this 'two-step, just-about' axial logic is not hard to conjecture. It has the simple effect that when you are going from one 'place' – be it a slightly larger space, or a major line, or a key building – to another, then there is always likely to be if not a point from which both origin and destination can be seen then at least a section of line from which both are visible. Since we can also see that each line passes through a series of convex spaces, and that each convex space, however small, will usually have building entrances opening onto it,[5] we can see that the axial organisation and convex organisation of space combine with the location of building entrances to create a consistent type of pattern yielding both intelligibility and order out of what might otherwise seem a formless aggregation of buildings.

Once we see this, then it is easy to see that the City has everywhere if not a two-step axial logic then at least a few-step axial logic. Axial organisation is consistently used to make larger-scale links from one place to another than the apparent irregularity of the plan would initially suggest. Axiality is used, we might say, coupled to the convex and building entrances properties we have noted, as the general means to provide larger-scale intelligibility and spatial orientation in a system that appears from other points of view to be rather freely growing. 'Just-about' axiality is the product of this minimalist approach to the problem of global form in urban layouts. Even more strikingly, it is the means of linking the local 'place' to the global structure and through this of achieving that compression of scales – the sense of being in a locally identifiable 'place' and part of a much larger 'city' at one and the same time and by the same spatial means – which is the distinctive excellence of good urban design.

But this axial compression of scales goes beyond the creation of internal coherence in the space of the City. It is also the means by which interior and exterior, heart and periphery, are brought into a direct relation. Distance from edge to centre is, as it were, obliterated by the repetition of the 'few step' trick on the fatter spaces that define the major routes into and through the City – Cheapside, Bishopsgate, Aldgate High Street, Gracechurch Street, and so on. It is notable that these edge-to-centre fatter spaces do not, as we have already noted, contain the longest lines in the City. Intelligibility through axiality is not simply a matter of length. These fatter spaces by their very amplitude lend emphasis to the marginal axial displacement and the shading of building surfaces which is the architectural essence of the two step logic and the means by which the abstract principle of axial connection is converted into a style in the architecture of urbanity. These larger spaces stand for this style because it exemplifies it most clearly in the overall structure of the City.

As we saw in chapter 4, it is also this profound architecture underlying the plan that creates the pattern of natural movement in the city. And of course this is the key to its logic. Space in the city is *about* movement. It does not seek to express the relations of major buildings to each other. It seeks to minimise the effect of buildings, even the largest and most public, on the pattern of movement on which the life of the city as a centre of business always crucially depended. In the city therefore space is fundamentally instrumental, and the axis its primary instrument. Its symbolic

and ideological role is subordinated – though never eliminated – by
the dominance of the practical. The axis is – can be – both symbol and
instrument. Here, it is primarily instrument.

Does this mean then that axiality is doomed to the ambiguity that
renders so much of architecture opaque to analysis. I do not believe so.
The ambiguity is a structured ambiguity and the architectural conditions
in which axiality takes on a predominantly symbolic or instrumental form
are, I suggest, quite strictly defined. To understand this, we must look
closely not only at the axiality of space itself, but at the buildings and
their facades which are, in the last analysis, the only means by which
these spatial differences are created.

Consider for example London's other city, the centre of government in
Westminster, again as it was around 1800 before the Victorian 'modernisation' of the plan (see figure 6.3b). At first sight, the plan appears rather
less irregular than the City of London, largely due to a sense of greater
rectilinearity underlying the block structure. This should not, however,
lead us to misread its axial structure. If we look for long lines, then there
turn out to be relatively few, and their extension seems much less pronounced than in the City of London. Looking more closely, we see that
more links just fail to be axially direct, and in many cases this appears to
be directly related to the greater rectilinearity of the plan. In retrospect
we can see that the greater geometric deformity of the City of London
plan gave a greater sinuousness to the space which in turn gave rise to
greater rather than less axial extension. In Westminster, lines are on the
whole shorter than in the City. This all but eliminates any sense of a two-
step logic, and this in turn increases the sense that the parts of
Westminster are more separated from each other. This can be confirmed
by an 'integration' analysis, which shows that Westminster is in fact substantially less integrated than the City of London.

The longer lines that we do find are, however, very interesting. One
of them, Tothill Street, is both the most integrated line in Westminster and
the line which strikes the main facade of the Abbey, albeit slightly off centre.
It is also, in the sense that was common in the City of London, a 'just-about'
line. Another 'just about' line, King Street, strikes the northern facade of
the Abbey, this time full centre. This line is not an integrator within

Figure 6.3a

Westminster, but it is a critical integrator of the Westminster street pattern to the areas to the north and east. In other words, the Abbey, instead of being axially cut off from the main City as was the case in the City of London, acts as a kind of pivot for the most important internal line and the most important internal-to-external line in Westminster. Neither line slips past the facade. Each is fully end-stopped. The Abbey literally holds the structure together by occupying its key syntactic location, while also of course creating a disjunction from a purely spatial point of view. The major building has, it seems, intervened in the urban structure in a dramatic way.

Now this axial disjunction by means of major public buildings is an architectural commonplace, but its very obviousness should remind us that it is exactly what did not happen in the City of London. The dominant

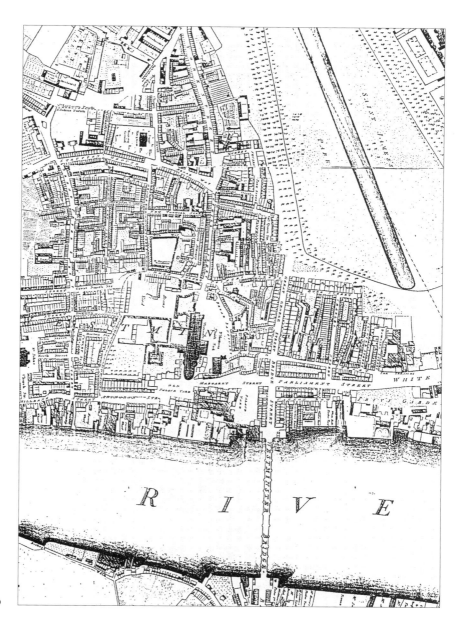

Figure 6.3b

axial structure was 'constituted' not by the facades of major buildings but consistently by the facades of the everyday buildings, which, wherever possible, opened directly onto the axes. Where major public buildings

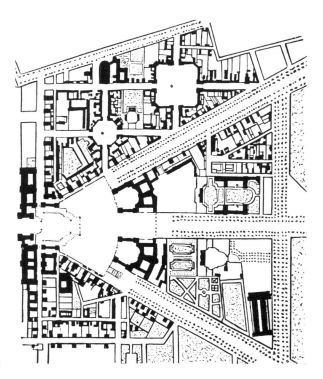

Figure 6.4

occurred they were treated no differently from the point of view of the axial structure. Even the famous City churches received no special treatment, but are embedded in the urban fabric and related to the axial structure in exactly the same way as the everyday buildings. The global, few-step logic of the City of London is created almost exclusively by the arrangement and orientation of the ordinary buildings. Responsibility for the space structure is as it were 'distributed' – and distributed more or less equally – amongst the largest possible number of buildings. Where major buildings received special axial treatment, it was usually to bury them unobtrusively in the urban fabric. In Westminster the public buildings are much more obtrusive, in spite of the overall reduction in spatial scale and axial integration.

But they do not yet dominate the urban structure in the sense we find in, say, eighteenth-century downtown Versailles, shown in figure 6.4. Here we find three powerful axes striking the palace head on, one at right angles, two at about forty-five degrees. All therefore lead essentially nowhere but the Palace. In terms of natural movement, the Palace acts as a negative attractor. The effect of this is immeasurably increased by two further spatial devices. First, the width and uniformity of the spaces through which the major axes pass, so that axiality is quite the contrary to 'just about'. Axiality is equal everywhere in the space. Second, the everyday buildings – thinking of these mainly in terms of their size and larger numbers – are unlinked as far as possible from the major axes. Following this logic to its extreme, of course, we end up with a space structure in which only the public buildings and monuments constitute the major axial structure, while everyday buildings are removed as far as possible. We are in effect back in Teotihuacan.

This formulation even helps us to begin to make sense of Tikal (figure 6.1b) surely one of the strangest proto-urban objects in the record. This we can now see to be an extreme case of such a spatial logic. All that can be termed a global urban structure lies in the complex of causeways and ceremonial centres that lie at the heart of the area. The scatter of everyday buildings is distributed, apparently randomly, in and around this global complex. They have no consistent spatial relation to the complex (apart from a consistent randomness), no relation to each other, and above all no relation to a system of space which might begin to constitute an overall urban structure. The disjunction of the ceremonial and the everyday, and of the local and the global, is in this case about as complete as it could be.

We may then attempt to summarise the complex of properties that seem to be associated with the axis as symbol rather than as instrument. There seem to be four headings: first, the degree to which axiality is 'just-about' rather than filled out into continuously fat spaces; second, the degree to which there is a few-step logic throughout the system rather than a one-step logic in some parts combined with a many-step logic in others; third, the degree to which strong and weak axiality is related to the entrances of buildings, everyday or public; and fourth, the angles of incidence of axial lines on building facades, varying from striking full on or glancing off.

Let me first suggest that there seems to be a rigorous social logic to these spatial choices. This social logic shows itself in the ways in which we find these properties concatenated in real cases. For example, the City of London combined 'just-about' axiality everywhere, with few-step (rarely one-step) logic, constitution of space by everyday buildings and glancing off angles of incidence of axial lines on facades. This is the opposite of the Teotihuacan or Versailles kind in which fatness is made greater and evened out along the length of the axis, one-step logic for public buildings and many-step logic for everyday buildings, constitution of major axes by major buildings and elimination of everyday buildings, and angles of incidence which are usually orthogonal, both creating the large-scale one-step logic and the small-scale many-step logic. We thus find a natural tendency for greater geometry in the plan – presumably implying a power able to conceive of a form all at one – to be associated with less integration of space and a greater tendency towards the symbolisation of the axis.

We easily associate the first type of concatenation with instrumental axiality and through this with urban situations in which the exigencies of production and distribution are the dominant social requirements. The latter concatenation is just as easily associated with what we may call symbolic axiality which prevails where bureaucracies or religious hierarchies, with their primary concern for symbolic expression rather than movement and communication, are the dominant forces shaping space, that is where the needs of social reproduction are dominant over the needs of social production. It is through the use of the axis as symbol that forms of social power most naturally express themselves through domination of the urban landscape. This is fundamentally why we have two types of city: the common type of working city, and the more exceptional type of city specialised by the need to reproduce the formal structure of a society.

Time as an aspect of space

But why these spatial forms rather than others? To answer this we must build a small armoury of concepts. In *The Social Logic of Space*[6] it was suggested that the concept of time is useful, even necessary, to the description of space. Two concepts were suggested. The *description* of a space was the set of relations – or as we would say now, the configuration – in which that space was embedded, that is which described how that space fitted into a complex of space: its relations to building entrances, its convex structure, the lines that pass through it, its convex isovist, and so on. The *synchrony* of that space was then the quantity of space invested in that description. These concepts were a response to the problem of finding a way of saying how two identical spaces with different named functions might be formally different from each other. The motivating case was a pair of hypothetical spaces, identical in shape and size, but one a military parade ground, the other a market place. Are the spaces the same other than in how they are used?

The answer proposed was that the spaces have identical synchrony – they have the same area in the same shape – but different descriptions – that is, the identical spaces are embedded in quite different syntactic contexts. The parade ground has the spatial relations of a military camp, that is, it is related to certain military buildings which are likely to be free standing and have a certain geometrical layout reflecting military statuses, and relations to camp entrances and ceremonial routes, symbolic objects like flagpoles, and so on. The market has the spatial relations of a certain location in a street complex and the buildings which constitute it. The description of the space is its social identity. The synchrony, or quantity of space invested in that description, is the degree of emphasis accorded to that description in the complex. Synchrony, we may say simply, reinforces description. The synchrony of the parade ground and market place may be identical, but the descriptions are different. Therefore a different description is being emphasised. Therefore the spaces are different.

Intuitively, it seems reasonable to use the term 'synchrony' to describe metric scale in space, since we must use movement, which occupies time, to overcome space, and since visibility substitutes for movement in this sense, expanding space metrically brings more of it into a single space-time frame. Underlying this there is a model of space in which space is seen and understood by a human subject who is essentially peripatetic. Any spatial complex is a system which can only be seen one part at a time and which requires movement to see and understand as a whole. To the peripatetic subject, to say that spatial relations are synchronised is to say that they are simultaneously present to the peripatetic observer within the same space-time frame. Therefore the fact of progressively moving

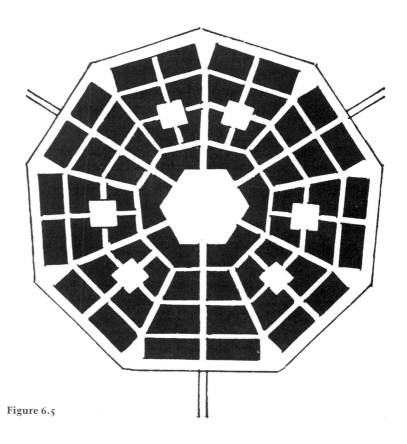

Figure 6.5

through a spatial complex such as a town or building successively syn-
chronises different sub-complexes of spatial relations. In these sub-
complexes, the larger the convex space or the longer the axial space
then the stronger this synchronising effect will be. Hence synchrony
as the descriptor of the quantity of continuous space within which
the same relations prevail.

    Now consider another distinction, due to a colleague of mine,[7]
between *structure* and *order*. Spatial complexes are intelligible to us in
two ways: as artefacts we move about in, and learn to understand by *living*
in them; and as overall rational *concepts*, which can be grasped all at once,
and which often have a geometrical or simple relational nature. The first
we may call *structure*; the second *order*. Town plans make the distinction
particularly clear. Ideal towns are dominated by rational *order*, and can be

grasped as a single concept. Most real town plans, however, lack such simplicities. They appear irregular, almost disordered – though they are not so when we live in them and move around them. On the contrary, it is the ordered town that is usually confusing 'on the ground'. Real towns, as we have seen, have 'structure' which we discover by living and moving, but not an obvious rational 'order'.

Now consider this definition in terms of the time concepts we have introduced in relation to two town plans. One the 'ideal' town plan of Palmanova, shown in figure 6.5, and the 'organic' layout of the plan shown in figure 4.3a. The ideal town can be grasped as a pattern *all at once* , or *synchronously* , provided we are in a position to see it all at once, as we are if we consider it as a plan on the page or from the air. The reason it can be grasped all at once is not so much because it has a regular geometry, but for a simpler and more basic reason: it is made up of *similar parts in similar relations*. Such compositions immediately reveal their nature because the mind easily grasps the repetitivity of the elements and relations that make up the form. It is this property of being made up of similar parts in similar relations we call *order*. We tend to associate it with the constructive activity of the human mind. Order is fundamentally rational. It can be grasped all at once because it is imposed all at once.

The 'organic' town has no such order. Elements can scarcely be identified, let alone repetitive elements. The same is true of relations. Very little repetition can be identified, if any. However, we now know that such 'organic' towns have powerful spatial patterning which appears to originate in function. For example, the distribution of integration in the axial map defines an 'integration core' which generates not only a movement pattern but also a distribution of land uses such as shops and residences which are sensitive to movement. We can call such patterns *structures*, and contrast them with *orders* because they have quite different, almost contrary, properties. Structures cannot be seen all at once, nor are they imposed all at once by minds. They are *asynchronous* both in their genesis and in the way we experience them. They arise from a lived process, and are intelligible through the processes of living in the town, and, most especially, by the process of movement. Without movement, an asynchronous system cannot be seen, let alone understood.

It is an empirical fact that, regardless of their relative prevalence in geographical or planning texts, by far the great majority of towns and cities in human history display more structure than order. The reasons are not hard to find. For the most part, towns arise for essentially functional reasons, and, naturally enough, evolve according to a functional logic. However, if we consider another aspect of urban intelligibility, that is the formal configuration of built forms, and especially of their facades, then we find that, intriguingly, matters are more or less reversed. Facades typically display a good deal of order, and anything we might call structure by analogy to the semi-regular patterns of the organic town is rare, if it can be identified at all. There is a simple reason for this, centred about the relations between space, form and time. Unlike urban space structures, which are asynchronous because they require the passage of time required for movement in order to see them piece by piece, building facades are, in their very nature, synchronous. They are intended to be read and understood all at once. They therefore do not require time for their understanding. Order, we might suggest, is as prevalent over structure in built forms as structure is prevalent over order in space. In both, both kinds of case exist, but order is natural to form because it is intended to be read synchronously just as structure is natural to space because of its essentially asynchronous nature.

How forms, and especially facades, relate to space is then likely to be of interest. Let us then consider space from the point of view of the facades of buildings. It is clear that every facade will be partly visible from certain points in urban space and wholly visible from others. Both sets of points form a shape, defined by all that can be seen from the facade. We can draw both shapes, and call the first the 'part-facade isovist' and the second the 'full-facade isovist'. To draw them we first project each vertex of the facade as far as possible in all directions from which any part of the facade can be seen. The combination of the shapes swept out by the two vertices is then the part-facade isovist, and their intersection is the full-facade isovist. Figure 6.6 shows a hypothetical case, in which the part-facade isovist is darkly shaded and the full-facade isovist lightly shaded. Evidently, the full-facade isovist will be the region of space from which the facade is synchronously visible for the peripatetic observer.

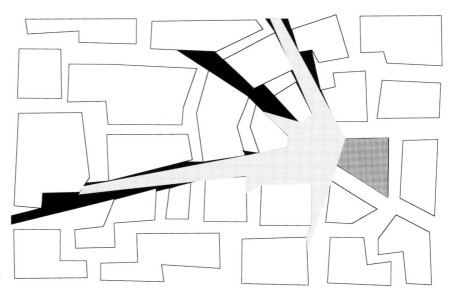

Figure 6.6 Facade isovist

Now let us consider the effects on facade isovists of different kinds
of axiality. First let us look at the City of London again, but this time
from the point of view of its facade isovists. Two points can be made. The
guild buildings are available to the street from rather short isovists, usually ending in right angles, and also usually ending in an enclosed space.
Interestingly, the only exception to the short line rule is the Guildhall,
and here the long axis also ends in an enclosed space, suggesting some
consistency in the rule for that type of building. Public buildings are in
general on larger-scale spaces, but have very restricted isovists which we
can for the most part only see sideways, and with a relatively small-scale
isovist. This is particularly true of the three major buildings at the heart of
the city: the Mansion House, the Bank of England and the Royal Exchange.
Major buildings do not seem to occur at the points where major axes strike
whole building facades.

This quasi-concealing of the public buildings has three marked
effects. First, the degree to which their views are axially synchronised is
very restricted. One comes across them rather suddenly. Second, one usually approaches them at an angle so that whatever order is present on the
facade is obscured by perspective. Third, and perhaps most important, the

effect of approaching the building sideways is that what one sees changes quite rapidly as one first arrives at the building and then proceeds beyond it. One might say that the effect of this type of facade isovist is that from the point of view of movement, the order in the facade of the building is never freeze-framed, but is constantly shifted and distorted.

Now consider how the contrary can be achieved. The most effective means would be a single long 'tunnel' isovist striking the building at a right angle. This would mean that the longer this tunnel isovist, the more protracted the time during which, for the moving observer, the facade of the building would be freeze-framed, and the more invariant would be any symmetry that facade possessed. By placing an observer moving through space on the axis of symmetry of the building facade, and extending the spatial axis as far as possible away from the building at a right angle, the presence of the symbolic building becomes more pervasive and more invariant. The more convex the axis, then, the more invariant would be this effect throughout the region passed through by the line.

We can also relate this to the global urban structure by bringing integration into the picture. The more integrating the 'symbolic axis', the more whatever is freeze-framed by the line would be dominant in the urban structure. The effect of converting space from instrument to symbol would be amplified by the fact that a large-scale object at right angle to a key axis will act as a negative attractor in the urban form, that is, whatever its degree of integration, natural movement rates will fall away in the direction of the negative attractor, though this may of course be compensated by the numbers of people attracted to the building for other reasons.

In short, the logic of the symbolic axis is in its way as consistent as that of the instrumental. Its object is not to organise a pattern of movement and through this to generate encounter, but to use the potential of urban space for another kind of emphasis: the communication throughout space of the symbolic importance of certain buildings or locations. The role of the symbolic axis tends to be focussed in certain locations rather than diffused throughout the form, but its role in creating the overall urban structure is no less powerful.

We can see then that Teotihuacan is built according to a 'formula' no less than the city of London, but the formula is different. In spite of initial doubts, its internal logic, and presumably its social logic, are just as consistent. Just as London is the expression of one kind of social logic, so our strange towns are consistent expressions of another.

Notes

1 Banister Fletcher's *A History of Architecture* (edited by Professor John Musgrove), Butterworth, London, 1987.
2 Hillier & Hanson, 1984, chapter 5.
3 The plan is by Horwood.
4 See Figure 4.3a in chapter 4.
5 See *The Social Logic of Space*, chapter 3.
6 Hillier & Hanson, chapter 3, pp. 95–7.
7 J. Hanson, 'Order and structure in urban design: the plans for the rebuilding of London after the Great Fire of 1666', *Ekistics*, Special Issue on space syntax research, vol. 56, no. 334/5, 1989.

Visible colleges

The problem of space according to Lévi Strauss

The previous chapters have studied urban space, the space that is, formed
by the relations amongst buildings. But what of the building interior?
How far can the techniques used and the lessons learned in the study of
urban space inform studies of the interiors of buildings more complex
than the house, where by definition, a more structured organisation than
an urban community is at work? It turns out that to study these relations
we must build a more complex model of what we are seeking, one which
takes into account how structured an organisation is, and how it is structured. Once we do this, we find that many of the principles learned can be
applied to the complex building interior. A crucial case is the research
laboratory, where until quite recently, spatial group dynamics were
thought to be entirely absent.[1] To begin our task of building a more complex model, we must look into some anthropological ideas about space.

In 1953, Lévi-Strauss formulated the problem of space as follows:

> It has been Durkheim's and Mauss's great merit to call attention
> for the first time to the variable properties of space which should be
> considered in order to understand properly the structure of several
> primitive societies ... [But] there have been practically no attempts to
> correlate the spatial configurations with the formal properties of the
> other aspects of social life. This is much to be regretted, since in
> many parts of the world there is an obvious relationship between the
> social structure and the spatial structure of settlements, villages and
> camps ... These few examples (camps of Plains Indians, Ge
> villages in Brazil, and pueblos) are not intended to prove that spatial
> configuration is the mirror image of social organization but to call
> attention to the fact that, while among numerous peoples it would be
> extremely difficult to discover any such relation, among others (who
> must accordingly have something in common) the existence of a rela-
> tion is evident, though unclear, and in a third group spatial configura-
> tion seems to be almost a projective representation of the social
> structure. But even the most striking cases call for critical study; for
> example, this writer has attempted to demonstrate that, among the

Bororo, spatial configuration reflects not the true, unconscious social organization but a model existing consciously in the native mind, though its nature is entirely illusory and even contradictory to reality.[2]

A little later he adds:

Problems of this kind (which are raised not only by the consideration of relatively durable spatial configurations but also in regard to recurrent temporary ones, such as those shown in dance, ritual, etc.) offer an opportunity to study social and mental processes through objective and crystallized external projections of them.[3]

It may seem natural that a 'structuralist' of Lévi-Strauss' stripe would see the spatial forms of settlements as 'projections' or 'reflections' of 'mental processes' and be puzzled when he finds it in some cases and not in others. But we find a curious blindness in his view. A short while previously in the same paper Lévi-Strauss had proposed a fundamental distinction in the analysis of social structure between what he calls 'mechanical' and 'statistical' models.[4] In a mechanical model, according to Lévi-Strauss, the elements of the model are 'on the same scale as the phenomena' they account for. In a statistical model the elements of the model are 'on a different scale' from the phenomena.

Lévi-Strauss illustrates the difference through marriage laws in 'primitive' and modern societies. In primitive societies, the laws of marriage can often be 'expressed in models calling for actual grouping of the individuals according to kin or clan'. Individuals are thus categorised and brought into well-defined relationships with individuals in other categories. This degree of determination is characteristic of a mechanical model. Modern societies, in contrast, specify no such assignment of individuals to categories, and therefore no such relations to other categories. Instead, 'types of marriage are determined only by the size of primary and secondary groups'. A model of the invariants of such a system could therefore determine only average values, or thresholds, and therefore constitute a statistical model.

What we find curious is that in using such terms as 'projection' and 'reflection' to formulate the problem of space, Lévi-Strauss seems to be taking for granted that spatial phenomena will be on the same scale as the mental processes that (so he imagines) must govern them, and therefore be expressible through a mechanical model. It is far from obvious that this should be so. On the contrary, everyday experience suggests that it is rarely so, and that space more commonly possesses the attributes of Lévi-Strauss' statistical model. The differences between the type of spatial mechanical models Lévi-Strauss has in mind for such cases as the circular villages of the Ge Indians of Brazil and the type of space characteristic of modern cities seems to have much in common with the differences he has already noted between types of marriage systems. Modern urban space is for the most part interchangeable and lacks well-defined correspondences between social categories and spatial domains. Insofar as such distinctions exist, they appear to be exactly of a statistical kind and are generated by a process of social action rather than simply reflecting a mental process. Considering the full range of cases with which ethnography and everyday life presents us, in fact, space seems to vary on a continuum with mechanical and statistical models as its poles.

The reason for Lévi-Strauss' unexpected conceptual blindness is perhaps that he lacks any concept of what a statistical model of space would look like. The need to formulate such a model underlies the attempted resolution of Lévi-Strauss' problem in *The Social Logic of Space*.[5] In that text it is argued that leaving aside issues of sheer scale, which are themselves morphologically significant, the investment societies make in space varies along three fundamental dimensions: the degree to which space is structured at all, the degree to which space is assigned specific social meanings, and the type of configuration used. Across the range of known societies, the first gives a continuum from non-order to order; the second gives a continuum from non-meaning to meaning; and the third gives fundamental differences in actual spatial form across a range of spatial variables.[6]

Morphogenetic models
The only type of model that might succeed in showing a field of phenomena with these dimensions of variability to be a 'system of transformations' (to use a favourite expression of Lévi-Strauss) is, it was argued in *The*

Social Logic of Space, a model in which rules are conceived of not as mental entities producing projections or reflections of themselves in the real world, but as restriction imposed on an otherwise random generative process – say, a cell aggregation model, or a model generating relationships in a graph. In such a model, rules and randomness can interact to produce not only known outcomes, but also new outcomes or *morphogenesis*. Cases were shown in which a morphogenic model based on cell aggregations randomised apart from purely local rules (i.e., specifying only relations of cells to an immediate neighbour) was able to generate – and by direct inference to 'explain' something about – common global topological properties of groups of apparently random settlement forms.[7]

But computer experimentation has shown that such morphogenesis occurs only where the rules restricting the random process are few, and local in their scope. The more the rules become too many or too global (i.e., specifying relations beyond those with immediate neighbours – for example by requiring lines of sight covering groups of a certain size), the more the generative process will tend to produce reflections or projections of those rules. Morphogenesis in such systems requires, it seems, the co-presence of randomness and rules restricting that randomness.

Such co-presence can arise only to the extent that the number of possible relations that cells can enter into in an aggregation process is significantly more than those specified by rules. The higher the proportion of possible spatial relations specified by the rules, and the more global those rules, the less the process has morphogenetic potential, and the more it will conserve the form given by the rules. Conversely, the lower the proportion of possible relations specified by rules, the greater the morphological potential. More succinctly, we can say that short descriptions, or 'short models' as we have come to call them, inserted in random processes tend to morphogenesis, while long descriptions, or 'long models', tend to conserve.

We also find that the shorter the model the larger the equivalence class of global forms that can result, and the more these forms will, while sharing 'genotypical' similarities, be individually different. The longer the description required, the smaller the equivalence class and the more individuals will resemble one another. In other words, short models tend to individuation as well as morphogenesis, whereas long models tend to conformity as well as conservation.

A further refinement of this theoretical model can incorporate another significant dimension: that of social meaning. In what has been described so far, it has been assumed that the elements of a generative process are interchangeable and do not have individual identities. If we now assign individual identities – or even group identities – to individual cells, and assign individuals or categories to specific relations with other individuals or categories within the system, then the description required to restrict randomness is still further lengthened, since relations between specific elements or groups of elements need to be specified – though this time by *transspatial* or conceptual rather than purely spatial rules.

This is most economically conceived of as the imposition of 'non-interchangeability' on the elements of the generative process. While appearing initially to be the addition of entities of an entirely different kind – those associated with social 'meaning' – the concept of non-interchangeability shows that these can be brought within the theoretical scope of long and short models. The limiting case of such a non-interchangeable system is one in which every cell has a specified relation to all others in the system. This limit seems to be approached in the famous case of the Bororo village used (though not originated) by Lévi-Strauss.[8]

The continuum of long and short models is, we believe, the general form of Lévi-Strauss' distinction between mechanical (long) and statistical (short) models. Unifying both into a single scheme of things, one is able to see that the statistical and the mechanical, while appearing to characterise quite different research approaches to human affairs (in that sociology tends to the statistical while anthropology tends to the mechanical), are in fact aspects of an underlying continuum of possibility that runs right through human affairs in all societies.

Simple examples can be set within the model and clarified. For example, a ritual is a set of behaviours in which all sequences and all relations are specified by rules – that is, it is a long-model event. Of its nature, a ritual eliminates the random. Its object is to conserve and re-express its form. A party, on the other hand, while it may be casually described as a social ritual, is a short-model event. Its object is morphogenetic: the generation of new relational patterns by maximising the randomness of encounter through spatial proximity and movement.

   Not the least interesting property of long and short models for our present purposes is that they appear to give good characterisation of both spatial patterns and types of human encounter (encounter being the spatial realisation of the social), so that one can begin to see possible generic relationships among them. Short models, it seems, require space to be compressed because they depend on the random generation of events, and this becomes more difficult to the degree that distance has to be overcome. Long models on the other hand tend to be used to overcome distance and to make relationships that are not given automatically in the local spatial zone. Societies typically use ceremonies and ritual to overcome spatial separation and reinforce relationships that are not naturally made in the everyday spatial domain. Informality, in contrast, is associated exactly with the local spatial zone and is harder to retain at a distance. Greater space, as Mary Douglas once observed, means more formality.[9]

   Looked at this way, one can see that society actually has a certain rudimentary 'spatial logic' built into it, which links the *frequency* of encounters with the *type* of encounters. By the same logic, the typing of encounters between short and long models generates a need to pattern the local spatial domain to structure the range of encounter types. In this way, space as a physical arrangement begins to acquire a social logic.

   This reformulation of the problem of space leads to a research programme in which the object of investigation is how the two morphologies of space and encounter are patterned. Research can thus proceed without any presumption of determinism. If social encounters have their own spatial logic and space has its own social logic, and the task of research is to understand how they relate morphologically, then the naive paradigm of cause and effect between environment and behaviour can be avoided. Indeed one can see that the term 'environment' used in this context is in danger of itself setting up this false paradigm of the problem it seeks to address,[10] since it presupposes an ambient circumstance with some specific influential relation to the behaviours it circumscribes. This paradigm is unrealistic, and it has been criticised at length elsewhere. Even so it is worth uttering a word of warning that the fallacies of what has been called the 'man environment paradigm' can also be present in the notion of the 'setting'.[11]

These theoretical ideas have been set out at some length because we believe that the analysis of the relationship between 'the spatial setting and the production and reproduction of knowledge'[12] can proceed effectively only within this type of theoretical framework. It is this theoretical framework that the methodology of 'space syntax' seeks to convert into a programme of empirical investigation, by first investigating space as a pattern in itself, then analysing its relationship to the distribution of categories and labels (non-interchangeabilities), then systematically observing its use.

Before explaining something of the method and the modelling concepts it gives rise to, however, some careful distinctions must first be introduced about the way we use the word 'knowledge', since these have a direct bearing on how the reproduction and production of knowledge relate to space.

Ideas we think with and ideas we think of

To study space and knowledge, we must begin by making a fundamental distinction between two everyday senses of the word 'knowledge'. The first is when we talk of knowing a language, or knowing how to behave, or knowing how to play backgammon. The second is knowing projective geometry, or knowing how to make engineering calculations, or knowing the table of elements.

Knowing in the first sense means knowing a set of *rules* that allow us to *act* socially in well-defined ways: speaking, listening, attending a dinner party, playing backgammon, and so on. Knowing in this sense means knowing something *abstract* in order to be able to do, or relate to, something *concrete*. Knowledge of abstractions is used to generate concrete phenomena. Let us call this kind of knowledge *knowledge* A, or *social knowledge*, since it is clear that the ubiquity of knowledge A is one of the things that make society run.

Knowledge A has several important characteristics. First, we tend to use it *autonomically*. We are not aware of it when we use it, in the sense that when we are speaking sentences, the last thing we wish to give attention to is our knowledge of the rules of language. The rules of language are *ideas we think with*, whereas the concepts we form through language are, for the most part, *ideas we think of*. It is necessarily so. To be effective as speakers, we must take it for granted that we know, and others share, the rules of language.

Second, in spite of the evidently abstract nature of such knowledge, we normally acquire it by *doing*, rather than by being explicitly taught. As we learn words and sentences, we are not aware we are learning abstract rules. On the contrary, what we are learning seems fragmentary and practical. Nevertheless, as linguists have so often noted, such knowledge must be abstract in form since it allows us to behave in novel ways in new situations – the familiar 'rule-governed creativity'.

Third, we should note that knowledge A works so effectively as social knowledge precisely because abstract principles *are* buried beneath habits of doing. Because they are so buried, we become unconscious of them, and because we are unconscious we also became unaware that they exist. Ideas we think with are everywhere, but we do not experience them; they structure our thoughts and actions, but we have forgotten their existence. The trick of culture, it might be observed, lies in this way of making the artificial appear natural.

Knowledge B, in contrast, is knowledge where we learn the abstract principles consciously and are primarily aware of the principles both when we acquire and when we use the knowledge. Thus we learn and hold projective geometry, or how an engine works, or the table of elements, in such a way that abstract principles and concrete phenomena seem to be aspects of each other. We might very loosely call this 'scientific knowledge', making the only criterion for this term the fact that principles as well as cases are explicit and can be written down in books and taught as aspects of each other.

Now it is unimportant to our argument that there is no clear demarcation between knowledge A and knowledge B. On the contrary, the lack of clarity as to what belongs where is often an important debate. For example, in the field of space there is a theory called territoriality, which claims scientific status. We believe this theory not only to be wrong but also to be knowledge A masquerading as knowledge B. That is, we believe it to be in the main a projection into a quasi-scientific language of normative beliefs and practices that are deeply ingrained in modern Western society – ideas that have indeed become ideas we think with in architecture (Hillier 1988) and now need the reinforcement of scientific status.

The reason we need the distinction between knowledge A and knowledge B for our purposes here is that all human spatial organisation involves some degree of knowledge A. How much knowledge A is involved is indexed by the length of the model that structures space. But it is not a one-way process in which space *reflects* knowledge A. In short-model situations, space can also be *generative* of knowledge A.

Examples of this range of possibilities are given in the next section. However, knowledge A is not our principle subject here. We are interested in space and knowledge B, trivially in its reproduction, non-trivially in its production. The essence of our answer is that the conditions for the production of knowledge B are likely to exist to the extent that knowledge A is absent in spatial complexes, and that the short-model conditions that permit the generation of knowledge A also have a bearing on the generation of knowledge B.

This does not mean that the absence of knowledge A in space will always lead to the production of knowledge B, or that knowledge B can be produced only when knowledge A is absent. What it means is that in the absence of knowledge A the spatial conditions exist for all kinds of *generation* – new relationships, new ideas, new products, and even knowledge – just as in the presence of knowledge A, the spatial conditions exist for all kinds of *conservation* – of roles and positions, of social praxes and rituals, of statuses and identities.

More briefly, the proposition put forward in this paper is that buildings, which insofar as they are purposeful objects are organizers of space, can act in either a *conservative* or a *generative* mode. The place of the spatial reproduction of knowledge lies in the conservative mode. The place of the spatial production of knowledge lies in the generative mode. What this means in practice may surprise the proponents of scientific solitude.

Space and knowledge A
The argument can be made more precisely by illustrating the presence of knowledge A in some simple examples of domestic space. Social

knowledge is built into domestic space in many ways, but one of the most important is through *configuration* – that is, through the actual layout of the plan.

A key syntactic measure of configuration is *integration.* This is initially a purely spatial measure, but it gives a configurational analysis of function as one simply looks at the integration values of the spaces in which functions are located. As soon as we can identify common patterns in the degree of integration of different *functions* or *labels* in a sample of dwellings, then it is clear that we are dealing quite objectively (i.e., in terms of the properties of objects) with cultural genotypes acquiring a spatial dimension – that is, with social knowledge taking on a spatial form.

In chapter 1 this notion was illustrated by three examples. The order of integration of the different functions was similar in all three cases. In other words, the way in which spaces are categorised according to the ways in which culture arranges activities – what goes with what, what is separated from what, what must be adjacent and what separate, and so on – finds a repeated form. This, we saw as one of the 'deep structures' of the configuration. We called this kind of configurational repetition across a sample an 'inequality genotype', since it is an abstract underlying cultural form, assuming many different physical manifestations, and expressing itself through integrational inequalities in the ways that different functions feature in the domestic-space culture.

This would seem to be a clear case where knowledge A is embedded in spatial configuration. It could even be said that the spatial configuration *constitutes* rather than *represents* social knowables. It belongs in the domain – largely unconscious, because habitual – of the lived pattern of everyday life, rather than in the representation of these patterns through symbols.

The list of invariants in an inequality genotype can be extended by analysing more subtle spatial properties, such as the relation between permeability and visibility among the spaces. The more the list can be extended and remain invariant – or approximately so – across a sample, the more it can be said that the genotype is a long model or a Lévi-Straussian mechanical model. In the case of the French farmhouses, the genotype is far from being a mechanical model. There is much that varies, apparently randomly, among the houses, ensuring that each retains its individual spatial character.

Set into the general theoretical scheme we are proposing, we might say that the list of invariants over the list of possible invariants across the sample would be the length of the model. For our present purposes, we will not pursue precise measurement too far, since to show the possibility in principle is sufficient. But it can easily be seen that a more stereotyped housing type – say the English suburban house, where most spatial and function rules are invariant across very large samples – will have a much longer model than the French farmhouses, where much individuation still prevails over an underlying genotypical pattern.[13] We can also say, therefore, that the length of the models indexes to the degree to which the houses, through their configuration, reproduce knowledge A. English suburban houses reproduce more social knowledge than do the French rural examples.

Strong and weak programs

Let us now consider two more complex examples, which take the model to its extremes. To do this we need to invoke movement. In architectural terms, movement is a very dull word for a very critical phenomenon. Although we are accustomed to taking a static view of buildings by being concerned primarily with the aesthetics of their facades, there is no doubt that from the point of view of space, buildings are fundamentally about movement, and how it is generated and controlled. The type of 'inequality genotype' just discussed may be present in, say, a factory (through the different degree of integration of managers, foremen, supervisors, workers, different departments, and so on),[14] but it is rather shadowy and far from being the most important feature of the spatial layout and its dynamics. To understand these more complex situations we must internalise the idea of movement into our theoretical model.

Let us begin with an example of what we call a 'strong-programme' building. The programme of a building is *not* the organisation it houses. An organisation, by definition, is a list of roles and statuses that has no necessary relation to a form of space, and its description – although not necessarily how it functions – would be the same regardless of its spatial configuration. We must give up the idea that it is the organisation that is reflected in the layout (another Lévi-Straussian case of a mechanical expectation that is usually unfulfilled) and look for some aspect of the organisation that does have some kind of spatial dimension.

'Programme' is the name we give to the spatial dimensions of an organisation, and the key element in any programme is the interface, or interfaces, that the building exists to construct. An 'interface' is a spatial relation between or among two broad categories of persons (or objects representing persons) that every building defines: *inhabitants*, or those whose social identity *as individuals* is embedded in the spatial layout and who therefore have some degree of control of space; and *visitors*, who lack control, whose identities in the buildings are collective, usually temporary, and subordinated to those of the inhabitants. Thus teachers, doctors, priests, and householders are inhabitants, while pupils, patients, congregations, and domestic visitors are visitors. An interface in a building is a spatial abstraction associated with a functional idea. It can vary in its form – think, for example, of the many ways in which the interface between teachers and pupils in a school can be arranged – but the building does have to construct its key interfaces in some form or other. The notion of interface thus extracts from the idea of organisation the spatial dimensions that must be realised in some way in the spatial form of the building.

A strong programme exists in a building when the interface or interfaces constructed by the building have a *long model*. Take a court of law, for example, which has probably the most complex strong-program interface of any major Western building type. The complexity of the programme arises from the fact that there are numerous different categories of persons who must all be brought into the same interface space in well-defined relations. The length of the model arises from the fact that spatial configuration must ensure that each of these interfaces happens in exactly the right way, and that all other possible encounters are excluded.

The interface in a court of law is, of course, static and 'synchronised' – meaning that all parties are brought into the same space-time frame. But the way the interface is brought about has to do with movement. The court of law has as many entrances as categories of participant, and all entrances have the property of noninterchangeability. Usually each independent entrance is associated with an independent route, or at least with a route that intersects only minimally with others. Each category is likely also to have an independent origin and destination in and around the courtroom space.

The essential characteristic of the court of law, considered as a system of movement and stasis, is that everything that happens is programmed in advance in order to structure the interfaces that must occur and inhibit all others. Movement is thus constructed by the programme, and the role of spatial configuration is primarily to permit the necessary movements and inhibit others. A strong-programme building is one in which it is not the layout that generates the movement pattern but the programme operating within the layout. In terms of the model, it can be said that the whole space structure for stasis and movement is controlled by knowledge A: its aim is to reinforce certain categoric identities and create strongly controlled interfaces between them.

Now let us consider a contrary case: the weak-program building. Fig. 7.1a shows the editorial floor of a leading London daily newspaper. Impressionistically, it is the opposite of the courtroom. It appears to be a hive of activity, with a high degree of apparently random movement and static encounter. If we now analyse the space structure using the axial convention (in which the longest and fewest lines of sight and access are drawn through all the open space), then analyse its integration pattern, we find that it has an integration core (the 10 per cent most integrating lines) of a type familiar from syntactic studies of urban grids (fig. 7.1b): a semigrid near the heart of the system links to strong peripheral lines by a series of routes, keeping it shallow from the outside as well as across its width. If we carefully observe the pattern of movement and stasis, we find that integration values of axial lines are powerful predictors of the degree to which space will be used (fig. 7.1c).

We see here what we believe to be a general principle: as the program of the building becomes weaker and moves toward an all-play-all interface, the distribution of space use and movement is defined less by the program and more by the structure of the layout itself. This is because the high number of origin/destination pairs coupled to the integrated nature of the

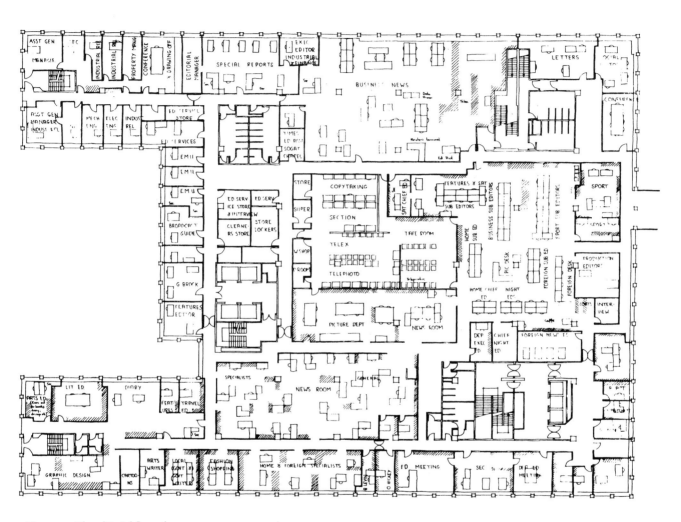

Figure 7.1a The editorial floor of a leading London daily newspaper, including the main items of furniture and equipment.

layout means that the by-product of movement – moving through inter-vening spaces – reflects the pattern of routes from all points to all other points. In this way the editorial floor comes to resemble an urban system, where movement and space use also have a weak programme. In this case we can say that the grid is behaving generatively: it is optimising and structuring a dense and random pattern of encounter, rather than simply restricting it to reflect a pre-existing social knowledge pattern.

Theoretically it can be said that the editorial floor is a short-model setup; and through its integrating layout, its density of movement, and

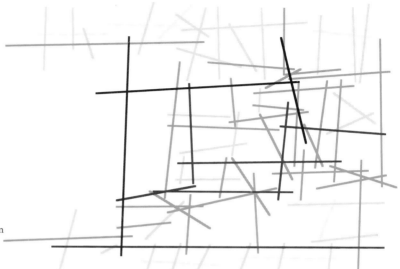

7.1b The axial integration map of the open space structure of the editorial floor.

7.1c Scattergram showing the correlation between the integration value of a space on the horizontal axis and the observed density of space use on the vertical axis averaged over twenty observations at different times of the day. The outflying point (highest use) is the photocopy space. The degree to which it is removed from the regression line of the remainder of the points indicates the degree to which it attracts use due to its function rather than to its spatial location. This shows how it is possible to detect the 'magnet' effect of facilities against the background of the use pattern of the spatial milieu, r = .83,p<.001.

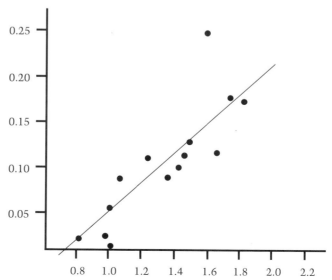

its structuring of the by-product of movement, it is generating new encounter patterns – that is, it is acting *morphogenetically* at the level of social encounter. Its content of social knowledge and non-interchange-ability is weak and ever changing. The function of space is to be creative by facilitating and extending the network of unprogrammed encounters necessary to the efficient running of a newspaper. Space in this sense is generative, or creative of knowledge A. It is generating new patterns of social relationship, which might not exist outside the spatial milieu.

This same construct can be applied to the *type* of social structure described by knowledge A. When we look for social structure in an organ-isation one of the first things we pick on as an indicator is the division of labour, and important for our purposes here, the more obvious the division of labour, the more strongly we consider an organisation to be structured. In this sense we can consider a social structure in terms of the length of the model needed to describe its division of labour. The shorter the model, the more the social structure required to carry out actual tasks will be generated through changing day-to-day needs. The longer the model, the more the division of labour itself will serve to reproduce the status quo.

In relation to knowledge A, therefore, both spatial structure and the organisation division of labour can act in either a *conservative* (reproduc-tive) or *generative* (productive) mode, and by and large this will be deter-mined by the length of the model governing the degree of randomness in the system.

Strong and weak ties, local and global networks
But what about the *production* of knowledge B – the key question? Can space influence the advance of science? Here there are no answers, but there are suggestive studies. Before describing them, we would like to present two pieces of research that, while not concerned with space, have a bearing on the matter.

The first is the seminal work of Tom Allen[15] on communication and innovation in R & D organisations in engineering. To quote his own summary:

> Despite the hopes of brainstorming enthusiasts and other proponents of group approaches to problem solving, the level of interaction with-in the project groups shows no relation to problem-solving performance.

The data to this point lend overwhelming support to the contention that improved communication among groups within the laboratory will increase R & D effectiveness. Increased communication between R & D groups was in every case strongly related to project performance. Moreover, it appears that interaction outside the project is most important. On complex projects, the inner team cannot sustain itself and work effectively without constantly importing new information from the outside world ... such information is best obtained from colleagues within the organization ... In addition, high performers consulted with anywhere between two and nine organizational colleagues, whereas low performers contacted one or two colleagues at most.[16]

The second piece of research is Granovetter's work on strong and weak ties, presented under the title 'The strength of weak ties'.[17] The argument is that any individual has a close network of strong ties – that is, friends who tend to know one another – and a more diffused network of weak ties – that is, acquaintances who normally do not know one another. Weak ties thus act as bridges between localised clumps of strong ties and hold the larger system together. The wrong balance can be disadvantageous. For example:

Individuals with few weak ties will be deprived of information from distant parts of the social system and will be confined to the provincial news and views of their close friends. This will not only insulate them from the latest ideas and fashions, but may also put them at a disadvantaged position in the labor market ... Furthermore, such individuals may be difficult to organize or integrate into politically based movements of any kind, since membership in movements or goal-oriented organizations typically results from being recruited by friends.[18]

Granovetter's work focusses primarily on social networks in the broader community, but he also reviews work on the role of weak ties in schools by Karweit et al.,[19] and in a children's psychiatric hospital by Blau.[20]

Although Granovetter's work refers in the main to the generation of knowledge A, while Allen's refers to the generation of knowledge B, the two arguments are similar, in that both cast doubt on the long-assumed benefits of spatial and social localism (small communities, small organisations, small groups of neighbours) and point to the need for a more global view of networks. I have put forward similar arguments about urban space.[21] Recent architectural and urban theory has been dominated by social assumptions of the benefits of small-scale communities, and spatial assumptions of the benefits of localised 'enclosure' and 'identification'. The effect of both, however, seems to be to fragment the urban space structure into overlocalised zones that become empty of natural movement through their lack of global integration, and often show signs of physical and social degeneration in a comparatively short time.

All our analytic studies of the structure and functioning of urban space suggest that it is the global scale that is critical, whether to the structuring of co-presence through movement, the sense of safety, the development of social networks, or the distribution of crime. The local sense of place arises not from the existence of segregated local zones, but from different types of deformity in the global grid. The same applies to social networks. Good urban networks are not self-contained groups but distributions of probabilities within a larger, continuous system. The key to 'urbanity', we have concluded, lies in the way the local and global scales of space and networks relate to each other.

All of these suggest that what is needed is a theory of space in which the relations between local and global scales and the dialectic of strong and weak ties and of structure and randomness (through long and short models) all interact. Because any spatial structure has the capability to generate patterns of co-presence through movement, it also has the potential to generate ties. Spatially generated ties will clearly in the first instance be weak ties. The more localised the tie, the more one might expect space to have the potential to help turn a weak tie into a strong tie. Indeed, in the local spatial milieu, one might well expect the spatial strategies of individuals to be concerned with the avoidance of the over-strengthening of ties – in much the same way as there are special forms of social and spatial behaviour to resist the spatial pressure to make relations with one's neighbours stronger than is comfortable. The ability of space to generate weak ties lies, we suspect, in the middle ground between the

immediate neighbouring group and the larger-scale trans-spatial network
that is more or less independent of space.

Probabilistic inequality genotypes in two research laboratories
We can now look at cases. Figure 7.2a is the open space structure of Lab X
and figure 7.2b the same for Lab Y. Lab X was constructed in two phases
according to a single planning system, but the Lab Y building is divided
into the 'old building' (horizontal in the plan) and the recently added 'new
building' (vertical in the plan).

Both Lab X and Lab Y belong to well-known organisations, but each
has a distinctive research style and management structure. Lab X is the
lab of a large, well-established public charity specifically concerned with
a certain range of diseases. Its director sets up and funds (according to
reputation, often lavishly) teams led by eminent research leaders, whose
task is to pursue specific goals laid down by the charity. The research programme is thus geared to specific medical and therapeutic goals. Lab Y is
oriented more to the academic production of knowledge and has a less
goal-directed, more individually entrepreneurial form of organisation, its
members for the most part define their own research programs. Both are
highly successful, but in terms of top-level performance (as measured by,
for example, the number of Nobel prizes) there is little doubt that Lab Y
would have to count as the higher flier.

What figures 7.2a and b show is a useful way of representing the difference in the spatial layout of the two labs. In each figure, all the 'free space'
– that is, the space in which people can work and move freely – is coloured
black. This shows that in spite of the basic cellular form of each building,
there are fundamental configurational differences between the spatial
layouts of the new and old parts of Lab Y, and between Lab X and the old
part of Lab Y. In the latter case, the differences have arisen from a protracted process of spatial mutation and adaptation.

The most important configurational difference between Lab X and
the old part of Lab Y is that while both have created internal permeabilities between groups of cells, links are deep (on the window side) in Lab X
and shallow (on the corridor side) in Lab Y. The new part of Lab Y, however,
seems to combine properties of both. These differences are shown more

7.2a The open space structure of Lab x.

7.2b The open space structure of Lab y.

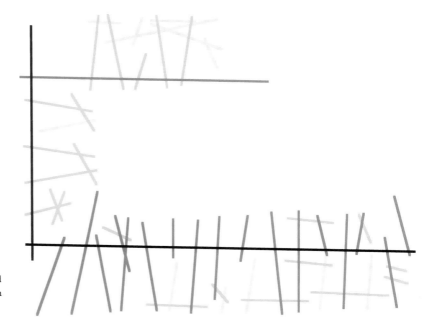

7.2c The axial integration map of Lab x. The axial map passes the fewest and longest straight lines of access through the free floor space.

7.2d The axial integration map of Lab y.

clearly in the 'axial' maps of each lab, given in figures 7.2c and 7.2d, showing the differences in the location of the intercell links. There are no discoverable technological reasons for this difference. However it is repeated on other floors of the same buildings. Even more strikingly, in a new building housing new labs of both organisations, the floor layouts adopted by each show exactly the same type of differentiation.

There also seem to be fundamental differences in the space use patterns of Lab X and the old part of Lab Y. The old part of Lab Y seems to the causal observer to be a hive of activity, whereas the new part and Lab X seem to be scarcely occupied at all until one leaves the corridor and enters the lab itself. This initial impression seems to be contradicted by the actual densities of use. In terms of number of persons divided by the full lab area, or the quantity of free floor area (the total area minus that occupied by benches and equipment) per occupant, average densities are almost identical in the two layouts.

However, the *pattern* of use is quite different, in each case following the pattern of spatial adaptation. The most obvious difference is that Lab Y has space use and movement rates in the main corridor about five times as high as those in Lab X, with a substantial component of interaction between two or more people occurring in the corridor.

We can make the pattern differences clear by dividing activities into four broad kinds: contemplative activities (such as sitting, writing), practical activities (such as working at the bench, which usually involves a certain degree of local movement), interactive activities (such as conversing or taking part in discussions) and non-local movement (i.e., movement that is basically linear and on a larger scale rather than describing a local convex figure, as would usually be the case for movement involved in working at a lab bench). We will describe an activity as occurring deep in the lab insofar as it occurs toward the window side of the lab and away from the corridor, and shallow insofar as it occurs toward the corridor side. Obviously since both buildings are corridor-based, most non-local movement will be in the shallowest space – that is, the corridor itself.

In Lab X, contemplative activity concentrates deep in the lab, by the windows (almost never in the offices provided for this!), practical activities are usually spread over the full depth of the lab, and interactive activities concentrate in the region of the axial lines linking the lab bays together (see table 7.1). These links occur deep in the lab, which means that interaction tends to occur in the same areas as contemplative activities, close to local movement but maximally far from non-local movement.

In Lab Y, contemplative activities again occur deep in the lab by the windows, practical activities tend to concentrate toward the centre and shallow areas, and interactive activities concentrate strongly in the shallow areas close to the corridor – as in the previous case, hugging the axial line linking the lab bays together (see table 7.1). This means that interaction occurs both close to local movement within the lab, as in the previous case, and close to non-local movement in the corridors, where a significant degree of interaction also occurs.

Put simply (and inevitably simplifying the real situation somewhat), we can say that in Lab Y, contemplative activities are deeper than practical activities, while interaction is shallow and close to non-local movement. Using the symbol '<' to mean 'shallower than' we can say that in Lab Y: *movement < interaction < practical < contemplative*. In Lab X, both contemplative activities and interaction are deeper than work, and remote from non-local movement, so we can say that in Lab X: *movement < practical < interaction = contemplative*.

Table 7.1 below gives the mean distance (in metres) of each of the activity types from the local intercell links in each building. Since the distance is the mean of a large number of observations of individual workers, it provides a 'statistical' picture of activity in the two buildings. This picture shows that interaction stays close to the intercell links in both buildings, but that this leads to its being close to global movement in Lab Y and removed from it in Lab X.

Table 7.1

	Movement	Interactive	Practical	Contemplative
Lab X	4.9	.93	2.85	1.09
Lab Y	1.3	1.17	1.41	2.03

These formulae summarising the spatial dynamics of each organisa-tion resemble the 'inequality genotypes' noted in domestic space. But whereas the domestic inequalities were an association of function labels with integration values, and were therefore more like a Lévi-Straussian mechanical model, in the case of labs the inequalities are purely proba-bilistic, representing activity types rather than social categories, and therefore resemble a Lévi-Straussian statistical model.

We might call these formulae expressing differential spatial dynamics 'probabilistic inequality genotypes' and note that while both are short-model they affect the dynamics of the organisation differently. In Lab X, the probabilistic inequalities would seem to work to reinforce local ties and make them stronger, thus reinforcing the local group at the expense of the larger group. In Lab Y the inequalities seem to act more to create weak ties at the larger scale and link the local group to a larger-scale level of between-group contact.

We cannot yet demonstrate that these have effects on research pro-ductivity. What we can say is that the pattern exists, giving rise to a mor-phological concept of work organisations as something like 'space-use types', with suggestive relations both to organisational objectives and also to the theories of Allen and Granovetter. In terms of the organisational nature and objectives of each lab, it would seem to be a matter of how the bound-aries of knowledge are to be drawn in space – that is, how the reproduction of knowledge is to be organised in support of the production of knowledge. In Lab X, the objectives are focussed and defined for the group by the organ-isation as a whole. The spatial structure of the lab and the spatial dynam-ics within it thus both mirror this structure and work to concentrate the efforts of a local, organisationally determined unit. In Lab Y, the more fluid organisation, based more on individual initiative than on group objectives (although defined by a commonality of academic interests), has created an intensively interactive spatial milieu at the scale of the floor as a whole. In both cases, specific forms of sociality are built into the work process itself, rather than being simply added on by special-event socialising – such as going to shared coffee locations or having joint seminars (although these also occur).

So far as the production of scientific knowledge – that is, knowledge

B – is concerned, we might propose that the two forms of spatial layout have radically different implications. Whereas the statistical effect of the layout in Lab X has led to the separation of interaction within a lab from large-scale movement between labs, in the old building of Lab Y the two are brought into close probabilistic contact. However, the existing state of knowledge B is defined to some degree by the organisational divisions into different research groups studying particular defined areas and physical scales of science. In the case of Lab X it is tempting to suggest that the predominant spatial milieu leads to the reinforcement of these local, pre-existing boundaries of knowledge. In the old building of Lab Y, however, the tendency would be to break the existing boundaries through the random action of the spatial milieu at the large – between existing boundaries – level.

More generally – more speculatively – we might suggest that while organisations always tend to localism, the statistical tendency of the building will be either to reinforce this or to weaken its boundaries. Everything depends on the level at which the spatial structure of the building introduces randomness into the encounter field. Our instinct is to suggest that the more fundamental the research, the more it will depend on the globalising of the generative model. In contrast to organised events, weak ties generated by buildings may be critical because they tend to be with people that one does not know one needs to talk to. They are, then, more likely to break the boundaries of the existing state of knowledge represented by individual research projects, organisational subdivisions, and localism.

We might suggest that the morphogenesis of knowledge B – like all morphogenesis – requires randomness. How can randomness be inserted into the process by which knowledge B is generated? Obviously, since science is done by human beings, it must be by randomising the knowledge A inputs. It is at this level, it seems, that a building can operate to generate or conserve. Space is morphogenetic of knowledge B precisely because it can randomise knowledge A.

Synthesis: creating phenomena and visible colleges
There is a debate as to whether basic science is an individual or a collective

activity. The evidence we are finding (and which we have presented only as examples) is that it is how the one relates to the other that is critical, at least as far as the study of space is concerned. Space, we would suggest, articulates exactly this double need for the individual and the collective aspects of research: how to combine the protection of the solitary with the natural generation of more randomised co-presence with others – the need for which seems to grow the more the objectives of research are unknown.

But it is not just that the nature of scientific work requires this kind of socialisation. There is something else, we suggest, intrinsic to the nature of scientific research that gives it a special dynamic. It is customary to see science as a dialectic between theory and experiment, with (psychologically incompatible) theoreticians working in one corner and experimenters in another. Under the influence of such theorists as Popper and Lakatos, the late twentieth century has been preoccupied with theory (correcting an early failure to understand the deep dependence of phenomena on theory), seeing experiment increasingly as no more than the servant of theory.

Hacking (1983) disagrees, and sees experiment and theory as bound up in a quite different way. 'One role of experiments', he writes, 'is so neglected that we lack a name for it. I call it the creation of phenomena. Traditionally scientists are said to explain the phenomena they discover in nature. I say they often create the phenomena which then become the centrepieces of theory'.[22] Phenomena, according to Hacking, are not the sense data of phenomenalism. Science is not made of such. Phenomena, for scientists, are significant regularities that are useful to speculation.

Phenomena are therefore not 'plentiful in nature, summer blackberries just there for the picking'. On the contrary, they are rare. 'Why', Hacking asks, 'did old science on every continent begin, it seems, with the stars? Because only the skies afford some phenomena on display, with many more that can be obtained by careful observation and collation. Only the planets, and more distant bodies, have the right combination of complex regularity against a background of chaos'.[23] Because phenomena are so rare, they have to be created. This is why the creation of significant phenomena plays such a central role in the advance of theory.

Hacking, like most people in the philosophy of science, is working on big science. We are not philosophers of science and cannot offer useful comment on his propositions at that level. But we can apply his strictures to our own situation. Speaking as researchers who are trying to run a lab setup in a soft science, we know that the creation of phenomena is the centre of what we do, even though we see our objectives as the creation of theory. Global spatial complexes with well-defined morphological properties, generated by a computer on a restricted random process, are created phenomena. So are inequality genotypes, integration cores, and scattergrams showing correlations between integration values and observed movement or crime frequencies.

Of course, much of our discussion is theoretical. But theoretical debate centres on created phenomena, and it is created phenomena that continually destroy and generate theory. Theoretical debate survives distance. The creation of phenomena is harder to share at a distance. It is not because one discusses theories but because one creates phenomena that people cannot be absent for long without beginning to lose touch. The creation of phenomena, it seems, is more spatial than is theory.

We suspect it may also underlie the more localised spatial dynamics of the laboratory. 'What's so great about science?' Hacking asks. He then suggests it is because science is 'a collaboration between different kinds of people: the speculators, the calculators, and the experimenters'. 'Social scientists', he adds,

> don't lack experiment; they don't lack calculation; they don't lack speculation; they lack the collaboration of all three. Nor, I suspect, will they collaborate until they have real theoretical entities about which to speculate – not just postulated 'constructs' and 'concepts', but entities we can use, entities which are part of the deliberate creation of stable new phenomena.[24]

The locus of this collaboration is, we suggest, the research lab. A lab is where thoughtful speculators are close to the creation of phenomena. To be absent from the lab is not to be unable to theorise, but it is not to know quickly enough or precisely enough what to theorise about. This is not of course to say that the collaboration between theory and the creation of phenomena cannot proceed at a distance. On the contrary, it is obvious that it often does. But what science cannot do without, we suggest, is the existence of lab-like situations *somewhere*, where the creation of phenomena and speculation – and probably calculation too, if our experience is anything to go by – feed off each other.

Such *visible colleges* are, we suspect, the precondition for the existence of science's ubiquitous *invisible colleges.* Where they occur, a spatial dynamic will be set up, which will mean that, for a while at least, a good place will exist in which science can happen. That good place is, probably, a *generative* building. Only when such concrete realities exist somewhere within the abstract realm of the invisible college can that peculiar form of morphogenesis that we have called the creation of knowledge B become a collective phenomenon.

Appendix

The full study of laboratories, of which the results reported in this chapter were a preliminary, eventually produced an even more striking spatial outcome. The design of the study was informed by some of the results from Allen's study[25] of factors influencing success in innovation. In paired studies of defence research projects in the USA where routinely two independent teams are commissioned with the same brief and the performance of their design solution tested, Allen studied the information and communication networks used by the successful teams in arriving at innovative solutions. The most important contacts from the point of view of innovative problem solving were not those within the project team, but those between people working on entirely different projects. It was conjectured that it was these relations between groups that might be affected by building design.

The main phase of research which followed the pilot study therefore took a sample of twenty-four building floors in seven sites in different parts of the United Kingdom. The sample spanned public, private and university sectors, and covered a range of scientific disciplines. All the laboratories selected were considered 'good' within their field. The study itself addressed a wide range of spatial and environmental issues, and included detailed surveys of spatial and equipment provision, observations of space-use patterns and a questionnaire survey to determine the strength of communication networks. The questionnaire listed by name all, or a large sample, of the people who worked in the survey area. Respondents were asked to score on a five-point scale the frequency with which they had contact with each individual name on the list. They were also asked whether or not they found that person useful in their work. Although the questionnaires were confidential they were not anonymous, since we needed to know for each respondent which contacts were within their research group and which were between groups. We expected that within the research group everyone would know everyone else, see them daily, and find them useful in their work, and this turned out to be the case, without variation attributable to spatial structuring.

Between group contacts, however, we thought might show spatial variation. To investigate this we looked at the data not from the point of view of each individual, but counting how often each name on the list was cited by every other respondent. The intention of this 'reversed citation' method was to eliminate possible effects from different interpretations of the questions by different respondents. Each name on the list had an equal chance of being cited by each respondent. Using this method to investigate between group contacts, the findings were interesting. For example, respondents who were found most useful outside their own research groups were neither the most or least frequently seen. Usefulness and frequency of contact were clearly not the same thing.

But the most striking findings were spatial. First, the mean rate of inter-group contacts on each floor correlated with the mean degree of spatial integration of the floor considered as a spatial complex on its own, rather than in terms of its embedding in the whole building. The rates of 'useful' contacts, on the other hand, were strongly related to building integration for the floors considered in terms of their embedding in the whole building. More spatially integrated buildings, it seemed, increased the level of useful work-related inter-group communication that Allen had found to be so important for innovation. In other words, local integration

predicted network density, but global integration predicted network usefulness.
A still more significant finding resulted from relating the local and global measures together. The more global integration – which we might expect to be less
than floor integration, due to the effect of vertical divisions or division of the
building into zones following the enveloped shape – approached local integration,
the better the ratio of useful to all contacts.

These are strong findings and suggest that spatial configuration in laboratory buildings can affect patterns of communication amongst researchers.
However, it does raise a question regarding the precise mechanism that could
give rise to these effects. Light has recently been cast on this through the work
of Paul Drew and Alan Backhouse at the University of York.[26] In a study of
large open-plan professional design offices they used careful observations and
video recordings to look at the behaviour of workers engaged in work-related
interaction. They found that when an individual is at his workstation he is
usually regarded by others as engaged in work and should not be disturbed. However, should that individual leave his workstation to move to some other area,
whether or not that movement is dictated by the needs of work, he is regarded
as 'free' and so available for 'recruitment' into interaction. They write:

> In plotting the movements of individuals when away from their worksta-
> tions, we found a markedly high incidence of 're-routings' – cases where
> a person notably deviated from his route of prior intention at the behest
> of another, or in order to recruit another person into interaction. As an
> individual moved into the vicinity of a 'significant' other, he would be
> (a) engaged or 'recruited', (b) his task orientation would be altered from the
> planned to the contingent, and (c) his prior task would become relegated
> to become a task 'pending' attention. The evidence for this was found in
> the high incidence of individuals responding to verbal and non-verbal
> recruitments, and altering their intended course of action to accommodate
> such recruitment. Interestingly, not only does the recruited undergo a task-
> reorientation, but the recruiter must also change his task as he cannot have
> planned or expected the appearance of the recruited. In this sense a clear
> division is apparent between the organisation of planned immediate work
> and the unplanned, contingent achievement. As such the accomplishment
> of 'work' is often a contingent and unplanned process.[27]

This micro-scale mechanism suggests that movement in buildings may be more intimately involved in the work process than has hitherto been recognised or allowed for. If, as Backhouse and Drew suggest, a certain proportion of work-related interaction arises in this 'contingent' and unplanned manner, then providing the opportunity for movement and recruitment and the recruitment which results may be the key to maximising work-related communication. The model has other attractive properties. To the degree that movement takes people from one part of the organisation past workstations of people from other parts of the organisation, the opportunity for recruitment will serve to create contacts between organisational segments. If as Allen has suggested, these are the important contacts from the point of view of innovative problem solving, we can begin to imagine the way that this might work.

We can also imagine what will happen if we set out to design our buildings and organisations simply with efficiency in mind. Let us assume that the state of knowledge in the task area covered by an organisation is broadly understood by management and that pains have been taken to structure the organisation in a relatively rational way. It follows that groups within the organisation will reflect the current understanding and existing state of knowledge of the task area. People who this understanding gives us to believe need to interact often will be located within a group, those between whom there seems to be no rational need for communication may be separated. Steps may even be taken in the interests of organisational 'efficiency' to minimise the intrusion of unrelated groups on each other and to minimise the need for movement on the part of staff by making sure that all facilities required for work are conveniently located near to each group. These would seem to be reasonable steps to take in order to produce a rational and efficient building plan.

What would be the effect of such a plan on the progress of the state of knowledge in the organisation? By and large the existing state of knowledge in a field is a pretty good starting point for problem solving, but slowly it would become apparent that other organisations were making the innovative breakthroughs. These breakthroughs are so rare in any case that their lack may never be noticed. The solutions to problems in the 'efficient' organisation would largely be produced as a result of the people put together for that purpose by the organisation on the basis of current knowledge, and because the opportunity to interact with people outside that definition of knowledge would be reduced in the interests of efficiency, the boundaries of knowledge would seldom be challenged or broken.

In this sense, organisational efficiency and true innovation may sometimes run counter to each other. Innovation requires probabilistic interaction and the opportunity to recruit provided by bringing the larger-scale movement structure closer to the workstation. Moreover it requires that the larger-scale movement takes people with knowledge in one field past people with problems to solve in another. In this way it seems possible that the spatial configuration of buildings and the disposition of the organisations that inhibit them are actively involved in the evolution of the boundaries of scientific knowledge itself.

Notes

1   Nuffield Division for Architectural Research, *The Design of Research Laboratories*, Report of a study sponsored by the Nuffield Foundation,Oxford University Press, 1961.

2   C. Lévi-Strauss, 'Social Structure' reprinted in *Structural Anthropology*. Anchor Books, 1967, pp 282–5.

3   Ibid., p 285.

4   Ibid., pp. 275–6.

5   BIll Hillier and Julienne Hanson, *The Social Logic of Space*, Cambridge University Press, 1984.

6   Ibid., p 5.

7   Ibid., pp. 55–63. See also: Bill Hillier, 'The nature of the artificial: the contingent and the necessary in spatial form in architecture' from *Geoforum*, 16(3), 1985, pp. 163–78.

8   C. Lévi-Strauss, *The Raw and the Cooked*, Harper Books, 1964.

9   Mary Douglas, *Natural Symbols*, Pelican Books, 1973.

10 Bill Hillier, and Julienne Hanson, 'A second paradigm', *Architecture and Behaviour*, 3(3), 1987, pp. 197–203 and Hillier and Hanson, *The Social Logic of Space*.

11 Bill Hillier, and A. Leaman, 'The man-environment paradigm and its paradoxes', *Architectural Design*, August 1973, pp. 507–11.

12 Ibid.

13 Julienne Hanson, and Bill Hillier, 'Domestic space organisation', *Architecture and Behaviour*, 2(1), 1982, pp. 5–25. See also B. Hillier, J. Hanson and H. Graham, 'Ideas are

in things', *Environment and Planning B: Planning and Design*, vol. 14, 1987, pp. 363–85.

14 See Peponis, J. 'The Spatial Culture of Factories' Ph.D. thesis, University College London, 1983.

15 T. Allen, *Managing the Flow of Technology*, MIT Press, 1977.

16 Ibid., pp. 122–23.

17 M. Granovetter, 'The strength of weak ties' from *Social Structure and Network Analysis*, edited by P.V. Marsden and N. Lin, Sage Publications, 1982, pp. 101–30.

18 Ibid., pp. 106.

19 N. Karweit, S. Hansell and M. Ricks, *The Conditions for Peer Associations in Schools*, Report No. 282, Center for Social Organization of Schools, John Hopkins University, 1979.

20 J. Blau, 'When weak ties are structured', Unpublished, Department of Sociology, SUNY, Buffalo, New York , 1980.

21 Bill Hillier, 'Against enclosure', *Rehumanising Housing*, edited by N. Teymour, T. Markus and T. Woolley, Butterworths, 1988.

22 Ian Hacking, *Representing and Intervening: Introductory Topics in the Philosophy of Natural Science*, Cambridge University Press, 1983, p 220.

23 Ibid., p 227.

24 Ibid., p 249.

25 Allen, *Managing the Flow of Technology*.

26 Backhouse A. and Drew P., 'The design implications of social interaction in a workplace setting', *Environment and Planning B: Planning and Design*, 1990.

27 Backhouse and Drew, 'Design implications', pp. 16–17.

Part three

The laws of the field

chapter eight

Is architecture an ars combinatoria?

Despite the merits of rectangular dissections as models of smaller plans, there is an increasing proportion of 'theoretical possibilities' for larger dissections which nevertheless become rather unlike the plans of buildings, and hence begin to lose their practical interest. Such dissections consist, certainly, of rectangular components corresponding to rooms, packed together in different configurations. But these configurations are not at all probable architecturally, in ways which are hard to pinpoint precisely, but are no less real for that. It is something to do with such facts as that real buildings tend to have limited depth, because of the needs of daylighting and natural ventilation, so that when large they become organised into regular patterns of wings and courts. Or that rooms are set along relatively simple and coherent circulations systems consisting of a few branching corridors which extend along the buildings' whole length. There are many dissections which are made up, by contrast, of a deep maze like agglomeration of overlapping rectangles, many of them completely internal and through which any linking pattern of circulation routes would be circuitous and confusing. If we could capture properties like these in explicit geometrical measures, then we might be able to limit the study of dissections, for example, to a much reduced class of arrangements which would all be 'building-like' in some well defined sense.

STEADMAN, 1983

The deepest root of the trouble lies elsewhere: a field of possibilities open into infinity has been mistaken for a closed realm of things existing in themselves.

HERMAN WEYL

Endless corridors and infinite courts

No idea in the theory of architecture is more seductive than that architecture is an *ars combinatoria* – a combinatorial art: the idea that the whole field of architectural possibility might be made transparent by identifying a set of basic elements and a set of rules for combining them so that the application of one to the other would generate the architectural forms which exist, and open up possibilities that might exist and be consistent with those that do. By showing architectural forms to be a system of transformations in this way, the elements and rules would be held to be a theory of architectural form – the system of invariants that underlie the variety to be found in the real world. The best-known statement of this hope is that of William Lethaby when he calls for 'a true science of architecture, a sort of architectural biology which shall investigate the unit cell and all possibilities of combination'.[1]

At first sight, this seems promising. Most buildings seem to be made up from a rather small list of spatial elements such as rooms, courts and corridors, which vary in size and shape but which are usually found in fairly familiar arrangements: corridors have rooms off them, courts have rooms around them, rooms may connect only with these or may also connect directly to each other to form sequences, and so on. Similarly, the aggregates of buildings we call villages, towns and cities seem to be constructed from a similarly small and geometrically well-defined lexicon of streets, alleys, squares, and so on. With such an encouraging start, we might hope with a little mental effort to arrive at an enumeration of the combinatoric possibilities in the form of a list of elements and the possible relationships they can enter into so that we can build a reasoned picture of the passage from the simplest and smallest cases to the largest and most complex.

Unfortunately, such optimism rarely survives the examination of real cases. If, for example, we consider the cross-national and cross-temporal sample of 177 building plans brought together in Martin Hellick's *Varieties of Human Habitation*,[2] we may well feel inclined to confirm at a very broad level – and with great geometric variation – the idea that there are certain recurrent spatial types such as rooms, courts and corridors, but we also note the prodigious variations of overall layout which seem to be consistent with each. The historical record of actual buildings and how they have evolved suggests that most buildings are morphologically unique, and it is far from obvious how any combinatorial approach could reduce them to a list of types.

Even if we isolate the problem of spatial relations from that of shape and size by, for example, analysing plans as graphs, then we still find cornucopian variety rather than simple typology. For example, a recent study of over 500 English vernacular houses built between 1843 and 1930 reveals exactly six pairs of duplicate graphs, even though the sample was taken from a single country during a period where some typological continuity could be expected.[3] Plans seem to be individual, often with family resemblances or common local configurations, but rarely consistent enough or clear enough to suggest a simple division into types.

Theoretical investigations of architectural possibility have led to an even greater pessimism. For example, studies which have attempted to enumerate architectural possibility, even within artificially constrained systems such as the dissection of rectangles into patterns of room adjacencies,[4] have invariably shown that at an early stage in the enumeration the number of possibilities quickly outstrips the number of conceivable cases, and a combinatorial explosion of such violence is encountered as to exclude any practical possibility of continuing from smaller to larger systems. Thus Steadman concludes in his review of modern attempts at the systematic enumeration of building plans that '...for values of n (the number of cells in a rectangular "dissection") much greater than 10, the extent of combinatorial variety becomes so great that a complete enumeration is of little practical purpose; and indeed that for values of n not much larger than this, enumeration itself becomes a practical impossibility'.[5]

There are in fact strong a priori grounds for Steadman's caution. Although by circumscribing what we mean by a building in unlifelike ways, for example, by dealing only with rectangular envelopes, or by standardising the size and shape of spaces, one can place limits on combinatorial possibility to the point where we can in principle count numbers of possible arrangements, however large, the more constraints one places on the combinatoric system, the less we seem able to account for the variety which actually exists. But if we relax these constraints, it is far from obvious that there are any numerical limits at all on architectural possibility. For example, if we require all cells to be the same size then no cell can be adjacent to more than six others. But if we allow cells to vary in size and shape as much as necessary, then we may construct a corridor so that arbitrarily many cells are directly adjacent to it, or a court so that arbitrarily many cells are around it. Endless corridors and infinite courts must surely lead us to abandon simple cellular enumeration as a route to a combinatoric theory of spatial possibility in architecture.

P-complexes in a-complexes

There is in any case a further profound problem in the understanding of buildings as cellular dissections or aggregations. An arrangement of adjacent cells, whether arrived at by aggregation or subdivision, is not a building until a pattern of permeability from one cell to the other is created within it. For example, figure 8.1a shows a single adjacency complex, which we may call an a-complex, in which figures 8.1b and 8.1c inscribe different permeability complexes, or p-complexes. For clarity, the p-complexes of b and c are also shown as graphs in 8.1d and e.

Evidently, the two will be spatially very different buildings, even though the a–complexes are identical and each p-complex has exactly the same number of open and closed partitions. Over and above the question, then, of how many a-complexes there are, we must therefore also ask how many p-complexes are possible within a given a-complex. We then find a second combinatorial explosion within the first: of possible p-complexes within a given a-complex. Although an a-complex whose graph is a tree (see chapter 1) can only have one single p-structure inscribed within it (and then only if we disregard connections to the outside) as soon as this constraint is relaxed we begin to find the second combinatorial explosion: that of the possible p-complexes within each a-complex.

Suppose, for example, that we start with a version of the 6×6 a-complex shown in figure 8.1a, in which each cell is demarcated from its neighbour by a two-thirds partition with a central doorway, as in figure 8.1f and g. Obviously, every time we close – or subsequently open – a doorway we will change the spatial pattern of the p-complex. The question is, how many ways are there of inscribing different p-complexes in this a-complex

Figure 8.1

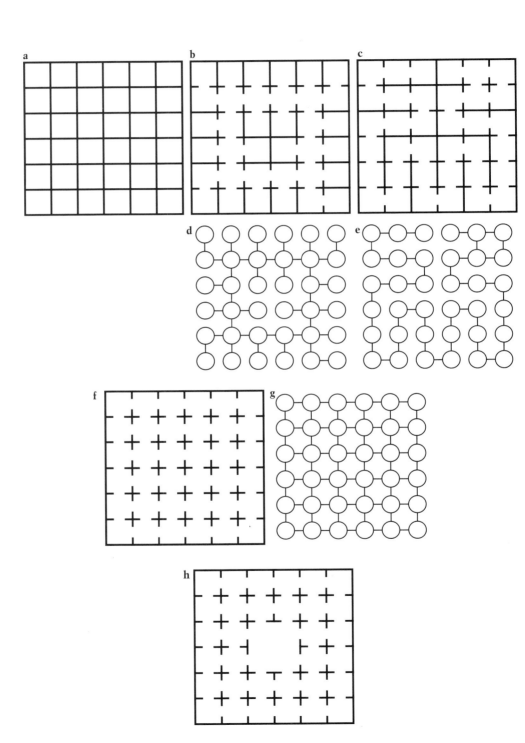

by closing and opening doors? We may work it out by simple combinatorial procedure. First we note that a regular n × m adjacency complex will always have $(m(n-1)+(n(m-1))$ internal partitions between cells, giving $(6(6-1)+(6(6-1)) = 60$ in this case. This means that the first time we select a door to close we will be making a choice out of 60 possibilities. The second will be out of 59, so there are 60×59, or 3540 possibilities for the first two doors. However half of these will be duplicates, since they differ only in the order in which the doorways were opened, so we need to divide our total by the number of ways there are of sequencing two events i.e. 60×59/1×2, or 1770. The third doorway will be chosen out of 58 remaining possibilities, so there will be 60×59×58 or 205320 possible combinations of three, but the number of duplicates of each will also increase to the number of different ways there are of ordering three events, that is 1×2×3 (= 6), so the total of different combinations for three doorways is 60×59×58/1×2×3 or 34220.

The total number of combinations for n doorways, will then be 60×59×58...×(60-n)/1 × 2 × 3×...×n, or in general, n(n-1)(n-2)...(n-m)/m! In other words the number of duplicates increases factorially rising from 1, while the number of total possibilities is multiplied by one less each time. This means that as soon as m reaches n/2, then the number begins to diminish by exactly the same number that it previously expanded. The numbers in effect pass each other half way, so that there are the maximum number of different ways of arranging 30 partitions in 60 possible locations, but this number diminishes to 1 by the time we are opening the 60th doorway, just as it was when we opened the first doorway. These calculations reflect a simple intuitive fact, that once we have placed half the partitions, then what we are really choosing from then on is which to leave open, a smaller number than the partitions we have so far placed. When we have placed 59 partitions, there is only one location in which we can place the 60th, and this is why if we carry out the calculation at this point it will give a value of 1.

What exactly are the numbers we are talking about? The procedure we have outlined can in fact be expressed more simply in a well-known combinatorial formula which can be applied in any situation where we are assigning a given number of entities to a given number of possible assignments. If the number of doorways is d, and the number of partitions p, then the formula p!/d!(p–d)! will give us the number of possibilities which we have just worked out. With p=60, the highest value that the formula can yield will be when d is half the possible number, that is 60/2×30, and the result of the calculation 60!/(30!(60 – 30)!) is 118,264,581,600,000,000 (a hundred and eighteen thousand trillion). The second highest value, 114,449,595,100,000,000, will be when d is 29 or 31, the next, 103,719,935,500,000,000, when d is 28 or 32, and so on, and the lowest, 1, when d is 0 or 60, and the second lowest, 60, when d is 1 or 59.

These kinds of numbers of possibilities, though quite modest by combinatoric standards, are almost impossible to grasp. To give an intuitive idea of the scale of possibilities we are dealing with in the modest complex, we might perhaps compare our maximum number of possible p-graphs for this comparatively small a-graph with another 18-digit number: the number of seconds believed to have passed since the big bang (provided it occurred 15 billion years ago), that is about 441,504,000,000,000,000. This means that if a computer had begun at the moment of the big bang to draw up all these possible configurations of doorways for this one modest adjacency complex, then it would have had to work at an average of one every four seconds to be finishing now. If we printed out the results on A4 sheets, and set them side by side, they would reach from Earth to the nearest star and back, or 141,255 times to the sun and back, or just short of a billion times round the world.

There are a number of ways of reducing these vast numbers. For example, each p-complex will have as many duplicates as there are symmetries in the system. We can therefore reduce all our totals by this factor. We may also decide that we are only interested in those p-complexes which form a single building, that is a complex in which each cell is accessible from all others without going outside the building. The maximum number of doors that can be closed without necessarily splitting the complex into two or more sub-complexes will always be (n-1)(m-1), or 25 in this case. No way is known of calculating how many of the p-complexes with 25 or less partitions will be single buildings, but, in any case, the realism of this restriction is doubtful because we have not so far taken any account of permeability to the exterior of the form, and in any case, a complex split into two is still a building complex and may be found in reality.

More substantively, we might explore the effects on imposing Steadman's 'light and air' restrictions on the form. Here we find they are far less powerful than we might think in restricting p-complexes. For example, we may approximate a form in which each cell has direct access to light and air by making an internal courtyard as in figure 8.1h give or take a little shifting of partitions to allow the inner corner cells direct access to the courtyard. Combinatorially, this has the effect of reducing the number of internal partitions by 4 to 56, and the maximum number that may be closed – without splitting the building by 1 to 24. The number of p-complexes that can be inscribed within the a-complex is therefore still in the thousands of trillions.

We will find this is generally the case. The imposition of the requirement that each cell should have direct access to outside light and air makes relatively little impact on the number of p-complexes that are possible, the more so since direct access to external light and air will also mean an extra possible permeability in the system which we have not so far taken account of. It is clear that although light and air are inevitably powerful factors in influencing a-complex, they place relatively little restriction on the possible p-complexes. We might even venture a generalisation. 'Bodily' factors like light and air have their effect on buildings by influencing the a-complex, but do not affect the p-complex which is determined, as we have seen in previous chapters, and as we will see more generally below, largely by the psycho-social factors which govern spatial configuration.

If we see buildings, as we must, as both physical and spatial forms, that is as a-complexes with p-complexes inscribed within them, then we must conclude that buildings as a combinatorial system take the form of one combinatorial explosion within another with neither being usefully countable except under the imposition of highly artificial constraints. Is the combinatoric question about architecture then misconceived? If it is, how then should we account for the fact that there do seem to be rather few basic ways of ordering space in buildings? What we must do, I suggest, is rephrase the question. Architecture is not a combinatorial system *tout court* any more than a language is a combinatorial system made up of words and rules of combination. In language, most – almost all in combinatorial

terms – of the grammatically correct sequences of words of a language have
no meaning, and are not in that sense legitimate sentences in the language.
It is how (and why) these combinatoric possibilities are restricted that is
the structure of the language. So with architecture. Most combinatorial
possibilities are not buildings. The question is: why not? How is the combinatorial field restricted and structured so as to give rise to the forms
that exist and others that might legitimately exist? It is this that will be
the theory of architectural form – the laws that restrict and structure the
field of possibility, not the combinatorial laws of possibility themselves.

How then should we seek to understand these restrictions that
structure the field of architectural possibility? There are a number of
important clues. First, as the results reported in chapters 4–8 show, the
configurational properties of space, that is of the p-complex, are the most
powerful links between the forms of built environments and how they
function. It is a reasonable conjecture from these results, and their generality, that, in the evolution of the forms of buildings, factors affecting the
p-complex may dominate those affecting the a-complex. Bodily factors
affecting the a-complex may create certain limits within which p-complexes
evolve, but buildings are eventually structured by factors which affect
the evolution of the p-complex, because it is the p-complex that relates
to the functional differences between kinds of buildings.

Second, the properties of p-complexes that influence and are influenced by function tend to be global, or at least globally related, configurational properties, such as integration, that is properties which reflect the
relations of each space to many, even all, others. For example, the average
quantity of movement along a particular line is determined not so much
by the local properties of that space through which the line passes considered as an element in isolation, but by how that line is positioned in relation to the global pattern of space created by the street system of which
it is a part (see chapter 4). In general we may say that configuration takes
priority over the intrinsic properties of the spatial element in relating
form to function.

These conclusions may be drawn as generalisations from the study
of a range of different types of building and settlement. However, there is
a further, more general, conclusion that may be drawn from these studies

which has a direct and powerful bearing on our present concerns. If we consider the range of cases studied as instances of real p-complexes within the total realm of the possible, we find that as complexes become larger they occupy a smaller and smaller part of the total range of possibility from the point of view of the total spatial integration of the complex, crowding more and more at the integrating end of possibility as complexes grow. For example, the recent doctoral study of over 500 English houses from the mid nineteenth to early twentieth century already referred to [6] with a mean size of 23.6 cells, has found most of the houses lie within the most integrating 30 per cent of the range of possibility and all within 50 per cent. Analysis of large numbers of buildings over a number of years suggests that at around 150 cells, virtually all buildings will be within the shallowest 20 per cent of the range of possibility, and most much below it, at 300 cells, nearly all will be within the bottom 10 per cent, and at around 500 most will be within the bottom 5 per cent. It is clear that as buildings grow, they use less and less of the range of possible p-complexes. The same is true of axial maps of settlements.[7]

In short, the most significant properties of p-complexes seem to be related to the degree and distribution of spatial integration – that is the topological depth of each space from all others – in the complex. It follows that if we can understand theoretically how these characteristic properties of integration are created, then we will have made some significant progress towards understanding how architectural possibility becomes architectural actuality. How then does integration arise in a p-complex in different degrees and with different distributions? The simple fact is that the properties of any p-complex, however large, are constructed only by way of a large number of localised physical decisions: the placing of partitions, the opening of doors, the alignment of boundaries, and so on. What we need to understand in the first instance is how the global configurational properties of p-complexes space are affected by these various types of local physical change. It will turn out that the critical matter is that every local physical move in architecture has well-defined global spatial effects in the p-complex, including effects on the pattern and quantity of integration. It is the systematic nature of these effects by which local physical moves lead to global spatial effects that are the key to how combinatorial possibility in architecture is restricted to the architecturally probable, since these are in effect the laws by which the pattern and degree of integration in a complex is constructed.

Once we understand the systematic nature of these laws, we will be led to doubt the usefulness, and even the validity of the combinatorial theory of architecture in two quite fundamental ways. First, we will doubt the usefulness of the idea of spatial 'elements', because each apparent spatial element acquires its most significant properties from its configurational relations rather than from its intrinsic properties. Even apparently intrinsic properties such as size, shape and degree of boundedness will be shown to be fundamentally configurational properties with global implications for the p-complex as a whole. In effect, we will find that configuration is dominant over the element to the point where we must conclude that the idea of an element is more misleading than it is useful.[8] Spatial elements, we will show, are properly seen not as free-standing 'elements', with intrinsic properties, waiting to be brought into combination with others to create complexes of such properties, but as local spatial strategies to create global configurational effects according to well-defined laws by which local moves induce global changes in spatial configurations.

The second source of doubt will follow from the first: it is not combinatorics per se which create complexes but the local to global laws which restrict combinatorics from the vast field of architectural possibility to certain well-defined pathways of architectural probability. The theory we are seeking lies not in understanding either the theoretically possible or the real in isolation, but in understanding how the theoretically possible becomes the real. We will suggest that the passage from possibility to actuality is governed by laws of a very specific kind, namely laws which govern the relation between spatial configuration and what I will call 'generic function'. Generic function refers not to the different activities that people carry out in buildings or the different functional programmes that buildings of different kinds accommodate, but to aspects of human occupancy of buildings that are prior to any of these: that to occupy space means to be aware of the relationships of space to others, that to occupy a building means to move about in it, and to move about in a building depends on being able to retain an intelligible picture of it. Intelligibility and functionality defined as formal properties of spatial complexes are the key 'generic functions', and as such the key structures which restrict the field of combinatorial possibility and give rise to the architecturally real.

The construction of integration

Let us begin with figure 8.1f, a 6×6 half-partitioned a-complex with an isomorphic p-complex inscribed within it, that is, all partitions are permeable. What we are interested in is how the key global configurational property of integration is affected by closing and opening the central sections of the partitions. To make the process as transparent as possible, instead of using i-values, we will use the total depth counts from each cell from which the i-value is calculated. Half-partitions may be turned into full partitions by adding 'bars', in which case the cells either side become separated from each other, without direct connection. Half-partitions can also be eliminated, in which case the two cells become a single space. If all partitions to a cell are barred, then that cell becomes a block in the system.

Now as we already know from the analysis of shape in chapter 3, the p-complex of figure 8.1f will already have a distribution of i-values, which we can show in figure 8.2a as total depth values, that is the total depth of each cell from all the others, with the sum, 5040, shown below the figure. It is important for our analysis that we understand exactly how these differences arise, since all is not quite as it seems. We will, it turns out, need to make a distinction between the shape of the complex and the boundary of the complex. At first sight, it is clear that the differences between the cells are due to the relation of the cell to the boundary of the complex. Corner cells have most depth, centre edge rather less, then less towards the centre. If we change the shape of the aggregate, say into a 12 × 3 rectangle, as in figure 8.2b then all the individual cell total depths will change, as will the total depth for the aggregate as a whole (6330) reflecting the changing relations of cells to the boundary.

However, if we eliminate the boundary by wrapping either of the two aggregates first round a cylinder so that left joined to right, and then into a torus so that top joined to bottom, then the total depths for all cells in each aggregate would be the same, since starting from each and counting outwards until we have covered all the cells, we will never encounter a

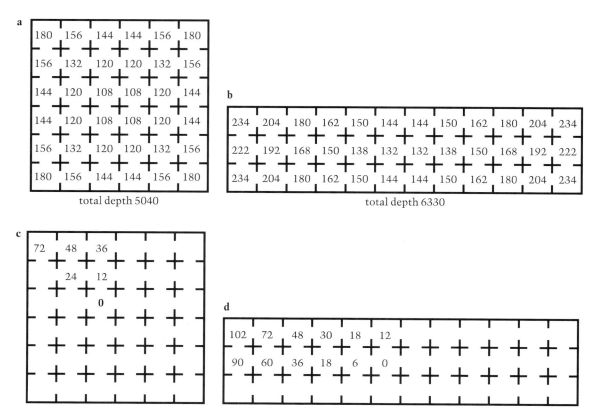

Figure 8.2

boundary and so will find the same pattern of depth from each cell. The total depths of the cells would in fact be equal to the minimum depth of the cells in the bounded aggregate, that is the group of four at the centre of the square form, whose value is 108, and the pair at the centre of the rectangular form, whose depth is 132. However, this implies that in spite of the removal of the boundaries, these differences between the square and rectangular shapes still survive. These differences in total depth values are it seems the product of the shape of the aggregate but not of its boundary.

This can be demonstrated by a simple thought experiment. Take a cellular aggregate, say the six by six square and wrap it onto a torus, thus removing the boundary. Select any 'root' cell and construct a justified graph – that is a graph in which levels of depth of nodes from an initial node are aligned above a selected root node in a series of layers representing depth – in which all cells sharing a doorway with the root are the first layer, all those sharing a doorway to a first layer cell are the second layer, and so on. When the graph reaches any cell adjacent to the boundary in the original bounded aggregate in the plane, any next, deeper cell with which a cell in the justified graph shares a doorway will already be in another branch of the graph. Thus the justified graph finds the limits of the original shape of the aggregate, even though the boundary has been eliminated by wrapping on the torus.

It follows that the uniform depth value that will be found in any shape on a torus will reflect the shape and will be equal to the minimum depth of the original aggregate in the plane. This will be 108 for the square form and 132 for the rectangle. A depth of 108 per cell (three times the number of cells in the complex) can therefore be said to be the depth due to the square form having a square shape and 132 the depth due to the rectangular form having a rectangular shape. When dealing with a standard shape, therefore we may if we wish eliminate this amount of depth from each cell, and deal only with the depth due to the boundary. These remaining depths are shown for the 6 x 6 square and the 12×3 rectangle in figures 8.2c and d. These boundary related depths are due to the fact that the aggregate boundary is barred from its surrounding region. If we were to open all cells to the outside by opening the boundary, and treating the outside region as an element in the system to be included in depth calculations, then clearly the depth values would all change, particularly if we counted the outer region as a single space, in which case cells close to the boundary would have less depth than cells at the centre. This alerts us to the fact that in considering the barring – that is the conversion of half partitions into full partitions – in a cellular aggregate, the boundary is itself an initial partitioning, and like any other partitioning it has effects on the distribution of depth in the aggregate. Bearing this in mind, we may now return to the plane, and hold shape and boundary steady by considering only the square form, in order to explore the depth effects of adding further barrings within the aggregate.

Figure 8.3

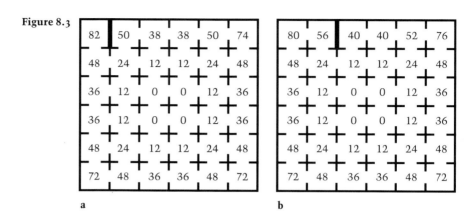

a   b

It is obvious that further internal barring will increase the total depth for at least some cells, since it will have the effect of making certain trips from cell to cell longer. It is perhaps less obvious that the quantity, as well as the distribution, of extra depth created by bars will vary with the location of the bar in relation to the boundary. For example, if we place a bar in the leftmost horizontal location in the top line of cells in figure 8.1, as in figure 8.3a, the total depth in the aggregate will be increased from 5040 to 5060, an additional 20 steps of depth, while if we place the bar one to the right, as in figure 8.3b, then the increase in total depth will be from 5040 to 5072, an additional 32 steps.

How does this happen? First, all the 'depth gain' in figures 8.3a and b is on the line in which the bar is located. On reflection, this must be the case. Depth gain happens when a shortest route from one cell to another requires a detour to an adjacent line. Evidently, any other destination on that adjacent line or on any other line will not require any modification to the shortest path, unless that line is itself barred. Depth gain for a single bar must then be confined to the line on which the bar occurs. But placing the bar at different points on the line changes the pattern of depth gain for the cells along the line. Each cell gains depth equal to twice the number of cells from which it is linearly barred, because each trip from a cell to such cells required a two-cell detour via an adjacent line. Evidently this will be two way, and the sum of depths on the two sides of a single bar

Figure 8.4

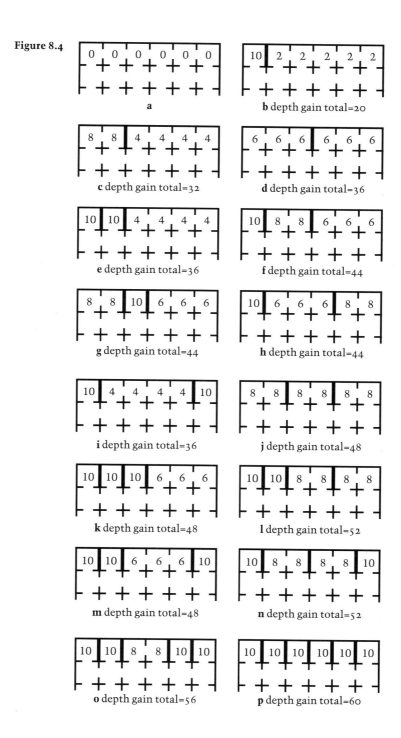

will thus always be the same. It follows that the depth gain values of individual cells will become more similar to each other as the bar moves from edge to centre, becoming identical when the bar is central. It also follows that the total depth gain from a bar will be maximised when the bar is at or near the centre of the line, and will be minimised at the edge. This is illustrated for edge to centre bars on a 6-cell line in figure 8.4 a, b c, and d.

The fact that an edge location for a partition minimises depth gain but maximises the differences between cells, while a central location maximises depth gain but minimises differences is a highly significant property. It means that decisions about where to place a bar, or block a doorway, have implications for the system beyond the immediate region of the bar. If we define a 'local physical decision' as a decision about a particular bar within a system, and a 'global spatial effect' as the outcome of that decision for the system as a whole, it is clear that local decisions do have quite systematic global effects. In these cases, the systematic effects follow what we might call the 'principle of centrality'.

It might be useful to think of such 'local-to-global' effects as 'design principles', that is as rules from which we can forecast the global effect of a local barring decision by recognising what kind of barring we are making. In this case the design principles are two: that the depth gain from a bar is minimised when the bar is placed at the edge and maximised when placed at the centre; and that edge bars make for greater depth gain differences between some cells and others, while central partitions equalise depth gain.

Similar principles govern local-to-global effects when we add a second bar in different locations as in figure 8.4e-j. Depth gains for each cell are equal to twice the number of cells on the far side of the nearest bar. For each cell, bars other than the nearest on either side do not affect depth since once a detour to an adjacent line has been made, then it can be continued without further detour to reach other cells on the original line, provided of course there is no bar on the adjacent line (see below). Figure 8.4k–p then shows that depth effects of three to five bars are governed in the same way, ending with the fully barred line in which each cell gains depth equal to twice the number of other cells in the line. These examples illustrate a second principle: that once a line is barred, then depth gain from the next bar will be minimised by placing it within the shortest remaining line of

cells, and maximised by placing it in the longest. We can call this the
'principle of extension': barring longer lines creates more depth gain than
barring shorter lines. Within each line, of course, the principle of centrality continues to hold, and the distribution of depth gains in the various
cases in figure 8.4 follow these both in the principle of extension and the
principle of centrality. Thus taking figures 8.4g and j, each has a bar in
the second position in from the left, but e then has its second bar immediately adjacent in the third position in from the left, while f has its second
bar two positions away, equidistant from the right boundary of the complex. This is why g has less depth gain than j in spite of its second bar
being in a more central location in the complex as a whole, because, given
the first bar, then what counts is the position of the next bar in the
longest remaining lines, and in j, the bar is placed centrally on that line.
This shows an important implication of the principles of centrality and
extension: when applied together to maximise depth gain, they generate
an even distribution of bars, in which each bar is as far as possible from all
others; while if applied to minimise depth gain, bars become clustered as
close as possible to each other along lines.

Suppose now that instead of locating the second bar on the same line
we locate it on an adjacent line. Figure 8.5a–j shows the sequence of possibilities for the location of the second bar, omitting, for the time being
(but see below) the case where we join bars contiguously in a line. When
barred lines are adjacent, then for each line, the depth gain is greater than
for each bar alone, but the effect disappears when the two barred lines are
not adjacent, as in the final two cases, k and l. The effect is identical if
the two bars are on adjacent lines away from the edge. These effects are
best accounted for by seeing each barring of two adjacent lines as dividing
the pair of lines into an 'inner zone', where there is only one bar to circumvent in each direction, and two 'outer zones' from which two bars
must be circumvented to go from one to the other. The conjoint effect is
entirely due to the outer zones, in that to go from one outer zone to the
other, there is a further bar to circumvent once a detour to the adjacent
line is taken to circumvent the first bar. Depth gain for a cell is therefore
equal to twice the number of cells that lie beyond bars on either line.
Thus the value of twelve in the leftmost example in the top row is the

292 The laws of the field

Figure 8.5

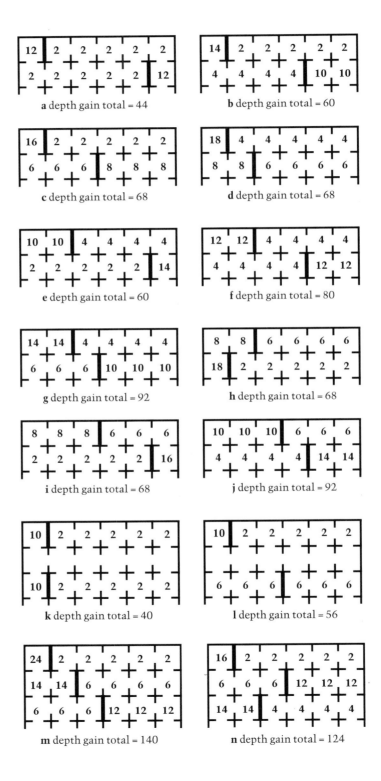

product of twice the five cells on the far side of the bar in the top row, plus twice the single cell on the far side once you move from the top to the second row. Similarly, the total depth of two for each of the cells to the right of the bar in the top row reflects the fact that only one cell is on the far side of the bar in the top row, and none are in the second row. This calculation of depth gain will work for any number of rows of cells, providing that the bars are non-contiguous. Non-contiguity of bars means that there is always a 'way through' for a shortest path.

If we then add a third (non-contiguous) bar on a third line, then there are two alternative possibilities. If the three bars are in echelon, as in figure 8.5m, then 'outer zone' cells on all three lines will gain depth additively equal to twice the number of cells in all the opposite outer zones. This is because when the bars are in echelon, then every detour to an adjacent barred line means that the bar on that line is still beyond where you are on that line, so a further detour is necessary. Inner zone cells gain only twice the number of cells in the outer zones of their own lines.

If the bars are not in echelon, as in figure 8.5n, then the gain will only be as from a pair of adjacent lines since the bar on the central line must be so placed as to allow a 'way through'. The central line will, however, gain depth from its relation to both adjacent lines, and can be counted first in a pair with one, then with the other. If four non-contiguous bars are on four adjacent lines, then the depth gain is according to whether trios of lines are in echelon or not, and so on. If there are two or more bars on the same line, then the calculations will be according to the formula already outlined. If one of the adjacent lines is an edge line, then likewise, this can be calculated according to the formula already explained.

These are the possible non-contiguous barrings on the same general alignment (i.e in this case all are horizontal). What about the addition of a second (or more) non-contiguous bar on the orthogonal alignment, as in figure 8.6a? We already know the effect of the second bar on its own line. Does it have an effect on the line of the first bar? The answer is that it does not and cannot, provided it is non-contiguous, because while it is non-contiguous there will always be a 'way through' for shortest paths from cells on other alignments. Depth gain resulting from a bar on a certain alignment can never be increased by a bar orthogonal to that alignment, while the bars are non-contiguous.

What then are the effects of contiguous bars? There are two kinds: linearly contiguous bars, in which two or more partitions form a single continuous line; and orthogonally contiguous bars, in which two or more bars form a right-angle connection. Within each we can distinguish contiguous bars which link with another bar at one end, and those which link at both ends. First let us look at the right angle, or L-shaped, case for the single connected bar. Figures 8.6b–e shows the depth gain pattern for the simplest case, a two bar L-shape, located at four different positions. The first thing we note is that in all cases the depth gains on 'either side' of the L are in total equal, though very differently distributed. In 8.6b, where the L faces into the top left corner, the depth gain forms a very high peak within the L, which is made up of two elements: first, the depth gains along each of the lines of cells partitioned by the bar, of the kind we have seen already; and second by the conjoint effect of the two bars forming the L, in creating a 'shadow' of cells, each with a depth gain of 2, which mirror the L shape on the outside diagonal to it. This is a phenomenon we have not see before, since with non-contiguous bars all depth gains can be accounted for by the effects of individual bars.

As the L-shaped bar is moved from top left towards the bottom right, while maintaining its orientation, as in 8.6c,d and e, we find that although the individual effects of each of the constituent bars making up the L remains consistent with the effects so far noted, the conjoint 'shadow' effect diminishes, because there is less and less scope for the 'shadow' as the L moves towards the bottom right and the L shape follows, rather than inverts, the L formed by the corner of the outer boundary. We see then that in this case the effect of moving the L from the centre towards the corner will be to diminish depth gain, as expected, as the L moves towards a corner from which the L faces outwards, but to increase it as the L moves towards a corner where the L faces inwards towards the corner.

At first sight, this seems to contradict the principle that edge partitions cause less depth gain and central partitions more. In fact, what we have is a stronger instance of the effect noted in figure 8.4a, where the most

Figure 8.6

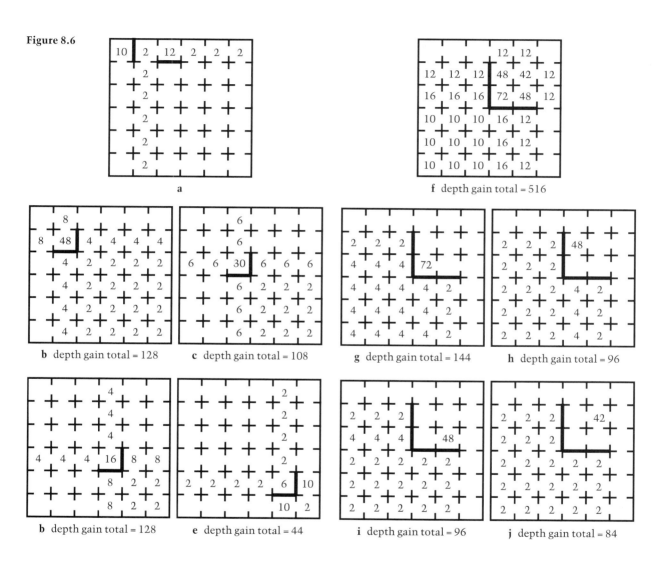

a

f depth gain total = 516

b depth gain total = 128

c depth gain total = 108

g depth gain total = 144

h depth gain total = 96

b depth gain total = 128

e depth gain total = 44

i depth gain total = 96

j depth gain total = 84

peripherally located partition created the least depth gain overall but the greatest depth gain for the single cell. The depth gain was focused, as it were, in a single cell. In 8.6b, the depth gain is even more powerfully focussed in a single cell, both because it focusses both the gain from the two bars making up the L, but also from the 'shadow'. In other words, what counts as the 'other side' of the partition is expanded by forming contiguous partition into an 'enclosure'. Enclosure, we might say, means 'enclosure with respect to what'. The greater the area 'with respect to which' an 'inside' region is enclosed, then the greater the enclosure effect by the focussing of depth gain. This is, in effect, a generalisation of the 'principle of extension' by which greater overall depth gain arises from the greater scope of the effect of the partition. In figure 8.6b, this extension on the 'other side' of the enclosure includes the area between the two alignments affected by the partition, and this increases its extension.

This effect will increase if we add new contiguous bars to the original L-shape. Figure 8.6f for example shows the depth gain pattern for an L-shape whose arms are twice as long as in the previous figure. The depth gain pattern is similar to that for single L-shapes, but even more extreme. Figures 8.6g–j break this down by taking each of the cells on the open side of the barring and showing the shadow due to that cell. This is calculated by taking each open side cell in turn and calculating the detour value for each shadow cell. The shadow shown in figure 8.6f evidently, is the sum of these sub-shadows of figure 8.6g–j, plus those of the four cells on the 'open' side of the L (which are not shown).

Next consider the linear contiguity of bars. Figure 8.7a–g shows a series of cases in which bars are first extended linearly to double unit length and moved across from edge to centre, and then triple unit length. Depth gains are larger even than for L-shaped bars, and the rate of gain increases not only as the line of bars is moved from edge to centre, but also, even more dramatically, as the number of bars formed into a continuous line is increased. For example, the depth gain from a single edge bar is 20, rising to 36 as the bar moves to the centre, but if we expand the bar linearly to a pair, the gain is 180 and if we add a third then the gain is 504. This reflects a simple fact that to detour round one bar – say an edge bar – to a cell that was initially adjacent requires a 2 cell detour. However, if a second bar is added in line, then the detour will be 5 cells, and if a third is added, the detour will be 7 cells, and so on. The contiguous line of bars is the most effective way of increasing depth in the system first because it is the most economical way of constructing an object requiring the longest detour from cells on either side to the other, second because the longer the bar the more it has the effect of increasing the number of cells on either side of it, that is, it has the effect of barring the whole aggregate. Evidently, this 'whole object barring' will have more depth gain to the degree that the object is barred into two equal numbers of cells. Thus in figure 8.7g the long central bar comes as close as possible to dividing the whole object into two equal parts.

Figure 8.7h–j then demonstrates the effect of linearity on three contiguous bars. In all three, at least two bars are located in the second position from the edge. In 8.7h, the bars are formed into a U-shape giving a total depth gain of 124, 28 more than would be gained by the lines independently if they were non-contiguous, and with a very strong peak inside the enclosure. In figure 8.7i, which is a three-bar L-shape, the total depth gain is 200, 104 more than the lines would have independently, and with a less strong peak within the enclosure. In 8.7j, the total gain is 336, 240 more than for the lines independently, and with a much more even spread of values, without any single peak. These differences thus arise simply from the shape formed by the three contiguous lines. The principle is that the more we coil up bars, and create a concentrated peak of depth gain within the coiled up bars, then the less the overall depth gain. Depth gain in the whole system is maximised when bars are maximally uncoiled and construct a maximally linear 'island' of bars. Since the U-shape of 8.7h approximates a 'room', we can say that the most integration efficient way of arranging three contiguous bars is to form them into 'rooms'. Such 'rooms' will not only have the least depth gain effect on the spatial complex, but will also maximise the difference between the depth-gain of a single space (i.e. the 'room') and that in the other spaces of the system. This is the phenomenon we first noted for edge partitions in figure 8.4.

Now if we reflect on figure 8.7j, we can see that all the depth gain apart from that due to the individual bars is to the central bar and to the fact that it connects two ways to form the line of three. This means that if we start from a situation in which we have the two outer bars, then the addition of the single bar connecting the two outer bars into a line in itself adds a depth gain of 272. This double connecting of bars to form a line is the most powerful possible move in creating additional depth, not least because it must necessarily have the effect of eliminating a ring from the system.

Figure 8.7

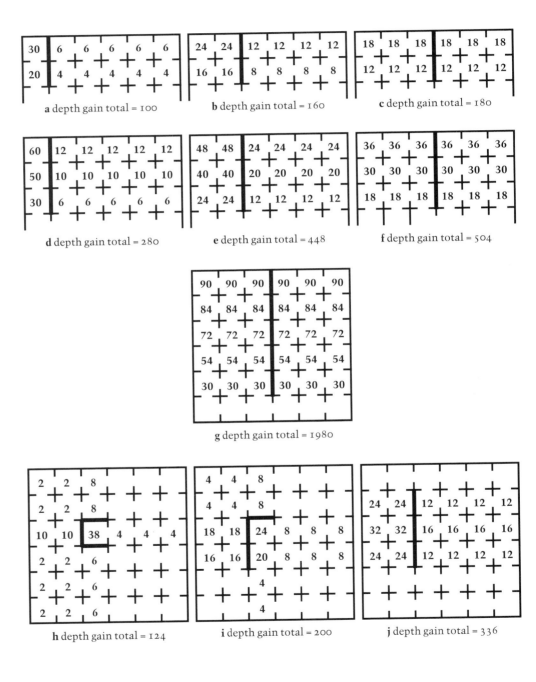

We may summarise all these effects in terms of four broad principles governing the depth gain effects of bars: the principle of *centrality*: more centrally placed bars create more depth gain than peripherally placed bars; the principle of *extension*: the more extended the system by which we define centrality (i.e. the length of lines orthogonal to the bar) then the greater the depth gain from the bar; the principle of *contiguity*:contiguous bars create more depth gain than non-contiguous bars or blocks; and the principle of *linearity*: linearly arranged contiguous bars create more depth gain than coiled or partially coiled bars. All four principles govern *local-to-global* effects in that each individual local physical move has quite specific global effects on the spatial configuration as a whole. At the same time these effects are dependent on the number and disposition of bars and blocks that already exist in the system. The four principles allow us to keep track of the complex inter-relationships between what is already in the system, and the global consequences of new moves. We may therefore expect to be able to construct processes in which different sequences of barring moves will give rise to different global configurational properties.

Elementary objects as configurational strategies

We will see shortly that this is the case. But first we must show that the same principles that govern the opening and closing of partitions, also govern all other types of spatial moves which affect integration such as the creating of corridors, courts or wells, and even changes in the shape of the envelope of the complex. Let us first consider wells. Wells are zones within a complex which are inaccessible from the complex and therefore not part of the spatial structure of the complex. They act in effect as blocks in the system of permeability. We will see that the effects of blocks of different shapes and in different locations have configurational effects on the whole system which follow exactly the same principles as those for bars.

First, let us conceptualise blocks in terms of the barring system we have so far discussed. A block is an arrangement of bars we have so far disallowed, that is an arrangement of four or more bars in such a way as to form a complete enclosure, so that one or more spaces is completely separated from the rest of the spatial system, and effectively eliminated

Figure 8.8

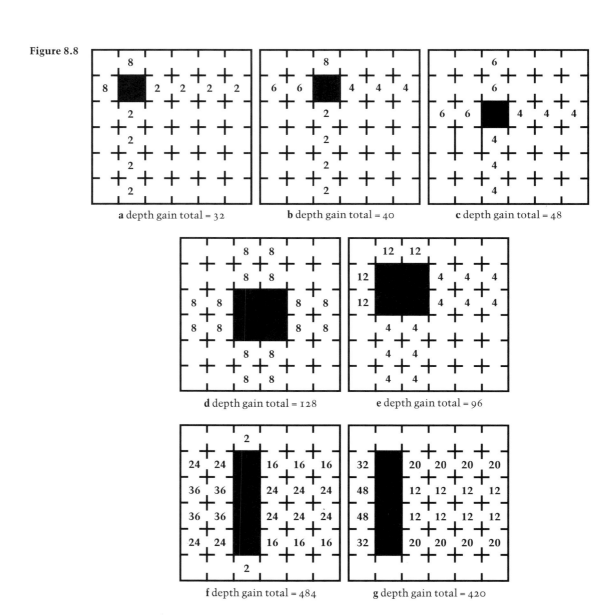

a depth gain total = 32   **b** depth gain total = 40   **c** depth gain total = 48

d depth gain total = 128   **e** depth gain total = 96

f depth gain total = 484   **g** depth gain total = 420

from it. A block is in effect the elimination of one or more cells from the spatial system. Three possible cases of single cell elimination are shown in figure 8.8a, b and c with the resulting depth gains. Because the block bars lines in two directions all that happens is that the pattern of depth gain resulting from the blocks follows the edge to centre rules, as for bars. There will not, for example, also be 'shadow' effects, as with L-shaped bars, because the relation between the enclosed space and those on the other side of the L-shape, which created the 'shadow' has been eliminated by the complete closing off of the block. We must note of course that the depth gains figures are less than for a simple barring, but this is simply because one cell has been eliminated from the system. We may if we wish correct this by substituting i-values for depth gains, since these adjust depth according to the total number of cells in the system, but at this stage it is simpler to simply record the depth gains and note the effect of the elimination of a cell.

Figure 8.8d–g then shows four possible shapes and locations for blocks of four cells, together with the depth gains for each cell and the total depth gain indicated bottom right of the complex. As we would expect from the study of bars, the compact 2×2 block has much less depth gain than either of the linear 4×1 forms, and the linear forms have higher depth gains in central locations than peripheral locations (as would compact blocks). We may note that, as we may infer from bars, the depth gain effects from changes of shape are much greater than those from changes of location. But also of course the locational effects of high depth gain shapes – that is linear shapes – are much greater than the locational effects of low depth gain – or compact – shapes.

It is clear that in this way we can calculate the depth gain effect of any internal block of any shape and that it will always follow the general principles we have established for bars. However, there is another important consequence of this, namely that we can also make parallel calculation for blocks placed at the edge of the complex. The reason this is important is that such peripherally located blocks are not 'wells' which by definition are internal to the complex, but changes in the shape of the envelope of the complex. It is clear from this that we may treat changes in the external shape of the complex in exactly the same way as interior 'holes' within the complex. Since we have already shown that such 'holes' are special cases of barring, then there is a remarkable unification here. From the point of view of the construction of integration – which we already know to be the chief spatial correlate of function within the

Figure 8.9

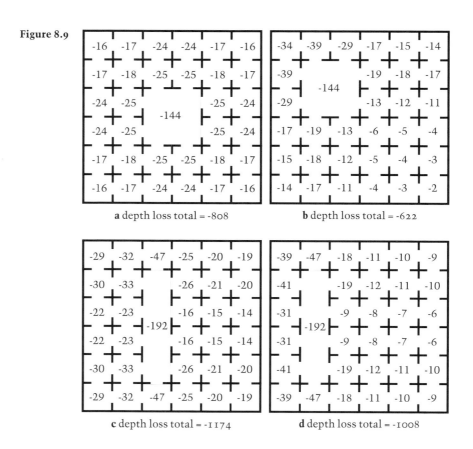

a depth loss total = -808

b depth loss total = -622

c depth loss total = -1174

d depth loss total = -1008

complex – it seems that partitions within the complex are the same kind of thing as changes to the shape of the complex, whether these are internal, as with wells, or external, as with changes in the envelope shape.

We will now show that the creation of larger spaces within a complex such as courts and corridors can also be brought within the scope of this synthesis and be shown to be the same kind of phenomenon and subject to the same laws. First, we must conceptualise what we mean by the creation of larger spaces in terms of a barring process. Larger open spaces in the complex are created by eliminating the existing two-thirds partitions instead of completing the partition, and in effect turn two neighbouring spaces into what would then be identified as a single space. Figure 8.9a–d does this so as to substitute open spaces for the blocks shown in

Figure 8.10

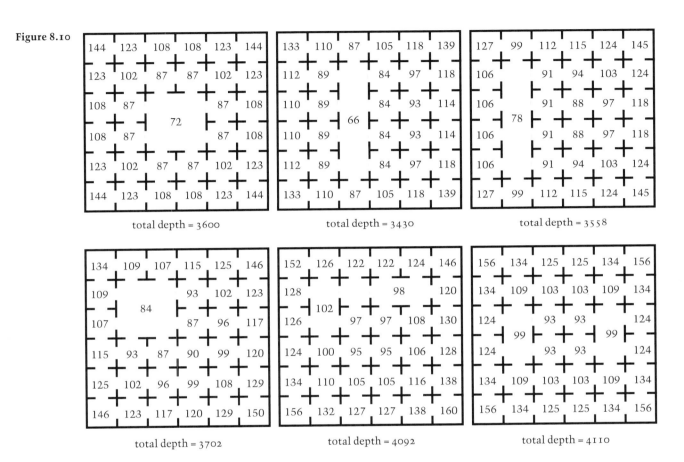

the previous cases, and gives the consequent depth *loss* (that is, integration gain) for each cell. The depth loss for the larger space is calculated by substituting the new value for the whole space for each of the values in the original form and adding them together. Total depth loss for each form is shown below the figure.

The first point to be noted is that the depth loss for a shape of a given size is a constant, regardless of location in the configuration. This is because from the point of view of the large space, the effect of substituting a single space for two or more spaces is to change the relations of those spaces with each other – that is to eliminate a certain number of steps of depth – but not to change the relations of those spaces to the larger system. However, although the depth loss for the larger space is constant, its effects on the rest of the system are not. In fact they vary in exactly the opposite way to the blocks. Whereas peripherally located blocks add less depth to the system than centrally placed blocks, peripherally placed open spaces eliminate less depth than centrally placed spaces; and a linear arrangement of cells into a single space has a greater depth loss (more integrating) effect than a square arrangement, and this effect is greater when the linear space is placed centrally than when it is placed peripherally.

The first four complexes of figure 8.10 show the same cases but marking each space with its total depth from the rest of the system rather than its depth loss. Here what we note is that identical larger spaces in different locations will have different total depths reflecting their location in the complex. It is only the depth loss from making two or more spaces into one that is identical, not the depth values of the location of these spaces in the complex. Thus we can see that a centrally placed open 'square' is more integrating (i.e. has less total depth) in itself than a peripherally placed one, and that a linear form will be more integrating than a compact form. These effects are of course exactly the inverse of those of blocks, and we may therefore say that they are governed by the same laws. In the two final examples in figure 8.10 the four open cells are arranged as two two-cell spaces rather than a single four-cell space and show another inverse principle: that contiguously joined spaces will always create more integration than a comparable number of discrete spaces.

Thus the four principles of centrality, extension, contiguity and linearity which governed the depth gain effects of bars and blocks also govern the depth effects on the global system of creating larger open spaces, though in the contrary direction. More centrality for larger spaces means more integration, more extended lines from larger spaces means more integration, more continuity of larger spaces means more integration and more linearity of larger spaces means more integration. A useful bonus is that in the case of larger spaces we can actually see that the effects are not within the spaces themselves but are to do with the effect of the spaces on the remainder of the system.

We can now draw a significant conclusion. Not only partitions, internal walls and external shape changes but also rooms and larger linear or compact open spaces such as corridors and courts have all been shown to be describable in the same formal terms and therefore to be, in a useful sense, the same kind of thing. This has the important implication that we will always be able to calculate the effects of any spatial move in any system in a consistent way, and indeed be able to predict its general effects from knowledge of principle. This allows us to move from a static analysis of the global implications of local changes in system to the study of dynamic spatial processes in which each local move seeks, for example, to maximise or minimise one or other type of outcome. When we do this we will find out that both the local configurations we call elements and the global patterns of the spatial complex as a whole are best seen as emergent phenomena from the consistent application of certain types of spatial move. We will call these dynamic experiments 'barring processes'.

Barring processes

For example, we may explore barring processes which operate in a consistent way, say to maximise or minimise depth gain, and see what kind of cellular configurations result. In making these experimental simulations, it is clear that we are not imagining that we are simulating a process of building that could ever have occurred. It is unrealistic to imagine that a builder would know in advance the depth gain consequences of different types of barring. However, it is entirely possible that within a building tradition, a series of experiments in creating cellular arrangements would lead to a form of learning of exactly the kind we are interested in: that certain types of local move will have global consequences for the pattern as a whole which are either functionally beneficial or not. We may then imagine that our experiments are concerned not with simulating a one-off process of building a particular building, but with trying to capture the evolutionary logic of a trial-and-error process of gradually learning the global consequences of different types of local barring moves. In this sense, our experiments are about how design principles might be learnt rather than how particular buildings might be built.

First some definitions. We define a barring *move* as the placing of a single bar whose only known (or, on the evolutionary scale, discovered) consequence is its depth gain for the system as a whole. A barring *manoeuvre* is then a planned series of two or more moves where the depth gain effect of the whole series is taken into account, rather than simply the individual moves. Manoeuvres may be 2-deep, 3-deep, and so on according to the number of moves they contain. Moves are by definition 1-deep manoeuvres. A move may be made in the knowledge that one move eliminates more of a certain type of possibility than another. For example, a bar placed away from the boundary eliminates two possible locations for non-contiguous bars, whereas a bar contiguous with the boundary eliminates only one. This is important, since the location of one bar will often affect where the next can go, and it will turn out that in some processes in the 6×6 complex non-edge bars exhaust non-contiguous bars within about fourteen steps, whereas with edge bars it is twenty, and this makes a significant difference to a process. We allow this knowledge within moves, because it can be seen immediately and locally as a consequence of the move, provided the principles are understood.

Both moves and manoeuvres thus have foresight about depth gain, but only manoeuvres have foresight about future moves. A random barring process is one in which barring moves are made independently of each other and without regard for depth gain or any other consequence. We might say then that in describing moves and manoeuvres we are describing the degree to which a process is governed by forethought. At the opposite extreme from the random process, it follows, there will be the process governed by an n-deep manoeuvre, where n is the number of bar locations available, meaning that the whole set of bars is thought out in advance, and each takes into account the known future positions of all others.

Let us now consider different types of barring process. Figure 8.11a–d sets out a barring process of 24 bars, numbered in order of placement in which each move is designed to maximise depth gain. We choose 24 because 25 is the maximum that can be placed without dividing the aggregate into discontinuous zones (that is, in effect, into two buildings), and one less means that one 'ring' will remain in the circulation system (that is one cycle in its graph), so that if there is a process which maximises some property of this ring then we might find out what it is. Bars are numbered in order of placing, and we will now review this ordering.

Figure 8.11

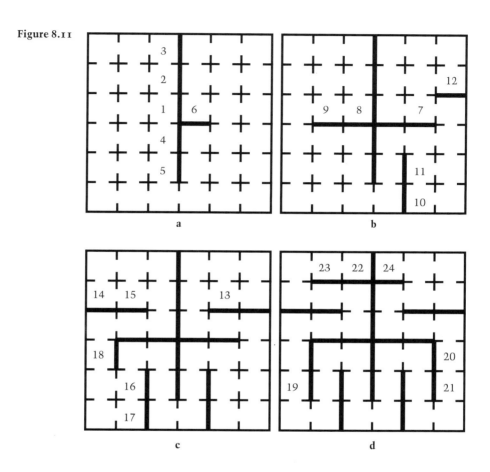

To maximise depth gain, our first bar – bar 1 – must be placed exactly to bisect a line of cells. It does not matter which we select, since the effect of all such bisections will be equivalent. But bar 2 must take into account the location of the first, since depth gain will be maximal only if it is linearly contiguous with it. The same principle governs the location of the bars 3, 4 and 5. After five moves therefore we must have a long central bar reaching to one edge, and we have in fact created the form shown in 8.7g, which is the most depth gain efficient way of using fewest bars to 'nearly divide' the aggregate into two. Thus we have arrived at a significant global outcome for the object as a whole, even though we have at each stage only followed a purely local rule. Although individual moves had a certain

degree of choice, the configurational outcome as a whole, we can see, was
quite deterministic.

Since the next move cannot continue on the central bar line without
cutting the aggregate into two, we must look around for the next depth
maximising move. We know we must bisect the longest sequence of cells,
and if possible our bar must be contiguous with bars already placed. To
identify the longest sequence, we must recognise that the barring so far
has effectively changed the shape of the complex. We could, for example,
cut the complex down the line of the central partition and treat it almost
as two complexes. As a result, there is now a longest sequence of cells
running around both sides of the central partition which does not form a
single line, but it does constitute the longest sequence of shortest available routes in the complex. It is by partitioning this line close to its centre
that we will maximise depth gain, that means placing the bar at right
angles to the partitioning line at its base in one of the two possible locations. The next bar must then take account of which has been selected,
and in fact extend that bar. The next two must repeat the same move on
the other side, thus taking us up the ninth bar in the figure. The same
principle can then be applied to the next sequence of bars, and in fact all
we must do to complete the process is to continue applying the same
principle in new situations as they arise from the barring process. By bar
24, the pattern is as shown in the final form in figure 8.11d.

Looking at the final form, we first confirm that once a 25th bar is
added no further bar could be added without splitting the aggregate into
two. We also note that the configuration of space created by the barring is,
excepting the small ring that would be eliminated by bar 25, a single 'unilinear' sequence of cells, that is the form with the maximum possible
depth from all points to all others. By maximising depth gain at every
stage of the process we arrive, perhaps not surprisingly, at a form which
globally maximises depth gain. We also note, that by applying simple
rules to the barring process, we have converted a process which theoretically could lead to an astronomical number of possible global forms, to
one which leads almost deterministically to a specific form.

Figure 8.12a–d now illustrates the contrary process in which each
move minimises depth gain, again with numbering in the order of the

Figure 8.12

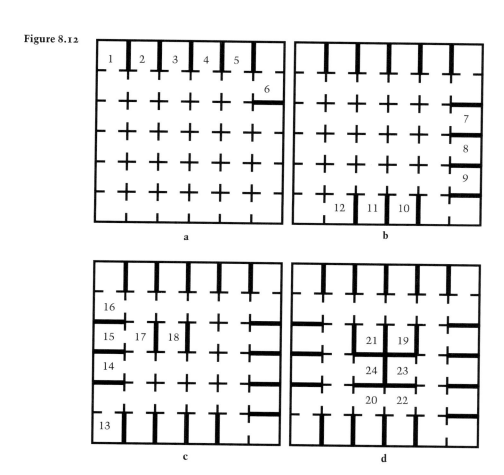

moves. Bar 1 must be at the edge of a line of cells, and to minimise the loss of non-contiguous bar locations it should also be on one of the outer-most lines of cells. Once we have bar 1, the following moves to minimise depth gain must continue to bar the already barred line, since this line is now shorter than any other line, and to do so each time as close to the edge of the remaining cell sequence as possible. As before, then, bars 1 – 5 are forced, and lead to a very specific overall pattern. A similar procedure is then forced on other edge lines, obviously omitting bars which would form a right angle with existing bars, since this would split the system into two. Bars 1–16 therefore continue this process until the possibilities are exhausted.

The next move must be non-contiguous and must be as near the edge as possible. Several identical possibilities exist, so we select 17. 18 and 19 must continue to bar the same line, leaving only one of two possible identical further non-contiguous moves. We select 20. Now no more non-contiguous moves are available, so we must select contiguous moves with the least depth gain. The best turns out that rebarring the already barred line on which 20 lies has the least depth gain, in spite of the fact that it creates a three-sided enclosure. But the next move cannot create the same pattern to the right, since this will also create a double line block as well as a three-sided enclosure. Barring the open line at 22 has less depth gain than barring the adjacent line to the right, at which point 23 becomes optimal. The final bar must then be on one of five still open lines, the four comprising the 'ring', and the one passing through the centre. Cutting the ring creates much more depth gain than cutting the centre line, because it creates a block in the system that is four cells deep from the boundary. Of the possible locations on the centre line, the central location has less depth gain because the location one to the right creates a two-deep enclosure, which creates more extra depth than the difference between the centre and one-from-centre location.

The depth minimising process has thus given rise to a form which is as striking as the depth maximising process: a ring of open cells accessing outer and inner groups of one deep cells. We have only to convert the doors in the ring to full width permeabilities to create a fundamental building form: the ring corridor accessing separate 'rooms' on either side. This has happened because the depth gain minimising strategy tends to two kinds of linearity: a linearity in dividing lines of cells up into separate single cells; and a linearity in creating the open cell sequences that provide access to these cells. Aficionados of Ockham's razor will note that both these contrary effects follow from the single rule that bars should always be placed so as to bar the shortest line of cells available as near the edge as possible. This means that once a line has been divided, then it minimises depth gain to divide it again, since, other things being equal, the remainder of an already barred line will always be shorter than an unbarred line. figure 8.13a and b shows the final forms from the two processes, together with depth values for each cell and the total depth for each bottom right.

Figure 8.13

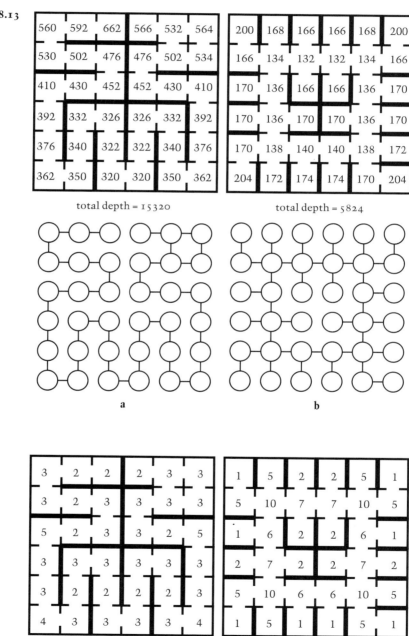

The total depth for the depth maximising process is 15320 while that for the depth minimising process is little more than a third as much at 5824. These differences are all the more remarkable in view of the fact that each form has exactly the same number of partitions. The only difference is the way the partitions are arranged.

But in spite of their differences, each of the forms generated seems in its way quite fundamental. The depth maximising form is close to being a unilinear sequence, that is the form with the maximum possible depth from all cells. The depth minimising form approximates if not a bush, then at least a bush like arrangement built on a ring. We have arrived at these forms by constraining the combinatorial process down certain pathways by some quite simple rules. These have created well defined outcomes through morphological processes which are objective in the sense that although the selection and implementation of rules is a human decision, the local to global morphological effects of these rules, whether for the individual move in the process or the accumulative result, is quite independent of human decision. The eventual global pattern of space 'emerges' from the localised step-by-step process. At the same time, processes whose rules are similar 'converge' on particular global types which may vary in detail but at least some of whose most general properties will be invariant – the tendency to form long sequences with few branches, the tendency to generate one-deep dead end spaces, the tendency to form smaller or larger rings and so on.

This combination of emergence and convergence is immensely suggestive. It appears to offer a natural solution to the apparent paradox we noted at the start of this chapter: that in spite of the vastness of the combinatorial field, intuition suggested relatively few ways of designing space. We may now reformulate this paradox as a tentative conclusion: consistently applied and simple rules arising from what is and is not an intelligible and functionally useful spatial move create well-defined pathways through the combinatorial field which converge on certain well-defined global spatial types. These laws of 'emergence-convergence' seem to be the source of structure in the field of architectural possibility. What then are these laws about? I propose they are about what I called 'generic function', that is properties of spatial arrangements which all,

or at least most 'well-formed' buildings and built environments have in
common, because they arise not from specific functional requirement,
that is specific forms of occupation and specific patterns of movement
but from what makes it possible for a complex to support any complex
of occupation or any pattern of movement.

The theory of generic function: intelligibility and functionality

The first aspect of generic function reflects the property of 'intelligibility'
which Steadman suggests might be one of the critical factors restricting
architectural possibility. In chapter 4 we suggested that the intelligibility
of a form can be measured by analysing the relation between how a complex can be seen from its parts and what it is like in an overall pattern, that
is as a distribution of integration. This was expressed by a scattergram
showing the degree of correlation between the connectivity of a line,
which is a local property of the line and can be seen from the line, and
integration, which is a global property relating the line to the system as a
whole and which cannot therefore be seen from the line. How might this
concept relate to the construction of spatial patterns by physical moves?
Visibility is in fact interesting since it behaves in a similar way to depth
under partitioning. For linear cell sequences the effect of bars on visibility exactly mirrors depth gain, though in a reverse direction: visibility lost
from a bar is exactly half the depth gain from the same bar, and as the bar
moves from edge to centre the total visibility along the line decreases,
while at the same time the visibility value of cells along that line become
more homogeneous, eventually becoming the same with a central bar.

In our two complexes, then, let us define visibility very simply as
the number of cells that can be seen from the centre of each cell. These
visibility values are set out for our two depth maximising and minimising
complexes in figures 8.13c and d. These visibility values and their mean
index the visual connectivity of the complex. We may also express these
by drawing an axial map of the fewest lines that pass through all the cells.
We can see how many cells each line passes through, and how this differs
from one complex to another. We can if we wish express this in a summary way by working out the ratio of the means depths for each cell and the
mean visibility of each cell. For the depth minimising form, the mean

Figure 8.14

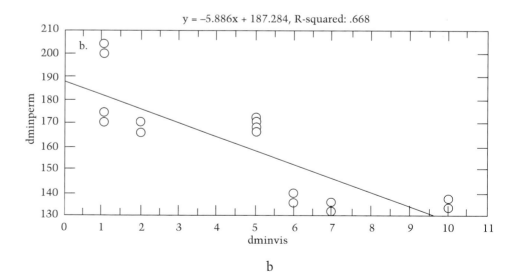

a.

y = –22.489x + 490.523, R-squared: .031

a

b.

y = –5.886x + 187.284, R-squared: .668

b

depth from cells is 5.3, and the mean visibility is 3.9. We might call this a
.74 visibility to depth ratio. In the depth maximising form, the mean depth
is 11.9 while the mean visibility is 2.8. a visibility ratio of .24, about a
third that of the depth minimising form. This seems to agree quite well
with intuition.

This shows how the visibility and depth properties of the complex
relate to each other. However, we may learn more by correlating the permeable depth figures for cells with their visibility figures and expressing
the relation in a scattergram. The better the values correlate, the more we
can say that what you can see from the constituent cells of the system are
a good guide to the global pattern of depth in the complex which cannot be
seen from a cell, but which must be learnt. The correlation thus expresses
the intelligibility of the complex. Figures 8.14a and b are the scatters and
correlation coefficients for our two cases, showing that the depth minimising form is far more intelligible than the depth maximising form.

This formally confirms our intuition that the depth maximising
form is hard to understand, in spite of being a single sequence, because the
sequence is coiled up and the information available from its constituent
cells is too poor and undifferentiated to give much guidance about the
structure of the complex as a whole from its parts. The opposite is the case
in the depth minimising complex. On reflection, we can see that this will
always tend to be the case with depth maximising processes since the
partitioning moves that maximise depth are also those which also maximally restrict visibility.

There are therefore, as Steadman suggests, fundamental reasons to
do with the nature of human cognition and the nature of spatial complexes
which will bias the selection of spatial forms away from depth maximising
processes and in the direction of depth minimising processes. Through this
objective – in the sense that we have measured as a property of objects
rather than as a property of minds – property of intelligibility then we can
see one aspect of generic function structuring the pathways from combinatorial possibility to the architecturally real.

There are, however, further reasons why depth minimising forms will
be preferred to depth maximising forms which have to do with functionality. Functionality we define as the ability of a complex to accommodate

Locally convex movement; when small movements intersect and form a local convex region.

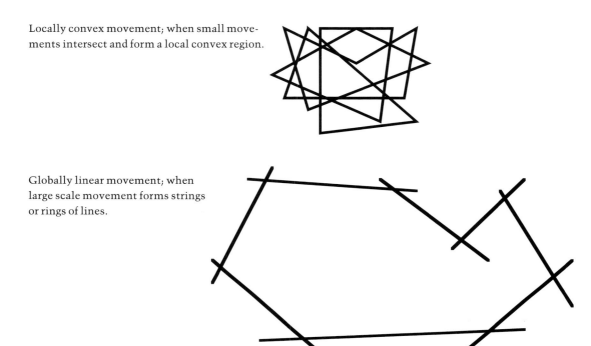

Globally linear movement; when
large scale movement forms strings
or rings of lines.

Figure 8.15

functions in general, and therefore potentially a range of different functions, rather than any specific function. Intuitively, deep tree-like forms
such as the depth maximising form seem functionally inflexible and
unsuited to most types of functional pattern while the depth minimising
form seems to be flexible and suited to a rather large number of possible
functions. Can this be formalised?

   It is useful to begin by considering in as generic a way as possible the
types of human behaviour that occur in buildings. We may do this best by
considering not the purpose or meaning of an activity but simply its physical and spatial manifestation, that is, what can actually be observed
about human activity by, say, an extra-terrestrial who had no idea what
was going on and could only record observations. Generically, such an

observer would conclude, two kinds of thing happen in space: occupation and movement. Occupation means the use of space for activities which are at least partly and often largely static, such as conversing, meeting, reading, eating or sleeping, or at most involve movement which, when traced over a period, remains localised within the occupied space, such as cooking or working at a laboratory bench, as shown in figure 8.15.

Movement we can define not as the small local movements that may be associated with some forms of occupation, and therefore to be seen as aspects of occupation, but movement between spaces of occupation, or movement in and out of a complex of such spaces. Movement is primarily about the relations between spaces rather than the spaces themselves, in contrast to occupation which makes use of the spaces themselves. We can see this as a scale difference. Occupation uses the local properties of specific spaces, movement the more global properties of the pattern of spaces.

There is also a difference between occupation and movement in the spatial form each takes. Because spatial occupation is static, or involves only localised movement, the requirement that it places on space is broadly speaking convex, even when this involves localised movement within the space. In particular, any activity that involves the interaction or co-presence of several people is by definition likely to be convex, since it is only in a convex space that each person can be aware of all the others. Movement, on the other hand, is essentially linear, and the requirement that it places on space is consequently linear, at least when seen locally in its relation to occupation. There must be clear and relatively unimpeded lines through spaces if movement is to be intelligible and efficient.

Occupation and movement then make requirements of space that are fundamentally different from each other in that one is convex and the other linear. Because this is so there is an extra difficulty in combining occupation and movement in the same space. There will always, of course be practical or cultural reasons why different forms of occupation cannot be put in the same space – interference, scaling of spaces, privacy needs, and so on – in spite of the fact that each is convex and in principle could be spatially juxtaposed to others. But to assemble movement and forms of occupation in the same space is in principle more difficult

Figure 8.16

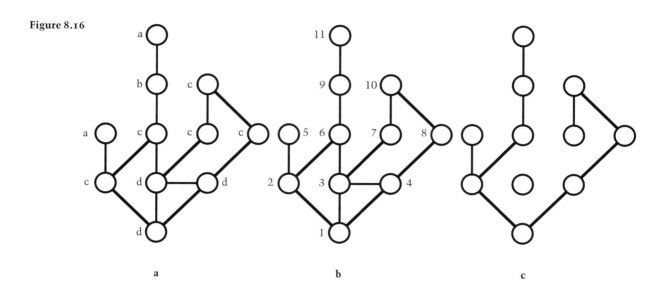

because over and above functional interference, occupation and movement have fundamentally different spatial shapes. The interference effect
from occupation to occupation and from movement to movement will be
of a different kind to that from occupation to movement because the spatial requirements are more difficult to reconcile.

Because this is so, it is common to find that the relation between
movement and occupation in spatial complexes is often one of adjacency
rather than overlap, whether this occurs in spaces which are fully open
(as for example when we have both lines of movement and static occupation in a public square), or fully closed, as when we have rooms adjacent
to corridors, or one is open and the other closed, as when houses align
streets. In each case, the linearity required for movement is achieved by
designing movement to occur in spaces which pass immediately by
rather than through occupation spaces.

Now let us consider the types of space that are available to meet the
requirements of occupation and movement. First we must consider the
most basic topological properties as embodied in the graph of a complex,
since even at this level topologically different types of space have quite
different potentials for occupation and movement. Let us first consider
a familiar graph, as shown in 8.16a, b and c.

In this graph, as in others, the spaces that make up the graph can be divided into four topological types. First, there are spaces with a single link. These are by definition dead-end spaces through which no movement is possible to other spaces. Such spaces have movement only to and from themselves, and are therefore in their topological nature occupation-only spaces. Examples are marked 'a' in figure 8.16a. The link from one-connected spaces to the rest of the graph is necessarily a cut link, meaning that its elimination must split the graph into two, in this case the space whose link has been cut and the rest of the graph. Because the cut link only serves a single space, the effect of cutting makes little difference to the remainder of the complex beyond minor reductions in the depth of the rest of the complex following the elimination of a space.

Second, there are spaces with more than one link but which form part of a connected sub-complex in which the number of links is one less than the number of spaces, that is, a complex which has the topological form of a tree. Such spaces cannot in themselves be dead end spaces, but must be on the way to (and back from) at least one dead end space. All links to spaces in such complexes, regardless of the number of links to each space, are also 'cut links' in that the elimination of any one link has the effect of splitting one or more spaces from the rest of the complex. Such spaces are marked 'b' in figure 8.16a. A consequence of the definition is that there is in any such sub-complex (or complex) exactly one route from each space to every other space, however large the sub-complex and however it is defined. This implies that movement through each constituent space will only be to or from a specific space or series of spaces. This in turn implies that movement from origins to destinations which necessarily pass through a b-type space must also return to the origin through the same space.

Third, there are spaces with more than one link which form part of a connected sub-complex which contains neither type a nor type b spaces, and in which there are exactly the same number of links as spaces. Such spaces are marked 'c' in figure 8.16a. The definition means that c-type spaces must lie on a single ring (though not all spaces on the ring will be c-type) so that cutting a link to a c-type space will automatically reduce the ring to one or more trees. Movement from a c-type space through a

Figure 8.17

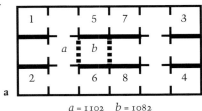
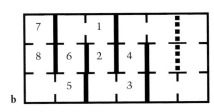

a

$a = 1102$ $b = 1082$

neighbour need not return through the same neighbour but must return through exactly one other neighbour.

Finally there are spaces with more than two links and which form part of complexes which contain neither a- nor b-type spaces, and which therefore must contain at least two rings which have at least one space in common. Such spaces must lie on more than one ring, and are labelled 'd' in figure 8.16a. Movement from d-type spaces through a neighbour has the choice of returning by way of more than one other neighbour.

We may also define subcomplexes of the a-, b-, c- or d-type as the space of that type plus all the spaces by reference to which it is defined as a space of that type, even though some of those spaces may belong also to other subcomplexes. (In other words, a subcomplex of a given type is a complex containing at least one space of that type.) Looking at numbered spaces in figure 8.16b, we can then say that spaces 5 and 11 are a-type spaces, and that the sub-complex formed by spaces 2 and 5 and that formed by 9 and 11 can be thought of as a-type subcomplexes. Space 9 is a b-type space, and that the subcomplex formed by spaces 6, 9 and 11 can be seen as a b-type sub-complex. Spaces 2, 6, 7, 8 and 10 are c-type spaces and each may be seen as forming part of a local ring, or c-type complex: thus 2 and 6 are part of the c-type subcomplex formed by spaces 1, 2, 6 and 3, and 7, 8 and 10 are part of the c-type complex formed by spaces 3, 7, 10, 8 and 4. Spaces 3 and 4 are d-type spaces and are part of the d-type subcomplex formed by spaces 1, 2, 3, 4, 6, 7, 8 and 10. Spaces are, in effect, unambiguously defined by their place in a complex, but this does not mean that spaces that contribute to that definition do not form part of other complexes. For example, an a-space may be part of a b-complex, or a c-space may be part of a d-complex without in either case compromising its unique identity as an a- or c- type space.

There are simple and fundamental relationships between these elementary topologies and the depth minimising and maximising processes. A depth minimising process will in its nature tend first to leave long lines of spaces unimpeded and to preserve their connection to other long lines, and second to coil contiguous bars up into small, one with deep 'rooms'. This is illustrated in figure 8.17a where the first eight bars cut the shortest lines, to create rooms at either end and potential rooms in the centre. The dotted bars marked 'a' and 'b' represent two possible choices at this point, and the figure on the right side shows the total depth in the system after each. The analysis shows that the two one-deep rooms add far less depth than one two-deep complex, in effect because the two-deep complex is created by five contiguous bars, whereas the one-deep spaces are each created by three contiguous bars. The depth minimising process thus tends to create a-type spaces linked by global c- and d-type complexes, as was the case in the 6 x 6 example in figure 8.13b. In contrast, the depth maximising process, as shown in figure 8.17b for example, will by contiguously barring the longest available lines, create b-type spaces and therefore sequences rather than a-type spaces, and localise c- and d-complexes at the earliest possible stage of generation, and with a configuration in which there are few a-type spaces, and these at the end of long sequences, with any rings in the system highly localised.

In other words depth minimising processes will tend locally to a-type complexes and globally to d-type complexes (in figure 8.13b it is only the final 24th bar that reduces a strong global d-complex to a global c-complex), while depth maximising processes will tend globally to b-type complexes and locally to small residual c-type complexes. This is instructive because it tells us how these elementary configurations are related to the product of the functionally critical property of integration in spatial complexes. Essentially, a- and d-type spaces create integration, while b- and c-type spaces create segregation. In other words, segregation in a complex is created almost entirely by the sequencing of spaces.

Since this is not obvious, it is worth illustrating. In figure 8.18 for example, in the left column, we increase the size of the ring from 8 to 12 spaces and the i-value increases (i.e. becomes less integrated) from .4285 for the 8-ring to .4545 for the 12-ring. In the second column, we add

Figure 8.18

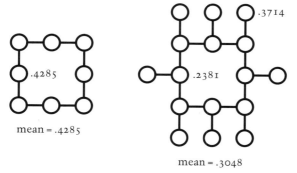

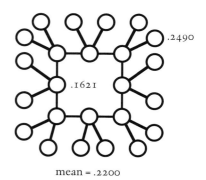

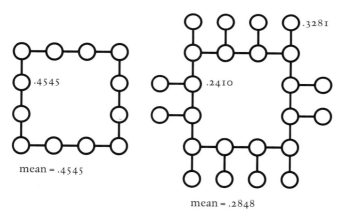

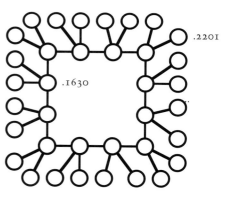

a single a-type space to each c-type space. Both complexes become on average more integrated, but the 12-ring complex below becomes relatively more integrated at .2848 than the 8-ring complex above at .3048. In fact, the ring spaces in the 12-ring complex are slightly less integrated at .2410 than those of the 8-ring complex at .2381, but the a-type space of the 12-ring complex are markedly more integrated at .3281 than those of the 8-ring complex at .3714. In the right column, we link two a-spaces to each c-space and the pattern becomes even more marked. The 12-ring complex is now more integrated at .2011 than the 8-ring complex at .2200, with ring spaces at .1630 compared to .1621, but a-spaces at .2201 compared to .2490.

We now have a more or less complete account of the relation between generative processes, the creation of different types of local and global space complexes, and the construction of patterns of integration. We can now formulate the question at the centre of our argument: what are the implications of these spatial variations for occupation and movement, that is, for the generic functioning of spatial complexes? In exploring this, we should bear in mind one of the major findings of the research reported in chapters 5 to 8: that the more movement in a complex is from all parts to all other parts, then the more the pattern of movement in a complex will tend to follow the pattern of integration.

First we must note that each of the types of space we have identified, and the type of complex it characterises, has generically different implications for space occupation and movement. As we have already indicated, a-type spaces do not have through movement at all and therefore do raise the issue of relating occupation to movement (other than movement to and from the space itself). b-type spaces raise the possibility of through movement but also control it strongly, both because each route through a b-type space is unique and also because return movement must pass through the same space. c-type spaces also raise the possibility of through movement while also constraining it to specific sequences of spaces, though without the same requirement for the return journey. d-type space permits movement, but with much less built-in control because there is always choice of routes in both directions.

It is clear then that b-type and to a lesser extent c-type spaces have a much more determinative relation to movement than either a-type or d-type spaces. While the a-type does not allow for through movement, and the d-type allows choice of movement, the b-type and the c-type permit but at the same time constrain it by requiring it to pass through specific sequences of spaces. The b-type is the most constraining. For any trip from an origin to a destination, every b-space offers exactly one way in and one way out of each space and every trip in a b-complex must pass both ways through exactly the same sequence of spaces. A similar, though weaker, effect is found for c-spaces and c-complexes, because although at the level of the ring as a whole there will be a choice of one direction or another, trips once begun must use a single sequence of spaces, and the trip therefore resembles a b-trip, though without the requirement that the return journey repeat the same sequence in reverse. This effect arises from the simple fact that b- and c-type spaces are from the point of view of any trip that passes through them, effectively two-connected, and two is the smallest number that allows entry to a space in one direction and egress in another. It is this essential two connectedness from the point of view of trips, that gives b and c-spaces their distinctive characteristic of both permitting and constraining movement.

Now this means that b- and c-type spaces raise issues for the relation between occupation and movement which are not raised either by one-connected or more than two-connected space, in that they *require* the resolution of the relation between occupation and through movement within each convex space. This has a powerful effect on the usability of spaces and space complexes of this kind. In general, it can only occur where the sequencing of spaces reflects a parallel functional sequencing of occupation zones, and movement is, as it were, internalised into the functional complex and made part of its operation.

For example many types of religious building use exactly this spatial property to create a sequence of spaces from the least to the most sacred, each space having different occupational characteristics. More commonly, we find the phenomenon of the ante-room, for example where a senior person in an organisation places a subordinate in a space which controls access to the office. In domestic space, such interdependencies are quite common. Indeed, the domestic dwelling may often be characterised as a pattern of such interdependencies. Figure 8.16, for example, has a maximally simple b-complex (spaces 6, 9 and 11) associated with male working activity and a near maximally simple c-complex (spaces 3, 7, 10, 8 and 4) associated with female working activity, as well as a maximally simple a-complex (spaces 2 and 5) associated with formal reception and a dominant d-type space (space 3 – the salle commune) in which all everyday living functions, including informal reception, are concentrated and which holds the whole complex together. It is notable that if this space (space 3) is removed from the complex, as in figure 8.16c, the whole complex is reduced to a single sequence with a single one-deep branch.[9]

In general we can say that the sequencing of spaces normally occurs when (and perhaps only when) there are culturally or practically sanctioned functional interdependencies between occupation zones which require movement to be an essential aspect of these interdependencies and therefore to be internalised into a local functional complex of spaces.[10] Such interdependencies are comparatively rare, and because they are so where they do occur they tend to be highly localised. There are simple combinatorial reasons for this. If interdependencies requiring internalisation of movement into a functional complex is unusual for pairs of occupation types, it is even more unusual for triples, even more for quadruples, and so on. This is why it tends to remain localised.

It follows that whereas in small buildings, such functionally interdependent complexes can form a significant proportion of the complex, or even the whole complex, as buildings grow large and acquire more and more occupation spaces, those that have the necessary interdependencies that require spatial sequencing will become a diminishing proportion of the whole. As buildings grow therefore more and more of the movement will not be of the kind which is internal to the functioning of a local subcomplex but will occur between subcomplexes which are functionally much more independent of each other.

This means that movement will be less 'programmed', that is, a necessary aspect of interdependent functions, and more contingent, or 'unprogrammed'.[11] It follows that the pattern of movement will follow from two things: first from the way in which the various occupation spaces are disposed in the spatial complex, coupled to the degree to which each acts as an origin and a destination for movement between occupation spaces; second, from how this disposition relates to the spatial configuration of the complex itself. The more movement occurs more or less randomly from all locations (or even all parts of the complex) to all others, then the more it will approximate the conditions that give rise to 'natural movement', that is movement through spaces generated by the configuration of space itself, and the more movement will then follow the pattern of integration of the building. The more this occurs, the movement will

be functionally neutralised, that is, it will not be an intrinsic aspect of
local functional complexes determined by the functional programme
of the building but as a global emergent phenomenon generated by the
structure of space in the building and the disposition of occupation
spaces within it.

Neutralised movement will then tend to follow the configurational
topologies that generate the pattern of integration in a building. a-spaces
will have no movement other than that starting and finishing in them;
b-spaces will have movement only to the spaces to which they control
both access and egress; c-spaces will have movement to spaces to which
they control either access or egress; while d-spaces will be natural attractors of movement. It follows that just as a-spaces are the most suited for
occupation because they are least suited for movement, so d-spaces are
the least suited for occupation, because they are the most suited to movement, especially where this movement is from all locations to all other
locations in the complex.

It follows that a growing spatial complex will need a decreasing
proportion of b- and c-complexes since these will only be needed for local
functionally interdependent groups of occupation spaces, and a growing
proportion of a-type and d-type complexes. In such complexes there will
be a natural specialisation of spaces into a-complexes for occupation and
d-complexes for movement, and therefore an equally natural tendency
towards the adjacency relation for occupation and movement.

As we have seen, it is exactly such complexes that are generated by
depth minimising processes. Such complexes also have other advantages.
First, because the mix of a-type and d-type complexes is in its nature the
most integrated, then journeys from all spaces to all others will be on
average topologically (and in fact metrically) shorter than for any other
type of complex. Second, such complexes maximise the number of a-spaces
for occupation while minimising the number of spaces in the d-complex
for movement, thus making the relation of occupation and movement
as effort-efficient as possible. Third, the more this is the case, the more
movement from specific origins to specific destination in the complex
will overlap and create a global pattern of co-presence and co-awareness of
those who are not brought together in the local functional subcomplexes

of the building. In other words, the movement pattern brings together in space what the occupational requirement of the complex divides. This reflects the basic fact that whereas the overlap of occupation type in the same space is likely to cause interference from one to the other, the overlap of movement in situations where movement is functionally neutralised, creates an emergent form of spatial use – co-presence through movement – which is essentially all of the same type. Overlap is therefore not likely to be read as interference. On the contrary, it is likely to be read as a benefit.

It is then in the nature of things that spatial complexes of this type will tend to become dominant as buildings grow in scale and occupational complexity. This type of configuration arises from generic function, that is from the fact of occupation and the fact of movement, prior to any consideration of the specific functions to be accommodated in the building. We only need to add the larger open spaces and longer linear spaces in the d-complex in accordance with the principles we have established to optimise the relation between occupation and movement in the complexes.

So, is architecture an ars combinatoria?

We have now answered the question asked at the beginning of the chapter, and embodied in the two prefatory quotes. No theory of architecture as an *ars combinatoria* of elements and relations is useful because, as with language, it is how combinatorial possibility is restricted that gives rise both to the 'structure of the language' and to the 'elements' of which the language is composed. The vast majority of combinatorial possibilities are as irrelevant to that language as random sequences of words are to natural language. The structure of the language, which eliminates most possibilities, arises not from basic rules for combining basic elements, but from local to global laws from physical moves to spatial configuration, which give rise at one level to the local stabilities we call elements and at another to the higher order patterns that characterise the general spatial forms of buildings.

The effects of understanding how restrictions on combinatorial possibility create the 'language of space' are two. First, we see that there are not in any useful sense basic elements. Elements arise from local spatial strategies that realise – and must then be taken as intending to realise –

Figure 8.19

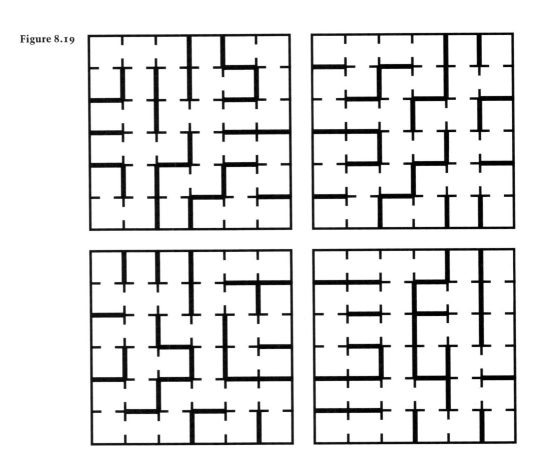

particular local to global spatial ends. All are describable as spatial
phenomena emergent from the consistent application of rules governing
either the completion or removal of a single type of fundamental spatio-
physical element: the permeable partition. It is the record of this consistent application that we see when we name a local configuration as a
certain kind of element. If we randomly partition a complex, as in the
four examples in figure 8.19, we do not find such consistencies, and we
are not therefore inclined to identify elements. We should properly see
'elements' as 'genotypes', that is, systems of informational abstractions
governing objects whose phenotypes are endlessly varied. It is only in this

way that we can reconcile the idea of a well-formed 'element' with the fact that such elements arise from and are given by configurational relations, not only those which generate their intrinsic form, but also those which define their embedding in the system as a whole. In one sense we might say that we have *reduced* the apparent fundamental elements of spatial complexes to something more elementary: a small family of local physical moves which by following different rules produce spatial effects in the complex. But in a more important sense, we have dissolved the element into two sets of configurational laws: the laws that generate the element itself; and those that generate the impact of the element on the complex as a whole.

Second, we see that it is not useful to think of global patterns as arising simply from relations among elements. In a spatial configuration, every local move has its own configurational effect, and it is the natural laws that govern these local to global effects that govern global configuration. It follows that it is knowledge of these laws that we require for a theory of space, not knowledge of combinatorial possibility. It is these laws that give rise to both the local configurational types we are tempted to call elements and to the global configurational patterns that commonly characterise buildings as a whole. We can thus solve the apparent paradox of vast combinatorial possibility and a few basic pattern types. It is the natural local to global laws restricting possibility that lead space to converge on the pattern types that we find.

The precise form of these laws governing the relation between possible spatial configuration and generic function lies in the fact that individual, localised design moves – say making a partition, or eliminating a doorway – have global configurational effects, that is effects on the overall pattern of space. These global pattern effects of local moves are systematic, so that different types of move, carried out consistently will give rise to very different configurational effects. These local to global laws are independent of human volition, and as such must be regarded as more akin to natural laws than contingent matters of human existence. This does not imply that the relationship of human being to space is governed by natural laws, but it does mean that the passage from the possible to the actual passes through – and has historically passed through – natural laws

which mediate the relationship of human beings to space. The built
forms that actually exist, and have existed, are not, as they are often taken
to be, simply subsets of the possible, but variable expressions of the laws
that govern the transition from the possible to the real. These laws, and
their relation to generic function, are therefore the true constraints on
spatial possibility in architecture and urban design, and a theory of space
must be an account of these laws.

Does this mean we should abandon combinatorics altogether? We
should not. Combinatoric possibility is the framework within which
architectural actuality exists, and the proper form of a theory is one that
described how possibility becomes actuality. We are now in a position
to suggest the general framework for such a theory. The huge number of
possible spatial arrangements, we suggest, pass through a series of three
filters before they become real buildings. The filters operate at different
levels, but all have to do with the human purposes for which we make
buildings; that is, these filters are functional filters of possible forms.

The first filter is the most general: that of generic function, as we
have described it above. This governs the properties which all spatial
arrangements must have in order to be usable and intelligible to human
beings at all, that is in order for human beings to be able to occupy space,
to move about between spaces and to find buildings intelligible. The second filter is the filter of cultural intent. This refers to the way in which
buildings tend to form culturally defined types so that buildings which
perform the same culturally defined function in a specific time and space
tend to have at least some common spatial properties. We may call this
filter that of the cultural genotype. The third filter is the level of the
specific building, where those aspects which are not specified by the cultural genotype can vary either in a structured or random way, giving rise
to individual differences in buildings. These three functional filters are
not independent of each other, but work in succession. For example, all
level-two cultural genotypes work within the limits set by the generic
function filter of level-one. Similarly, level-three filters work within
the constraints set at level-two.

There is, however, a further reason why we should not abandon
combinatorics. Although we have shown in this chapter that the combi-

natorial study of formal and spatial possibility in architecture cannot in itself lead to the theory of *architectural* possibility, this does not end the matter. Although the theoretical space of buildings is only a part of the theoretical space of spatial combinatorics, it nevertheless *is* a part of that field, and as such it must obeys its laws. If this is the case, then we find that having eliminated combinatorics as a theory of architecture, we must readmit it as meta-theory.

Let us argue from a precise example. In chapter 2, we discussed a thought experiment called the 'Ehrenfest game' as a model for the concept of entropy. In this experiment, 100 numbered balls placed in one jar eventually get more or less evenly distributed between two jars if we randomly select a number and transfer the corresponding ball from whichever jar it is in to the other. This happened because the half and half state is the most probable state because there are far more microstates, that is actual distributions of the numbered balls, corresponding to the half and half macrostate (that is the actual number of balls in each) than to macrostates in which the balls are unevenly distributed. The shifting probabilities of this process give an insight into the formal nature of 'entropy'.

Now the point of the 'Ehrenfest game' is that it is a useful analogue for the physical notion of 'entropy', as found for example in mixing gases. It is relevant to our argument because we can use the Ehrenfest model to explore a random partitioning process, and in doing so learn important lessons about partitioning in general. All we need do is set up a process for randomly partitioning our spatial complex by numbering our 60 partitions in the 6×6 complex and setting up the random selector to select a number between 1 and 60. We then spin the pointer to select numbers in succession, and each time a number is selected go to the partition with that number and change its state: that is, open a doorway in a partition without one, and close it off if it has one. What happens? Intuition says that the process will eventually settle down to a state in which about half the partitions have doorways and half do not, and that this is therefore the most probable state. We already know that this is the state where there are the maximum possible number of different arrangements.

We may show this, and understand its relevance, by thinking

through carefully what will happen in our random process. The first time a number is selected, the probability of opening a doorway rather than closing one is 60/60, or 1, meaning certainty. The second time, there is a 1/60 chance of closing the same door we have just opened (a .0167 probability) and a 59/60 chance of opening another (a .9833 probability). The third time, there is a 2/58 chance of closing one of the doors we have just opened (or a .0345 probability), and a 58/60 chance of opening another (a .9667 probability). Evidently as we progress, the chances of closing a door rather than opening another begin to approach each other until when we have 30 doorways open and 30 partitions closed, the chances are exactly equal. Opening and closing doors are therefore 'equiprobable'.

In other words, we have the same type of combinatorics for partitioning process as we do for an Ehrenfest game, and therefore for the concept of entropy. This conclusion has clear architectural implications. For example, it explains that, as we have already noted, there are far more partitioning states for about half the number of possible partitions than there are for smaller or larger numbers. There is then a greater range of states for partitioning close to the maximum for a single complex (as in the depth maximising and depth minimising examples) and it is also in this region that small changes to a partitioning have the maximum effect on the distribution of integration, as for example moving a single partition to cut a large ring. There are a whole family of such and similar questions which arise from the basic combinatorics of space, even though buildings occupy only a small part of the combinatorial range.

The laws of spatial combinatorics are not therefore the spatial theory of architecture but they do govern it and constitute the meta-structure within which the theoretical space of real architectural possibility exists. Spatial combinatorics is therefore the meta-theory of architectural space, not its theory. The relationship is exactly analogous to that between the mathematics of 'information theory' and the science of linguistics. The mathematical theory of communication is not itself the theory of language, but it is the meta-theory for the theory of language, because it is the framework of general laws within which linguistic laws come into existence. As with language, mathematical laws of combinatorics are everywhere present in architectural possibility because they are the framework for that system of possibility. They need therefore to be understood as a pervasive, containing framework for the theory of architectural space.

In the next chapter we will see that there is a much more pervasive sense in which combinatorics is the meta-theory of architectural possibility, that is when we come to study not the discrete sets of possibilities which we have considered so far, but when we look at aggregative processes of the kinds that prevail in urban system of all kinds, and in building complexes as they become large. Here we will see that, as discussed briefly in chapter 8, combinatorial probability actually plays a constructive role in architectural morphogenesis.

Notes

1   W. R. Lethaby, *Architecture*, Home University Library, London 1912.
2   Hellick M, *Varieties of Human Habitation*, 1970.
3   Trigueiro E, '*Change and Continuity in Domestic Space Design: a comparative study of houses in 19th and early 20th century houses in Britain and Brazil*', PhD thesis, UCL 1994.
4   As reviewed in P. Steadman, *Architectural Morphology*, Pion 1983, chapter 8 and Appendix.
5   P. Steadman, p 171.
6   Trigueiro, 'Change and continuity'.
7   These proportions are estimated from the results yielded by the 'second normalisation' to large numbers of cases. It must be stressed that they are at this stage only tentative approximations. The general point, however, seems secure.
8   An exactly analogous conclusion about the nature of 'elements' in language is reached by de Saussure in *Course in General Linguistics*, McGraw Hill, 1966 (originally in French, 1915). For example: 'Language does not offer itself as a set of pre-delimited signs to be studied according to their meaning and arrangement', p.104; 'We are tempted to think so if we start from the notion that the units to be isolated are words...the concrete unit must be sought not in the word, but elsewhere', p. 105; and 'Language, in a manner of speaking, is a type of algebra consisting solely of complex terms...language is a form not a substance...all our incorrect ways of naming things that pertain to language stem from the involuntary supposition that the linguistic phenomenon must have substance', p.122.
9   In other words, each kind of occupation is characterised by a distinctive local configuration, dependent for their integration into a single complex on the spatio-functionally central salle commune. It is the fact of being an assemblage of different local sub-complexes into a single configuration that makes the dwelling distinctive as

a building type. The dwelling is not, as it is often taken to be, the simplest building. On the contrary, seen as an intricate pattern of functional interdependencies mapped into space, it may well be the most complex.

10   In buildings where the organisation of a specific pattern of movement is a dominant functional requirement we can expect space to be dominated by sequencing. For example, galleries and exhibition complexes, which are designed explicitly to move people through the complex so that all spaces can be traversed without too much repetition, normally have a high proportion of c-type sequenced spaces, giving their justified graphs the distinctive form of a number of deep, intersecting rings. This is not, however, a clear case. If we examine the functional microstructure of gallery spaces we find that the lines of global movement pass through the sequenced space in such a way as to leave the viewing zones free for only local convex movement. Locally at least, the relation of convex and linear zones is one of adjacency rather than true interpenetration.

11   Or, as discussed in chapter 7, will follow long or short models.

chapter nine

The fundamental city

In dilating my surface I increased the possibilities of contact between me and the outside of me that was so precious, but as the zones of my body soaked in marine solution were extended, my volume also increased at the same time, and a more and more voluminous region within me became unreachable by the elements outside, it became arid, dull and the weight of this dry and torpid thickness I carried within me was the only shadow on my happiness – so perhaps I could say that I'm better off now than I was then, now that the layers of our former surface, then stretched on the outside, have been turned inside out like a glove, now that all the outside has turned inward, and enters and pervades us through filiform ramifications…

(ITALO CALVINO, BLOOD, SEA)

Cities as things made of space

In the previous chapter it was suggested that the relation between human beings and space was, at a deep level, governed by two kinds of law: laws of spatial emergence, by which the larger-scale configurational properties of space followed as a necessary consequence from different kinds of local physical intervention; and laws of 'generic function', by which constraints were placed on space by the most generic aspects of human activity, such as the simple facts of occupying space and moving between spaces. In this chapter we argue that, to a significant extent, the spatial forms of cities are expressions of these laws, and that if we wish to understand them we must learn to see them as 'things made of space', governed by spatial laws whose effects but not whose nature can be guided by human agency. One implication of this argument will be that twentieth-century design (as discussed in chapter 5) has often used spatial concepts for urban and housing areas which fall outside the scope of these laws, creating space which lacks the elementary patterning which these laws have normally imposed, in some shape or form, in the past. If, as is argued here, such laws exist, then it will be necessary to revise current concepts of the well-ordered city back in the direction implied by these laws.

There are, however, obvious objections to the idea that urban forms evolve according to general laws. The most obvious is that cities are individuals, and that this is because the forms they take are influenced by factors which are quite specific to the time and place in which they grow – local topographical facts such as harbours, rivers and hills, particular historical events such as trading developments, population movements and conquests and by pre-existing contextual conditions, such as route intersections and the existence of exploitable resources. Each type of influence might be expected to have generically similar effects on urban form, but taken together it is highly unlikely that any two cities would repeat the same grouping or sequencing of influences. These factors, then, in spite of initially suggesting bases for comparison, tend to make each city unique. And this, of course, is how we experience them.

A second objection is slightly less obvious, and a little contradictory to the first, since it is typological. The spatial and physical development of cities is – quite properly – held to be a reflection of the social and economic

processes which provide the reasons for their existence. Differences
in these processes are likely to give rise to differences in type between
cities. We saw a clear instance of this in the typological contrast drawn
in chapter 6 between cities of production and cities of social reproduction. Differences in spatial and physical form were there shown to be
reflections of differences in the essential functions of those cities.
Similarly, differences in the physical and spatial form of cities, say, to the
north and south of the Mediterranean, are manifestly connected in some
way to the social and cultural idiosyncrasies of the European and Islamic
traditions. It seems then to be specific social, economic and cultural
processes, rather than generic spatial laws, that are the driving forces
on urban form.

   Both objections seem well-founded. Seen in one way, cities are individuals; seen in another, they seem to be types. How can these facts be
reconciled to the idea that general spatial laws might play a role in their
spatial evolution? In fact, there is no incompatibility. It is simply a matter
of the level at which we are talking. The influence of spatial laws on
cities operates not at the level of the individuality of the city, nor on the
typology of the city, but at the deeper level of what all individual cities
and types of city have in common, that is, what, spatially, makes a city a
city. As settlements evolve under different social and topographical conditions, they tend to conserve, in spite of the influence of these differences, certain properties of spatial configuration 'nearly invariant'. By
'nearly invariant', we simply mean that the configurational properties we
find fall within a very narrow band of combinatorial possibility. Without
knowledge of these 'near invariants' we cannot easily understand what
cities are in principle, before we consider them as types or as individuals.

   What are these 'near invariants'? Let us begin by looking at a pair of
illustrative axial maps: plate 2c–e, which is part of London as it is now, and
plate 7, which is the central part of Shiraz, in Iran, as it was prior to twentieth-
century modernisation. The grids have clear differences in character. Line
structures are more complex in Shiraz, and are in fact much less integrated and intelligible. If we were to examine the relation of lines to convex
elements, we would find that in London lines tend to pass through more
convex spaces than in Shiraz. Looking at the integration core structures,

we also find differences. Although at radius-n (not shown in the case of Shiraz), both have strongly centralised cores, linking centre towards edge, at radius-radius, London has a 'covering' core, linking centre to edge in the way characteristic of European cities, while in Shiraz the radius-radius core is markedly regionalised. These differences in grid structure are associated with well-known behavioural differences, for example, in the ways in which inhabitants relate to strangers and men to women in Islamic as compared to European cities. We can call these associations of urban forms and social behaviour 'spatial cultures', and note that one of the main tasks of a theory of urban form would be to explicate them.

However, as can be seen from the two plates, underlying the manifest spatial differences, we also find much common ground in the urban grids. For example, in both cases, the spaces formed by the buildings tend to be improbably linearised in at least three senses. At the smallest scale, we find that buildings are placed next to and opposite each other to form spaces which stress linearity rather than, for example, enclosure. Second, at a slightly less local level, lines of sight and access through the spaces formed by buildings tend to become extended into other spaces to a degree that is unlikely to have occurred by chance. Third, we find that some, but only some, of the linear spaces are prioritised to form larger scale linear continuities in the urban grids, creating a more global movement potential. These properties are present in the two cases to different degrees, but they are nevertheless present in both cases. They will be found to be present in some degree in most settlements.

At a more global scale, we also find commonalities across the two cases, which are also 'near invariants' in settlements in general. Two of the most notable are that in both cases we will find a well formed local area structure of some kind, coexisting with a strong global structure. Both levels of structure are different in the two cases, but each case does have both levels of structure, and this we will find is generally the case in cities. At the most general level of the overall shape of cities, we also find 'near invariants'. One of the most significant is that cities, as they grow, tend to fill out in all directions to form more or less compact shapes, even in cases where they are linear in the early stages. The 'deformed grid', with all the properties we have just described, seems to be the aptest term to

summarise these, and other, 'near invariants' of cities, because, however
much urban space is articulated and broken up, buildings are still in general aggregated into outwards facing islands to define intersecting rings of
space, which then become improbably linearised to give rise to the local
area and global structures that are found by configurational analysis.

These commonalities, it will be argued, arise from what spatial cultures have in common, that is, from what in the previous chapter was
called generic function. This, it will be recalled, referred not to the different activities that people carry out in space, but to aspects of human
occupancy of space that are prior to any of these: that to occupy space
means to be aware of the relationships of a space to others, that to occupy
a spatial complex means to move about in it, and to move about depends
on being able to retain an intelligible picture of the complex.

Intelligibility and functionality, defined as formal properties of
spatial complexes, are the keys to 'generic function'. In the case of settlements, generic function refers not to the specificities of different cultural,
social and economic forms, but to what these forms have in common
when seen from a spatial point of view. The deep invariant structure of
urban grids is generated, it will be argued, from generic function creating
emergent invariants, while the typological differences arise from cultural,
social and economic differences, and individualities from topographical
and historical specificities. In effect, it is proposed that there exists a fundamental settlement process, which is more or less invariant across cultures,
and that spatial cultures are parameterisations of this process, by, for example, creating different degrees and patterns of integration and intelligibility,
and different degrees of local and global organisation to the overall form.
Our task here is to show what this fundamental settlement process is and
how it is a product of generic function and the laws of spatial emergence.

Before we embark on this, we must first be clear what exactly it is
we are seeking to explain. It is clear that when settlements are small,
they can take a great variety of forms. It is also clear that throughout history we find quite radical experiments in urban form, for example, the
cities which we examined in chapter 6. However, as cities become large,
these peculiarities tend to be eliminated, and grids become much more
like each other in certain ways. What we are seeking to identify here are

the invariants in the processes by which large cities tend to grow – that is, to try to describe the main lines of urban evolution. 'Strange' cities exist, and for a while even grow quite large, but they are essentially dead ends in urban evolution. Their principles of organisation do not support a large successor family of cases and types across the range of urban scales.

Because they operate at a very deep level and govern the common structure of cities, it might be thought that the fundamental city is too generalised to be of real interest. This is not the case. The influence of spatial laws on cities is pervasive as well as deep. It effects the level at which we see and experience cities, as well as at the level of their deep structures. In order to understand individual cities and types of cities at any level we must first understand exactly what it is that these general laws have contributed to their form. If we think of cities as aggregates of cellular elements – buildings – linked by space, then in the language of the previous chapter, spatial laws are the 'first filter' between the boundless morphological possibility for such aggregates and the properties of the vanishingly small subset we call cities. Social and economic processes are then the second filter, guiding the basic paths of evolution this way or that to give rise to recognisable types. Specific local conditions in time and space are then the third filter through which the city acquires its eventual individuality.

Our task in understanding the fundamental city is then to answer two questions: how and why should these particular invariants emerge from a spatial process of generation? And what aspects of the social and functional processes that drive settlement formation guide growing cities along these pathways? The answer to both questions will be essentially those we have discussed in the previous chapter: laws of spatial implication from local physical moves to overall spatial patterns in cellular aggregates – for such cities are – these being driven by 'generic function', in conjunction, of course, with prevailing socio-economic and topographical factors.

Two paradoxes
How then and why should these 'near invariants' *emerge* in a process of successively placing built forms in a growing aggregate? First, we must be

aware that aggregative processes are themselves subject to certain laws of 'emergence', which are not insignificant for urban growth. For example, a randomly growing aggregate will, if free from constraints, tend towards a circular form as it becomes large, simply because this is more probable than any other form.[1] This is relevant to urban growth because a circular shape is also the most integrating shape, and this means that to the extent that trips are from all points to all others, then mean trip length will be minimised in a circular form – that is, oddly, in the form that grows most randomly.

Such 'laws of emergence' are important to urban growth. But far more important is the fact that some of the most elementary laws of this kind affect urban growth not simply by being emergent properties of the growing system, but by imposing conflicting tensions on the system. The resolution of these then becomes the prime determinant of the pathway of the system. The laws of emergence operate, in effect, as paradoxes which must be resolved by the growth process. There are two such paradoxes. The first can be called the paradox of centrality, the second the paradox of visibility.

The paradox of centrality takes the following form. In a circular – that is the most probable – aggregate, integration runs from centre to edge, with the greatest integration in the centre, and the least at the edge. This prioritises the centre from the point of view of known effects of integration on the functioning of a spatial system. For example, more movement along shortest paths will pass through the central area than anywhere else, if movement is from all points to all other points, or if origins and destinations are randomised.

However, all this is only the case if we consider the urban system on its own, in terms of its interior relations. As soon as we consider its external relations, say to other settlements in the region, or even simply to the space outside the system, then the centre to edge distribution of integration no longer applies. In fact, the more integrating the form – that is the more it approximates the circular form – then the more its most integrated internal zone is maximally segregated from the external world, and, by definition, from any other aggregates that are to be found in the vicinity of the system. In other words, maximising internal integration also maximises external segregation. This is the 'paradox of centrality'.

Conversely, as we move from a circular form towards the most linear form, that is the single line of cells, or the least probable shape in a growing aggregate, then we find that the most linear form, which is the least integrated in itself, is the most integrated to the outside or to other systems in the region, since each of its constituent cells is by definition directly adjacent to the space outside the form. In short, the circular form is the least integrative with the space outside the form for the same reason that it is the most internally integrative: that it has the least peripheral cells for the maximum interior cells. The converse is true for the maximally linear form which has the most peripheral cells against internal cells.

Growing urban systems must respond to the paradox of centrality, because it has the simple consequence that if you try to maximise internal integration then you lose external integration and vice versa, and urban forms seem to need both internal and external integration. The tension between internal and external integration leads settlements to evolve in ways which overcome the centrality paradox. For example, the tendency for a growing urban system to increase the length of certain edge to centre lines in proportion to the growth of the system is one response to this. Exactly why this should be the case leads directly to our second paradox, which we will call the paradox of visibility, although this does not quite express its complex nature, since it arises from differences between the metric and visible properties of space.

The visibility paradox can be explained very simply. If we arrange elements in a single line, as in figure 9.1a and b (the corresponding graph), we maximise the metric or modular depth that those elements can have from each other in any contiguous arrangement. The more elements we so arrange, the greater the depth, and the worse the metric trip efficiency of the form if movement is to be from all points to all others. But if we are interested not in movement, but in visibility, then we find the contrary effect. Suppose, for example, we superimpose a line, representing a line of sight, on our linear arrangement of elements, as in figure 9.1c and d. The visible (as opposed to metric) integration of the form is then maximised because all cells are covered by a single line. In the graph, this means all other elements are connected to the graph element representing the line. In other words, the arrangement of elements in which metric segregation

Figure 9.1

a 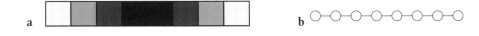   b

c 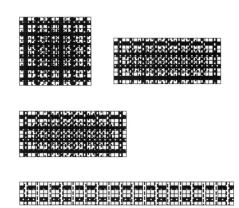   d

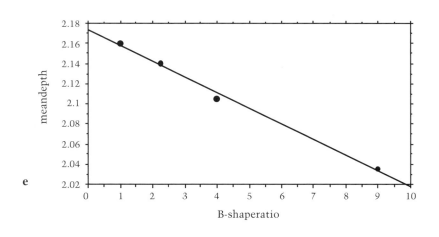

e

is maximised, that is the linear shape, is also the arrangement in which visual integration is maximised. For a linear shape without a line of visibility, mean depth increases with the number of cells, but with the superimposition of the line then, however long the line of cells, the maximum depth in the system will be 2, and in fact the mean depth of an expanding sequence must converge on a limit of 2.

In an important sense, then, the visual integration of a shape behaves in the opposite way to the metric integration. This will also apply to grids made up of elements and superimposed lines. Holding the number of elements steady at 36, and arranging them to be covered first by a 6×6 grid of lines, then 9×4, then 12×3 and finally 18×2, we find the mean depth of the system decreases with elongation. We can say then that visual integration increases with increase in the block shape ratio, that is the ratio of the long to the short side, as in the figures and scattergram in figure 9.1e. This is the opposite of the effect of elongation on a shape on its own, without superimposed lines.

In other words, when considered as elements in a visibility field the primitive elements representing locations in the form have the contrary integration behaviour to the same elements considered as a system of metric distances. If lines are superimposed on grids of elements, then the more elongated the grid, the more integrating; the opposite of the case for arrangements without superimposed lines. The linear form, which from a metric point of view, and therefore from the point of view of movement considered as energy expenditure, is the least integrated form, is visually the most integrated form. The implication is obvious, but fundamental. If we arrange a series of, say, urban areas in a line we maximise the mean trip length at the same time as we maximise visibility. The same principle governs the progressive elongation of grids.

Urban form must then overcome two paradoxes. First, it must create external integration for the sake of relations to the outside world, as well as internal integration, for the sake of relations amongst locations within, even though these properties are theoretically opposed to each other. We may add that urban form must achieve this at whatever level the paradox might become problematic. That is likely to include at least a local and a global level. Second, it must pursue both compactness and linearity, the former for the sake of trip efficiency, the latter for the sake of visibility and intelligibility. The characteristic 'near invariants' of urban grids that we have noted, are, it will be argued, essentially responses, at different levels, to these two paradoxes.

How then does urban form resolve these paradoxes? It is proposed here that two paradoxes set the questions to which the structured grid, whether 'deformed' or 'interrupted', give us the answer.[2] A structured grid is one in which integration and intelligibility are arranged in a pattern of some kind, which supports functionality and intelligibility. Essentially, lines and areas are prioritised for integration and intelligibility to varying degrees in order to create a system of differentiation, and it is this differentiation that we call structure in the system. This is why integration cores and area scatters are such fundamental functional properties in urban systems. They reflect the process of constructing a differentiated structure in the system. The distribution of integration in an urban system, together with its associated built form and land use patterns, is not a static picture of the current state of the system, but a kind of structural record of the historical evolution of the system. The 'structural inertia' imposed by this evolved structure is of course also the prime constraint on the future evolution of the system.

The task is then to show how urban form comes about in such a way as to resolve the two paradoxes, that is, to show how the structured urban grid is discoverable as an *emergent* pattern through the pursuit of more elementary properties of space arising from the disposition of buildings. This poses a methodological difficulty. All the spatial analyses we have made in this book so far are analyses of existing complex systems, that is systems that have already evolved or already been constructed. The question we have posed about urban form is about the construction of systems, that is how systems evolve and grow in what is initially a void. The spatial void seems to be structureless. How then can we conceptualise and analyse aggregative processes which are initiated and evolved in a spatial void?

The answer is simple, and will lead us into new theoretical territory. Space is not a structureless void. We only believe it is by using an implicit analogy with physical systems. What we call structure in a physical system, whether artificial or natural, has to be created by putting elements together in some way. Space is not like this. In its raw state, space already contains all spatial structures that could ever exist in that space. It is in this sense that space is the opposite of 'things'. Things only have their own properties. Space has all possible properties. When we intervene in a space by the placing of physical objects we do not create spatial structure, but eliminate it. To place an object in space means that certain lines of visibility and movement which were previously available are no longer available. When we talk of a structured grid in a city, brought about by the placing of built forms, this grid already existed, in co-existence with all other possible structures, within the 'substrate' space (that is, the space prior to our intervention in it) now occupied by the city, before the city came into existence. The spatial system we call the grid was not created by the placing of built forms. Others were eliminated. The grid was constructed in an important sense negatively. It was not assembled in itself. Its existence was drawn attention to and highlighted by the elimination of other 'virtual' structures.

This view of space is as true practically as it is philosophically. A dance sketches out a possible structure of space within an infinite set of possibilities. The dance is an exploration – a celebration perhaps – of the infinite structurability of space. Any open space is a space in which no possibilities have yet been eliminated, and every open space is continually structured and restructured by the human activity that takes place in it. If we do not conceptualise space in this way we have no way of reconciling human freedom and the human structuring of space. Human activity is never actually structured by space. In structuring space by physical objects we suggest possibilities by eliminating others. But the spaces in the interstices of physical forms are still 'open'. Within these limits, the infinite structurability of space still prevails. In our cells we may dance.

All-line visibility maps
In order to understand how the placing of physical objects in a substrate space creates spatial structure by elimination, we must have a formal conception of the substrate space as containing all possibilities prior to our intervention in it. In view of the 'unreasonable effectiveness' of line-based

analyses in understanding the space structure of cities, suppose then that
we regard the substrate as a matrix of infinitely dense lines of arbitrary (or
infinite) length in all directions, and call it the 'line substrate'. An object
placed in a 'line substrate' will block some lines and leave others intact,
and this will have the effect of creating some degree of structure in the
line substrate.

How can we identify and measure the structure in the line substrate
produced by an object? Clearly, we cannot at this stage use the 'axial maps',
which have proved so useful in analysing the structure of real cities, since
we cannot yet draw them. A single object placed in a line substrate will
have infinitely many lines incident to it, and also infinitely many lines
tangent to it, as well as infinitely many other lines in its immediate
vicinity. Such infinite line matrices do not at first seem to be usefully
analysable.

However, there is a way we can proceed which seems to lead to a
fundamental description of objects and sets of objects in terms of their
structuring effect on the line substrate. Within the set of lines which pass
in the region of an object – let us think of it as a simple building – there
will be a subset which are as close as possible to the object but which are
unaffected by it. These will be the lines that are tangent to the vertices of
the object, including those that lie along any straight surfaces. A slightly
smaller subset will be those that are tangent to exactly one vertex of an
object. This will eliminate those that actually lie along a face, since such
a line would necessarily be tangent to two vertices, one at each end of the
face, but include those which are as close to the face as we wish – in practical computing terms, as close as a single pixel.

Defined this way, each vertex still has an infinite set of lines tangent to
it, which we can think of as forming an open fan shape around that vertex.
These line sets have the useful property of defining the limits of the
object in the substrate – exactly if we use the larger subset, to within one
pixel if we use the smaller subset – without making use either of the lines
incident to the object or those in the region which are not tangent to a
vertex. The tangent subset is, in a useful sense, a well-defined set of lines
selected by and in that sense generated by the presence of the object. We
have at least simplified the situation a little.

However, as soon as we add a second object in the vicinity of the first, we can define a new subset: that of the lines that are tangent to at least one vertex in each object. By finding each line tangent to a vertex on one object which is also tangent to a vertex of the other, then continuing that line till it is stopped by being incident either to a further object or to any boundary which we decide to place around the region, we define exactly the kind of line matrix that was demonstrated in chapter 3. The set of lines is in effect made up of all lines drawn tangent to vertices that can 'see' each other, and therefore have a straight line drawn tangent to them. We may call this the 'all-line map' generated jointly by the vertices of the two objects that can see each other. Like any other connected line matrix, such 'all-line maps' can be subject to integration analysis. If we do so, we find that any set of objects will create some kind of structure.

We can now use this as a general method for analysing the effects of objects placed in a line substrate, by finding all lines tangent to the vertices that can see each other for all objects in the substrate, then subjecting the resulting all-line map of those objects to integration analysis. To do this we must define a boundary to the system. To limit the effect of the boundary on the analysis we can allow the substrate to adapt its shape to form a more or less regular envelope around the group of objects. By proceeding in this way, a structure of integration is created in the line substrate which reflects the shapes and positions of the objects we have placed in the substrate with respect to each other. For example, in plate 3a, we have found the all-line map created by a number of objects and then its pattern of integration. It is reasonable to think of this as an analysis of the field of visibility created by the placed objects, since every line defines a limit of visibility created conjointly by a pair of vertices from a pair of objects.

These analysed visibility maps are quite remarkable entities, and appear to synthesise aspects of configurational analysis which had previously seemed to be quite independent of each other. For example, it is clear that, by definition, axial maps are subsets of the lines that make up the 'all-line' visibility map. Visibility maps, we may say, 'contain' axial maps. It follows that they will also contain some account of the global structure of a pattern of space in a configuration because axial maps do. We shall see shortly that this is the case.

However, we also find that visibility maps reproduce some aspects of the analysis of shapes set out in chapter 3. For example, if we construct a regular five-by-five grid of blocks, and carry out an all-line analysis, we find that whereas a simple axial map would give each line the same integration value (because all are equally connected to exactly half of the total) the integration structure in the all-line analysis distributes integration from edge to centre. This is shown in plate 3b. The central bias in the integration core arises because in addition to the global structure of lines, as would be found in the axial map of the grid, there are also everywhere a large number of lines of every length specified by pairs of vertices which can see each other, including a large number of lines only a little longer than the blocks of built form. This dense matrix of short lines acts as though it were a tessellation, and not only distributes integration from edge to centre in the short lines, but also necessarily transmits this bias to the longer lines. In other words, the all-line integration analysis reproduces both the global structure of the form through its long lines which are equivalent to the axial map, but also reflects the local structure of the shape as would be found in the tessellation.

All-line visibility maps also reproduce some of the conjoint effects of tessellations plus lines noted in figure 9.1. For example, if we take 36 blocks and arrange them 6×6, 9×4, 12×3 and 18×2 (calling the ratio of length to breadth the 'block shape ratio') and use each to generate all-line visibility analyses, we find that as the arrangement elongates mean depth diminishes. If we maintain the number of blocks constant, the mean depth in the all-line map is minimised by reducing the 'pile' (that is, the number of lines of blocks in the arrangement): a 2-pile arrangement of cells has less depth in the all-line map than a 3-pile arrangement, which has less depth than a 4-pile arrangement, and so on up to squareness. Greater elongation means greater integration.

On closer examination, the '2-pile' grid, as instanced in the 18×2 grid of figure 9.1, turns out to be even more interesting. If, instead of maintaining the number of blocks constant and rearranging them with different 'pile' (that is into the 4 pile 9×4, the 3 pile 12×3 and so on), we maintain pile constant and increase the number of blocks, then we find that mean depth increases with increasing numbers of blocks, but with different curves for different piles. For example, figures 9.2a and b show respectively the growth curves for mean depth in 1-pile and 4-pile arrangements with increasing numbers of blocks, and therefore increasing block shape ratio. Experimentation with larger systems so far suggests that mean depth continues to increase with 1-pile and 4-pile, at least up to the scales of a reasonable city system. Figure 9.2c, however, shows a quite different behaviour for 2-pile systems. In the early stages of growth, mean depth rises rapidly, and continues, slowing rapidly up to 18 blocks (2×9). With 20 (2×10) or more blocks, mean depth then begins to decrease, and continues to decrease as blocks are added, at least up to the normal limits of urban possibility. The reason why 2-pile systems, and only 2-pile systems, behave in this unique way is as simple as it is fundamental. Remembering that blocks which are aligned do not see each other through intervening blocks (because lines tangent to vertices do not include those that are tangent to two vertices on the same block, that is lines which lie flat on the face of a block are excluded), the 2-pile system is the only system in which all blocks see more than half of the other blocks. In all other cases, blocks which are not on the same alignment interfere with the mutual visibility of at least some of the blocks. As 2-pile systems grow, therefore, the privileged visibility over all other arrangements increases.

2-pile systems therefore have a unique theoretical status among block arrangements as far as the degree of integration in the all-line map is concerned. We should not then be surprised that it corresponds to one of the primary spatial types – perhaps the primary type – that cities offer. Streets, avenues, alleys, boulevards, roads and so on are all variants on the fundamental 2-pile linear type. It is at least a suggestive inference that these unique integration possibilities of the visibility fields created by 2-pile systems are the reason for this privileged typological status.

A related interpretation might be possible for that other dominant urban spatial type: the large open space known variously as the 'piazza', 'place' or – with inappropriate geometricity in English – 'square'. If we create a square in a grid – say by eliminating the central four blocks in a 6×6 grid, as in plate 3c, the effect is to reduce the mean depth and thus increase the overall integration of the system. If we then move the square

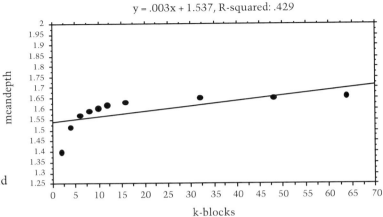

Figure 9.2

y = .003x + 1.537, R-squared: .429

a Growth of one pile grid

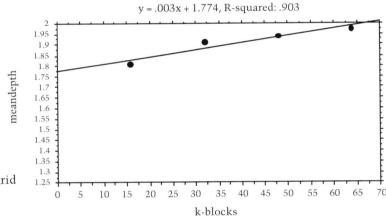

y = .003x + 1.774, R-squared: .903

b Growth of four pile grid

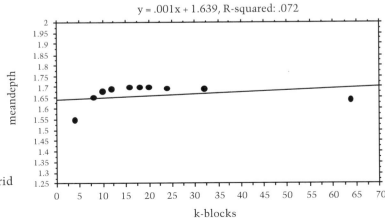

y = .001x + 1.639, R-squared: .072

c Growth of two pile grid

towards the corner, as in plate 3d, we find that the mean depth of the system is still reduced compared to the 6×6 grid, but to a lesser degree than with the central space. In other words, the effects are exactly what we would expect from the principles for the construction of integration set out in the last chapter. A centrally located larger space integrates more than one that is peripherally located. The effects of replacing the open spaces with equivalently shaped blocks, as in plate 3e and f, are also exactly what would be expected. A centrally placed block reduces integration more than a peripherally placed block. Replacing square spaces and blocks with linear spaces and blocks of equivalent area will also follow these principles.

In other words, all-line visibility maps reproduce the local to global effects by which the global configurational properties of spatial complexes were shown to arise from local physical moves. We may therefore pose interesting questions such as: what local physical moves give rise to the characteristic structures that are found in the various types of urban grids? For example, beginning with the 6×6 grid, whose all-line mean depth is 1.931, in plate 3g a double sized block is created across the centre line near the 'northern' edge. The effect is to reduce the integration of the central line, previously (along with the central east-west line) the most integrating because of its central location. Also the overall mean depth of the system increases to 1.949. In plate 3h, the block is brought closer to the centre. The effect is to de-integrate the central north-south line even more, as can be seen from the deepening of the blue to the north and south of the block. There is a second effect. The east-west central lines are now less integrated than the north-south lines adjacent to the double block. This is because one of the crucial connections that gave them this value – the north-south central line – has been blocked. In fact this effect was also present in plate 3g, but less strongly, so that it did not reach the threshold at which the colour would be changed. In plate 3j the block is moved away from the central line and returned to the northern edge. Comparing with plate 3g, it can be seen that the segregative effect is less. In plate 3k, the block is moved away from the edge. The segregative effect is greater than for plate 3j, but less than for plate 3h.

It is clear that these effects follow from the principles set out in the previous chapter. The more centrally a block is placed, the greater the

'depth gain' or loss of integration. It should therefore be possible to explore
how the deployment of blocks in general create differently structured
grids. For example, if we place four double-sized blocks adjacent to the
centre as in plate 3l, we immediately create a kind of 'deformed wheel'
integration structure, with hub, spokes and a rim one block in from the
edge. This happens because the double-sized blocks all eliminate connection to the central lines, which are naturally prioritised by the form, and
make the 'rim' lines, which are still maximally connected, relatively
stronger in integration. The interstitial zones defined by the wheel are
defined by the rather sharp segregation created behind the double blocks
by cutting them off not only from their lateral neighbour zones, but
also from the central lines. This structure is therefore characterised by
diffusing integration to create the wheel, and rather strongly segregated
zones close to the centre of the form. In contrast, plate 3m, by placing the
blocks away from the central lines, creates stronger integration in the
central lines, but weaker in the rim lines. The four zones adjacent to the
centre are still marked out by comparative segregation, but much less
than before because in all cases direct links to both neighbour zones and
the central lines are retained. The resulting form is overall more integrated
than the previous case, with a stronger central structure, but a less strong
zone structure and a less marked deformed wheel effect.

In each case, these effects are expressions of the principles for the
creation of structure in spatial complexes set out in the previous chapter.
They show that comparatively simple local changes in a spatial complex
can have powerful structural effects on the configuration of the whole.
Even on the basis of what we know, we can suggest generative processes
which either minimise or maximise integration and, it will turn out,
intelligibility (as defined in chapter 3). In general, loss of integration and
intelligibility results from placing blocks so that they bar lines generated
by existing blocks at 90 degrees. The most general form of this would seem
to be a process in which we locate rectangular blocks in non-contiguous
T-shapes, as in plate 3n. The non-contiguous T has the effect that both
lines parallel to the long faces of existing blocks are inevitably stopped
by blocks placed in the vicinity, and lines along the surface of the block
therefore change direction at 90 degrees. We can call this the 90-degree

generator. As the scattergram shows, the aggregate form arising from the 90-degree generator has very poor intelligibility and it is clear that it will always do so if applied as the principal generator for the block placing. A similar 90-degree effect will arise in a square block process by similarly placing each next block so as to block the face line on at least one existing block. In order to make this process work in all directions, it is necessary to create slightly wider spaces near the corner of each block, as in plate 3p, in which the loss of integration and intelligibility is even greater than to the rectangular 90-degree process.

The 90-degree process depends on creating the 90-degree relation at the point where a new block is added to the system. Suppose then that we avoid such relations at least for one line parallel to a face in an existing block. In other words, suppose we add blocks so as to create at least one 'zero-degree' relation for the new block (i.e. continuing the line) and an existing block. Plate 3q is an example of a random process following only this rule. It will of course create 90-degree relations as well as zero-degree relations, simply as the result of the non-contiguous L-shape. The process creates a number of lacunas, and lines of all different lengths. But at this scale the outcome has a fairly strong edge-to-centre structure, and the degree of integration and intelligibility are high. We can then add to this process the 'extension' rule from the previous chapter and require the process always to conserve the zero-degree relation for the longest line available. One possible outcome of such a process is shown in plate 3r. The effect of introducing the 'extension' rule by which the longest line is conserved where each new block is added is to create not only a much stronger structure, but also a structure that is much more differentiated between high and low integration than before. Overall integration and intelligibility are also very high. We can now see that the pure orthogonal grid is a simple extension of this principle: line length is conserved in all directions by making all-line relations along faces zero-degree continuations.

However, there is no such thing in reality as a pure grid, if for no other reason than because certain lines will be spatially privileged at the expense of others by being continued outside the settlement into the routes that connect it with other settlements, while other lines will not. In practice we also find that geometrically ordered grids, such as those found in

ancient Greece and Rome, ancient China and modern America, are not
internally uniform. Sometimes lines in one direction are privileged at the
expense of others by the overall shape of the settlement, but, more commonly, some lines are internally stopped at right angles by built forms,
while others continue. This is why we called such grids 'interrupted
grids', and noted that they were just as structured as 'deformed' grids.

These simple cases illustrate the kind of thing we need to know:
how spatial structure in grids arises from local action on blocks. One whole
class of grids – interrupted grids – is based almost entirely on what we
have so far explored, that is grid shape and interruption. We can have the
outline of a theory of interrupted grids on the basis of the methods we
have so far set out. However, the commonest kind of grid is not interrupted
but deformed. The difference between the two is easy to describe. In the
interrupted grids we have so far considered all major lines – that is the
subset of the all-line map that constitutes the axial map – are either tangent
to a vertex of a block or end on a block at close to ninety degrees. In practical terms this means that lines either continue with no change in direction, or compel a ninety-degree change in direction. We could call such
grids zero-ninety grids, because all movements proceed with a zero-degree
change in direction or a ninety-degree change in direction. Deformed
grids are, quite simply, grids that use all the whole range in between.

What the two types of grid have in common is that, whatever the
technique for creating angles of incidence between lines, the outcome is
variation in the lengths of lines. These variations are one of the means by
which structure is created in the urban grid. In both deformed and interrupted grids, this structure most commonly arises from the application
of the 'extension' principle: longer lines tend to be conserved by zero- or
low-degree line relations, allowing ninety- or high-degree line relations
to occur away from the longer lines. This is why in deformed grids we
typically find the dominant structure is made of sequences of longer
lines whose intersections are low degree, and shorter, more localised, lines
whose intersections are high degree. In chapter 4, for example, we found
that in the City of London, there was a pervasive tendency for longer lines
to be incident to others at open angles while the more localised shorter
lines tend to be incident at, or close to, right angles. In spite of other

differences, similar observations can be made about many Arab towns, though the lines that intersect at open angles tend to be less long, and less differentiated in length from some of the more localised lines. This is an example of a parametric difference expressing cultural variation in the fundamental settlement process. We should also note of course that this relation was exactly inverted in the 'strange towns' of chapter 6. It was the longest lines that ended in ninety-degree relations by being incident to major public buildings.

In fact, the situation is slightly more subtle. If we consider the structure of the grid from the point of view of how its local sub-areas are fitted into the larger-scale grid in both western and Arab cities, we find that in both cases this relation is most often formed by using a ninety-degree relation to join the internal streets of the local area to the larger-scale grid. However, the sub-area line that links to the main grid at ninety degrees will itself then tend to avoid ninety-degree relations as it moves into the heart of the sub-area, and continue out in another direction. In other words, the lines that form the dominant structure in sub-areas follow the same type of logic as the line of the main grid, though at a smaller scale. Linearity is being used to create an integration core linking edge to centre for the sub-areas in much the same way as the larger-scale grid is creating it for the town as a whole.

The pattern of angles of incidence of lines created by different ways of placing blocks of built form, and particularly the variation between low- and high-degree angles of incidence in deformed grids, and zero- and ninety-degree angles of incidence in interrupted grids, therefore seem critical to our understanding of how real urban structures are put together as spatial systems. Since most large cities are deformed grids, and there is reason for believing that the structure of deformed grids is in some senses more complex and subtle than interrupted grids, we must now explore the implication of what we have learned for deformed grids.

How emergence overcomes indeterminacy to create local order
If we are to begin without the assumption of an underlying grid, to guide the placing of blocks, then we must first show how *local* order arises in a growing aggregate in the first place. By local order, we mean constant

relations between one block and its neighbours. This excursion will lead us to a conclusion of as much theoretical as practical importance. The reason we find urban systems invariably display local as well as global order, is that without local order there is indeterminacy in the emergent structure. Very small changes in the positioning and shape of objects can lead to a radical difference in the structure of integration in the all-line map created by those objects. For this reason, large-scale layouts cannot be constructed on the basis of local indeterminacy, and this is why we invariably find local as well as global order in urban systems. The role of local rule following is to make the emergence of local structure predictable. These local 'emergences' then stabilise the situation enough to permit the emergence of more global order 'on their back', as it were. This is why we find, at smallest urban scale, 'near invariants' in the form of continuous definition of local external spaces by building entrances, and the local linearisation of built forms. Local order in this sense will be seen to be the necessary foundation of global urban form. Without it, the local system cannot be stabilised sufficiently to allow global patterns to be constructed.

We must begin by considering the most elementary relations in a system, beginning with one object in the vicinity of another. Plate 4a, b and c shows a series of possible cases which are then subjected to all-line analysis. As we can see, in each case the precise pattern of integration is different, depending on the shapes of the objects and their positions with respect to each other. But there is also an invariant effect. Regardless of the shape or relative locations of the cells, all the pairs of objects create a focus of integration between them in the all-line map. Further experiment would show, and reflection confirm, that given any pair of objects in a substrate, then other things being equal integration will tend to be drawn to the region jointly defined between them. This means also that each object is adjacent to a shared set of integrating lines, and therefore potentially permeable to it, in the direction of the other object. This is an instance of what we mean by an invariant. It is a structural condition that is always the case even under considerable and geometric variation. It is also an emergent effect, in that it was not defined in the initial rule which placed the second object, but emerged from this placing wherever it occurred. In this particular case, the invariant emergent effect gives a meaning to the spatial concept of 'betweenness'.

As soon as we begin to consider systems with more than two objects, however, we lose this invariance in the emergent outcome and instead discover a profound problem which seems initially completely incompatible with the idea of a local order: that of indeterminacy in the emergent outcome. As soon as we have a third object, we find that structures emergent from analysis of the all-line maps arising from those objects are highly unpredictable and subject to great variation in outcomes with very small changes in the shape and positioning of any of the objects. Fortunately, it is in finding the answer to this problem that we will be able to set the foundations for a full theoretical understanding of settlement space. Only by placing and orienting objects in certain ways in relation to each other can local indeterminacy be overcome and local order created in the evolving system.

Suppose then we add a third object to the pairs we have already considered, as in plate 4d and e. It seems there is no reliably emergent pattern. On the contrary, the structure changes from 4d to e following very minor changes in the locations of the blocks. Plate 4f and g shows the same effect in a much more complex system. The only difference between the two is a change in the size – but not the shape or position – of one of the objects, yet the outcome in the all-line map is quite different. Further experimentation will show that this is always the case. There is of course a local determinism operating. But it is so dependent on very small changes in the shape and positioning of objects that it is virtually impossible to predict without this very detailed knowledge.

Now everything that has been learned about real spatial systems in the earlier chapters of this book suggests that structural indeterminacy in spatial patterns is the last thing we expect to find. On the contrary, we have found that spatial systems of all kinds and at all levels tend to organise themselves according to certain genotypes, that is common patterns that often cross quite different-seeming cases. It is clear that such systems are not indeterminate. Nor are they altered in their structure by minor changes. On the contrary, their structures are highly robust, and can usually absorb quite significant modifications without undergoing great changes in structure. In this sense, we can say that real systems have a great deal of redundancy. This redundancy, and the consequent robustness in the structural outcome, can only arise from consistencies of some kind in the way that objects are placed, that is from a local rule following behaviour in the placing of objects. Since we have seen that real systems seem to follow rules about local linearity of built forms, and the relation of lines to entrances, we should first consider the structural effects of these.

Suppose then that we align a series of blocks, as in plate 4h. Now there is an emergent invariant. Integration in the all-line map will align itself one side or other of the alignment of cells. On reflection, it is evident that this must always be so. Integration must always be dominated by the outer vertices that can see each other. However, which side is selected is still highly indeterminate. It depends on quite minor differences in the nature of the cell surfaces, and the inter-relations of these differences on either side of the alignment. Plate 4i, for example, shows a slight realignment of the same blocks as in h, in that the positions of the three internal blocks are rearranged. The effect is that the dominant lines of integration shift from one face of the alignment to the other. The reasons for these differences can always be traced, but they are often quite hard to find. In this case it depends on the relative length of the longest alignments along the face, and this depends on very small differences in the degree to which blocks protrude. The all-line integration analysis of the system is therefore not yet robust. We have solved half the problem. We know we will find a linear pattern of integration in the all-line map. But we do not yet know where it will be.

One way of making the outcome determinate will of course be to align the objects perfectly and standardise their shape. If we do this, then integration will distribute itself equally on both sides of the alignment. However, there is a second factor that can bring redundancy into the alignment, one which does not require us to attain geometrical perfection, and that is the relation of external space to building entrances. If we model even a single cell not simply as a convex object, but as a building-like entity with an interior and an entrance (and creating a finite substrate mirroring the shape of the built form) then we find that this on its own will have the immediate – and on reflection obvious – effect of bringing

integration onto lines passing the entrance, as in plate 5a. In other
words, the effect on the all-line map of considering internal as well as
external space, as related through the entrance, is to integrate the area
outside the entrance to the building in a direction orthogonal to the
orientation of the entrance. It would not stretch things too far to suggest
that the effect of even one such building with an entrance is to create a local
spatial pattern which is already street-like. It is easy to see that this is a
necessary emergent effect. Other things being equal, the relation to the
interior of the 'building' will always create an extra degree of integration
in the local all-line map, and in the absence of other influences, this relation will dominate the structure of integration.

Now it is clear that if we both align cells with interiors and face
their entrances more or less in the same direction, then integration in the
resultant all-line map will powerfully and reliably follow the line orthogonal to (and therefore linking) the alignment of entrances, as in plate 5b. We
are in effect using the alignment and the entrance effect to reinforce each
other, and so create redundancy in the resulting structure. This effect will
be lost if we face a pair of cells in opposite directions, as in plate 5c, or
place one behind the other, as in plate 5d. Stabilisation requires alignment and entrances to coincide in creating the same effect.

We now see that these two most localised invariants in urban form,
the relation of space to entrances and the local alignment of forms,
together reliably create exactly the emergent local structure in the substrate
that we have observed to be the case. Cell alignment 'means' the creation
of a linear integration structure along the surfaces of aligned cells; entrance
orientation specifies on which side this is to occur. In the absence of one
or other we will not find the invariant pattern we have noted. The two
together have the effect of eliminating local indeterminacy in the form,
and creating a robust emergent pattern of integration in the aggregate.

There is, moreover, a second way in which an emergent pattern of
integration can be stabilised in a small aggregate: by creating a second
alignment of cells more or less parallel to an existing alignment. This
second alignment does not have to be complete, but the more complete
it is the more it will eliminate indeterminacy in the resulting pattern of
integration in the all-line analysis. In the two cases in plate 5e and 5f for

example, quite minor changes in the shape and alignment of cells – the lower left cell in f has been moved slightly to the left of its position in e – is enough to realign the dominant line of integration from left right to diagonally top down. However, if, as in plate 5g, we add a third cell on the second line, it is very hard to find an arrangement of the cells or shape change which does not lead to the main axes of integration running left to right between the two alignments. The pattern of integration has again become robust. It is not likely to change under small variations in the shape and position of cells.

There are then three ways in which the local indeterminacy of integration patterns can be overcome in small cellular aggregates. One is alignment of the cells. The second is alignment of entrances. The third is parallel alignments. What we find in real settlements is that all three are used to reinforce each other. It seems an unavoidable inference that, at this localised level, settlements pursue integration in the emergent structure by using all three ways of achieving it to reinforce each other. In other words, even at the most localised level we find that settlements exploit emergent laws of space. We can then be quite precise as to the respective roles of human agency and objective laws. The human agency is in the physical shaping, locating and orientation of built forms. The laws are in the emergent spatial effects consequent on those physical decisions. Built forms, we may say, are shaped, located and oriented by human agency, but in the light of laws which control their effects.

The laws of growth

If this is so at the most localised level, what of the higher levels of area and global structure? Here we must remind ourselves of the contrary influences of two underlying principles: linearity integrates the visibility field, compactness integrates the movement field. Urban form, we proposed, reconciled these two imperatives of growing systems through the 'deformed' or 'interrupted' grids, both of which tend to maximise linearity without losing compactness. We shall see now that this principle can be seen to operate at every level of the evolution of urban form, right down to the level of certain very small settlements whose layout seems to contain the very seeds of urban form.

In *The Social Logic of Space*[3] it was shown that the basic topological forms of certain small and apparently haphazard settlement forms, in which irregular ring streets with occasional larger spaces like beads on a string – hence the 'beady ring' – could be generated by 'restricted random' cell growth processes in which cells with entrance and spaces outside the entrance were aggregated randomly, subject only to the rules that each cell joined its open space onto the open space of a cell already in the complex, and that joining cells by their vertices was forbidden (since joining buildings at the corner is never found in practice). Plate 6a shows an example.

It was also suggested that many settlements which began with this type of process progressively introduced 'globalising' rules as they grew larger. These globalising rules took the form of longer axial lines in some parts of the complex, and larger convex spaces, usually with some well-defined relation between the two. The effect of globalising rules was that certain key properties, such as axial depth from the outside to the heart of the settlement, tended to remain fairly constant. Such contents tended to create a structure more or less on the scale of the settlement as it grew. Analysis then showed[4] that the effect of these rules was to maintain both the intelligibility and the functionality of the settlement, to maintain a strong relation between the different parts of the settlement and between the settlement and the outside world.

In these 'beady ring' forms, two key local spatial characteristics were noted, which then tended to be conserved under expansion. First, virtually all local 'convex' spaces, however small or narrow, were 'constituted' by entrances. Second, these convex elements tended to be linked by lines of sight and access. Since we knew that both of these arise as emergents from the conservation of integration in the form, it seems reasonable to believe that we now have a theory for these local aspects of the form. But what of the globalising processes?

We should note that beady rings already resemble urban systems in ways which are significant for urban structures. First, the distribution of integration in the open space is not undifferentiated, but biased strongly towards certain lines and certain locations. Second, the lines that are prioritised tend to be among those that link the settlement to its exterior. Theoretically, of course, this is likely to be the case, because in any small collection of objects, the lines which are wholly internal (in that both ends stop on built forms), are likely to be shorter than lines which connect the interior to the exterior. This is particularly significant, since it seems to contain the seeds of a key aspect of urban structures: that is the tendency for the integration core to link at least some key internal areas to the periphery of the settlement.

To explore how this becomes a key factor in settlement growth, we must bring into place the 'four principles' set out in the previous chapter, and reinterpret them for the aggregative process in which built forms progressively construct patterns of open space. The reader will recall that the four principles were *centrality* : blocks placed more centrally on a line create more depth gain – that is reduce integration – than peripherally placed blocks, and vice versa for the creation of open space by block removal; *extension* : the longer the line on which we define centrality, the greater the depth gain from the block, and vice versa for space; *contiguity* : contiguous blocks create more depth gain than non-contiguous blocks, and vice versa for space; and *linearity* : linearly arranged contiguous blocks create more depth gain than coiled or partially coiled blocks.

Seen from the point of view of the line structures that are created by block aggregation processes, the four principles begin to look much simpler. The centrality principle and the extension principle can be expressed as a single principle: maximise the length of the longest available line. If there is a choice about placing a building to block a longer or shorter line, block the shorter line. This does not quite work in a void, since too many lines are infinite, but it would be progressively more and more possible to make such discriminations as an aggregate becomes more complex. The effect of this rule would be always to conserve the longest existing lines in the growing aggregate and gradually evolve these lines into yet longer lines. A similar simplification is possible for the principles of contiguity and linearity when considered from the point of view of line creation. Both imply the minimisation of deflection from linearity. Placing objects contiguously will clearly increase deflection, and so will the linear placing of objects, rather than in a 'coiled up' form.

We might then transcribe the four principles into a simpler form which runs something like: select longest lines for maximum linearity, and on others (where maximum linearity is by definition not being conserved) keep deflection to the minimum. We can easily see how such a rule, operating in the context of the need to resolve the paradox between compact metric integration and linear visual integration would lead naturally to the structural bias we find in the beady-ring form. It is less obvious, but nonetheless the case, that it can also lead to the much more complex structural biases in larger urban grids that we identify as 'integration cores'. In due course, we will also see that it can in itself lead naturally to the commonest kinds of local area structure that we find in larger cities.

How then and why do these global properties of urban systems arise? Consider the earliest stages of growth in deformed grids, beginning with the hypothetical 'beady-ring' settlement of plate 6b, with its all-line analysis and intelligibility scattergram below. The integration core links edge to centre and the scattergram shows that the intelligibility is high (from which we may be sure that the correlation of local and global interaction will be even higher). Now we know that in any such system the longest available lines are unlikely to be those that make interior connections, since these by definition stop on buildings at each end, but will be among those that link interior to exterior. Suppose then that we simply follow the rule of placing new blocks so as to extend longest lines. A possible outcome after a while would be as in plate 6c.

This is a fairly common form of development, but as a principle to guide the evolution of larger systems it is insufficient, since the effect is to create lacunas in the form and make it non-compact. We also find, on analysis, that the core becomes focused very strongly in the centre, with edges that become very weak. This is what we would expect, since it is the lack of compact development in all directions that led to the lack of structure at the edges. We also find intelligibility, as shown in the scattergram, beginning to break down in the more integrated areas, reflecting the independence of growth along different alignments. In fact we find this type of development is quite common in small-scale settlements, but is rarely found in larger ones. Morphologically, there seem to be sound reasons for this limitation. None of the properties we have come to expect in growing systems are conserved beyond a certain stage in this type of development.

Let us then experiment by expanding the hypothetical settlement
compactly. We will explore two possibilities. In the first, we pursue our
dual rule of optimising the linear extension of existing longest lines, and
avoiding undue linear deflection in the remainder of the system. In the
second, we reverse the first principle, and block longest lines at ninety
degrees with blocks that also cause substantial deflection of lines elsewhere in the system. Plate 6d shows two possible outcomes after a further ring of growth complete with all-line analyses and intelligibility
scattergrams. In the first outcome, the integration core continues to link
centre to edge, and maintain overall integration and intelligibility in the
system. In the second, chicanes on all lines from centre to edge mean that
these lines become hard to differentiate from other lines. The result is a
much more centralised core, which no longer covers the diameter of the
system. The overall degree of integration and intelligibility are accordingly substantially less than in the first case. If we then continue the
same pair processes as in plate 6e and f, we find similar outcomes, though
with the additional effect that the integration core in 6f has now split into
two. The levels of both integration and intelligibility are significantly
lower in 6f than 6e.

These are of course considerable simplifications of real urban
growth processes, but they serve to illustrate a fundamental principle:
that given that we follow the rules of local alignment of built forms and
entrances to stabilise integration in the local system, then simply following the rule of selecting the longest lines for extending linearity, and
keeping deflection to a reasonably low level in the rest of the system, will
in itself tend to create an integration core that links centre to periphery in
several directions. This not only tends to solve the paradox of linearity
and compactness, by creating spaces that link centre to edge, but also
creates a system which is internally integrated, and intelligible. Thus the
paradox of centrality is overcome, at least from the point of view of visibility and intelligibility. All this happens because the integration core
structures the settlement in such a way as both to integrate the settlement
internally while at the same time integrating it to its exterior. In other
words, the combined 'centrality' and 'extension' principles – simply
by being applied in a growing system – have the effect of overcoming the

centrality paradox by exploiting the visibility paradox. In this sense
at least we can say that some of the key invariants of global order in the
fundamental settlement process are simply products of generic function
applied to growing systems in the light of the paradoxes of growth in such
systems.

One question then remains. How do local area structures arise? Let
us then pick up the story of the expanding deformed grid that we left at
plate 6e. We know that systems can evolve a centre-to-edge integration
core which will guarantee certain key system properties under growth.
However, as the system grows farther, it will generate more and more the
structural problem we saw in plate 6c: as the lines that form the integration core drive outwards, they tend to become farther and farther apart
creating larger and larger lacunas in the system. As the system grows,
this problem must become more acute. The scale of the lacunas means
that it cannot be solved by simply avoiding overly deflecting lines. There
must be structure within the lacunas just as previously there was a need
for structure in the main settlement as it grew. The structure, we might
say, that resolves the centrality paradox at the level of the whole settlement recreates it as a more localised problem, by partly enclosing areas
that must by filled in with built forms if the compactness rule is to be
retained. It follows that structure must evolve to overcome this problem.

All we need to specify is the continuation of the process we have
already described for the growing centre into the lacunas between the
radials. Since built forms will already exist at the edge, the process must
begin there. A process of placing blocks in order to maximise the longest
lines created by the built forms will first tend to create a linear space penetrating the lacuna laterally, so that in spite of the fact that the process has
begun at the edges of the lacuna, a structure will be created which is dominated by edge-to-centre lines in at least two and possibly more directions.
The interstices will then be filled with blocks that avoid overly deflecting
linearity, and these will then form the less integrated zones within the sub-
area. Because initially the conditions of this local process are structured
from the periphery, the conditions for radial growth do not exist here. On
the contrary, the initial moves in the system under these more structured
conditions necessarily begin to sketch a more orthogonal grid.

Accordingly, we tend to find a greater tendency towards orthogonal order in these interstitial areas than in the initial urban form. It is literally suggested by the process itself.

In cases where this process subsumes an earlier settlement – say an existing village – then this may initially be the natural magnet for the lines penetrating the lacuna from the edge. This will tend to form a local deformation of the grid evolving in the lacuna. It is exactly such a process that gave rise to London's 'urban villages'. These are invariably the foci of the integration core of local deformed grids which, like other London areas, take the form of a 'deformed wheel' (that is, an integration core with a hub, spokes and a rim, with quiet areas in the interstitial zones) in which the periphery, instead of being the space outside the settlement, is formed by the radials of the larger-scale urban process. It is this process that gives rise to the fact that in cities like London the 'deformed wheel' structure is repeated twice, once at the level of the whole city and once at the level of the local area. It is also this that gives rise to the geometry of the local and larger-scale organisation of the city that we noted earlier in this chapter, in which length of line and angle of incidence were the key variables.

Not all cities, of course, have this kind of local area structure. But this is the difficult case. London embodies the continuation of the operation of generic function, and the spatial processes to which it gives rise, into the local area structure of the growing city. It is this that makes London, in spite of initial appearances, such a paradigmatic case of the well-structured city. Perhaps because throughout its history planning intervention was of the most parsimonious kind, the greatest latitude was created for the fundamental settlement process to evolve in one of its purest forms.

It is this that gives London its unique theoretical interest. Other cities have very different ways of constructing their local area structure, but they are *more* structured, that is they are a product more of cultural parametrisation of the fundamental process than of the fundamental process itself. In Shiraz, for example, local area structures are much more axially broken up than in London, but they are also smaller and less complex as areas. Most local areas in Shiraz are made up of sequences of right-angle

lines connecting in one, two, three or four places to the dominant structure of the integration core. Their relation is predominantly to the outside, and that relation is constructed by simple, but deep, sequences of
lines. We do not therefore find that the correlation of radius-3 and radius-
n integration gives the structure of the local area. We do find, however (as
shown by Kayvan Karimi, a doctoral student at UCL), that the correlation
of radius-6 and radius -n integration does capture this structure, as shown
in the two cases picked out in plate 7. We also find a geometric correlate
to these properties: each line that forms part of a local area belongs entirely to that area. No line which is internal to an area also crosses a core line
and becomes part also of another local area. Local areas in Shiraz are, we
might say, linearly discrete. This was much less the case in London where
at least some lines which were part of local areas also continued into
neighbouring areas. As we have found before, configuration of properties
are constructed eventually out of the line geometry constructed by
blocks of built form.

Shiraz is a fairly extreme case, where local structures are small, segregated and highly dependent on the global structure of the settlement.
At the opposite extreme we find cities like Chicago, where the high mean
average length of line and the fact that some cross the entire system mean
that integration is very high. There is then in the settlement *as a whole* a
high correlation between connectivity and integration, and a fortiori a
high correlation between local and global integration. In Chicago there is
very little tendency for whole lines to be confined to any plausible sub-area
in the city. On the contrary, a major characteristic of the structure of the
city is that all areas are made up of lines that include many that are global
lines in the system. But this does not mean that there is no local area
structure. On the contrary. If we select for areas all lines within that area
and those that pass through the area, we find reproduced at the local level
even stronger correlation between connectivity and integration than prevails for the system as a whole. In other words, the local area structure of
the city is characterised in the case of Chicago by the correlation between
connectivity (that is, radius-1 integration) and radius-n integration, in
London by the correlation between radius-3 and radius-n integration and
in Shiraz by the correlation of radius-6 and radius-n integration. This

then is a parameter by which each city adapts the fundamental settlement process to its own structural needs.

However, all of the invariants that were specified in the original description of cities hold in all three of these cases. Not only do we find these deep structures in common, but also a common geometrical language of line length and angles of incidence through which not only these structures, but also the parametrisations through which cultures identify themselves in spatial form, are realised. It is the existence of this common geometric language which permits both invariants and cultural parametrisations to proceed side by side. At the deepest level of what all cultures share – that is of what is common spatially to humankind – is the geometric language that we all speak.

Notes

1   This was explored in the early seventies by Daniel Richardson in 'Random growth in a tessellation', *Journal of the Cambridge Philosophical Society*, 74, 1973, pp. 515–28.

2   The difference between a 'deformed' and 'interrupted' grid is that the controlled irregularity of the former comes about essentially through geometric deformation of the line structure, in the manner of European cities, while that of the latter comes about by placing buildings and other facilities to 'interrupt' some lines rather than others, in the manner of Graeco-Roman or American grids. Both usually achieve the result of a well-defined pattern of integration in the axial map of the city. For a further discussion, see below.

3   See B. Hillier & J. Hanson, *The Social Logic of Space*, Cambridge University Press, 1984, chapter 2.

4   B. Hillier et al. 'Creating life: or, does architecture determine anything?', *Architecture & Behaviour*, vol. 3, no. 3, Special Issue on Space Syntax research, Editions de la Tour, 1987.

Part four

Theoretical syntheses

Space is the machine

Of what things is space the cause? None of the four modes of causation can be ascribed to it. It is neither cause in the sense of the matter of things (for nothing is composed of it), nor as the form and definition of things, nor of ends, nor does it move things.
(ARISTOTLE: *PHYSICS* BOOK IV CHAPTER I)

Forms and functions, buildings and societies

Common sense affirms, and the ordinary use of language confirms, that there is an association between the form and function of a building. If we name a kind of building – say 'school' or 'house' or 'church' – and try to disentangle what we mean, then we find at least two sets of ideas present in the word. One is the idea of a particular form of social organisation. The other is the idea of a particular form of building. Perhaps *an* organisation and *a* form is too specific. A family of possible organisations and a family of possible forms might convey more accurately what is in our minds. These seem in some way to be bound up with each other in the intuitions of 'school' or 'house' or 'church', so that we think we recognise one from the other. This association of ideas is not confined to cognition. It affects behaviour. By recognising types as form-function pairings, we anticipate how to behave in the kinds of spaces that we expect to find in a building. We are preprogrammed by our intuitions of building types to behave in ways appropriate to the form.

However, in spite of the apparent closeness of the association, the relation between form and function in buildings has always proved resistant to analysis. Although the relation seems intuitively clear on a case by case basis, and architects design buildings to fit different functions for the most part without too much difficulty, it is very hard to be explicit about what it is that distinguishes the form-function relation as it appears in one type of building from the way it appears in another. One might say that a designer will design a possible version of the form–function pairing for a certain purpose, but that does not mean that any aspect of what is designed is necessary for that purpose. Knowledge of what is necessary implies knowledge of the limits of possibility. Such limits are not at all well understood. In the present state of knowledge, it is not unreasonable to doubt their existence. The form-function relation may not be well defined enough to allow such knowledge. The fact that buildings so easily change their function supports these doubts. The form-function relation may not be quite as specific as the uncritical use of the language of building types suggests.

To some extent this state of affairs may be due to failure to distinguish between the specific functions buildings perform, and 'generic function', as set out in the last two chapters. Generic function implies that what makes buildings functionally interchangeable is what buildings must have in common spatially in order to fulfil any function. The more generic function is sufficient to account for spatial organisation in any particular case, then the more we would expect functional flexibility. However, this does not solve the problem in hand. Intuition clearly anticipates, and language institutionalises, specific functions and warns us that in some important sense a school is a school, and a house a house. Are intuition and language then wrong in this affirmation?

There are two aspects to the problem. First, our ideas about buildings already come replete with social ideas. Second, our ideas about social institutions come with ideas about buildings attached to them. Each presents a problem for architectural theory. The first leads to the form-function question as we have described it. Does common sense deceive us in affirming a well-formed typological relation between the form a building takes and what it is for? If it does not, is this association contingent, in that it just happens that this function leads to this form and that function another? Or is there some more systematic sense in which variations in functions are associated with variations in form? If the latter is the case, then there can be a form-function theory in architecture. If not, there cannot be. The second leads to questions about buildings as social objects. Does it matter that our ideas about social institutions come with ideas about buildings attached to them? Is the building in some sense a part of the definition of the social entities we name as schools, monasteries, and so on? If so, is this simply an association of ideas, or is there some well-defined sense in which variations in social forms are expressed through variation in the forms of buildings?

On reflection, our reaction tends to be against the idea of systematic relations. At first sight, a social organisation – say a school – is a set of roles and relations that can be fully described without invoking a building. However, the matter is not so easily settled. The *idea* of a school, if not its organisational diagram, implies more than roles and relations in the abstract. It implies roles and relations realised in spatial form in some way. There must, for example, be spatial interfaces of some kind between teachers and taught. Such interfaces define a kind of minimal spatial content not simply to the building, but to an organisation and therefore to the building. These spatial dimensions of organisation arise not from the form of the organisation but from its functioning. An organisation can be described without reference to space, and therefore without reference to buildings, but the way in which the organisation works usually cannot.

The idea of a school does after all seem to imply some type of realisation in space. It was a recognition of this minimal spatial context in organisations that gave rise to the theory of buildings as 'interfaces' between 'inhabitants' and 'visitors', (such as priests and congregations, teachers and taught, families and guests), and between different categories of inhabitant that was set out in *The Social Logic of Space*[1]. Interfaces seem to define the essential spatial 'genotypes' of the buildings we name as belonging to this or that functional type. However, this leads to a difficult question. If societies regularly produce spatial genotypes in buildings, then surely there must be some sense in which these genotypes are necessary to, even a part of, society. An even more difficult question follows. If we find it hard to conceptualise how a building can have necessary social dimension to it, it is even harder to conceptualise how a society can have a necessary built dimension to it.

Our puzzle is then twofold. Buildings seem to be physical things, and societies and organisations seem to be abstractions. Yet our ideas of buildings seem to contain social abstractions, and our idea of social organisations seems to contain ideas of buildings. The common coin of both relations seems to be the idea of space. Space both gives the form to the social abstractions which we name in buildings, and space seems to be the content of the building that can be taken back to the more abstract conceptions of society and organisation. The first defines the form-function problem in architecture. In what sense is there a regular relation between the forms of buildings and the ways in which the bits of society that inhabit them work? The second is the problem of the building as a social object. Is there any real sense in societies needing buildings to make them work? These two related problems will be dealt with in turn, beginning with a little recent history.

Recent history

It is sad, but true, that the theoretical nature of the form-function relation in architecture mainly comes to public attention through failure. When an architectural scheme – say an inner city redevelopment or a large housing estate – goes wrong in a public way, it is common to blame architects for their crazy theories. It is a one-sided game. Buildings and places that work rarely attract such epistemological comment. Good buildings and places are taken to be as nature intended rather than as artificial products of thought. No one ever praises architecture for the excellence of its theories. Only failure, it seems, alerts the man or woman on the upper level walkway or in the empty piazza to the highly theoretical nature of architecture.

But what exactly is it about architecture that these theoretical critics are referring to? They seem not to be talking about construction, since that would be regarded, rightly or wrongly, as a matter of fact, of knowable technique, and therefore a matter of competence rather than theory. Nor do they seem to be talking about aesthetics or style, since that would be regarded as a matter of taste or of art, and therefore a matter of sensibility rather than theory. Theoretical criticism of architecture seems squarely aimed at the second term of the Vitruvian triad of 'firmness, commodity, and delight'.[1] It addresses the way in which the physical and spatial form of buildings impinges on the way we live our lives – that is, the form-function relation.

As we have seen, the form-function relation is easy to talk about in a generalised way, but difficult to talk about precisely. It is not even clear how we should talk about it. The form-function relation, unlike construction, does not seem to belong to architecture as science, since there seem to be no clear facts, let alone explicit and testable theories. Nor does it belong to architecture as art. We cannot seriously see the North Peckham estate or Pruitt Igoe as failures of art. Yet the form-function relation does seem to be what people expect architectural theories to be about. On reflection, we might find that both architects and their theoretical critics agree that this is right. Architecture is a technique and an art with social consequences which are intrinsic rather than extrinsic. They lie in the nature of the object itself, as well as in its associations and symbolic meanings. Architectural theories do not therefore in general take the form of propositions about construction or propositions about art: they are in essence propositions about the relation between architecture and life; that is, about what architecture is *for* in relation to what it *is*. This is perhaps the distinctive feature that makes architecture unlike anything else that human beings do. At least part of its social implications lie in its very form, and our notions of what a theory is reflect this.

A great deal more of the current public debate about architecture than we allow is aimed at the form-function relation. People are worried about places that seem not to work; about developments in cities that lack the life that is the source of urbanity; about housing estates that do not seem to generate the elementary decencies of community life. They believe, rightly or wrongly, that architecture is in some way implicated. This creates a problem between architecture and its public that is more than one of communication, because, in spite of the fact that designing forms to fit functions is one of the foundations of architectural practice, the fact is that most of our usable knowledge about it comes from precedent and individual experience. There is very little theoretical understanding of the form-function relation. We even find it difficult to talk about in a consistent and rational way. Fortunately, when push comes to shove, the theoretical critics on the upper level walkway share our incoherence, and need only a little encouragement to conspire with us in talking about the problem as though it could be reduced to construction or aesthetics, or maybe the lack of shops, or transport or nursery facilities.

The idea that there is so little theoretical understanding of form and function in architecture may surprise many, since it is widely believed that the failures of twentieth-century architecture are largely to be laid at the door of a 'functionalist' theory.[2] The conventional wisdom is that modernism failed because it was more concerned with the relation between form and function than with the relation between form and meaning, and that this was so because architecture, under the peculiar social pressures of the *post bellum* decades, had become more preoccupied with social engineering through architecture than with architecture itself. The subsequent disillusion with functionalism as the normative basis of design also became a rejection of the form-function relation as the primary focus for a theory of architecture, in favour of the form-meaning relation. Modernist functionalism was rejected not only as a false theory, but as a theory aimed at the wrong problem.

In retrospect, it is far from obvious that the rejection should have
been so thoroughgoing. It was always clear that the 'failures' of modernism were not simply failures of a functionalist philosophy, but also
functional failures. The new housing forms simply did not work to meet
the benign social engineering objectives – community, interaction, identity, and so on – that were written into their programmes. The proper
inference from this would seem to be that the functionalist theories used
by the designers were wrong, but that functional failure had confirmed
the central importance of the form-function relation. There could, after
all, be no functional failure if the relation between form and function were
not powerful. The call should then follow for a new theory of function.
Instead, there was an abandonment of functional theory in general and an
intellectual abandonment of the form-function problem at exactly the
moment when functional failure had brought it dramatically to public
attention.

   To understand this apparently perverse reaction – and also see that
in a certain sense it was justified – we must understand exactly what it
was that was rejected. What was rejected, it will be argued, was not the
form-function relation per se, since that continued to play the same practical role in architectural practice that it has always played, but a specific
formulation of the form-function problem that provided the foundation
for architecture as social engineering. This we will call the 'paradigm of
the machine'. The paradigm of the machine was the necessary foundation
for the practice of architecture as social engineering, and originated in a
debate between architecture and the social sciences. As a result, certain
theoretical problems in the social sciences pertaining to the relation
between the social world and the material world, were transmitted into
architecture. To the extent that architecture became social engineering,
the paradigm of the machine invaded architectural thought, took over its
language and its institutional structures, and became pervasive and
destructive.

The metaphor of the machine and the paradigm of the machine
We must begin by making a clear distinction between the paradigm of the
machine and the metaphor of the machine. The most famous – some

would say infamous – proposition of architectural theory in the twentieth-century is probably Le Corbusier's 'A house is a machine for living in'.[3] On the face of it, this seems to assert a direct analogy between buildings and machines. In fact, a closer reading quickly suggests this is not to be taken seriously. A machine is an organisation of matter that transforms other matter through its operation. Nothing like this conception is to be found in Le Corbusier's text. Translating from machines to buildings would have to centre on the plan as the organiser of the life that goes on in a building. If the building is to be seen as a machine, then this implies that the relation between the plan and the life that takes place in the plan – is in some sense mechanistic, and that the former is either determinative, or a strict expression, of the latter. This belief is not to be found in Le Corbusier's text. On the contrary, when in his 'Manual of the dwelling' he explains in more detail 'the house as a machine for living in', he describes rooms, and exhorts clients to demand a whole range of rooms for new functions, but he does not discuss the organisation of rooms into a plan in any way.[4] It is clear that his preoccupation is not with the machine as formal analogue for the organisation of the dwelling, but with the machine as the metaphor for a style uncluttered with the decorative detritus of the past.

This interpretation is confirmed when, later on in the book, Le Corbusier does talk of plans. His approach is passionate, historical, and preoccupied with the symbolic potential of space.[5] It is clear that Le Corbusier sees the plan as part of architecture, and the space that is organised by the plan as a prime expression of architectural creativity. His spatial philosophy is specific. The principle spatial element is the axis. The organisation of the building is the organisation of its axes, that is, of its sequences of experience. The axis is fundamental because the experience of architecture is an experience of movement. 'Arrangement is the grading of axes, and so it is the grading of aims, the classification of intentions.'[6] There is no determinism in this view, only a strict rationalism by which the mind imposes its geometric self on the geometric potential of the external world, and calls it architecture. One finds in Le Corbusier then the metaphor of the machine, but not the paradigm of the machine. In general we will find this is the case in high architecture. One scours the architectural manifestos of the twentieth-century in vain for a thoroughgoing statement of the determinism from spatial form to function, or its inverse, that would be the true architectural embodiment of the paradigmatic, as opposed to metaphoric, idea of the building as machine.[7]

Where then do we find the notorious functional determinism for which twentieth-century architecture has become famous and for which modernism has been so commonly blamed? The answer is that it is to be found in the social and political theorising that increasingly became the intellectual context of the practice of architecture as architecture moved towards a social engineering practice. The central proposition of architecture as social engineering is that specific social outcomes can be engineered by manipulating architecture this way and that. In other words, the relation between form and function in architecture is analogous to similar problems dealt with by engineers. If architecture is indeed social engineering then it needs a theory to explain how it works. The paradigm of the machine filled this need. We should call this the paradigm of the machine, not the theory of the machine, because a paradigm is a set of model ideas and assumptions about the fundamental constitution of a field of phenomena which tell us what there is to theorise about. It functions as a framework for thought and for the setting of objectives, both theoretical and practical. It tells us in effect what kind of a problem we are dealing with. A theory tells us how phenomena work, and therefore suggests how we might solve problems.[8] The paradigm of the machine, it will be argued sets up the form-function problem in such a way that it could never generate a credible form-function theory.

The reader might object at this point that the possibility of pursuing social objectives through architecture has been reaffirmed throughout this book, since spatial form in architecture has been shown to have social determinants and social consequences. This is a correct accusation. But the substance of the proposal here is different. The central argument in this book is that the relation between form and function at all levels of the built environment, from the dwelling to the city, passes through the variable of spatial configurations. The effects of spatial configuration are not on individuals, but on collections of individuals and how they interrelate through space. All that is proposed, in effect, is that a pattern of space in a complex can affect the pattern of co-presence and co-awareness of collections of people who inhabit and visit that complex. This is a very obvious thing to say. The most likely answer is: 'Well of course ...' One is more likely to object to its triviality than to its metaphysics. All that has been done in earlier chapters is to show very carefully exactly how this occurs, and how these low-level effects link to more interesting, more obviously social effects.

Now the essence of the social engineering approach to the form-function relation in architecture was that it had no conception of spatial configuration, and without this the effects we will find ourselves looking for are not effects from one type of pattern to another, but from physical forms directly to individuals. The building itself is seen as the machine, and the physical form of the building the determinant of behaviour. Such relations do not exist, or at least not in any interesting sense. Belief in their existence really does violate common sense. How can a material object like a building impinge directly on human behaviour? Even so, it is exactly this that we are expected to believe if we abandon spatial configuration as the intervening variable. The paradigm of the machine in effect asks us to believe that the relation of form to function in archi-tecture passes not, credibly, from a pattern of space created by the build-ing to a pattern of co-awareness and co-presence, but, incredibly, directly from building to individual.

There are many versions of this belief. Some assume that direct relation between building and behaviour should take the form of 'fitting' activities to spaces. Others stress the intervening role of cognition, for example, that the built environment acts as a series of 'clue and clues' to behaviour or as a kind of theatrical back cloth which is 'appropriate' for the activity happening in front of it. All have in common that they pre-suppose a relation between built form and behaviour unmediated by spatial configuration.[9] That such relations do not really exist in any sys-tematic sense seems amply confirmed both by the lack of research results which show such relations, and by the fact that the only relations we can find are those that pass through spatial configuration. The effect of the paradigm of the machine on the theory and practice of architecture was therefore to base architectural practice on a theoretical foundation which

generated no research results and could predict no outcomes from design.
Architecture as social engineering was in effect founded on a postulate of
a relation between built form and human function which could not be
verified because it was not there.

It was this naive formulation of the form-function relation in architecture that was rejected with the demise of modernism. Unfortunately,
by then it had become, through its normative role in design, so fully
enmeshed with the whole idea of the form-function problem in architecture, that the rejection of the paradigm became, for a while at least, the
rejection of the problem, and consequently of the need for a form-function
theory in architecture at all. This chain of events is evidence of the ability
of paradigms to exert covert power on human thought. The paradigm of
the machine was always strange to architects, but it became the foundation for modernism in action, through its role in the programmes of social
engineering that architecture was enjoined to carry out in the post-war
decades. The paradigm of the machine was an idea about architecture
that never became a properly architectural idea, for the simple reason that
the relations on which the paradigm were posited simply do not exist.
Their hypothetical existence was an illusion of the paradigm.

Once we have located the paradigm of the machine as the necessary
belief system of architecture as social engineering, we can begin to trace
its origins and understand its true nature. Its origins turn out to be a great
deal older than we might think, and link up to a much wider spectrum
of ideas that began to prevail in intellectual life towards the end of the
eighteenth and in the early part of the nineteenth-century. This broader
underlying scheme of thought that gave rise to the paradigm of the
machine constitutes what I will call the 'organism environment paradigm'.
To understand its nature we must understand the origins of its key
conceptual constituent: the idea of 'environment'.

The origins of the environment

'Environment' is one of those curious words which we assume have always
been around, but which are in fact quite recent additions to our vocabulary,
and to our system of common concepts. It is an interestingly complex
idea. It implies not only the milieu in which we exist, but a milieu which

surrounds us. Environing means to surround, so an environment is not only
a physical milieu but one which actively and significantly surrounds, so
that the environed thing in some way is aware of, or affected by, its 'environment'. Environment as a surrounding thing implies an experiencing
subject at its centre. In the late twentieth-century, we confirm this complexity in the term environment by using it to express not only a new
awareness of the importance of our milieu, but also of our relation to it.

In this form, the idea was barely present in common consciousness
until well past the turn of the century, and it is only in the past three
decades that it has become a dominant element in our view of ourselves
and our place in the world. Because of the importance of the concept in
current thinking, the argument that is about to be proposed needs very
careful definition. In being critical of the effects of the concept of environment in the formation of certain paradigmatic schemes, there is no implied
criticism of the change in our awareness of our surroundings that the idea
of environment has helped to bring about. There are however, hidden
dangers in the concept. In particular, we must investigate the origins and
meanings of the word if we are to fully understand the origins, and the
malign effects of, the paradigm of the machine in architecture.

According to Canguihem,[10] we must look for the origins of the concept of environment in its modern sense in the eighteenth-century, and
some very significant developments that took place then in the development of scientific thinking about the natural world. To understand the
scientific developments, we must know the problem to which they were
addressed, and for this we must go all the way back to Aristotle. In looking at the natural world, especially those areas which are covered by such
modern sciences as biology and zoology (but also including the areas now
covered by physics and chemistry), what Aristotle saw in nature was a
general form-function problem: how was it that the forms of species (or
other natural forms) were so well adapted to how they functioned? We
might say that for this reason Aristotle saw nature as a design problem,
and sought an answer which would explain how nature managed to
design such successful form-function relations.

Aristotle answered by making an analogy with architecture. This
analogy is so pervasive in Aristotle's accounts of nature that it should be

thought of as Aristotle's paradigm. The form of a house, Aristotle argued, cannot be explained by a purely material process of laying stone on stone. This 'material' process had to be guided by a pre-existing idea of the form the house was to take. What is the nature of such ideas and where do they come from? They are, according to Aristotle, purposes. The form of a house arises from human purposes. Forms are therefore expressions of purposes and indeed in a sense are purposes. As it is in architecture, Aristotle argues, so it must be in nature, since we find the same agreement between form and apparent purpose. Aristotle then generalises. Material causes explain little. Final causes are purposes. The source of order in nature must therefore be purposeful design. It would not be too much of an exaggeration to say that the entire Aristotelian system of nature was erected on this architectural foundation.[11] Its flaws are well known. From a scientific point of view, arguing from design explains nothing. It does no more than remove one mystery by invoking another, and explain one kind of order by assuming another anterior to it.

Now the reason these ideas are an important background in the eighteenth-century is that in key areas of science such as physics theories had arisen which seemed not only to be true, but also showed how it was possible to explain order without the assumption of anterior order. How surprising this apparent emancipation of human thought seemed can best be explained by a contrast with Aristotelian physics. The fundamental assumptions of Aristotelian physics were common sense. If something moved, it was because something else had moved it. All our experience confirms this. Yet it leads to an impossible physics. For example, according to these assumptions, it was self evident that the forces that impelled movement could not work in a void. From this it followed that space was a plenum, rather than a vacuum. In such a universe, the chain of movement must be endless. Whatever moves, something else must itself be moved. What then is at the end of the line? Aristotle answers with a verbal conjuring trick: the unmoved mover.

Newton's solution to the paradoxes of Aristotelian physics is as well known as it is extraordinary. Following earlier incomplete formulations by Galileo and Descartes, he proposes a principle which contradicts all experience available at the time, the 'principle of inertia' which states

that all bodies move 'in a right line' forever until impelled by some external force to change their course.[12] This reformulation puts motion 'on the
same level of being as rest',[13] so that motion is no longer a change, as it
was in Aristotle, but a state. This is why it can continue forever, and this
is why the principle of inertia can be used as the fundamental assumption
of a mathematical physics, whose task was then to describe how forces
work on inert bodies to produce the patterns that we see in the universe.

    Of course, some of Newton's contemporaries objected that in elimi-
nating common sense Newton had also eliminated physics, and was
offering a mathematical description but not a physical theory.[14] On the
other hand, Newton's theory, with the minimum of assumptions and
with the greatest simplicity, gave an astonishingly accurate account of a
vast range of previously disparate phenomena, and permitted an uncanny
accuracy of prediction across many fields. In other words, although it did
not show why the world worked the way it did in any way which satisfied
common sense intuition, it showed how it worked with unprecedented
precision. Most important of all, Newton's theory showed how there could
be observable order in the universe without invoking some pregiven order
which gave rise to it. To accept that the universe worked mathematically
needed no stronger presupposition than that a soap bubble is spherical
because that represents the most probable distribution of forces.

    It was this discovery of order without anterior order that provided
the conceptual model for the attempts in the century following Newton
to make a parallel emancipation in our understanding of other natural
phenomena. From this point of view, the problem that had originally
motivated Aristotle, the forms of species in nature and their relation to
function, seemed intractable. How could there be a theory of the origina-
tion of order in natural species without anterior order, or design in some
guise, the more so in view of the fact that in this vastly rich and diverse
area of forms Aristotle's original objection that mathematics could not
be the language of science because it was too precise and abstract, seemed
still to hold force, despite the conquest of physics by mathematics?

    The modern concept of 'environment' took its form essentially as
the first attempt to formulate a solution to this problem: namely, the
environmental determination of species. In different parts of the world –

and therefore in different ambient conditions – very different patterns of speciation had occurred. The idea of the environmental determination of the forms of species quite simply turned the problem into the solution. If different speciation was to be found in different regions, what more natural proposition was there than that it was the conditions prevailing in these regions that had led to differential speciation in the first place? There were many variants on this underlying scheme of environmental determination, and no clear idea was proposed of how the mechanism of environment determining form might actually work.[15] But since Newton we did not need to be sure of mechanism before we believed in a theory, and the idea of environmental determination had great force because it showed for the first time how in the perplexing world of natural forms order could, in principle, arise from a natural process without the existence of pregiven order. In that sense, the epistemological force of environmental determinism captured something of the glamour that surrounded the theories of the physicists. It is within this scheme of thought that our modern notion of 'environment' originates. An environment not only surrounds: it affects and influences. The idea of environment is closely bound up with the idea of a being or organism at its centre drawing in to itself these effects and influences, and also creative contributing from its own interior nature to the interactive process by which its form, and hence the relationship between its form and its behaviour, developed.

The organism-environment paradigm

This scheme of thought is so important in the history of western cultures that it deserves a name – perhaps the 'organism-environment paradigm'.[16] By this is meant not simply the idea of environmental determination but also the vitalistic and subjectivistic objections to it which sought to involve the organism itself in the process of the evolution of its form,[17] since these ideas are virtually called into existence by environmental determinism. The organism-environment paradigm is the scheme of ideas that forces us to choose between objective determination by the 'environment' and the subjective objections to this. It is an intellectual framework which still influences certain fields of scholarship much more than it ought, since within a century of its inception, the whole scheme

of thought had been replaced in the field where it has originated by the far
more sophisticated paradigm of evolution theory, in which the environment was no longer seen as mould, but as a selector, and the relation of
organism to environment not as a direct physical relation of cause and
effect, but as an indirect relation, mediated by what we would now call
genetic information structures, passed from one generation to the next,
and gradually evolving, but not on the timescale of individuals. The Darwinian scheme is not an adjustment within the organism-environment
paradigm, but a replacement of it by another paradigm, one in which the
dominant process is not an interaction between the physical organism
and its environment but an abstract statistical mechanism in which
informational structures built into organisms diffuse and decay in the
evolving population according to the probability of randomly generated
mutations leading to greater success in leaving progeny.[18] The substitution
of random variation of forms for the environmental determination of
forms has, we may note, exactly the same epistemological function as
the substitution of inertia for caused movement in Newton's theory.
Through this it shows the way to order without pregiven order in nature,
and to an emancipation of the study of nature on to the level of physics.

From the point of view of the origins of the machine analogy in
architecture, we have to understand that the organism-environment paradigm, while showing little scientific explanatory power in the late eigh-
teenth- and early nineteenth-centuries, had great metaphorical power. Well
before Darwin, through that little understood process by which scientific
ideas become absorbed into culture, we find the organism-environment
idea diffusing with paradigmatic force well beyond the bounds of 'natural
history' (as it was then called). Balzac, for example, used it explicitly as
one of the guiding ideas in his *Comédie Humaine*, seeing social species
as products of milieu, and his novels as their natural history. 'The idea
(for his *Comédie Humaine*)' wrote Balzac 'originated in a comparison
between humanity and animality...As we read the writing of the mystics
who studied the sciences in their relation to the infinite, and the works
of the greatest authors on Natural History...we detect in the monads of
Leibnitz, in the organic molecules of Buffon, in the vegetative force of
Needham, in the correlation of similar organs of Charles Bonnet...we

detect I say the rudiments of the great law of Self for Self, which lies at the root of Unity of Structure. There is but one animal. The creator works on a single model for every organised being. 'The Animal' is elementary, and takes its external form, or to be accurate the differences in its external form, from the environment in which it is obliged to develop. Zoological species are the result of these differences...I for my part, convinced of this scheme of nature long before the discussion to which it has given rise, perceived that in this respect society resembled nature. For does not society modify Man, according to the conditions in which he lives and acts, into men as manifold as the species in Zoology?...If Buffon could produce a magnificent work by attempting to represent in a book the whole realm of zoology, was there not room for a work of the same kind on society?'[19]

It is in Balzac's novels that we find some of the earliest examples of that exact, atmospheric description of physical environments, presaging personages and their misfortunes, and creating in the reader's mind a quasi-naturalistic association between environment and human being, which is so characteristic of the technique of the nineteenth-century novel.[20] More significantly for our present theme, environmental determinism provided the intellectual spark for the late eighteenth and early nineteenth-century fashion for 'architectural determinism': the mechanistic idea that architectural design could, if handled right, directly cause beneficial effects on the moral and social lives of people. This became a pervasive influence on social reformers of the period, as well as on the builders of prisons and asylums.[21] It was this that established the paradigmatic idea that architecture could be both understood and exploited by direct analogy to machines, a reconciliation attractive and understandable to early nineteenth-century thought. Architectural determinism seemed to normalise the problems of architecture by making them look like problems of engineering. Through its association with the expanding social engineering purposes of early nineteenth-century architecture, and the increasing sponsorship of the state, architectural determinism came to be seen as a powerful, scientific and action-orientated reformulation of the form-function relation in architecture.

Architectural determinism, of course, is no more true than environmental determinism had been, nor should we expect it to be. As with

Lamarckism, no results have been produced which even begin to compel
our belief. However, unlike environmental determinism, architectural
determinism survived Darwin. There were probably three reasons for
this improper survival. First, environmental determinism was a scientific error, and therefore refutable, whilst architectural determinism was
a more diffuse cultural paradigm, often below the level of conscious
thought, and not exposed therefore to direct refutation. Second, because
it was a cultural belief, it tended to become institutionalised. If you spent
money on architecture as moral engineering, then you had to believe in
it. Third, the Darwinian revolution left many of the cultural by-products
of environmental determinism behind because the metaphorical impact
of Darwinism on culture lay elsewhere, in the survival of the fittest and
the descent from monkeys, with the reformulation of the form-function
problem in nature only in the small print read by the specialist.

For whatever reason, the organism-environment paradigm survived
into the twentieth-century. Partly through its association with the determinism associated with architecture as social engineering, it became the
default position for the formulation of all problems dealing with the relation of human beings and their built environment. This default survival
takes many forms: the study of human 'response' to the built environment;
the study of cognitive schemes by which we represent the built environment to ourselves; the study of built environments as theatrical sets or
back cloths providing cues and clues for the activity that is intended to
take place in the foreground; the study of 'territory' that is the study of
the space exterior to the individual insofar as it is constructed and interpreted through drives emanating from inside the individual – all these use
the same underlying paradigmatic scheme of an individual surrounded by
an environment which that individual seeks to interpret or affect.

It is through engagement with this default intellectualisation of the
form-function problem that architecture, as it engages in social engineering, also engages the paradigm of the machine, and the assumption it
implies of the direct and mechanistic relation between an individual and
that individual's immediate environment. The metaphor of the machine,
we might say, met the paradigm of the machine, and the prison of ideas
was complete. Through the powerful effects of customary language on

our habitual patterns of thought, this has become the natural and inevitable formulation of a whole class of problems, so much so that the appeal of writers like Giddens[22] to bring space and time back into the 'constitution of society' is in effect largely forbidden by the continuing invisible effects of this paradigmatic background, because they make it appear as a return to nineteenth-century mechansim.

The covert power of the paradigm is reinforced by the ease with which the organism-environment scheme ingests and reinterprets more ancient dualities. For example, the Cartesian duality of *res cogitans*, the thing that thinks, and *res extensa*, the thing that is, is re-expressed as the relation between abstract, individual minds and concrete surrounding environments. Similarly the distinction between subject and object becomes the experiencing mind and the experienced environmental object. Even the rival historical speculations of rationalism and empiricism find a resting place in the superordinate, apparently empirical concept of an individual mind, receptive and constructive, surrounded by a material environment, emanating and malleable. A history of errors is, it seems, confirmed as a progressive orthodoxy by the new formulation.

However, the worst outcome of the paradigm of the machine, and its intellectual parent the organism-environment paradigm, is that by representing the human subject as the object of concern at the centre of an influencing and influenced environment, the appearance is set up of a humane science concerned with understanding the effects of built environment on the social, cognitive and emotional life of people. But within this formulation no such effects are discoverable, other than those that do arise from the simple physical presence of an individual in an environment, such as the effects of air pollution on health, or the effect of sun on diseases of the skin. The appearance of the humane science is, in the last analysis, an inhumane deception.

At root, these consequences follow from the fact that the paradigm of the machine sets up the built environment as no more than an inert physical background to the behaviour and experiences of people. In effect, the artificial environment is being treated as a natural environment. This blinds the enquirer to the most significant single fact about the built environment: that it is not simply a background to social behaviour – it is itself a social behaviour. Prior to being experienced by subjects, it is already imbued with patterns which reflect its origin in the behaviours through which it is created. These patterns are reflected first and foremost as spatial configurations. As we have seen in earlier chapters, it is only when we understand the configurational nature of space and the origins of spatial configuration in the built environment in social behaviour, that we can begin to understand its effects on social behaviour. Both of these fundamental facts – the fact of spatial configuration and the fact of the social construction – the paradigm of the machine renders invisible.

What the paradigm of the machine defines instead is a quest for material, cognitive or symbolic influences that, as it were, emanate from the built environment surrounding individuals, and somehow 'cause' behaviour or response in those individuals. Yet the built environment that is expected to do this has no history, no immanent social content and no relation to the larger-scale society. The relation of people to environment is thus reduced to one that is both localised in physical space and decontextualised in logical space. The effects sought are for those individuals in that space at that time, free of spatial or social context. There is no evidence that any such systematic effects are anything but imaginary.

Wherever architecture sought interaction with the social sciences – that is, to the extent that architecture sought social engineering objectives – this was the dominant paradigm within which questions were formulated, and research initiated. It is this mechanistic formulation of the form-function problem as one of a mechanistic relation between an experiencing subject and an objective environment, unmediated by spatial configuration, that was decisively rejected with the fall of modernism. It was rejected because it had led architectural practice and theory into an impasse in which the form-function relation seems paradoxical. The paradox is that if architectural determinism is true then effects should follow from design that simply do not follow in reality. Yet if architectural determinism is untrue, then design does not seem to matter since no adverse or beneficial social consequences can follow whatever we do. This paradox was eventually crystallised by the architecture that most thoroughly embodies the idea of architecture as social engineering: the innovative housing estates of modernism. These estates were the embodiment of the benign intentions of architecture as social engineering. Yet it was exactly as social engineering that they seemed to fail. Architectural determinism had failed. Yet architecture it seemed had determined the failure.

Unfortunately, by the time this became clear, the invisible effects of paradigms to take over language, and guide thought by unconscious constraint, had made this seem the only possible formulation of the form-function problem. The abandonment of form and function as the central problematic of architectural theory, and its substitution by the form-meaning problem, was the result. In architectural polemic, the metaphor of the machine was succeeded by the metaphor of language, and in research the fallacious paradigm of the machine was succeeded by the – as we will see in a future text – equally fallacious paradigm of language. The paradigm of the machine had effectively 'structurally excluded from thought' exactly the pattern relations between space and people that are the essence of the form-function relation in architecture.

Let us then review the idea we wish to dispense with. Architectural determinism, the paradigm of the machine, and the organism-environment paradigm are all different names for the same underlying scheme of thought whose foundations we have hopefully now fatally undermined. Architectural determinism is the way in which the scheme of ideas appears within architecture, and confronts its practice and its theory. The paradigm of the machine is the invisible scheme of thought which history implanted in architectural discourse as the framework within which the form-function relation, seen as social engineering, should be defined. The organism-environment paradigm is the broader and older master scheme of quasi-scientific ideas on which the whole fallacious structure was erected. The three-level scheme constructs an apparatus of thought within which neither the form-function relation in architecture, nor the role of space in society – can be formulated in such a way that research can be defined and progress made in understanding.

This whole tripartite edifice of thought is dissolved by the proposition that the form-function relation in architecture, and the relation of space to society, is mediated by spatial configuration. Spatial configuration proposes a theory in which we find pattern effects from space to people and from people to space that in no way invokes mechanistic determinism. At the same time, the configuration paradigm saves the idea that architecture has social effects. By changing the design of a building or complex we do change outcomes. There is after all some kind of mechanism between the built world and people. But the machine is not the building. Space is the machine.

Space is the machine

We saw in chapter 2 that every theory must exist within a broader paradigmatic scheme of ideas that defines the nature of the field and what types of problems are to be opened up to research. How then should a general paradigmatic scheme for this redefinition of the relation between buildings and people be formulated? One thing is clear. Previous definitions of the relation have been based on analogy with fields other than architecture. The redefinition proposed here has no external analogue. It is, shall we say, the paradigm of architecture – and, if we are right, the paradigm of architecture is a configuration paradigm. How may the configurational paradigm of architecture then be formulated as a general scheme of ideas? Let me suggest what may seem at first an odd manoeuvre: a thoroughgoing comparison between buildings and machines. It turns out that this may after all be illuminating, especially in the light of the research results reported in earlier chapters.

If we think of form and function in a machine, then it is clear that a description of the form would be a state description of a system of differentiated parts that make up the machine, and a description of function would be a dynamic description of how the parts move in a co-ordinated way to impel and process some material. Conceptually, we might say a machine has three aspects: what it is, how it works, and what it does to something else. If we try to apply this to built forms (obviously leaving aside the building's mechanical plant, which is a normal machine) then we encounter difficulties in all three aspects. First, as spatial elements the parts of a building tend to be weakly differentiated. There is a more or less universal list of space types – rooms, corridors, courts and so on – which vary in their size and shape but not in their basic nature. In chapter 8 we saw how this came about, and that these spatial types were essentially configurational strategies. Even so, for practical purposes, this also shows why the apparent lexicon of spatial types is so limited. This, we saw, was one of the reasons why buildings designed for one set of activities are often easily adapted for others. Second, the parts of buildings don't move. There is only a state description of them. Third, people, the hypothetical processed material, do move, but not under any impulse from the buildings. On the contrary they move independently and under their own motivation. To caricature Aristotle, in buildings people are unmoved movers. As we will see in a moment, this reference back to Aristotelian physics is not idle.

However, through configurational analysis and empirical investigations we now know a number of things about buildings which bear directly on the differences between them and machines. First, although the types of space in a building are fairly universal, they differ significantly when seen from the point of view of configuration. How the rest of the building is available as a configuration from a space, as shown by an 'integration value' is one of the most marked types of differentiation between spaces. Configuration, it seems, does after all turn the building into a system of differentiated parts, not in a machine-like sense, but in a quite unique, architectural sense.

Now, we also know that there are two ways in which these differences relate to function. First, function can use configurational differences to give a picture of itself in the spatial form of the building, so that the building comes to embody social and cultural information in its form. The building thus is no longer a mere physical object, any more than (after Darwin) an organism was a mere physical object. Through configurations, buildings, like organisms, both contain and transmit information. Second, we know that although the parts of a building do not move, through their configurational differences they do affect the pattern of movement, in that other things being equal, the degree to which spaces are used for movement is a function of their configurational position. This is not an effect of the building on individuals, but a *system* effect from the space structure of the building to the probabilistic distribution of people. We do not therefore need hypotheses about how the building enters the mental state of individuals and compels them in this or that direction, as would be required by architectural determinism. We have transformed the mechanism from the Aristotelian to the Newtonian mode. Natural movement is a kind of inertia theory: it says not how individuals are impelled by buildings to move in this or that direction, but that, given that they move, then their distribution in a spatial configuration will follow certain mathematical and morphological laws, given only that movement is from all – or at least, most – parts to all others, and follows some principle of economy in route selection.

Now in the first, Darwinian, sense that buildings are, through their spatial configurations, embodiments of social information governing what must happen and where, we can then say that the building is a dependent variable in a social process. Its spatial form is, in a well-defined though limited sense, a product of its social function. However, in the second, Newtonian, sense that spatial configuration is generative of movement configuration, and thus of potential co-presences among people, then we can also see that the building as an independent variable is a social process. Its function is, in an equally well-defined sense, created by its spatial form. In other words, buildings can both receive information from society through spatial configuration, and also transmit effects back to society through configuration.

How do these bifurcating tendencies relate to each other? There are two aspects to the answer. The first is that, the two tendencies are dynamically interrelated. A functional genotype in a building is a temporary fixation of cultural rules in configurational form. But its expression has already been constructed within the laws of 'generic function' as discussed in chapter 8, that is, on the one hand, by local-to-global laws by which local physical changes have, both in themselves and when applied successively, global effects on spatial configuration; and, on the other, laws which link these local-to-global effects to generic function, that is the properties of intelligibility and functionality that permit a spatial complex to be adapted in principle for human occupation and movement. In other words, the building in its 'Darwinian' mode as a spatial complex embodying social information already embodies the 'Newtonian' laws by which a building already constitutes, in itself, a field of potential movement and co-presence. For example, an integrated space for everyday living is one in which generated movement is natural to its function, while a segregated space for use only on special occasions is one where generated movement is not.

Thus the genotypes which order cultural patterns of space use already tend to reflect the generative laws of space. Where they do not, it may be a failure of design, or it may simply be a reflection of the fact that cultural patterns tend to be more complex than the possibilities offered by space, and it may not be possible to give a spatial form to all the social rules that operate in a situation. In either case, we find that the shortcomings of space tend to be compensated by reinforced behaviours by individuals to ensure that the cultural pattern survives. In spite of the lawfulness of space, and its relation to human life in space, there is still some degree of interchange between the structure of space itself and human activity realised in space, in that if space does not provide adequately for the realisation of some set of rules for social relations in space, then this lack may be compensated for by special behaviours. For example, as Justin de Syllas showed in a pioneering study[23] (which still remains unpublished because of the reluctance of professional journals to allow serious analytic criticisms of architects' buildings), in a children's assessment centre the failure of the building to provide for natural surveillance of the children by the staff through everyday patterns of activity, combined with the excessively complex and permissive layout of the building, created a situation in which staff had to compensate for the lack of spatial controls by behaving like gaolers themselves, continually locking doors, and attempting to police restrictive rules.

The second aspect of the answer is that the two contrary tendencies are unequal, in the sense that the 'Newtonian', or generative, properties of the building will always operate unless there are social rules and practices to restrict their operation, whereas the 'Darwinian', or informational, properties of buildings usually require the support of social rules and practices. In other words, spatial configurations will naturally tend to follow the generative laws except insofar as they are restricted by social rules. We thus find that, as discussed in chapter 7, buildings vary between those which tend to express and restrict social relations and those which tend to generate social relations. Where we find strong genotypes, we find them associated with strong rules of behaviour, because the form of the building is already a mapping of that behaviour. But when the social rules decay, or are no longer enforced, then the spatial configuration reverts to the generative mode. Its spatial patterns will generate only the patterns of co-presence that would be expected by the theory of natural movement. Thus a courtroom stripped of judges and judged, and set in a funfair, ceases to be a courtroom and becomes a pure expression of the generative laws of space. The relation of spatial configuration to people is unmediated by social rules. The only effect of that space will be the effect of those patterns, on patterns of movement even though they were originally created to express social rules. The system is, as it were, reduced to its own inertia. This inertia, however, is still lawful.

Buildings are thus probabilistic space machines, able to absorb as well as generate social information through their configuration. In a very restricted sense then, we can say that buildings are machine-like, in that they are physical systems which through their spatial properties produce well-defined functional outcomes. In another, equally restricted sense, buildings are language-like, in that they embody, impart and transmit social information. But we would not understand either of these restricted truths unless we had first understood that, in their essential nature and dynamics, buildings are neither machine nor language. In that they are probabilistic space machines, buildings resemble nothing else.

As probabilistic space machines, buildings are subject to three types of law. First, there are the self-contained 'laws of space', which take the form of implications from local physical design moves to global spatial configurational effects. Second, there are laws which link the field of possibility created by the first type of law to 'generic function', that is to basic intelligibility and functionality, especially natural movement. Third, there are laws by which social formations, and the patterns of rule-governed spatial activity they give rise to, make use of these two types of law to give a picture of themselves in space-time, and through this to give rise to the sense that buildings are in some far-reaching sense, social objects, and as such important to society, and even, in some sense, part of it. This points us to our second question.

Buildings as social objects

Through the mechanism of the form-function relation, as it has just been described, it has been shown how, starting from the building as physical objects and society as abstraction, through the intermediary of space, social abstractions become embedded in buildings and can also be influenced by buildings. This led to an answer to the question: how is it that buildings are replete with social ideas? We will now consider the reverse question: how is it that social institutions contain ideas about buildings, and does it matter that they do? What, in short, is the role of buildings in society?

We may begin by reminding ourselves of a basic distinction made in chapter 1, a distinction that was the foundation on which the whole configurational theory was erected. This is the simple proposition that human beings inhabit two types of co-existent world: a continuous material world of objects and spaces which we occupy and move about in physically; and a discontinuous world of expressive forms, signs and symbols which we occupy cognitively. The former is 'real' space, the latter logical space. The act of building, through the creation of configuration in space and form, converts these into a single world. A configurational world is a continuous spatial world constructed so that expressivity also has become continuous. Building is the meeting point of the two worlds, where real space is converted into logical space.

Through its combination of the real and expressive worlds, buildings convert the material world which we inhabit into a non-discursive world of culture, indeed into culture's densest locus. Through this conversion, the material world becomes for us information and idea rather than thing. Because culture functions non-discursively, and makes the artificial appear natural, the built world we have made into information and idea comes to appear natural to us. We become less and less aware of it precisely because it supports our cultural identity by acting as its embodied basis. The building becomes seemingly dematerialised into non-discursivity and therefore into culture, while remaining at the same time the physical and spatial milieu in which we live bodily.

Through this assimilation of the material world in the cultural world, building becomes a puzzle for us. We become so used to its autonomic culturality that we are taken by surprise when we remember its physical nature. We begin to make distinctions between house and home, and between building and dwelling,[24] protesting that building is 'mere material' while something else, some immaterial human stuff, is the essence of what appears at first to be a physical object. Underlying these distinctions is a serious philosophical difficulty: how *can* the material world be involved in our social and cultural lives when our experience of society and culture seem centred in our minds? We encounter the same difficulty when we try to separate social institutions from the buildings they occupy. It is clear that the centre of what we mean by a social institution is an arrangement among people. Such an arrangement can surely exist without a building. Thus we say that a church is 'mere bricks and mortar', nothing without priest and congregation. The truth of this seems affirmed by the abandoned church building without either.

But the fact that a church building without its social set up is no longer 'really a church' does not imply that *with* its social set up the building is a mere physical appendage.[25] The fact that the social set up 'gives a meaning' to the building is more than an association of ideas. Once a social set-up with its building exists, then the building is much more than a stage set or background. In itself it transmits through its spatial and physical form key aspects of the form of the social set up. The case of the church is particularly clear, since the entire form of the building is dedicated to the support of a spatialised ritual of some kind, and the provision of an audience for that ritual. By providing a spatial form adapted to a particular ritual the building becomes part of the means by which that ritual is enacted by its community. Since rituals only survive insofar as they are enacted in real space-time, the building becomes a powerful part of the means by which that ritual is perpetuated, and transmitted into the future.

However, the matter is yet more complicated. The difficulty in understanding how a house is an aspect of a home, and a building an aspect of an institution, reflects our inability to understand how what appear to naive perception as abstractions and physical things – that is social institution and buildings – can be genuinely interrelated. In fact, this is only one aspect of a more general difficulty. We have the same problem in trying to decide whether social institutions, or whole societies, actually exist, or are simply common ideas in the minds of collections of individuals. How can the abstraction we call society take on physical form, as it seems it

must do if it is to be real in the normally accepted senses of the word?
If society does exist, then in what sense does it exist? Clearly, there is a
problem in assigning society a material existence in the same sense that
we assign an individual a material existence. Yet if societies do not exist
in a material sense, then in what sense can they be said to 'really exist'?
This problem is a further obstruction in the way of understanding the
relations between buildings and society. If we do not assign society some
kind of material existence it seems unlikely that we can formulate answers
to questions as to why and how spatialisation through the house as home
and the church building as an aspect of the church institution should be
so consistent an aspect of society. We may pose it as a question: if society
does not require spatialisation, then why does it give itself spatial form in
such consistent ways? If society is immaterial, then surely it would not
require this consistency of materialisation.

Fortunately, the idea of society 'really existing' is not exhausted by
the possibilities of existing in the same sense that individuals, or material
objects, exist, that is as continuous, finite entities occupying a well-defined
region of space-time. Once again we find paradigmatic ideas obstructing
the formulation of the problem, and indeed once again these ideas are
essentially ideas which are overly mechanistic, and obscure the relation
between the abstract and material world. At root our inability to conceptualise society as a thing has its origins in the most fundamental of our
materialistic prejudices: the idea of a thing. Things, it will turn out, are
not as simple as they seem.

We may begin with a famous problem in philosophy, allegedly
originating with Heraclitus and discussed at length (and recently by
philosophical standards) by Quine,[26] about the definition of rivers. How
can we say that a river is a thing when its constitutive elements – water
molecules – keep changing, and will be found now here, now elsewhere in
the river, then in a nearby sea, then as falling rain? Once said, the difficulty
ramifies. Perpetual elimination and replacement of parts is also true
of human beings. We should see ourselves not as things, perhaps, but as
processes. The common sense definition of individuals as things, and
even of things in general, seems after all to be illusory, the result of a
naive perception of the world.

But where does it end? Is all 'flux and change', and are all assertions of the 'thingness' of the world just temporary fixations? Or can we save the idea of thingness by a more careful definition? Consider three entities which seem to have different degrees of thingness: a one-metre cubed empty box lying on the ground below a tree on a warm summer evening with a light wind; a swarm of gnats three metres above the box; and a cubic metre of gnat-free air three metres to the east of the swarm. The box is clearly a thing, the cubic metre of air not, even though it is a finite physical entity in time and space. The swarm we instinctively name as a thing, even though it seems dubiously to satisfy common sense criteria. Can we then arrive at a general definition which clarifies what is and is not a thing?

First, what does the swarm have that the cubic metre of air does not? Let us reflect on how the swarm comes into existence. The swarm appears random but it is not. It is a partially random system subject to at least one restriction: that individual gnats move randomly only until they see a field of vision empty of gnats, when they turn and fly back in the direction of gnats. This rule, followed by each individual gnat, is enough to convert a set of individuals into a swarm. Every now and then a gnat will be lost and another gained, but this does not affect the existence of the swarm because the swarm does not depend on any individual. It arises from certain consistencies in the behaviour of a collection of individuals, without any individual needing to have a conception of a swarm.[27]

However, we do have a conception of a swarm, and are inclined to call it a thing. Why? How can we conceptualise this sense of thingness? The answer requires two stages. First, the sense of thingness appears because we note through time relational persistences among gnats, that is, ways in which gnats relate to other gnats, that manifest themselves in space and persist through time. Because these relations are multiple and simultaneous we may call them configurational persistences. Second, these configurational persistences have the quite objective effect that the thing we think we see, the swarm, offers some resistance to determination by forces external to itself, for example the light wind that we noted was blowing. In both these senses, the swarm differs from the cubic metre of air. There are no relational persistences arising from the air molecules such that these persistences resist determination by external forces. The light wind blows away the air molecules and replaces them with others, but leaves the swarm of gnats. Of course if the wind were a strong wind, then both the cubic metre and the swarm might be blown away. But that does not eliminate our point. The configurational persistence of the swarm offers a certain resistance to externalities that manifests itself as a temporary stability in space-time, and this seems enough to call it a thing.

By these criteria, the cubic metre of air is clearly not a thing, but the box on the ground clearly is. Its configurational persistences are of a more durable and fixed kind than those of the swarm, but nevertheless it is clearly these persistences that lead us to call it a box rather than a collection of pieces of wood. As with the swarm, also, these configurational persistences, while stronger than the swarm do not offer endless resistance to externalities. A major explosion for example could disperse the box sufficiently for us to say that it no longer existed. The passage of sufficient time would have a similar effect. Taking the definition of things farther afield, it seems to work for rivers, which we can see as configurational persistences amongst banks, water molecules and land gradients, rather than simply as water molecules. From here, it clearly works for less difficult cases such as human beings. If it has configurational persistences, we might say, then it's a thing.

Now an interesting aspect of this definition of what we see and say is a thing is that what we are defining is a process, or, more precisely, a particular stage of a process, with the particular attributes of configurational persistence. In other words, we have made our problem in defining things – that what we see appears to be process rather than fixation – into the centrepiece of our definition. We can now see that the philosopher's problem arose in the first place because, believing that at any moment in time we see states, we form the naive notion that states are primary, and that processes are interesting only in that they give rise to states. This is to misconceive what we see. When we see a universe, a human being, a box or a swarm, what we see is a constructive process unfolding in space-time under morphological necessity. It is from this conjunction that the appearance of the stable states arises that in turn gives rise to the notion of things.

Let us agree to call these configurational persistences 'structures', noting that they are invariably stages of processes, and that named thing-ness seems to arise from such structures. How does this allow us to refor-mulate the question: does society 'really exist', that is, is it some kind of thing? We may begin as usual by noting what we see and experience in space-time. What we see of society in space-time – apart from its physical and spatial milieu – is individuals interacting, transacting, encountering and perhaps also seeking refuge from all these. Is society then the sum of the interactions that we see in space-time?

It cannot be so. Whatever society is, one thing about it is clear: it must persist through time. Whatever interactions are, they cannot in themselves be society since they do not persist. Even allowing for social change, societies relate not only individuals at one point in time, but also individuals across time. Even when all individuals currently alive in a society are dead and replaced by their descendants, something survives as a 'society' which is recognisably descended from the original society, even though it may have changed considerably. Society is, at the very least, something that outlasts individuals. In spite of the claimed realism of those who reduce society to individuals, this reduction is in fact the one thing we logically cannot do, since it fails to explain the primary property of society, namely its persistence beyond the lives of any collection of individuals who make it up at any point in time. It follows that we cannot reduce society to individual interactions.

If we are not talking about interactions in space-time when we say 'society' then what are we then talking about? On the basis of our reflec-tions about things in general, the question can be better put: what *persists* under the myriad of human interactions that we observe in space-time? The answer is almost immediate from the formulation of the question. What persists is not interactions, but certain configurational patterns underlying the interactions. Individual interactions are endlessly replaced. But certain underlying patterns in these interactions persist. It is these patterns that we name as 'society'. The patterns can be the result of any number of different pattern formers: forms of production, social institu-tions, and so on. But it is the patterns themselves that we name as 'soci-ety'. Usefully, this distinction allows us to include the spatial form of

society among the pattern formers. Space is one thing that can generate
and restrict encounter and interaction probabilities, indeed, and this is
how space becomes involved in society.

Society then is not the space-time manifestations of society as the
interaction fields that continually occur in space-time, but the configurational persistences underlying interaction fields. There is an unavoidable
inference from this: the entity which we name as 'society' is not a thing
but an abstraction. Does this then mean that society is imaginary, a virtual product of consensus among individuals, without physical affirmation
in the world? It does not. It is real. Where then does this reality come? The
answer is stunningly simple: from being realised in space-time. The observable material world of interaction in which we live is not itself society
but it is the means by which society, the abstraction, realises itself in
space-time and thus projects itself from past to future. The realisation in
space-time is the means by which society as a system of configurational
persistence achieves this persistence and transmits itself across time.

Now the important thing about this definition of society from our
present point of view is that it immediately allows us to see the role of
buildings and physical environments. Our sense of being separated from
our physical circumstances is founded in the very nature of our social
existence whose nature is to overcome space, by forming this abstract
configurational entity, society, whose existence seems not in itself spatial but beyond and above space. Society is in this sense an abstraction. It
is the genotypes of social arrangements that are reproduced through time,
and which are therefore recognisable in the relational complexes which
are realised in a specific form at one point in time. Society is in this sense
a dematerialised thing, and this is why we find it hard even to acknowledge
its existence as a real thing.

However, although society is this dematerialised genotypical thing,
the means by which it is projected through time is anything but dematerialised. On the contrary, while the material form of society at any moment
of time *is* not that society, it *is the means by which that society is transmitted into the future* . The material form of a society as a system of relations at a point in time is not that society and certainly not its structure,
but, by being a realisation of the underlying genotypes of society, the

material form is the means by which the society as an abstraction is realised in space-time and then reproduced. Society is not in itself its material form, but even so only exists through its material form. This curious double-take is why all social practices take the form of abstract structures, like the grammars of languages, which are never seen as part of any material reality, but nevertheless dominate that reality by structuring what can happen in it, and by creating the real space-time events through which those structures are themselves perpetuated.

Buildings happen within this double-take. Like the social events which they contain, they themselves are space-time realisations of abstractions. They are less than social events, in that they are not made up of acting and thinking human beings, but they are also more in that they are long lasting, almost permanent, transformations of the real world in the image of the abstractions that govern their form. Buildings are not maps of human interaction. They are maps of the social genotypes of human interaction. This is what makes them so powerful. Social interactions as spatial events are momentary realisations of abstractions, of which they are therefore the phenotypes. Buildings only contingently house the phenotypes of human interaction. The most fundamental error of the paradigm of the machine was to seek order in the relation of people to the built world precisely in these localised phenotypes. The built world fixes in stone not the phenotypes but the genotypes of social behaviour.

The mystery of the social nature of the building now becomes clear. Manifestly a physical object, its essential nature is to give form to an abstraction, and through this to give that abstraction the realisation which enables it to be projected through time. Buildings do not reflect the particular materialisations of society that occur at any moment in time, but aspects of the generic abstractions which constitute society itself. It is these abstractions rather than any particular realisation of them, that need to be transmitted through time. Buildings make this doubly powerful by building these genotypes into the very materiality of our existence, and at the same time, through the omnipresence of configuration, rendering these same social 'things' non-discursive.

Buildings are thus among the most powerful means that a society has to constitute itself in space-time and through this to project itself into the future. In this sense, societies in spite of being in themselves a-spatial, are thoroughly dependent on space. The act of building is, as a consequence, inevitably a social act. As such it entails risk, risks that the forms will not be those that permit the society to reproduce its essential forms. In a modern society, these risks are carried between architecture and the social agencies through which architecture is legitimated and controlled. Architecture persists both because society changes and must change its built world in order to perpetuate itself in a slightly different way to its predecessor, and because the risks to society are not posed at the level of the individual buildings or particular projects. These must always experiment with the future. The real risk is in the persistence of error through time, so that forms inconsistent with the perpetuation of a good society become dominant. It is exactly from such high risks that we, in the late twentieth-century, seem recently to have made our escape.

Notes

1   Or 'durability, convenience and beauty' in the translation by Morris Hickey Morgan as Vitruvius, *The Ten Books on Architecture*, Book 1, Chapter 3 originally Harvard University Press, 1914, Dover edition, 1960.

2   But for important comments on this view see Stanford Anderson, 'The fiction of function', *Assemblage* 2, February 1987; and also J. Habermas, 'Modern and post-modern architecture', 9H, no. 4, 1982; and A. Colquhoun, 'Typology and design method', in *Meaning in Architecture*, eds. C. Jencks and G. Baird; Barrie & Rockliff, 1969.

3   Le Corbusier, *Vers une architecture*, 1923; translated by Etchells F., *Towards a New Architecture*, Architectural Press, 1927; Version used: 1970 Paperback of 1946 edition, p. 89.

4   Le Corbusier pp. 114–5.

5   Ibid., p. 173 et seq.

6   Ibid., p. 173.

7   In fact, the clearest statement of the basic ideas behind the philosophy are probably retrospective. For example, Sir Leslie Martin's classic 'Architect's approach to architecture' in the *RIBA Journal* of May 1967 is probably the most lucid account. However, even here there is a certain amount of confusion. Martin announces at the beginning of his text that he does not intend to talk about forms, but about the processes that give rise to them, then goes on to talk about little apart from forms. It may indeed be that one has to wait for the nineteen sixties when modernism was taking over the schools of architecture for a proper academic formulation of a modernist form-function theory,

as set out for example in the *Notes on the Synthesis of Form* of Christopher Alexander, 1964, which will be discussed in detail in the next chapter.

8   For a post-Kuhn discussion of the nature of 'paradigms' see M. Masterman, 'The nature of a paradigm' in ed. I. Lakatos & A. Musgrave, *Criticism and the Growth of Knowledge*, Cambridge University Press 1970.

9   The most extensive treatment of this issue is in Necdet Teymur's complex and difficult, *Environmental Discourse*, London, 1982.

10   G. Canguilhem, 'Le vivant et son milieu', in *La Connaissance de la Vie*, Librairie Philosophique J. Vrin, Paris, 1971. See also 'Machine et organisme' in the same text.

11   The two most important references to the 'architectural analogy' in Aristotle are probably in the 'Physics', Book 2, Chapter 8, pp. 250–2 in the McKeon edition of 1941, and in the 'Parts of animals', Book 1, chapter 5, pp. 657–9 in the same edition. But the idea is pervasive throughout Aristotle, as shown by the conceptual importance assigned to it in the references cited.

12   'The *vis insita*, or innate force of matter, is a power of resisting by which every body, as much as in it lies, continues in its present state, whether it be of rest, or of moving uniformly forward in a right line' I. Newton: Definition III from Definition & Scholium Book 1, *Principia Mathematica*, version used: ed. H. Thayer, *Newton's Philosophy of Nature*, Haffer, New York and London, 1953.

13   Koyre's excellent formulation in 'Newton and Descartes', in A. Koyre, *Newtonian Studies*, Chapman & Hall, 1965, p. 67.

14   See A. Koyre, 'Huygens and Leibniz on universal attraction', Appendix, '*Attraction an occult quality?*' p. 140.

15   For a discussion on this see C. Gillispie, *The Edge of Objectivity*, Princeton University Press, 1958, chapter 7, 'The history of nature'. For example, Gillispie discusses the highly developed version of the scheme of thought due to Lamarck who saw the organism as itself contributing to the evolution of its forms through the interaction between the creative forces emanating from the organism itself and the moulding effect of the environment, making an analogy to the geological processes of erosion that gave rise to rivers and valleys (p. 275).

16   See my earlier (with Leaman) 'The man-environment paradigm and its paradoxes'; *Architectural Design*, August 1973. I see the earlier term for the paradigm as technically incorrect, rather than simply politically incorrect.

17   See Gillispie, *The Edge of Objectivity*.

18   Again, one of the best accounts of the history of this idea is to be found in Gillispie, chapter 8, 'Biology comes of age'.

19   H. Balzac, Author's Introduction (to La Comédie Humaine) 1842; available in English as 'Author's Introduction' in *At the sign of the Cat and Racket and other stories*, Dent, London, 1908.

20   The best example is probably the opening pages of *Eugenie Grandet*.

21   See for example D. Rothman, *The Discovery of the Asylum*, Little, Brown & Co
      Boston-Toronto, 1971 – for example on p. 84: 'As a result of this thinking, prison
      architecture and arrangements became the central concern for reformers of the
      period. Unlike their predecessors, they turned all their attention inward to the
      divisions of time and space within the institution. The layout of cells, the
      methods of labour, and the manner of eating and sleeping within the peniten-
      tiary were the crucial issues. The most influential benevolent organisation
      devoted to prison reform, the Boston Prison Discipline Society, appropriately
      considered architecture one of the most important of the moral sciences. 'There
      are', the society announced, 'principles in architecture, by the observation of
      which great moral changes can be more easily produced among the most aban-
      doned of our race…There is such a thing as architecture adapted to morals; that
      other things being equal, the prospect of improvement, in morals, depends, in
      some degree, upon the construction of buildings'. Those who would rehabilitate
      the deviant had better cultivate this science…As with any other science, the
      advocates of moral architecture anticipated that the principles which emerged
      from the penitentiary experiment would have clear and important applications
      in the wider society. An arrangement which helped to reform vicious and
      depraved men would also be effective in regulating the behaviour of ordinary
      citizens in other situations. The penitentiary, by its example, by its discovery
      and verification of proper principles of social organisation, would serve as a
      model for the entire society'. Pessimists might be tempted to conclude that this
      is exactly what happened at least to public housing in the late nineteenth and
      twentieth-centuries. See also the late Robin Evans, *The Fabrication of Virtue*,
      Cambridge University Press, 1983.
22   See A. Giddens, *A contemporary critique of historical materialism*, MacMillan,
      1981, chapter 1, 'The time-space constitution of social systems'.
23   J. de Syllas, *Aesthetic order and spatial disorder in a children's home: a case study
      of the Langtry Walk Children's Observation and Assessment Centre in the
      London Borough of Camden*, January, 1991; based on research carried out for an
      MSc thesis for the MSc in Advanced Architectural Studies in the Bartlett, UCL, 1981.
24   M. Heidegger, 'Building, dwelling, thinking' in: *Basic Writings*, Routledge &
      Kegan Paul, 1987, pp. 319–39. Originally in German.
25   This basic fact is now increasingly recognised through important new studies
      such as those reported by Tom Markus, *Buildings and Power: Freedom and
      Control in the Origin of Modern Building Types*, Routledge, 1993.
26   W. Quine, 'Identity, ostension, hypostasis' – in *From a Logical Point of View*,
      Harper and Row, New York, 1953, pp. 65–79.
27   See R. Thom, *Structural Stability and Morphogenesis*, Benjamin, 1972,
      pp.318–19.

chapter eleven

The reasoning art

An intention is embedded in its situation, in human customs and institutions. If the technique of the game of chess did not exist, I could not intend to play a game of chess. In so far as I do intend the construction of a sentence in advance, that is made possible by the fact that I can speak the language in question.

LUDWIG WITTGENSTEIN, PHILOSO-
PHICAL INVESTIGATIONS I, 337.

My present belief, formed over the past six years, is that there exists a designerly way of thinking and communicating that is both different from scientific and scholarly ways of thinking, and as powerful as scientific and scholarly methods of enquiry when applied to its own kinds of problem.

L. BRUCE ARCHER (1984 p.348)

The creative paradox

There is, in architecture, a certain creative paradox. Most architecture is made by individuals, and the more significant the architecture, the more it is valued as the product of a unique individual creativity. Yet with the passage of time, even the most innovative architecture comes to be seen also as a product of the time and society within which it was created. This does not lead to a lower valuation of individual architects, but it does add to the appreciation of architecture a sense of the social and intellectual milieu in which the architecture was brought into existence, which may not have been clear at the time of its creation. Such effects are not confined to style and appearance, where they are most obvious. Many writers, most notably the late Robin Evans[1], Mark Girouard[2] and more recently Tom Markus[3], have noted similar effects for space organisation.

It might be said that this retrospective shift in perception arises simply because architecture is a 'social art', and that it is only with the social distance brought about by time that what was always present can be seen clearly. But this is to restate rather than resolve the puzzle. Architecture is a social art in two senses: in the narrow sense that buildings have social purposes, and in the broader sense that built environments seem to reflect society. At the time of its creation, it is usually clear that a work of architecture is a social art in the first sense, but not always in the second. We see easily that a building is an expression of social purposes, but not how the forms of this expression are in some sense a product of time and place. It is only with the passage of time that the second effect seems to emerge with any clarity.

The puzzle is that the individual act of architectural creation seems able not only to express the social purposes of a building but also to carry within it messages from the society in which it was created which only become clear with the passage of time. How, then, we may ask, does society get into the head of the designer during the process of creative design, and come out in the form of the building? We have, of course, seen how this can happen in the vernacular. Consistency of cultural and social expression is maintained through vernacular buildings, in spite of the great variation between individual cases, because the process of making the building is guided by configurational ideas-to-think-with. These

govern the ways in which forms and spaces are assembled into a whole,
and it is this that conserves some level of configurational affinity from one
building to the next. But architecture is, at the very least, the taking into
conscious and reflective thought of exactly those configurational aspects
of space and form by which cultures reproduce themselves through buildings.
How can architecture be at once an individual expression and an expression of society, if the essence of architecture lies in transcending the conventions that tie buildings into the idiosyncrasies of particular cultures?

Intentions and realities

This question has been posed in an extreme form by events in the twentieth-
century. From about mid-century, massive changes were brought about
in cities in the name of architecture. Vast swathes of what had previously
been plausible urbanity were excised and rebuilt as residential zones which
were, in comparison to the urban tradition they replaced, as strange as
Teotihuacan. In most languages, these areas have a special name – in
English it is 'estates' – to distinguish them from the rest of the urban fabric. These linguistic distinctions express fundamental differences in spatial form. Continuity with context is in general sharply broken, if not by
barriers then at least by changes in formal and spatial arrangement. The
effect is that no one goes into these areas unless they have to. They
become, in Alison Ravetz's accurate term, 'reservations'.[4]

 Within the areas, differences are even more pronounced. Public space
is no longer constructed in smoothly changing yet readable patterns by the
careful alignment and orientation of buildings. Instead, at the small scale,
there are endless courts, plazas, greens and walkways, apparently intended to create an intimate sense of locale through the zealous pursuit of
neighbourliness, but seeming to have the effect at the aggregate level of
contributing to a general sense of fragmentation in space. At the larger
scale these fragments are linked into abstract patterns in which space
seems the accidental by-product of a geometric order beyond the reach of
experience, graspable in the plan, but not at the experiential scale of architectural reality.

 These are the forms of 'pathological' space which were examined in
detail in chapter 5. As we saw, the spatial nature of social experience was

decisively altered by these architectural interventions. Within the areas created the inhabitants (whose experience could, because of their structural isolation, never be shared by those outside), witnessed the destruction of the everyday normalities of urban life and their replacement by a caricature urban lifestyle in which fear and alienation in empty spaces became as normal as the decent anonymities of the populated spaces of urbanity had been previously.

These outcomes were never of course intentional. In fact the intentions were exactly the contrary: to use new forms of space to create new forms of community. These intentions mutated with time, first taking the form of futuristic visions, then of a more technical enterprise of the invention of community by spatial engineering, then finally of nostalgia for a – probably imaginary – urban past. One after another, all these visions failed, leaving wherever they were attempted the same sense of an urban landscape despoiled of its essential features and replaced by a landscape as puzzling as it was unwelcome. If an architectural intention is a proposal to create a social outcome through a form, there was, at the very least, a monumental mismatch between architectural intentions and lived realities.

However, these intentions were never purely architectural. Belief in the possibility of new forms of communal existence through spatial engineering was shared widely amongst the multiplicity of political and executive agencies that brought about the re-structuring of the urban landscape. The apparent causes, as well as the outcomes, of these architectural changes were profoundly social. It is this that puts our question about the relation of architectural creation to society into sharp focus. Were the changes authentic architectural products, in which case the mismatch of intentions and realities is architectural error? Or was architecture somehow subverted by social forces of which it became for a time a willing agent and advocate? We have the question of how architecture can be at once a creative and social act in its most extreme form. Did society get into architecture and come out in built form? If so, then it is a matter of urgency to know how this can happen, the more so if we are to save our definition of architecture as the taking into conscious thought of the non-discursive, and therefore social, content of building.

To understand that this was indeed possible, we must understand much more than we do about the nature and origins of architectural intentions, and how architects convert these into built realities. That is to say, we must understand how architects do what they do: design. Understanding the process of design has been one of the vexed themes of architectural theory in the second half of the twentieth-century.[5] However, questions about design have always been posed in terms of the process of design: how do architects go about their task of designing, and can it be improved to provide a greater likelihood of success?[6] In this chapter we will try to pose the question in an entirely new way: that is, by inquiring into its products: how is it that these products can be – or at least seem to be – at once individual and social? What is the nature of design, that it is at once a creative individual activity and at the same time capable of influence, even subversion, by social forces and values?

Is design reason or intuition ?
Interest in design as an activity arose initially in the nineteen sixties, partly through a general interest in the possibility of applying 'scientific methods' in the pursuit of social objective in architecture,[7] partly because the possibility of using computers in design seemed to be predicated on a better understanding of how designers worked – but mostly perhaps because the possibility of design fields such as architecture being constituted as formal disciplines seemed to stand or fall on the possibility of a theoretical understanding of the design process.[8]

It would cause little offence to those who have written in this field to suggest that in spite of these efforts the design process today remains largely opaque. As a consequence, enquiries into the nature of design and the polemics to which they give rise are frankly unfashionable, and have been stagnant for some years. For the academically minded, enquiry into the objects of design rightly seems to offer more promise than enquiry into the nature of design. However, if we are to answer the question we have set ourselves, we cannot avoid reopening this enquiry in a limited way and reconsidering at least some of the key issues that past attempts to analyse design have highlighted. We cannot, for example, avoid the principal stumbling block to previous enquiries into design: is the activity of design a process of reasoning, and therefore one which can to some extent be explicated, or is it a purely 'intuitive' process, and one which must therefore remain a mystery?

At first sight, the claim that architectural design is 'intuitive' is likely to be greeted with some caution. Whatever else it is – and the more so if we follow the definition of architecture set out in the first chapter of this book – architectural design seems to be the imposition on the material world of the ordering activity of the human mind. Through architecture, we come to see, in the built world in which we live, patterns of order whose origins lie in human thought. It might then be expected that architects would see design as a process centred on those ordering powers of human minds which we, for want of a less general term, call reason. But if we listen to architects talking about design, they rarely talk about reason. If pressed to describe the mental process of design, they are more likely to invoke intuition.

We might of course take a cynical view and see this preference for the art over the science of architecture as no more than a trick to maintain professional mystique, since art is a mystery and science, by definition, accessible to open enquiry. However, I suspect there is a deeper and more justifiable reason for stressing intuition in design, one which has to do with the nature of design itself as an activity. For purely technical reasons, I believe, what we normally call intuition is unavoidably the motor of the design process. It is not a question of whether we should prefer an intuitive approach to design or a reasoning approach. It is simply that for design to take place at all mental structures must be deployed and used in such a way as to make the use of the term 'intuition' hard to avoid in any reasonable account of the process.

This does not mean that reason is not involved in the design process. On the contrary, I will try to show that reason is also intimately involved in design activity. It is the polarisation between intuition and reason that is wrong. Reason is involved in design for much the same reasons as intuition is. Architecture, I will try to show, is the deployment of intuition within a field structured by reason, and in this sense we may call architecture the reasoning art.

At first sight, this may seem a strange idea. Reason and intuition are usually opposed, even seen as incompatible, in our accounts of human thought processes. A typical dictionary definition is 'immediate apprehension by the mind without reasoning ... immediate insight'. Reason, used to describe processes of thought (as opposed to innate faculties), stresses externalisation of the structure of arguments as in 'form or try to reach conclusions by connected thought'. The question: is design a matter of intuition or reason? refers to this distinction. How far is design carried out through inchoate, 'black box' processes inside the mind which cannot be made explicit? And how far is it carried out by forms of externalised reasoning which in their very nature are, or can at least be made, explicit and therefore open to enquiry?

This question has, for two decades, had practical urgency since it might well prescribe limits to the ways in which we might seek to use computers to support architects in the creative aspects of their work. Unfortunately, efforts to solve this problem have led at best to a wide gap between theory and practice, and at worst to downright paradox. The fact is that as soon as we try to look at it closely the process of design becomes more and more puzzling.

Design as a process

At first sight, the process of design seems straightforward enough. It is usually initiated with a 'brief', which describes, summarily or at length, what the building must do. It then passes through a series of stages during which a possible building is first sketched and then gradually realised in more precise form, and ends when the designer hands over a proposal for a building, drawn and explained in such a way as to show what the building will be like and how it will provide what the brief asks for, or something better.

This seems simple enough. But if we look a little more closely, matters are not so clear. The 'brief' which initiates the process may be a lengthy formal specification, or it may be a few spoken words, but whatever form it takes, the essence of a brief is that it describes not a building but what a building must do, that is what functional programme it must satisfy. The brief specifies the functional programme rather than the building because what the building will be like, visually and spatially, is the speciality of the architect, the reason we employ one in the first place.

If we know what the building is to be like, as opposed to what it must do, then we do not seek the help of an architect.

Finding the form that satisfies the functional constraints set out in abstract form in the brief is then a reasonable way of describing the architect's useful skill. The brief initiates the 'design process', at the end of which – and often after much trial and error – the designer hands back to the client a proposal for a building, drawn and explained in such a way as to show both what the building will be like and how it will do what the brief asks for. This has led many to believe that to understand the design process we must show some process of thought by which a formal and spatial object may be derived from written instructions about function. Initially, this sounds innocuous enough, but on reflection it raises profound difficulties. By what possible means could there be a mental process which translates from written instruction to physical and spatial forms? The two domains are not commensurable. The same applies to the idea of translating from notions of function to notions of form. The 'form-function' relation is, as we have seen, perhaps the least understood problem in architectural theory. No wonder the design process appears mysterious. It is not at all clear that there could be an explicit process by which these two translations between incommensurable domains could be achieved.

However, many who have sought to explain the design process in terms of what goes on – or should go on – in the mind of the designer have taken this as the definition of the outline of the design process, and set up the question as one of explaining by what form of reasoning, or other thought process, designers go from information about function to a proposal for a physical and spatial object. It is worth examining this idea closely, since in doing so we will at least expose the full difficulty of our problem.

Design as a procedure

The most powerful statement of the procedural view of design is probably still Christopher Alexander's *Notes on the synthesis of form*[9] and it is worth commenting on, even thirty years after it was written, because although wrong, and known by its author to be wrong, it is sufficiently rigorous in its conception and execution to raise in a stark and simple way the profoundest problems in conceptualising the act of design.

The argument in the Notes is grounded in one of the fundamental polemics that modernism had introduced to architecture: how far was it satisfactory to regard design as an intuitive process, dominated by imagination and perhaps impeded by reason, and how far could the intuitive process be progressively replaced by a reason-based procedure in which the architect could draw on ever expanding knowledge? The fundamental argument against intuitionism in design was that it was through the unquestioning reliance on intuition that architecture was tied both to imagism – the domination of architecture by the visual rather than by the functional – and to historicism – the domination of architectural creativity by the forms of the past.[10]

Alexander's was the first utterly serious and formal attempt to put this into effect. It was based on seeing the design process, from the abstract statement of function in the brief to the crystallisation of a physical form, as a process of analysis of information followed by synthesis of form. Several models were proposed at the time, but all shared the central notion that a process from abstractly stated function to concrete architectural solutions could and should be a process of the analysis of the problem followed by a synthesis of the solution. Analysis-synthesis seemed the natural scheme of thought by which we could seek to replace an intuition based process with a reason based process.

It would not of course appear so now. With hindsight, it is easy to see that analysis-synthesis is not at all a natural scheme of thought but something more akin to a paradigm of thought, an understanding of which requires a minor excursion into the history of ideas. We tend to think of 'analysis-synthesis' as a very twentieth-century idea (we make the same error over 'architectural determinism'), but it is not. It was first set out clearly in the seventeenth-century by the mathematician philosopher René Descartes in his *Discourse in Method*.[11] Descartes's objective was very similar to that of the twentieth-century design theorists. Descartes wanted to rid the mind of the clutter of preconceptions embodied in natural language, and, starting only from indubitable, simple notions, to rework the whole structure of human knowledge. His model was geometry, where we begin from a small number of indubitable (as he thought) postulates and axioms, and use them to create chains of reasoning (theorems, lemmas, proofs, and so on) and eventually large structures of secure knowledge.

Descartes believed that by starting equally simply and working with similar rigour, all fields of knowledge could be rendered as well-structured and secure as Euclidian geometry. Descartes's metaphor for the restructuring of language was the well-ordered town, laid out on geometrical principles, which he contrasted with the town that had grown up, like the human knowledge embodied in language and habit, by a chance process of accretion.[12] In Descartes, we find all the elements in the modernist philosophy: the desire to get rid of preconceptions, to make a break with the untidy past, and to derive a whole new structure of ideas through analysis of foundations and rigorous development of more complex ideas.

Alexander's version of this in the Notes was to propose 'the analytical nature of the programme, and the synthetic nature of its (architectural) realisation'. He summarised this in a pair of related hierarchical diagrams. On the one side is the 'downward' hierarchy of the analysis of 'needs', in which the broadest statement of 'need' is first broken down into its major components, then these are broken down, and this is repeated until the most elementary level of need is reached. The 'upward' hierarchy of architectural forms then works the other way, with the most basic level as the foot of the pyramid, then the next level in which these are combined, and repeating this till the whole form is 'synthesised'.

Alexander offers a worked example of his method: the redesign of a village in India. His procedure was first to list all the 'misfit variables' (that is, the things that could potentially be put into the wrong relationship) as 'needs or requirements that must be satisfied in a properly functioning village'. These include all those 'explicitly felt by the villagers as needs', those 'called for by national and regional economy and social purpose' and those 'already satisfied implicitly in the present village (which are required but not felt as needs by anybody)'. Examples of the 141 needs identified were: 'Harijans regarded as ritually impure, untouchable etc.', 'Efficient and rapid distribution of seeds, fertiliser etc. from block HQ', 'Simplify the mobility of labor, to and from villages, and to and from fields and industries and houses', and so on. All the interactions between the needs are then listed, so that we have a graph made up of the 'needs' or elements of the graph and the 'interactions' or links in the graph.

The graph is then analysed and decomposed into 'four major subsets' each made up of between two and four 'minor subsets'. Minor subsets are groups of interrelated needs, and major subsets are groups of groups. Each 'minor subset' is then translated into a 'constructive diagram' indicating approximately how the subset of need could be satisfied by a spatial arrangement. These diagrams are then grouped together into more complex 'constructive diagrams' representing the 'major subsets' of needs, and the four major subsets are then grouped to form a constructive diagram for the whole village. In this way, Alexander claims to have begun with the analysis of needs as a field of information and ended with the synthesis of a design solution, that is an outline of spatial design for the village as a whole.

Many modern readers will be as repelled by the ethnocentric arrogance of the time as by the bizarreness of the solution proposed. But this is not the point at issue here (though it may well be epistemologically linked to it). The issue here is what Alexander has actually done. Has he actually derived an object, the village, from information, the abstractly stated needs, by means of a formal procedure? If the answer is yes, then he can truly claim to have succeeded in his aim of replacing intuitive design with a systematic procedure.

In fact, there is a devastating flaw in Alexander's procedure, one which entirely vitiates his aim of replacing intuition with reason, and leads him only to conceal intuition – even prejudice – under a veneer of reason. This is not a single flaw but a pervasive flaw. It vitiates every stage of the argument. The flaw can be stated as follows. What Alexander is opposed to is intuition based design, which, he argues, leads the designer away from a proper understanding of functional needs and the subsequent synthesis of a solution on the basis of that understanding. In practical terms this means that he is opposed to the idea that to be asked to design a 'school', say, immediately activates in the mind a range of given solutions to that design problem, solutions in which the functional patterns of a 'school' such as having classes, assemblies, teachers and taught, head and teachers, and so on are already arranged in specific ways according to certain conventional patterns through the ideas of built form which the word 'school' immediately brings to mind. Alexander objects, in effect, to the fact that in the ordinary use of language, words like 'school' already associate intuitively what the architect seeks to relate analytically and synthetically, that is, the functional and spatial pattern. This immediacy of association between function and form is precisely the means by which past conventions are reproduced. Alexander's programme therefore depends on doing something different from this.

Does he? Of course not. This is exactly what his procedure cannot do. However much you disaggregate the 'programme' analytically, there are no analytic means to move from a programme or functional element to an architectural or spatial element. This can only be done by using pre-existing knowledge or assumptions about how functional ideas translate into spatial ones. In other words, to make the crucial step in the whole procedure, that is to go from information to object and from function to form, Alexander has recourse to exactly what he said he was avoiding: the use of intuitively held assumptions about what the relation is or should be.

Alexander does not, however, draw the proper conclusion from this, that is, that his technique does not avoid intuitive design, but in fact conceals the use of intuition and assumption under the guise of a procedure. This is probably because he is overly impressed by the technique he uses in order to make the transition from information and function to spatial and physical design, that is the 'constructive diagram'. Alexander introduces this through a disingenuous example. He shows that if you draw vehicular movement at a road intersection, representing the amount of movement by the thickness of the lines, then both the lines of movement and the thickness are a representation of the actual spatial solution required. However, this is almost the only kind of case where such a close correspondence of 'constructive diagram' and reality can be found, and it is so because it is a matter of engineering, not culture. The idea that this can be duplicated in to cases where the passage from function to form involves cultural patterning can only have the effect that Alexander proposes to ignore cultural patterning and impose his own cultural assumptions through the design.

By this disregard of culture and covert imposition of his own Alexander betrays the whole essence of his technique: at every stage of moving from function to form he has no alternative but to have recourse to his own existing, taken-for-granted knowledge of how function relates to form, and therefore how information relates to objects. In other words, however much he disaggregates the design problem, Alexander still proceeds in the way he originally objected to: that is, by already 'knowing' the relation between form and function. This prior knowing covers exactly those aspects of design that we called 'non-discursive' in chapter 1, where we noted that they were handled in the vernacular as the unconscious relational by-products of the manipulation of objects. We can then say of Alexander's procedure that, far from replacing intuitive design with a procedure, he has retreated to a vernacularistic mode of design but only in order to transmit – and covertly – highly personalised values at the expense of those sanctioned by a culture.

Once this is seen, then it clearly also applies to the relationships among elements in the analysed programme, and to the relations among spatial elements in the 'synthesised' built form. In other words, in spite of all the 'methodology', it is intuitive knowledge that has actually done the entire design. The curious thing is that Alexander seems to have known this, and actually discusses it to some extent in his book: 'The designer', he says, 'must already have some physical ideas about the problem in his mind when he starts.' Indeed the designer must, and in fact they are invoked at every stage of the process. It is clear that these objections must afflict any non-trivial version of the analysis-synthesis model. To make the transition from information to object or from function to form we must use knowledge that we already have. This has an important implication: that design as a process of cerebration is not simply a procedure that draws on knowledge, but one where the process is actually based in knowledge and how the designer handles it.

On reflection, perhaps, we may see where the error lay in the analysis-synthesis model of design. The process from written brief to the proposal for an object describes the externalities of the process and how it is embedded in a wider social scheme of things. There is no reason to suppose that it is at the same time a description of the internalities of the process, that is of the thought process by which the designer conceives the object. From what we have seen of Alexander's methods, and from what we may infer from vernacular and intuitive design, the internalities of design are centred not around a procedure but around knowledge. The procedure proposed by Alexander may conceal knowledge, but it does not eliminate it. On the contrary, as we have shown, it is at every point based on knowledge of a certain kind. If we are to understand the internalities of design, then it is clear that we need, as a starting point, a model of design which acknowledges the centrality of knowledge rather than concealing it. How then can such a model be constructed?

Design as conjecture-test

The first step is easy. The analysis-synthesis model is, at root, a misunderstanding about scientific method, and the twentieth-century has seen a revolution in the notions of 'scientific methodology'. Our conception of science has moved on from one in which scientists were data gatherers who proceeded by 'inductive generalisation' (if the sun rises often enough, then we may assume it always rises) to construct theories which were 'certain' because they had been derived by 'induction'. We now see science as a highly imaginative activity in which 'data' is not so much seen as the foundation for theory, as the means of testing and eliminating theories[13] and as the source of intuitive theoretical leaps.[14] Karl Popper has been the most influential philosopher in this revolution. He argued that induction was not only unreliable, but also that one could not logically 'induct' complex models of the inner working of nature. Such models have to be first imaginatively conjectured, then refuted, or supported, by rigorous testing against data. No theory can ever be 'proved'. Every theory is forever uncertain, and likely to be replaced by a better one. Even if the induction of theories (as opposed to simple statements about suns rising or sequences of numbers) were logically possible, then it would still be of little use to science since if theories were argued as having been derived from data, there would never be any further need to test them against data. Since often rival theories were supported by all but a very few items of data, then it followed that science could never progress unless it used those few items of data to refute, rather than the many to support, theories.

If, then, science remains a rational activity in spite of being led by imagination and intuition, it is not clear why we should seek a stronger model for rationality in design. On the face of it, design looks much more like a process of conjecture-test than a process of 'analysis-synthesis'. The usefulness of this argument (which I and others proposed in the early seventies)[15] is that it relates intuition and reason in a lifelike way, and also suggests that design is not so very different from other types of human activity. For example, conjecture-test seems a reasonable model for speaking: one first conjectures a semantic complex, then tests it out by trying to say it.[16] What distinguishes design from other activities is not its procedure but its object, and what makes design difficult is what is to be designed. Theorists should therefore, it was argued, shift their attention from the process of design to its product if their efforts were ever to be useful.

Now this argument is helpful as far as it goes. But it is clearly point-less to claim to have solved the problem of the design process simply by proposing an analogy to science. Design is a process which those who undertake it find quite different, and indeed it is clearly quite different in its outcome. All we have learned from the analogy with science is to dis-pense with an illusion: that rationality in thought is necessarily and only the rationality of a process or procedure. How may the argument then be developed further?

In fact, the relevance of the analogy with science is not yet quite exhausted, and we may usefully extend it a little. Just as a scientist can-not 'induct' a complex theoretical model from a series of 'inductive gen-eralisations', so, as we have seen through Alexander, a designer cannot 'induct' a building from an analysis of the parts of a programme. The rea-son is simple and fundamental. Seen either as space or as form, a building is a configuration, and it is as a configuration that it works and is experi-enced. Now we know that the fundamental characteristic of a configura-tion is that every time it is changed, say by the addition or subtraction of an element or part, then the properties of the whole configuration change. The effects of regular changes, that is those made by following consistently applied rules, can be broadly predicted, but the effects of small or inconsistent changes where no rule is applied from one to the next, cannot be predicted. There is, as we saw in chapter 9, some degree of local indeterminacy from configuration to its structure.

It follows that designers must think configurationally, and of course this is exactly what they do. The very centre of architectural design is the bringing together of parts to form a whole. Design is, manifestly, a configurational activity. Two consequences follow. First, since a configuration is a 'whole', whose properties may be significantly changed by quite minor changes, it follows that the designer must on the whole tend to design top-down. The object of the architect's thought is a configuration, and a configuration is a whole entity, not an accumulation of parts. This of course is what we mean by a design conjecture. It is a configurational guess. It cannot be otherwise, since configuration cannot be arrived at by an additive process. Second, because a conjecture is configurational, and we know that configuration is handled by the human mind non-discursively, it follows that configurational conjectures are likely to be generated non-discursively. This of course is why architects talk of intuition. A process of configurational conjecture cannot proceed other than non-discursively. It cannot therefore either follow a reasoned procedure, nor can it proceed additively from the bottom up. Design is by nature a holistic, intuitive process, and this conclusion follows from a reasoned analysis of the process of design.

We therefore have a problem. If design is both a process of non-discursive conjecture, and at the same time a knowledge based process, how can these two facts be reconciled? How can we, that is, construct a model of the internalities of the design process which both 'saves' the apparent priority of intuition over reason in design, while at the same time saving the idea of design as a knowledge based process in which human reason is, par excellence, deployed?

The answer, as we will see, will lie in exploring the implications of the non-discursive in building – that is, the putting together or composing of a formal and spatial structure – for design as a cognitive process. We have already noted in a previous chapter that, in the vernacular, the non-discursive aspects of the building, that is the pattern of form and the pattern of space which give the building its cultural character, are recreated unconsciously through the manipulation of objects. The form, the spatial pattern and the functional pattern – the form-function relation, in short – are known in advance and need only be recreated. Because architecture of its nature unlinks the pattern aspects of the building from their dependence on social knowledge, then it is these non-discursive aspects which become uncertain. It follows that the problem we must solve in understanding design as a knowledge based process requires us to show exactly how those non-discursive aspects are handled, those aspects that is that Alexander concealed so thoroughly in his procedural theory.

The design process closely observed
Let us then define architectural design as a knowledge problem as clearly as we can. We must begin with a basic fact: a design is a representation, not a thing. To design a building is to create a representation of an unknown and original object whose properties must be well enough understood in advance in order for the act of building to proceed with confidence. The properties that must be predicted include of course all 'technical' aspects, that is those aspects which are governed by some kind of physical laws, such as the structural or climatic performance. However, they also include the non-discursive properties, that is the putting together or composing of a formal structure and a spatial structure. The former is a matter of foreseeing the aesthetic and cultural significance of the proposed building, the latter a matter of foreseeing how the building as a spatial entity will work for the programmes of activity that are projected to take place in it (as well as others, as yet unforeseen, that might in time be added).

In architecture, it is these non-discursive aspects to which attention is most drawn since it is in these areas that architecture claims to create an entity 'over and above building'. This means that in the design process there are two non-discursive problems: the generation of the proposed form, and the prediction of its functional properties. Our problem is to explain how each of these can happen, and in particular how each draws on and uses some kind of knowledge.[17] The best way to begin might be actually to examine what happens – or what seems to happen – during the course of the design process. What can be seen to happen should at least be an outward and visible sign of the interior process of design.

If we observe the design process as it happens, then we find ourselves noting two apparently very different but closely interrelated kinds of activity. One is the proposing of conjectural forms as possible solutions to the problem in hand, usually through a series of sketches or drawings. The other is talking about forms, that is explaining them, defending them, criticising them and proposing modifications, in effect discussing what they will be like if built. We may usefully note that the conjecturing of forms appears to happen largely in non-discursive mode, but that reasoning about forms happens primarily in discursive mode.

Let us look first at the more discursive aspects of the process, that is at the issue of prediction. How is it possible to predict the performance of an unknown and original object? Considering the problem in the abstract, it would seem that the possibilities are limited. Prediction can either be made on the basis of analogy with known cases, or by appeal to principle, that is to what is held to be true of all possible cases, or perhaps some mixture of both of these such as 'experience' which usually takes the form of a provisional principle based on personally known cases.

We will find this a useful guide in listening carefully to what is being said in the studio, and in particular, to how designers comment on design conjectures and predict what they will be like. One kind of inchoate comment, for example, tends to reflect non-discursivity quite directly. For example, 'This is great' or 'I really go for this.' However, this is rarely all that is said when offering such evaluations. Quite commonly it will be followed by some remark like: 'Am I right in being reminded of ...?, or 'You seem to have in mind such and such.' In other words, there is usually some attempt in talking about projected forms to invoke existing forms.

Noting this allows us to formulate a useful thought. Even if the spatial and physical forms of buildings are non-discursive, this does not mean that the process of pointing to comparisons between them is non-discursive. On the contrary, a process of comparison can be conducted without violating the non-discursivity of form. One does not have to describe a form to make a comparison. A comparison can be agreed or disagreed with verbally on the basis of appreciations of the form which remain in non-discursive mode. We therefore find that even though the object of evaluation remains non-discursive, we still find discursive reasoning being employed explicitly in a way in which it does not seem to be – or at least is not manifested – in the process of generating design conjectures. Designers rarely claim 'I got this bit from here, that from there', since this would suggest pastiche rather than originality. But discursive comparisons are a legitimate aspect of the process of design evaluation and prediction once the conjecture exists.

This tendency to invoke existing buildings becomes much more noticeable when it comes to predicting the functional performance of the building as opposed to evaluating its form aesthetically. We commonly find that the most persuasive and powerful arguments are comparisons with known cases which in some sense or in some aspect the design proposal resembles. There is an obvious reason why we should expect this to be the case. Architects design form, but hope for function. The most difficult aspect of prediction from an architectural conjecture is the prediction of function from form. It is only in existing buildings that function as well as form can be seen. By an empirical appeal to cases, then, function, the key unknown in the design process, can become part of the predictive reasoning about forms which characterises the design process.

For this reason, the forms of discursive reasoning that are used in foreseeing the architectural nature and predicting functional performance tend to be of an empirical kind. All other arguments seem to be weak compared to these, and in practice we find that empirical appeals are often the final arbiters. This is why, in the discursive or predictive phases of design, we note the predominance of reasoning which is at once empirical and discursive. Indeed, it is their empiricism that makes these phases discursive.

It is good that it should be so. If design conjectures were justified by appeal to principle, then there could be little effective critique of designs on the one hand, and little development of principle on the other. The situation would be analogous to the pre-Galilean situation in science when, under the influence of the Aristotelian methodology, science attempted to proceed from general axioms to particular phenomena, with the effect that no learning from unexpected phenomena was possible. In design, the situation is analogous. The testing of designs against known cases will always be the most flexible and potentially undermining technique for the evaluation of design conjectures. Through it, the real world is brought into the world of design, and is held there in much the same way and for much the same reasons as it is in science.

We have then it seems defined at least one phase of design as a knowledge based process, and one kind of knowledge that is deployed in the design process. Empirical knowledge of the non-discursive aspects of buildings, especially the relation of spatial form to function, are fundamental to the predictive or discursive phases of the conjecture-test sequences which characterise the design process. We may also note that, as we learn from Hacking,[18] in science empirical phenomena may also be the spark for theory, not by any logical procedure but by exactly the kind of non-discursive leaps which characterise scientific theorisation. In architecture, similarly, existing cases – that is, known architectural phenomena – can be the spark for a new and original design.

Where do architectural ideas come from ?

But what about the first non-discursive phase of the process, that is the generation of conjectural forms? Let us begin again by looking at the evidence that design shows of the process of conjecturing forms. Observing the process, what we usually see is a series of drawn conjectures. We rarely find a single conjecture and quite rarely a single kind of conjecture. More commonly we find families of conjectures reflecting different possible strategies in solving the problem in hand. What we actually see, then, is a range of possible forms, a range which clearly derives from a much greater possible set and which will in time be reduced to a single proposal.

In other words, on the face of it, what we see evidence of in the conjectural phases of design is not a translation from information to object or from function to form, but something much more easily conceptualised: a translation from architectural possibility to architectural specificity. It may of course be objected that this proposition is self evident. But from the point of view of how we conceptualise design as a knowledge-based process it is very important. It implies that the generation of form, the most problematic of all aspects of design from the point of view of the analyst, is not a matter of translating between incommensurable domains, but a process contained, in the main, within a single domain: the domain of architectural form. If this is the case, then it follows that the most important element in the process will be how the designer understands the field of formal and spatial possibility.

This is not all that we see on the surface of things. A design conjecture is not simply a conjectural form but a formal conjecture embodying a functional conjecture. The formal conjecture in effect comes to us already replete with a functional prediction which offers a solution to the problem posed by the brief. We must then conclude that notions of function and their relation to form are also present in the designer's understanding of architectural possibility, at least in such a way as to support a formal conjecture which is at the same time a function prediction. In effect the designer is mapping not only from knowledge of formal possibility to a conjecture for formal specificity, but also from knowledge of functional probability to a functional prediction.

We might say that seen as a cognitive act the conceptualisation of a form seems to be a matter of translating from knowledge of formal and spatial possibility to formal and spatial actuality, and from functional probability to functional prediction, in the light of an abstractly stated brief. In other words, design is not a matter of translating between incommensurable domains, but a process of transformation within domains, exactly those domains which are linked in the very nature of buildings. It follows that the knowledge that designers use in the generation of design conjectures is, like the knowledge used in testing conjectures, in some sense knowledge of buildings, but in this case, knowledge of possibility rather than actuality. The question is: what is this knowledge like? In the testing phases the knowledge was clearly empirical knowledge of real cases, and it was possible to argue that this was the best form for the necessary knowledge to take. Does the same hold for the generation of design conjectures?

Let us immediately set up a guide post. We saw in analysing the vernacular that the creation of a vernacular form meant holding steady ideas-to-think-with about relational structures in order to manipulate the ideas-we-think-of, that is, the physical and spatial elements that are composed into a building. The analogy was with language where the creative act of language is only possible by holding steady these relational ideas to think with that we call grammatical and semantic knowledge. It was also suggested that architecture meant taking these non-discursive structures into the realm of reflective thought, in much the same way as the scientist takes into conscious reflective thought the conditions for the existence of phenomena presupposed by the craftsman. Through this transformation of knowledge, architecture meant not simply reproducing a culturally sanctioned non-discursive pattern, but by reflective abstraction on the possibilities of such patterns, to create new non-discursivities.

But how does reflective abstraction come to be embodied in the act of design? To understand this we must first recognise that design is not itself an act of reflective abstraction. On its own, reflective abstraction can only lead to the understanding of forms. Design is about the creation of forms. It is a process of concretion dependent on abstraction but not in itself a process of abstraction. This process of concretion must incorporate reflective abstraction, but not in itself be simply reflective abstraction. How can this happen? The answer is simple, and, once stated carefully, quite obvious. *It is in the nature of creative acts of concretion, like design, that some set of ideas to think with must be held steady, temporarily at least, in order to manipulate and experiment with the ideas the designer thinks of in searching the field of possibility.* This is because the act of – let us call it non-discursive concretion, the creation of a non-discursive conjecture for a physical and spatial form – is not in itself a simple application of reflective abstraction, but a deployment of reflective abstraction to construct and search a field of possibility, in such a way that the reflective abstractions construct that search and inform the designer when he or she might be near what is being sought.

In other words, in architecture the reflective abstractions are inserted into the design process as ideas-to-think-with to be temporarily taken for granted in order to construct and search a field of possibility in terms of those reflective abstractions. In design, ideas-to-think-with are necessary because they inform the designer what he or she is looking for and constructs the field in such a way as to allow it to yield to his or her efforts. A good designer in effect constructs his or her own ideas-to-think-with and deploys them as structuring mechanisms to search the field of possibility and guide him or her as to the degree of success or otherwise of the search.

The act of design is such that it must, temporarily at least, hold steady ideas to think with in order to manipulate and experiment with the ideas that a designer needs to think of. It is necessary in the logical structure of the act. In order to propose such and such a form and such and such an outcome the designer must know, or believe he or she knows, not only the non-discursivities of form and space but also what in general is the effect of forms on outcomes.

Solution typologies

The question is: what are these ideas like? and where do they come from? Again we can most usefully begin by looking at the evidence provided by the design process itself in action. This time we should look at the earliest stages, since it is the sources of design conjectures for which we are now looking. We cannot begin earlier than the brief itself, that is the information that initiates the design process in the first place.

We have already discussed the problem that when we name a kind of building, say, a 'school', we are already referring to a very complex set of ideas which include not only buildings with certain characteristic appearances, but also certain patterns of activity carried out by people with well-defined social roles in certain kinds of spatial arrangements. In other words, the commonsense use of a word to name a building already describes possible relations among exactly those non-discursive aspects of buildings which the designer will seek to relate through design: that is, a functional programme, a spatial pattern for that functional programme and an expression of 'schoolness' through the physical form of the building. On reflection, we must expect this. It is the other side of our analysis of the vernacular. All of us, not only builders, already take part in an ongoing building culture, through which we are able to understand and use buildings, for more or less the same reasons that builders are able to build them. As with the builder, however, the cultural knowledge of building that we have is non-discursive insofar as it deals with the building as a relational complex of form and space. We must note also, that, as with the vernacular builder, non-discursive knowledge, because it is relational, is essentially abstract, although we may hold it together by images of physical objects, just as the builder reproduces it by manipulating physical objects.

If a whole field of non-discursivity in which forms of human activity, spatial patterns and formal expressions are interrelated is activated by the use of words like 'school', then it follows that it is also activated by the brief. The complex of ideas activated is unlikely to take the form of a single cultural type, as we would expect it to be in the vernacular, but that of a set of possibilities which reflects current, recent or historical solutions to that kind of design problem, and which manifest themselves to the designer as a field of strategic choice. We need a name for such fields of strategic possibility defined by past practice, and since elsewhere[19] it has been called a 'solution typology' we can continue to use this expression. Now the critical fact about a solution typology is that it already constitutes a set of non-discursive ideas of exactly the kind the designer requires, and so it offers an immediately available set of 'ideas-to-think-with' in searching the solution field. In exactly the same way that the vernacular builder uses the phenotypical means at his disposal to transmit abstract non-discursivities through the organisation of the form and the space, so the designer reviewing precedent, consciously or unconsciously, absorbs the non-discursivities contained in each of the solutions. The solution typology is therefore made of genotypes, or rather of phenotypes which imply genotypes. The designer does not have to use these genotypes, but the ideas are there, and their essentially unconscious and abstract nature means that it will not be easy to be free of them. For any design problem, we may then note that there exists a pregiven historical set of non-discursive genotypes reflecting the recent history of that problem. On reflection, the existence of such historical sets is the precondition for being able to identify a 'design problem' in the first place. In spite of first appearances, a 'design problem' is a historical conception.

One way in which designers often recognise that design, even the most innovative, happens within this context of ideas defined by the history of architecture to that point is by making a review of existing solutions to the type of design problem posed by the brief. There is a well established term for the cases so reviewed. They are called 'precedents'. Precedents are existing examples of solutions to a particular design problem. Reviews of precedent rarely look at one single kind of solution. They usually show as wide a range of solutions as possible,[20] including those that are not considered good. We rarely find however that the review of precedent is followed by emulating one precedent or other. On the contrary, where the review of precedent is explicit in this way the subsequent design usually makes it clear that the purpose of the exercise was not to provide a best case exemplar to follow, but to set up something like markers in the field of possibility for a new departure. The review of precedent is not intended to reduce the originality of the new design, but on the contrary to ensure its originality by laying out precedent in a clear and explicit way. In making a review of precedent a designer is acknowledging the historical continuity not only of architectural solutions but of architectural problems. It acknowledges that in architecture at any point in time we have that kind of problem because we already have that kind of solution.

Solution typologies, because they imply a range of non-discursivity in a relatively abstracted form, can in themselves provide cognitive mechanisms through which the designers can structure the field of possibility. But they can do so in two ways, either explicitly, as we find when a conscious review of precedent is made, or implicitly, when precedent is used in an unacknowledged way to structure the search for a solution. The latter strategy will always be a conservative one, in the obvious sense that it will always tend to conserve the existing solution typology. The former strategy, by acknowledging the solution typology, will tend to be more progressive since by setting out precedent it creates architectural conditions in which the simple following of precedent is more difficult.

Now whether or not the designer makes an explicit review of precedent, it is unavoidable that existing genotypes are at least a powerful, if ghostly, presence in the process through which design conjectures are formed. Established genotypes can invade the process of architectural creation by becoming part of the ideas to think with that inform the search for a design conjecture, with or without the compliance of the architect. It is entirely to be expected then that architects will while exploring formal possibility find cultural genotypes attached to at least some of the ideas they are thinking with. The evidence of architectural history is that the process of cultural evolution which we call the history of architecture is to a considerable extent informed by the cultural stability induced by the use of existing solution typologies – or rather their genotypes – as ideas to think with in searching the field of possibility for design conjecture.

We could think of this type of architectural production as 'normal' architecture by analogy with Thomas Kuhn's conception of 'normal' science as 'puzzle solving' within an unchallenged paradigm.[21] The analogy is not precise. The architectural field is more fluid. There is no one paradigm. Even so the broad analogy is probably correct. The act of architectural creation transmits some degree of cultural continuity because existing solution typologies are the most powerful and naturally available ideas to think with in the generation of design conjectures. It is this that creates the sense that in spite of each building's being an individual, buildings do form gradually evolving species. We see now how the genotypes of those species are transmitted through the comparative indeterminacy of individual creation.

Solution typologies and normal architecture

There are, however, serious dangers in the use of solution typologies. Epistemologically, we can say that the existence of solution typologies and their powers to transmit non-discursive abstractions, tends to vernacularise architecture, that is to return it from its aspiration to a universal transculturality back in the direction of socially normalised intentions and forms. Is 'normal architecture' then, defined as architecture in which the influence of prevailing solution types is paramount, the same as the vernacular, that is, no more than the transmission of culture through artefacts?

The answer is that it is not. Normal architecture uses similar cognitive mechanisms to the vernacular in producing designs, but this does not mean that the non-discursive knowledge that informs designs is of the same type. On the contrary, it is likely to reflect two fundamental new facts: first, the existence of architects as a specialised knowledge generating and knowledge using group, and, second, the fact that this specialisation is legitimised and made viable by the wider social structures of which it forms a part. This creates a new possibility: that 'architectural knowledge' may come to reflect not simply knowledge that architects share with other social members through common culture, but knowledge which reflects the fact that architects act on behalf of others in certain social situations. In other words, architecture has the potential to represent cultural partisanship as much as cultural agreement.

The degree to which this happens depends on a new factor which arises alongside the coming into existence of architects as a specialised group: the continuing debate between society and its architects about the aims and purposes of architecture. We can follow current fashion and call this 'architectural discourse'. Architectural discourse arises from the simple fact that because through building social life is constituted in organised space, and social values are represented in visible form, architecture cannot be socially neutral. On the contrary, every architectural act directly engages the social, and remains in a permanent dialectic with it. It is the intimacy of this relation that ensures a second, higher level dialectic between architecture and society: one between architectural theory and social ideology in the formation of architectural 'intentions'. Architectural intentions are the general propositions that stake out the points of aim for architectural design. They are likely to involve quite complex propositions about the relation of architecture to life. Such propositions are theoretical in that they propose, however broadly, an approach to spatial and formal configuration. As such they engage with theoretical debate within architecture. On the other hand, these proposi-tions are also social propositions, and as such inevitably provoke and become part of wider social debate.

Because this is so, statements of architectural intent cannot and should not be taken at face value. The sheer technical intimacy of the involvement of architecture with the social leads it into a permanent danger: that the theoretical and intentional abstractions which inform design and tell it where to aim will become subordinated to prevailing social ideologies. This leads architecture into a continuing intellectual struggle. On the one hand, the closeness of this involvement of architec-ture with society necessarily draws architecture into the permanent debate that every society has with itself about its nature and direction. On the other, the nature of architecture as reflective thought and action in exactly those aspects of buildings which are by their nature social, leads architecture to draw back from this debate into preoccupation with its own autonomy. This can appear paradoxical, but it is a structural necessity. Architecture is technically enmeshed in society, yet its reason for existence is to break free from this enmeshing, and to propose new forms and freedoms altering the terms of this enmeshing.

This two-sided debate is what we call architectural discourse, that is the continuing debate about architectural ideas and their relation to social values that is conducted between architecture and its public. In spite of its need for autonomy, discourse in architecture, as elsewhere, is not a freestanding thing, but a constantly shifting bundle of ideas which reflect and contribute to more general patterns of discourse through which a society debates itself with itself. Architectural discourse is one of the means by which architecture both ties into and struggles to be free from the gradual evolution and adaptation of the cultural and institutional structures which mark every modern society. Thus although architecture is in principle a freeing of building from the specific constraints of a culture, the need to embed this freedom in discourse in order to sustain it ensures that architecture can never assume its freedom from intellectual and social context. The question 'where do architectural ideas come from?' is a question to which an undermining answer is always possible: that any architectural idea may present itself as free-standing and clear of social construction, but time may show to have been an unwitting implement of a specific ideology.

A constant question-mark therefore hangs over statements of architectural intent. Are they autonomous constructs of architectural thought, and therefore constructive offerings from architecture to society, or are they ideas which are in some sense already received from society, imprinted on architecture through the common processes by which social and cultural change become normalised into social behaviour and institutions? In short, are the notions about architecture and society, that are expressed through the changing language of architectural 'intentions', in some sense socially constructed?

This question is most pressing in the matter of space. An architectural intention is usually a proposal to create a social outcome through a spatial form. Intentional statements in architecture therefore inevitably associate social values with spatial concepts, and become in effect propositions about the relation between architecture and how life should be lived in space. Theoretically, they are form-function propositions. For example, propositions about the relation between housing layout and community formation, or between open-plan offices or schools and organisational functioning, or between domestic space design and family behaviour, are all form-function propositions relating space to concepts of normal or desirable social behaviour. Sometimes such propositions are quite explicit, but quite commonly they become implicit, transmitted through the accepted forms of building and supported by the common words and terms we use to talk about them.

Because this is so, architectural theory has two objects of study, which were at the same time its primary sources. One is the objects of architecture, that is, the buildings and places that exist and could exist. The second is the study of 'intentions', and especially of the 'ideas-we-think-with' that underlie intentions in architecture, that is the shifting array of concepts that underlie architectural discourse and which seem often to govern the broader changes in architectural forms that we see over time. Many would see the latter study as primary, arguing that discourses are prior to buildings and buildings can only be rendered intelligible as social and architectural products through their relation to discourses. However, a key lesson from architectural experimentation in the twentieth-century is that there has often been a mismatch between the discourse of archi-tectural ideas and intentions, and the actual performance of the building and spatial forms which express those intentions. We cannot proceed on the assumption that there is a tight relation between idea and reality. We may well choose to study the two in parallel, but in order to do this we must also learn to study each separately. The parallel influence of social-ly constructed intentions on the one hand and available solution typolo-gies on the other together constitute a potential prison of idea through which architecture, while still pursuing its aim of freedom and autono-my, becomes in effect the inchoate and unwilling servant of social forces.

A case study
There is a paramount example of this, which concerns the origins of the strange landscapes described and discussed in chapter 5, and which were

the subject of an earlier paper called 'Against enclosure'.[22] In this paper it
was reported that by examining a large number of cases of social housing
design, in the mid-twentieth-century[23] a consistent set of spatial ideas
could be identified, coupled to equally pervasive social ideas. The spatial
idea centred around the idea of 'enclosure': that good space was enclosed
space. The social idea was that such 'enclosures' had to be identified with
well-defined, and preferably small, groups of people, and exclude others.
The guiding idea that linked the two was that if a group of neighbours was
forced into face-to-face relations, and others were excluded, then this
group will begin to form a small community. The same idea was applied
at the higher level of the 'enclosure of enclosures', or 'cluster of clusters',
to create 'local communities'. Architecturally, these led to a preoccupation with grouping dwellings so as to associate identifiable and distinct
external spaces with each group of dwellings, coupled to an overarching
geometry so that the relation of the local group element with the larger
whole would be clearly manifested in the plan. The whole scheme of
thought was describable in terms of three linked principles which could
be applied to generate a 'layout', regardless of context: 'enclosure, repetition, hierarchy'. These three linked ideas were so pervasive, and could be
found under many different types of building and spatial geometry, that
they seemed in themselves to constitute a kind of 'design paradigm' – one
which was constantly transmitted through the solution typologies which
embodied it and which offered themselves as precedent for public housing.

Unfortunately, it was exactly this set of ideas that created the frag-
mented and segregated landscapes that were the object of our pathological
investigations in chapter 5. The notion that small-scale localised 'enclosures', each one corresponding to a small, identifiable community[24]
should be the primary element of the new housing area, was exactly the
means by which the virtual community, brought about by the natural
co-presence and co-awareness arising from everyday movement in street
based areas, was destroyed. The true effect was to convert what had been
previously a community linked by the continuous, unbounded public
space of the street system, into a series of discrete pockets, each as
removed from the humanising influence of the public realm as the next –
in effect to create a complex and labyrinthine zone between the dwelling

and public space. As we saw in chapter 5, the crisis of modern public housing was the crisis of this space. Whatever the declared communitarian intention of the creators of these 'estates', the effect was to remove the least privileged groups in our societies from the public realm, and consign them to zones which no outsider entered without a strong reason, and which were therefore known only to their inhabitants. This is the durable legacy of the bureaucratisation of architectural thought which brought these zones into existence.

Even at the small scale of the 'enclosure' itself, commonsense, and a little more pragmatic thought, could have warned designers that their intentions were unlikely to be fulfilled. Human beings tend to have special social rules of politeness and avoidance to govern their relations to neighbours, precisely because these relations, because they are ever-present, could easily become too pressing and obtrusive. Exaggerating this face-to-face relation by spatial design, and at the same time eliminating the leavening of strangers as found in ordinary streets, seems far more likely to reinforce these rules of control and avoidance than to alleviate them. We should expect more avoidance, and more investment in the control of over-pressing neighbourliness in these isolated face-to-face groups. The question is not so much: how did the neighbourliness paradigm fail? but: how could the fiction of forced interaction have prevailed for so long?

The historical work to trace the evolution and constant transmutation of this set of spatial and social assumptions that underpinned so much mid-twentieth-century public housing has not been done, but three things can be clearly said. First, that in spite of its 'soft' expression in terms of neighbourliness and community, the essential idea of enforced face-to-face interaction is thoroughly mechanistic in exactly the sense that was argued in the discussion of the 'paradigm of the machine' in the previous chapter. Second, we can note the frequency with which the 'enclosure, repetition, hierarchy' paradigm was proposed as a novel solution to exactly the problem that it had itself created. For example, in the same year that Kirschenmann and Munschalek published their book from which so many of our cases of 'enclosure, repetition, hierarchy' were drawn, the Greater London Council published new design guidance on housing layout[25] intended to correct the errors of the past and propose new principles. In fact, in spite of much new language, what was proposed took exactly the same form as what it was seeking to replace: 'enclosure, repetition, hierarchy', dressed up in new words and diagrams. Third, each element of the design paradigm can be found at each stage of the evolution of social housing policy, and in fact can be traced back to its very beginning in the 'philanthropic' housing programmes of nineteenth-century London. So pervasive are the ideas, in fact, that it is hard not to see them as the design paradigm of social housing, a design solution which society, through architecture, imposed on certain sections of its population.

Both of these facts suggest that the design paradigm of 'enclosure, repetition, hierarchy' was a means by which those very same social engineering aims in architecture that it sought to supersede were perpetuated. We should not be surprised at this. It is in the nature of paradigms that they can guide apparently new proposals along the same underlying conceptual tramlines as those from which escape is sought. The widespread availability of a solution typology based on this scheme, linked to habitual statements of social intention legitimised by the public agencies which at the time controlled a social housing programme on a huge scale, must go some way to understanding the power of this idea to be constantly reformulated and accepted as new, when it manifestly was not.

The social knowledge embodied in the solution typologies in a society with architecture is not then the same as that which underpins the vernacular forms of societies without architecture. On the contrary, they are likely to be influenced by the types of structure prevalent in a society, and therefore to reflect its biases. The problem with such solution typologies, especially if they are sanctioned by explicit design guidance, is that their social origins tend to be as concealed from view as their theoretical nature is obscure. Non-discursivity is as it were turned on its head. It becomes a means not of expressing culture but of imposing culture, often for social ends which are not explicit. In such circumstances, architectural intentions become an object of legitimate enquiry, but the natural non-discursivity of solutions make it very hard to bring to the surface any concealed ideological content. However, an architectural tradition which fails to free itself from such a conceptual prison, as happened during the modern housing programme, is in danger not only of losing its identity as architecture, but also of acquiring another, more dangerous identity: that of an unwilling and servile agent of social forces of which it has as little understanding and over which it has no control.

Style as non-discursive idiolect

The essence of the 'enclosure, repetition, hierarchy' paradigm is that it substitutes a social ideology of 'desirable separation' for an analytic theory of the relation between space and community. It then works in the manner of a vernacular, in that ends – in this case in my view malign ends – are guaranteed through the manipulation of things, that is the given solution typologies. At the same time, it creates the appearance of architecture, in that an illusion is set up of an architectural debate over ends in the light of means. What is really going on is vernacular in the sense that covert ends are being transmitted by the manipulation of means, but the ends are no longer those of a shared culture, but those of partisan social programmes.

This debased mode of architectural operation has played such a significant role in the twentieth-century history of architecture that it deserves far more intensive study than has so far been devoted to it. It amounts to nothing less than the subversion of architecture towards what we might call bureaucratic vernacularisation, in the name of a partisan social engineering by spatial means. The question for a theory of design in architecture is then: how may these apparent consequences of the existence of architects as a special interest group in a society with inequities be avoided? The question has two aspects. How can solutions be generated outside the prevailing influence of solution typologies, with all the dangers that their uncritical use can bring? And how may innovative solutions be predicted? Only if these questions can be answered can we see the grounds of the existence of architecture in the sense that we have defined it, that is as an autonomous domain which debates with, responds to and creates new possibilities for society, but is not subservient to it. It follows from all our previous analysis that these are knowledge questions. What then are the knowledge conditions for an autonomous architecture?

Once again let us begin by looking at the evidence provided by the design process, and especially by its visible products. The most obvious thing that we notice in a creative designer's work is that it is recognisable. It constitutes what seems to be in some sense a species of architecture in itself. It has, in short, what we call style. Now style is clearly a non-discursive concept. Style exists where we note in a set of cases non-discursivities, whether formal or spatial, which appear to be unified by common principle. To use a form of words which is effective while being fashionable, we might say that by style we mean a non-discursive idiolect.

Style gives rise to the sense of a species of architecture where the genotype does not seem to arise from the transmission of a culturally normal form-function solution within the existing typology, but through a characteristic structuring of the non-discursive means themselves, again either formal or spatial. The existence of style means that what is taken into reflective abstraction is not a range of possible solutions but the formal and spatial non-discursive means by which solutions can be created. A style, in short, is a genotype of means. It creates an individualised species of architecture which cross cuts the architecturally normal cultural typing and may indeed run across a range of building types.

Because the sense of style arises directly from the non-discursive means, and because we can be sure that we could not recognise the existence of a style through a single case – though a single case might generate a style – it follows that our sense that the non-discursive idiolect that constitutes the style is essentially an abstraction. It is the common ground of a set of cases. It is yet another instance of our ability to extract the abstract from the concrete, the genotype from the set of phenotypes, and to recon-cretise the abstract genotype in a different form in a new phenotype.

Our concept of style in architecture tends, of course, to be bound to its most obvious manifestation in how a building appears to the eye, that is to the non-discursivities of form. Such a limited view would not survive a careful examination of the works of individual architects. Good architects have spatial, as well as formal, styles. Sometimes this is quite easy to see, for example in the work of Frank Lloyd Wright. But even in such cases, it is difficult to explicate. Experimental studies[26] suggest that explicating architectural genotypes of means is rather more difficult than explicating

vernacular genotypes of ends. But it can be rewarding, and is essential to
our understanding of individual architects' work. For example, in a comparative analysis of five houses by Loos and five by Le Corbusier, a graduate student at UCL[27] was able to show that although in each house there
was configurational differentiation of functions, there was no consistent
pattern within either architect's work of the kind that one so often finds
in vernacular samples (see chapter 1). It was not that the different functions were not spatially differentiated, but that the pattern of differentiation was not consistent across cases. It was as though each recognised the
principle that functions should be spatially differentiated, but that this
was regarded as a matter of experiment and innovation, rather than the
reproduction of a culturally approved genotype.

   However, what the student was able to show was that each architect
had a distinctive spatial style, in that whatever each was doing with the
functional pattern, distinctive spatial means were used to achieve the
ends. For example, in the Loos houses, adding visibility relations to permeability relations increased the 'intelligibility' (as defined in chapter
3) of the space pattern, whereas in the Le Corbusier houses it did not.
Similarly, in the Loos houses, the geometry of the plan reinforced aspects
of the spatial structure of the plan, in that major lines of spatial integration
coincided with focuses of geometric order, whereas in the Le Corbusier
houses they did not. By examining the houses as sequences of isovists,
the student also showed that in Loos houses the isovists are very large
and complex, but relatively uniform, whereas in Le Corbusier the isovists
are more selective in the spatial relations they show from the line, with
each episode tending to be dramatically different from the others. In
these respects, the student argued, the two architects were adumbrating
more fundamental – almost philosophical – differences through architecture: Loos to create houses which are novel expressions of culturally
defined habitability, Le Corbusier to create less habitable, more idealised
domains of rigorous abstraction. Neither Le Corbusier nor Loos was seen
to be denying the social and cultural nature of the domestic interior. But
each, by satisfying the need to give space cultural meaning through functional differentiation first one way then another, but with a consistent
spatial style, is giving priority not to the functional ends of building but

to the architectural means of expressing those functional ends. The genotype of these houses lay, it was suggested, not in functional ends, as in the
vernacular, but in the way the architectural means are used to express the
ends. But the means modify the ends by re-expressing them as part of a
richer cultural realm.[28]

This distinction between ends and means is, I believe, fundamental
to the definition of architecture offered earlier. It suggests that we can
make a useful distinction, in architecture as elsewhere, between the
realm of social meaning and the realm of the aesthetic – in this case the
spatial aesthetic. The cultural and functional differentiation of space is
the social meaning, the spatial means is the basis of the spatial aesthetic.
The former conveys a clear social intention, the latter an architectural
experience which recontextualises the social intention. Meaning is the
realm of constraint, the spatial aesthetic the realm of freedom. The spatial
meaning of form expresses what architecture must be to fulfil its purpose
as a social object, the spatial aesthetic expresses what it can be to fulfil its
purpose as architecture. But although space moves outside the realm of
specific codes of social knowledge, it does not lose its social dimension.
The relation between spatial and social forms is not contingent, but follows patterns which are so consistent that we can hardly doubt that they
have the nature of laws. The spatial aesthetic carries social potentials
through these laws. The autonomy of architectural means thus finds
itself in a realm governed by general principle, with its freedom restricted
not by the specific spatial demands of a culture but by the laws of space
themselves.

Two types of theory

This analysis of the notion of style suggests that it is more than a matter
of recognisable appearances. It seems to go to the heart of the nature of
architecture. This is the case, and a further review of the generative stages
of design will suggest why this is the case. We may begin by reminding
the reader of a distinction made in chapter 2 between theories as they
were used in art and theories as they were used in science. In science a
theory was about understanding, and once understanding was achieved
then action could follow. A theory in art is about creation, in essence

about *possibility*. Theories in art work by suggesting new ways to structure the search of the field of possible forms. Such theories are not universal, but simply generative in that they use abstract thought to generate new possibilities in art that had not been seen before.

It is clear that the idea of style as non-discursive ideolect and as a 'genotype of means' has a directly analogous role. Its effect is to construct an abstract means of searching a solution space, that is, to act as an 'idea to think with' at the level of the non-discursive means of architecture, opening up routes to possible architectures through the taking hold of the means by which non-discursivity is created. Because it is so, it leads to quite new ways of searching the field of possibility. While a solution typology structures the field of possibility by identifying a series of discrete islands, so that search tends to be restricted to the vicinity of those islands, a style as non-discursive idiolect defines a continuous web within the whole field of possibility, creating a density, richness and potential originality of solutions far exceeding that of any typology. Mitchell summarises this succinctly: 'Possession of a style is essential. Without it, an architect attempting to design is like the scholars Gulliver encountered at the Academy of Lagado, who tried to write books by randomly combining words. That way, one would never get to the end.'[29] This is true in a profound sense. It arises from the nature of solution spaces and how they can be searched without the guidance of pregiven solutions. One might add of course, that this is only the case if one wants to create architecture.

But however much we complicate the idea of style, its relevance is confined to the first phase of design, the generation of a possible solution, not the second stage of predictive testing. It was suggested in chapter 2 that the distinctive feature of architecture is that it requires both theories in the sense in which artists use the word and also theories in the sense in which scientists use the word, that is theories of possibility and theories of understanding, theories which tell us where and how to search, and theories that tell us what we have found. We now see clearly why this is the case. It is precisely because the solution field has been searched without the functional guarantees that solution types seem to offer (however misleadingly) that the designer is now in greater need than ever of ways to solve the second aspect of design: the phase of predicting functional and experiential outcomes. The problem is now a great deal more difficult, since by definition the solutions found, because we have not been led to them by known solution types, are more likely to be remote from experience and from precedent. In such cases, the means of prediction in design must move away from precedent and towards principle. Since these are the only two possible modes of foreseeing future performance, the designer is forced, through the very nature of the freedom that has been exercised in generating solutions, into the realm of theory. The more original the architecture, the greater will be this dependence.

In a sense which is critical to the very existence of architecture, then, style and theory are parallel freedoms. Innovation can only be within the realm of the humanly possible on the basis of theoretically analytic knowledge because only this can guide the predictive aspects of design where no guarantees of cultural or ideological conformity are available through the vernacular or solution types. Theory is fundamental knowledge of possibility and therefore of limitation. There is therefore an objective need to associate non-discursive idiolect with analytic theory. Of course this would only be the case if there were objective limitations to what is architecturally, as opposed to technically, possible. We have seen that there are such limitations. Fundamentally, theory is knowledge of these limitations.

On this basis, and only on this basis, the idea of analytic theory can be built into that transformability of culture which is architecture. Without analytic theory, as we have seen in some phases of twentieth-century architecture, architecture defeats itself by pursuing freedoms which are beyond its theoretical powers. Analytic theory is the price that architecture must pay for freedom. Without it, the two sides of architecture – that it is at once individual creation and social transmission – move into arbitrary and uncomprehending conflict. With analytic theory, the debate over architectural ends is an open debate, without it, a concealed paradigm. Analytic theory is, in short, the price of architectural freedom. What is no longer interesting is the idea that architectural freedom can be exercised outside the limitation that the laws of human spatial existence and the laws of space itself place upon possibility.

We can now at least see how important our original question was: if architecture is the taking hold of the configurational content of building, and making it the basis for reflective creation by freeing it from cultural stereotyping, how is it that the individual act of architectural creation is able to carry within it messages from the society in which it was created? The answer, we now see, is simple and fundamental. Architecture is a social art because the primary material of the art – the field of configurational possibility for space and form – is also the means by which buildings have intrinsic social contents. Space constitutes and form represents the presence of the social in the very form of the milieux in which we live and work. In the vernacular, the fit between forms of life and built forms is given by the common cultural programming of both. Architecture dispenses with the programming but it does not dispense with the relation that is guaranteed by the programming. The relation of form to life becomes a question to be resolved, no longer a matter of cultural habit. The relation can only be formulated on the basis of knowledge of some kind. The designer has to assume knowledge of the form-function relation, and assume that it is of sufficient generality to be used in a range of situations. Design can only proceed on the basis of assumed knowledge about the relation of spatial form to life. This is why most statements of architectural intention are statements of this kind, just as most architectural theories are attempts to formulate these relationships in a more general way. It is at this point, through the need for propositions, both specific and general, that link form to function, that architecture is tied to society and becomes the social art. In a sense, architecture is tied to society by its theoretical needs.

It is then a simple fact that the logic of the design process makes the link between architecture and society. But it does so either on the terms of architecture or on the terms of society. It depends on how far the guiding theoretical ideas are social knowledge or genuinely analytic knowledge. In the worst case, the takeover of areas of architecture by ideological formulations instead of analytic theories can lead architecture into its opposite: a kind of degenerate quasi-vernacularism, lacking the natural cultural fitness of the vernacular or the considered strangeness of genuine architecture.

The only alternative form of knowledge is theoretical knowledge. Theoretical knowledge is by definition the attempt to make the non-discursive discursive, that is an attempt to acquire knowledge of non-discursivity. Like all theorisation it is of course liable to error. But its orientation towards the explicitness of non-discursive knowledge means that its errors cannot be so easily perpetuated as are the errors institution-alised in solution typologies. This in the last analysis is why the project of architecture and the project of architectural theory are the same pro-ject. Theory is the precondition of the liberation of architecture from the social knowledge which dominates vernacular design and which continu-ally threatens architecture with bureaucratic extinction through typolo-gical guidance. Architecture as we know it necessarily oscillates between these two poles of theoretical and social knowledge, sometimes not knowing when it is informed by one and by the other. One thing is clear. It is only through the theoretical study of architecture that we can begin to become truly aware of when we are being creatively free in the realm of the non-discursive and when we are without being fully aware following the hidden dictates of society.

This is why great architecture tends, if not to objectivity, then at least to a belief in its own objectivity. Lesser architects assert that they create. Great architects believe they discover. This difference is due to the inter-vention of that peculiar brand of reflective thought which stands on the foundation of theory, yet when applied in creative mode breaks bounds and changes the architecture of the past into the architecture of the future.

Notes

1   For example, Robin Evans, 'Figures, doors and passageways', *Architectural Design*, 4, 1978, pp. 267–78; also 'Rookeries and model dwellings: English hous-ing reform and the morality of private space', *Architectural Association Quarterly*, 10, 1, 1978, pp. 25–35.

2   Mark Girouard, *Life in the English Country House: A Social and Architectural History*, Yale University Press, 1978; subsequently Penguin, 1980.

3   Tom Markus, *Buildings and Power; Freedom and Control in the Origin of Modern Building Types*, Routledge, 1993.

4   Alison Ravetz, in conversation.

5   Ed. N. Cross, *New Developments in Design Methodology*, Wiley, 1984.

6   B. Lawson, *How Designers Think: the Design Process Demystified*, Butterworth, 1990; originally Architectural Press, 1980.

7   C. Jones and D. G. Thornley, *Conference on Design Methods*, Pergamon, Oxford, 1963; eds. Broadbent G. and Ward A., *Design Methods in Architecture*, Lund Humphries, London, 1969; ed. G. T. Moore, *Emerging Methods in Environmental Design and Planning*, MIT Press, Cambridge, Mass., 1970; N. Cross & R. Roy , *Design Methods Manual*, The Open University Press, Milton Keynes, 1975; ed. S. A. Gregory, *The Design Method*, Butterworth, London, 1966.

8   H. Simon, *The Sciences of the Artificial*, MIT Press, 1971; and B. Hillier, 'The nature of the artificial' in *Geoforum*, vol. 16, no 2, pp. 163–78, 1985.

9   C. Alexander, *Notes on the Synthesis of Form*, McGraw Hill, New York, 1964.

10 How the argument about 'design method' was intimately related to one of the key philosophical objectives of modernism, that is to replace a historically and aesthetically dominated architecture with an analytically and socially based architecture, can best be seen in such texts as Sir Leslie Martin's lecture at the RIBA in April 1967 published as 'The architect's approach to architecture', *RIBA Journal*, May 1967.

11 R. Descartes, *Discourse on Method*, 1628; edition used: Trans: E. Haldane and G. Ross, *The Philosophical Works of Descartes*, Cambridge University Press, 1970, vol. 1, pp. 92–3.

12 Descartes p 87.

13 K. Popper, *The Logic of Scientific Discovery*, Hutchinson, 1934; *Conjectures and Refutations*, Hutchinson, 1968; and *Objective Knowledge*, Hutchinson, 1972.

14 I. Hacking, *Representing and Intervening*, Cambridge University Press, 1983.

15 See Hillier et al., 'Knowledge and design', in eds. Ittlesen and Proshansky, *Environmental Psychology*, 1976; republished in ed N. Cross, above, 1984. Originally EDRA Conference Proceedings, 1972.

16 B. Hillier and A. Leaman 'How is design possible?' in *Journal of Architectural Research and Teaching*, 3, 1, 1974.

17 The reader is also referred back to the discussion of this problem in chapter 2.

18 Hacking, *Representing and Intervening*, p. 220.

19 Hillier & Leaman, 'How is design possible?'

20 The terms 'problem' and 'solution' are used quite deliberately here. I am well aware that some theorists have doubted that designers 'solve problems' and even argue that this conception of design is likely to lead to an uncreative attitude and performance on the part of designers. The analysis of design set out in this chapter suggests that design, while a wholly creative act, is quite usefully thought of also as a problem solving act, not perhaps because it *is* an act of problem solving *tout court*, but because it *includes* one. The brief does pose a problem. A design does offer a solution. The key questions, and the ones with which this chapter is concerned are: what kind of problem? and: what kind of solution? and what kinds of knowledge are used in going from one to the other?

21   T. Kuhn, *The Structure of Scientific Revolutions*, University of Chicago Press, Chicago, 1962.

22   And which I discussed at greater length in B. Hillier 'Against enclosure', in eds. N. Teymur & T. Markus, *Rehumanising Housing*, Butterworths, 1988.

23   For the most part drawn from Kirschenmann & Munschalek, *Residential Districts*, Granada Publishing, London, 1980; originally in German as *Quartiere zum Wohnen*, Deutsche Verlags-Anstalt, 1977.

24   J. Hanson, 'The architecture of community', *Architecture & Behaviour*, Editions de la Tour, special issue on space syntax research, vol. 3, No. 3, 1987.

25   Greater London Council, *Introduction to the Housing Layout*, Architectural Press, London, 1978.

26   A pioneering study is by J. Hanson, 'Deconstructing architects' houses' *Environment & Planning B; Planning and Design*, 21, 1994, pp. 675–704.

27   Dickon Irwin, a student on the MSc in Advanced Architectural Studies at the Bartlett in 1989.

28   There is another account of this work in B. Hillier, 'Specifically architectural theory' *The Harvard Architectural Review*, no. 9, Rizzoli, New York, 1993. Also published as Hillier B., 'Specifically architectural knowledge', *Nordic Journal of Architectural Research*, 2, 1993.

29   W. J. Mitchell, *The Logic of Architecture: Design Computation and Cognition*, MIT Press, 1990, p. 239.

Index